ADVANCE PRAISE FOR

ORIGINAL SINS

"This book will transform the way you see this country, dismantling what you thought you knew about race and schooling in America and opening your eyes to realities that have been denied or avoided for too long. With a clear, unflinching voice, Eve L. Ewing shares an unforgettable origin story, one that challenges us to ask new questions about our own educational experience and our children's, starting with the Pledge of Allegiance first thing in the morning. You will come away from this book with a new capacity to imagine a different way to learn, grounded in the truth about our past and present and the potential of our future."

—Michelle Alexander, author of *The New Jim Crow*

"Eve L. Ewing is not only a remarkable writer, she is also a singular educator. And in *Original Sins,* she provides readers with one of the most powerful and illuminating lessons they may ever receive. In outlining the histories of Black and Native education she makes clear—in ways that feel at once engaging, unflinching, and revelatory—how our country's schools have intentionally configured the contemporary landscape of inequality. Exhaustively researched and exquisitely written, *Original Sins* is breathtaking."

—Clint Smith, author of *How the Word Is Passed*

"Carter G. Woodson, one of the twentieth century's greatest historians, asserted that lynching starts in the schoolroom. Eve L. Ewing, one of the twenty-first century's greatest intellectuals, proves that racism, colonialism, and carcerality started to enact these oppressive systems in the schoolroom as well. By reckoning with the violent, dehumanizing history of Black and Indigenous schooling, Ewing finds in the resistance of students, renegade teachers, and traditions older than the colonies a path toward a life-affirming, loving, caring education. But it will require dismantling racial capitalism, decolonizing our world and our minds, and burying America's original sins once and for all."

—Robin D. G. Kelley, author of *Freedom Dreams*

"*Original Sins* is a meticulously written invitation to gather alongside Ewing as she excavates the historical record to reveal how schools are instrumental in upholding racial hierarchy and diminishing the futures of Black and Indigenous communities. Reimagining schools through a communal practice of braiding, Ewing invites readers to consider the power of education toward liberation—schools as collective sites where we can dream and grow our knowledge toward building new worlds based on ethical relationships of care. *Original Sins* is a brilliant must-read for educators and all those concerned with Black and Indigenous futures."

—Leanne Betasamosake Simpson,
author of *As We Have Always Done*

"Calling for an interruption and not a repetition of the unforgivable harms done in the creation of the United States, Eve L. Ewing's *Original Sins* is a commitment to being true about the past in order to truly have a future. Fiercely hopeful, attending to the 'deep and furious power' of the shared histories between Black and Indigenous communities, Ewing uncovers the makings of other forms of relation that we want for our children and our children's children. This is a book you will read, and then want everyone in your life to read—a book to be read in community."

—Eve Tuck, co-editor of *Indigenous and Decolonizing Studies in Education*

"Eve L. Ewing lays bare the core project of dispossession and race-making in American education and statecraft. Careful attention to the distinct but shared trajectories of Black and Indigenous education forms the center of this project and is an extraordinary contribution to political history, studies in education, and shared futures. This book is a must-read."

—Audra Simpson, author of *Mohawk Interruptus*

"Eve L. Ewing's *Original Sins* is the book I longed for as a graduate student in educational studies, one that narrates the history of schooling as an extension of settler statecraft and racial hierarchy. In telling this story, Ewing takes readers on a journey through the works and words of leading Black and Indigenous scholars, cataloging the blatant and insidious ways that the nation's 'original sins'—Indigenous genocide and chattel slavery—structure both schooling and knowledge. She then reshapes this history into a provocation, a summons to collective struggle and imagining where dreams, memories, and ethics of care are woven together as the building blocks of a new vision of 'schools for us.' The world is clearly at a crossroads, between futures of more violence or more decolonial and abolitionist love. Futures of more freedom will need schools for us that refuse the carceral logics of miseducation and embrace Ewing's vision of relationality, care, and repair."

—Sandy Grande, author of *Red Pedagogy*

BY EVE L. EWING

Original Sins

Electric Arches

Ghosts in the Schoolyard

1919

Maya and the Robot

ORIGINAL SINS

ORIGINAL SINS

THE (MIS)EDUCATION OF BLACK AND NATIVE CHILDREN AND THE CONSTRUCTION OF AMERICAN RACISM

EVE L. EWING

ONE WORLD
NEW YORK

Published in the United States by One World, an imprint of Random House, a division of Penguin Random House LLC, New York.

One World and colophon are registered trademarks of Penguin Random House LLC.

LIBRARY OF CONGRESS CATALOGING-IN-PUBLICATION DATA
Names: Ewing, Eve L., author.
Title: Original sins / by Eve L. Ewing.
Description: New York, NY : One World, [2025] |
Includes bibliographical references and index.
Identifiers: LCCN 2024035575 (print) | LCCN 2024035576 (ebook) |
ISBN 9780593243701 (hardcover) | ISBN 9780593243718 (ebook)
Subjects: LCSH: Discrimination in education—United States—History. | Public schools—United States—History. | Segregation in education—United States—History. | Racism—United States—History. | Education—Political aspects.
Classification: LCC LC212.2 .E95 2025 (print) | LCC LC212.2 (ebook) |
DDC 379.73—dc23/eng/20241009
LC record available at https://lccn.loc.gov/2024035575
LC ebook record available at https://lccn.loc.gov/2024035576

Printed in the United States of America on acid-free paper

oneworldlit.com

1st Printing

FIRST EDITION

Book design by Barbara M. Bachman

To my great teachers—

oh, how abundant you have been!

In classrooms, in community, in kinship,

in ancestry, in archive, in love.

Wherever I have found you,

wherever you have found me,

I am grateful to you.

My country needs me, and if I were not here,

I would have to be invented.

—HORTENSE SPILLERS[1]

Our presence is our weapon.

—LEANNE BETASAMOSAKE SIMPSON[2]

CONTENTS

ORIGINAL SINS

INTRODUCTION

Life squeezes so tight that I can't breathe / and every time I've tried to be what someone else thought of me.

—LAURYN HILL, "THE MISEDUCATION OF LAURYN HILL"

What threatens white people is often dismissed as myth. I have never been true in America.

—NATALIE DÍAZ, "THE FIRST WATER IS THE BODY"[1]

When I teach courses on education policy, I always begin on the first day of class by asking my students a simple question: What is the purpose of schools? If you haven't ever thought explicitly about this question before, now is a good time to pause and ask yourself. Why do we have schools? What are they for?

I usually pose this question as part of a "think-pair-share" exercise. First, jot down your ideas on your own. Then, talk through them with the person next to you. Finally, we share them out with the class and brainstorm a list that goes up on the board to look at together. *Teaching you skills for a job. A place for kids to go during the day while people work. Preparing people to participate in a democracy. Socializing kids to play with other kids.*

All of these answers are, of course, correct. Or, to put it more precisely, all of these answers are or have been true at different times, in different places, and—perhaps most germane to our discussion in this book—for different people.

Horace Mann, who was the first secretary of the Massachusetts State Board of Education and one of the most well-known proponents of "common schools" (the precursor to what we now call "public schools"), famously put it this way: "Education, then, beyond all other devices of human origin, is the great equalizer of the conditions of men—the balance-wheel of the social machinery. . . . If this education should be universal and complete, it would do more than all things else to obliterate factitious distinction in society." Mann believed that the institution of schooling was the single most effective way to solve all of society's ills, stating that "without undervaluing any other human agency, it may be safely affirmed that the common school, improved and energized, as it can easily be, may become the most effective and benignant of all the forces of civilization" and that it would stand against "intemperance, avarice, war, slavery, bigotry, the woes of want and the wickedness of waste."[2]

Although Mann wrote those words nearly two centuries ago, his general sentiment has been shared by countless Americans across time, geography, culture, and political ideology. I've been an educator in one venue or another for about twenty years, in all kinds of settings—public schools, community centers, prisons, and universities; teaching three-year-olds and sixty-year-olds, and everyone in between. So I've been fortunate to have this conversation a lot. And I'm willing to bet that if, right this moment, you put down this book and ask someone—whether your mom or your roommate or the person who delivers your mail—what they believe is the key to the American Dream, to the promise of equal access to a good life, odds are good that education would be somewhere at the center of their equation.

But beneath the shining castle of that American Dream lie two cornerstones that irrevocably shaped the social fabric of this nation: the genocide and displacement of Indigenous peoples, and the institution of chattel slavery that held African people in bondage. We cannot truly understand the United States of the present without understanding these two original sins of the past and their structural afterlives, which lie at the basis of what we even understand race to be or to mean.[3] And the schoolhouse, that most venerable and beloved image of American aspiration, hasn't rested angelically on the sidelines, uninvolved with the construction of racial hierarchy. Rather, it has played a central role in furthering the work begun by slavery and settler colonialism.

"Race is socially constructed." This is a phrase we hear a lot. It means that what we call "race" is a thing humans build collectively. But who or what did the constructing? How did it happen? And, given that we might naturally expect a structure that is hundreds of years old to eventually crumble and collapse, who or what is doing the upkeep? In this book, I'm going to try to convince you that one answer lies in a place that shapes many of our earliest and most formative social interactions: the institution of schooling.

The genesis of what would come to be called the "New World" required an ideological foundation that would permit conquest and enslavement. These actions required an accompanying architecture of ideas to buoy them, to make them legitimate. The phrase itself—the "New World"—implicitly stands in contrast to the "Old World," the familiar territory of Europe.

But the Europeans who traveled across the globe to engage in violent conquest created a "new world" in another sense: they constructed a new social order, and new types of creatures.

The subhuman categories of the "Negro" and the "Indian" were invented through the entangled processes of colonial terror and enslavement. Countless disparate tribes, languages, spiritual practices, kinship networks, histories, and traditions were flattened under these new designations. Akan and Mina and Wolof became *Black.*[4] Muscogee and Haudenosaunee and Wampanoag became *Indian.* These are the *original sins* to which I'm referring in the title of this book. The sin lies not only in the act of violence, but in the creation of the *idea* that makes the violence morally permissible. I argue that the way Black and Native children have been treated in schools, from the earliest days of this country to the present, is an integral part of the way racial hierarchy is constructed and maintained; that school is a place where these ideas leave a lifelong mark on our sense of who we are, how we fit into the world, what is normal, and what is just.

And the *original* part matters. Begging forgiveness from Christian theologians, who will rightfully point out the diversity of views on the topic, I assert that the general idea of *original sin* is that it differs from the everyday transgressions each of us commits, the venial acts of greed and vice for which we can be forgiven. Original sin is inherited and fundamental. It doesn't go away.

The Race Machine

What do I mean by racial hierarchy? Well, when I visualize the way race works in U.S. society, I think of a kind of sorting machine. Sometimes in my mind it's like one of those Play-Doh factory toys where you insert clay at one end and out comes a star, a triangle, or a tangle of spaghetti-like threads. Other times I envision it as a complex Rube Goldberg machine, or a 1960s-era punch card computer, big enough to fill a whole room. Or a conveyor belt that carries people along. They enter on one end; on the other end they come out Having Race. Being Raced.

The Race Machine starts with complicated inputs: human beings, in our infinite diversity and complexity. We have different skin colors, hair textures, heights, weights, and body shapes. Our limbs and our eyes and our ears and our bellybuttons look different, across countless unknowable permutations. And that's just the part you can see! We also bring traces of parents and grandparents and great-grandparents, and the places where we are born, and the places where our parents were born. Plus there are the people who raise us, and all the things they believe and eat and sing and do, their faith practices, the ways they mark the day when someone is born or falls in love or dies. When I say infinite, I mean *infinite*.

But the Race Machine doesn't do infinity. It's a sorting machine. It takes all of that cumbersome infinity and turns it into something much simpler. For many folks, school is one of the first places where we encounter this sorting in highly visible ways.

Take a moment and think about it. When did you first realize that the world might look at you and not just see . . . *you*? Not your favorite music and least favorite foods, that toy you wanted more than anything for your birthday, the chore you always said you would take care of but did half-heartedly and hoped no one would notice, the scar from that time you fell once, lines from movies you had memorized. Not just *you,* but a category to which you belonged. A *type* of person you somehow were presumed to be, despite having played no discernible role in defining that type for yourself. This was your first encounter with what scholars call "race salience."[5] Was your memory in or around school? Did you notice that some kids in your class always seemed to be assigned to the "butterfly" reading group while others were always "caterpillars"? Did you have an intuitive sense of who was getting scolded all the time, who could get away with mischief while others never seemed to escape the teacher's watchful eye? Or maybe it was less about who *was* in the room with you and more about who *wasn't.* Did you know, even if nobody ever said it aloud, that *kids like that* live *there* and go to *that* school, while *people like us* go to *this* school? If you did make these observations about racial differences as a child, that makes you pretty much average, despite common misperceptions to the contrary. Research suggests that we are able to distinguish people by racial identity as early as infancy, begin to assign social meaning to those identities at preschool age, and become aware of racial stereotypes by the time we are about six years old.[6]

Maybe, in school, you were asked to check a box on a form in a way that made you hesitate. That matter of box checking is a troublesome one. The most frustrating part about this machine is that you don't get to decide how it sorts you, nor do you get to opt out. This is one of the ways that the notion of race, as sociologists see it, is different from the idea of other aspects of identity. "My mom's side is Irish," people will sometimes say, "but I was really close growing up with my dad's side of the family, so I really identify more as an Italian American." That is wonderful and interesting! But it is not the business of the Race Machine. The Race Machine says you are White.[7] The Race Machine, you see, is not about how you view yourself. Rather, it sorts you based on how other people see you and how the racial hierarchy of the country in which you live determines your place. Tiger Woods, who in 1997 told Oprah he was "Cablinasian" (a portmanteau of Caucasian, Black, Indian, and Asian), found this out the hard way when he was arrested by the Palm Beach County Sheriff's Office in 2017 and listed as "Black" on his mugshot. The Race Machine is not for the niceties of personal identity, heritage, or preference. The Race Machine is a sorting machine. And sort it does.

Sociologists Michael Omi and Howard Winant have termed this process "racial formation": "the sociohistorical process by which racial identities are created, lived out, transformed, and destroyed."[8] Sociologist Karen E. Fields and historian Barbara J. Fields call it "racecraft," intentionally calling to mind both the notion of *constant making and remaking* and the image of conjuring an illusion (i.e., a form of witchcraft). "If race lives on today," Fields and Fields write, "it does not live on because we have inherited it from our forebears of the seventeenth century or the eighteenth or nineteenth, but because we continue to create it today."[9]

Human societies sort individuals in many ways that are not endowed with cruelty or disparities in power. We sort people into Californians and New Yorkers, into Geminis and Leos, and people can find social meaning in those categories without using them to mistreat one another. Categories are not necessarily hurtful. But the trouble with the Race Machine is that these acts of sorting are attached to hierarchy. Racism is the technology that makes the machine go.

We usually think of "technology" as something that involves wires and circuits and electricity or machinery. The word is Greek in origin, from *tekhnē*—art or craft. Its derivative form *tekhnologia* meant "systematic treatment." So that's another way to think of the word "technology"—not quite the way we usually use it to refer to phones and jet propulsion systems and satellites. Rather, when I say "racism is a technology," I mean that racism is something *invented by humans* that creates a hierarchical pattern that is then applied or enacted *systematically* in various contexts. Those patterns are not static; they are ever shifting, historically and geographically contingent. Categories are made, challenged, erased, and remade. Generally, those with the most power in a given society consciously and unconsciously build the walls of racial hierarchy in the places that suit them best in their time. In response, folks at the grass roots also shift and shape racial identity through reflection and resistance.

This *shaping*, the way race is continually made, is a detail many people tend to forget. Despite the increased ubiquity of the phrase "race is a social construction," it can be hard in a racialized society to remember deep down that race is not something inherent to human beings or our bodies. Moses did not come down from the mountain and hand us our census categories. The boundaries of race are as arbitrary and malleable as the other borders and invented myths that define our lives.[10]

Part of this slipperiness comes from the ways Whiteness in the United States is defined—through absence. To be White is to be not-something, and during this country's formative years that meant Not-Black and Not-Indian. As Dakota historian Philip J. Deloria writes, "Savage Indians served Americans as oppositional figures against whom one might imagine a civilized national self," and "blackness, in a range of cultural guises, has been an essential precondition for American whiteness."[11] Hence the observation from Hortense Spillers with which we opened this book: the republic of the United States, which understands itself foundationally as a project for White people and Whiteness, needs to invent us, over and over.

In the face of these contradictions, some people will be quick to assert that race is not even real. "If it's socially constructed, it doesn't mean anything!" They're right—sort of—about the first thing and wrong about the second. If by "real" you mean generated outside the realm of human invention, then no, race is not "real." But because our society endows racial categories with meaning, the *consequences* of race are very much real. As sociologist and legal scholar Dorothy Roberts writes, "*Race is not a biological category that is politically charged. It is a political category that has been disguised as a biological one.* This distinction is important because many people misinterpret the phrase 'race is socially constructed' to mean that the biological category of race has a social meaning, so that each society interprets differently what it means to belong to a biological race."[12] This allows well-meaning people to dutifully assert that "race is a social construction" while still maintaining an unspoken belief that race is an objective, inherent biological fact. Instead, it is a set of political boundaries created by humans based on a set of fairly random and inconsistent criteria, endowed with profound social meaning over centuries and across every aspect of collective life.

As we watch the consequences of this hierarchy unfold, it's easy to talk about the workings of school as more or less orthogonal to the workings of race. Some people acknowledge that racial hierarchies keep schools from being the liberatory spaces they could otherwise be; the presumption is that if we solved this racism thing in society, schools would be all good. Paradoxically, we also hear the inverse argument—that schools are magical places that can somehow fix the racism endemic to the *rest* of society. In fact, neither articulation is quite right. Rather, school helps to keep the Race Machine running. School is one of the laboratories where the Race Machine and its technologies have been developed, honed, perfected, and maintained, generating the steam that makes the engine go.

The concept that schools are complicit in the maintenance of a bad thing is contrary to the most basic idea that supposedly animates education in the United States. We are told that schools are supposed to be places that inculcate fairness, where our life outcomes are tied to our individual efforts. But schools have been shaped by the same ideas that drove European colonists to stake property claims on faraway Indigenous lands and the ideas that shaped the formation of the Middle Passage. These original sins did not take place in a discrete moment of time; they linger, they fester, they grow and morph and change. They persist and persist and persist. They shape the tenor of our public discourse, the architecture of our buildings and towns and neighborhoods, the stories we are told, and the schools to which we send our children.

Carter G. Woodson made this point aptly in his classic work *The Mis-Education of the Negro,* toward which the subtitle of this book is nodding. The education Black people received, Woodson wrote, was "worked out in conformity to the needs of those who have enslaved and oppressed weaker peoples. For example, the philosophy and ethics resulting from our educational system have justified slavery, peonage, segregation, and lynching."[13] The mere fact of Black people attending school and receiving information was not only useless but actively harmful, Woodson argued, if it legitimized their own subjugation—

the process he termed "mis-education." He went on: "There would be no lynching if it did not start in the classroom. Why not exploit, enslave, or exterminate a class that everybody is taught to regard as inferior?"[14] The Self is made, the Other is made, and the school bell rings on.

This is a book about the stories the United States tells itself about Black and Native people, and the way that those stories uphold a racial hierarchy that shapes all of our lives—and about the roles of schools in perpetuating those stories.[15] Across the chapters that follow, I'm going to argue that there are three pillars of American racism that are cultivated in our institutions of schooling. Our schools not only *reflect* these values from the broader society in which they are situated, but actually play an active role in constructing, normalizing, and upholding them.

The first is the premise of *intellectual inferiority*. This is the idea that Black people and Native people are inherently less intelligent than other (implicitly, White) people, that we have less capacity for the complex thought that is understood to characterize human beings.

The second is *discipline and punishment*. This is the idea that Black and Native people have unruly bodies, and that in order for society to function, it is necessary to impose control, rules, and order upon those bodies above and beyond what would be considered necessary for any other human bodies.

And the third is *economic subjugation*. This is the idea that Black and Native people cannot be self-contained agents of our own labor, nor can we make choices about how we use that labor, benefit from it, or share the benefits with our communities; instead, we are assigned specific roles to play within a capitalist system, and the order of society is seen to be threatened if we deviate from those roles.

Each of these ideas has historically been the taken-for-granted law of the land that governs how our schools function. And because schools are a place where social norms are learned, reinforced, and reflected outward as normal, fine, and good, the prevalence of these ideas in schools has profound implications for the ways that racism manifests broadly all across our society.

The pages that follow include many stories of cruelty and hurt, and also of resistance and resilience. For Black and Indigenous people, having to tell and retell stories of suffering can itself feel like an act of violence—for the speaker as well as for listeners who may be all too familiar with these stories because they have *lived* them. But I hope this is an interruption, not a repetition.[16] I am not sharing these stories in the hopes of garnering sympathy from those who have inherited the legacies of violence. I am not sharing them to grant absolution. I share them in the hopes that they will inspire mutual recognition in Black people and Native people, points of departure for shared conspiring, for shared flourishing. I share them so that all educators—my people!—can have a robust conversation about the systems in which we find ourselves, and strive to change them.

Schools are supposed to be places for children. They are places where capable, trustworthy adults are supposed to be tasked with the work of teaching and nurturing. If the system we have built in this country does not see those children as human beings worthy of care, then any effort at "education reform" is completely pointless.[17] No amount of professional development, or access to technology, or equitable funding, or arts education, or after-school programs, or engaging curriculum, or higher teacher pay, or any possible idea you might have for remedying the ills of our school systems will ever make any difference in the lives of young people if the people and institutions that govern those reforms do not see those young people as precious, sacred beings deserving of respect and care.

In the final part of the book, I'll talk through what I see as some models for grounding our work in that notion of care, and of the particular gifts that a co-conspiratorial relationship between Black and Indigenous people can offer to the way we consider care work. I do so with an acknowledgment that, as education scholar Sefanit Habtom and Indigenous feminist scholar Megan Scribe (Ininiw iskwew, Norway House Cree Nation)[18] have written, "Black and Indigenous relationships are not easy or straightforward. At times, we have let each other down. Other times, we have lost sight of one another, seeking immediate gains over collective liberation. However, entangled within White supremacist settler states, there are many times—times like now—when it is increasingly clear that our interests and our survival tie us together."[19] To think through this idea of being "tied together," I'll use the metaphor of braiding as an act that helps us stay grounded in acts of loving reciprocity, in caring for ourselves and others.

What This Book Is and Is Not

This book is intended to be descriptive, not prescriptive. It's an invitation into a conversation, a tool for you to mark up and lend out and disagree with and share and highlight and bend out of shape, especially if you are a Black person, a Native person, an educator, a caregiver, a student, a person who has always felt like this school thing just feels a little off, or all of the above. The absolute best scenario is if you can find somebody else, or several somebodies, to read it with—use it for collective work, if you can. As you read these accounts of what has been, remember that we are all architects of what is to come. How does this knowledge of history shape the present and the future that you want to build?[20]

This is not a how-to-fix-your-school guide, or a how-to-unlearn-such-and-such guide. In fact, it's not a book about you, individually, and what you can or should do. Nor is it only a book about schools and schooling. Borrowing from Woodson and Ms. Lauryn Hill, I use the term "miseducation" expansively. Education does not happen only in schools; it happens in all the places where we receive messages about who we are, what we are, and how we ought to live together. I'll argue that Black and Native kids have been miseducated in schools, to be certain. But *all* of us—youths and adults, past and present, Black and Indigenous and otherwise—have received a profound miseducation. We have been offered a racial hierarchy that is violent, belittling, and ultimately unsustainable, and told that it's the only way for us to live. That hierarchy spins a web between home and school and work, ensnaring us. My hope is that in better understanding these ideas, and their rootedness in schooling, we draw them out from whence they hide. The matter of what we do with this knowledge is to be determined collectively: through conversation and action among educators and organizers. This is not an instruction manual. This is a book that makes ample use of the historical record because it is about the world as it has been. And yet, constructing something new requires feats of imagination. That work—the work of dreaming—is shared work.

Indeed, it's imperative that we don't just see the disdain and disregard for Black and Native children in school spaces as simply a matter of bias by individual people who harbor ill will out of ignorance. Rather, the project of creating the United States as a settler colonial racial project[21] was predicated on rendering Black and Native people into a state of beasthood, of savagery.[22] This "template" is the source code of the Race Machine—its prime directive, its innermost ticking clock.

By no means do I suggest that the experiences or social positions of Black and Indigenous people are equivalent; to the contrary, we will explore the many ways that this is *not* the case. For one thing, Native people within what is now called the United States are distinct from other groups in that they not only are made into racialized subjects, but also, as members of sovereign nations that predate this nation-state, face the ongoing aftermath of violent colonization.[23]

It's also obviously untrue that those three technologies of harm—the pillars I described above—have exclusively been used against Black and Indigenous people. I recognize that, for non-Black people of color, it can be frustrating to read accounts of "race" in the United States that exclusively discuss Black and White people. My intention in writing this book is not simply to expand that binary to a triad while still reinforcing feelings of invisibility among other people of color. My decision to focus on the histories of Black and Native people is not intended as an act of exclusion, but as an act of clarification—and invitation. If you are a reader who does not identify as Black or Native, I invite you to spend time here in a spirit of openness and reflection and, if you can muster it, a willingness to learn the specificity of these histories without the need to defend or deflect—and then, to consider the ways these technologies have been deployed against others. Let these connections be not a means for diminution, but rather grounds for a shared struggle. Many times you may find yourself saying, "But that's also true for my people!" I hope that these moments of recognition spur not the sense that something is therefore *not* true in some distinct way for Black and Native people, but rather a sense that we are all struggling to pilot our boats through the same tumultuous sea.

Examples abound: from the technologies of carcerality and surveillance that were used on Black political organizers during the COINTELPRO era, which have been expanded to control our nation's majority-Latine immigrant population through unjust arrests and detention centers and to entrap community leaders and activists in Muslim communities, to the phenomenon of what scholar and organizer Nick Estes (Kul Wicasa) refers to as "intifada on the plains"—resistance to the same militarized police tactics being used on both Standing Rock Water Protectors and Palestinians living under the ongoing Nakba.[24] Today, racism and settler colonialism continue—and so do the efforts to dismantle them. From Mexico to Colombia to Brazil, co-creative Black and Indigenous resistance movements have surged as activists respond to the tightly coupled assaults of anti-Blackness, anti-Indigeneity, racial capitalism, and settler colonialism.[25] I hope the book can illustrate places where our struggles converge and opportunities for us to work together, and I invite you to tell the stories of your people that have not yet been told.[26]

This book is not an "ultimate guide" or "definitive history" or any comprehensive attempt to cover everything; I hope it's a means to open space for conversation, not to close it. As education scholar Timothy San Pedro writes, "Harm is done when we try to hide the limitations of our knowing, when we try to present ourselves as complete rather than the in-process beings that we always are."[27] This book is an exercise in learning for me as well—and an exercise in striving, in gathering stories, in grieving. Through the work of writing, I have thought often of two of my "great-great-greats," both born in the 1840s. I think of my grandfather's grandfather Carl, who was born in Germany and was able to come to the United States and receive all the benefits of his position as a settler, farming and raising a family on land seized from Kickapoo people. I think of my grandmother's grandmother Adeline, who was born into enslavement in Alabama. As a White man, Carl had his life scrupulously documented, while Adeline's life is largely an archival mystery. Tiffany Lethabo King writes that "what the archives of slavery and Indigenous genocide and removal have in common is that they are almost impossible to retrieve."[28] I wish desperately that I knew more about Adeline's life, and about the lives of so many of the grandmothers, children, cherished friends, and beloveds whose stories fill these pages. So many of their names, the details of their hurts and their singing and their memories, are irretrievable to us on this plane, severed by cruelty.

Though much of their dreaming is obscured from us, I do know one thing about each of them. Each of them was somebody's baby. Each of them was loved. I hope you'll join me in calling them forth toward your heart, in honoring their memories even if we cannot always say their names. In this, we do the work of making a counterhistory together.[29]

Anishinaabe elder Garry Raven, speaking of the concept of *edbesendowen*—humility, one of the seven Grandfather Teachings of Anishinaabe tradition—cites the wolf as an important teacher. "The wolf always looks back when he leaves somewhere," says Raven. "The wolf teaches us that we need to look back on our life and learn from it."[30] The posture of the wolf calls to mind, for me, the Sankofa bird, the symbol that comes to us from the Akan people of West Africa, which has come to have so much meaning for people across the African diaspora. The Sankofa bird walks forward while looking backwards, an action said to represent a directive to "go back and retrieve."[31] In the pages that follow, with humility, I try to do just that.

PART I

WHAT ARE SCHOOLS FOR?

Because the Negro labored, he was considered a draft animal.
Because the Indian occupied large areas of land,
he was considered a wild animal. Had we given up anything else,
or had anything else to give up, it is certain that we would
have been considered some other thing.

—VINE DELORIA JR.[1]

To educate the Indian in the ways of civilized life,
therefore, is to preserve him from extinction,
not as an Indian, but as a human being.

—WILLIAM JONES, COMMISSIONER
OF INDIAN AFFAIRS, 1902[2]

Our public schools are filled with a conglomerate mass of
foreigners and children of foreigners sprung from generations
of ignorance and untrained intelligence. To make good citizens of
these through a few years of schooling is a stupendous task.

—*THE WALL STREET JOURNAL*, 1912[3]

The colored race is as yet, in general, only capable
of receiving and profiting by an elementary education,
which costs comparatively much less than that suitable for the
white race in its more advanced stages of civilization.

—REPORT OF THE FEDERAL SECURITY AGENCY,
OFFICE OF EDUCATION, 1893[4]

CHAPTER 1

Jefferson's Ghost

How does it feel to be a problem?

W. E. B. Du Bois famously posed this haunting question in 1903, in his classic work *The Souls of Black Folk.*[1] I think of it often, especially whenever I encounter one particular line from Thomas Jefferson's *Notes on the State of Virginia:* "Among the blacks is misery enough, God knows, but no poetry."[2]

It's stinging in its candor. It strikes me every time, sending me spinning through my own vignettes of the Black poets who set a course for my thriving. In eighth grade, my class took a three-day trip to Washington, D.C., my first time traveling without my family. We visited Monticello. No one brought up the poetry line. I would go through elementary school, high school, college, and my first master's degree, and no one would ever bring it up. Parts of Jefferson's legacy were omnipresent in my experience of schooling, and other parts were completely absent.

Before we dive into the three pillars of racism that I described in the introduction, I want to spend some time thinking about Jefferson as a titanic figure in American culture and the impact of his legacy on how we think about racial hierarchy in the United States; we'll then talk about how this vision has shaped the purposes of schooling along racial lines.

There's nothing coincidental about how Jefferson does and does not show up in schools and in curricula, or the fact that roughly half of U.S. states have public schools named "Thomas Jefferson."[3] Jefferson's beliefs about Black and Native people, and the ways he enacted those beliefs as a leader of singular magnitude, laid a cornerstone for the edifice of American racial hierarchy and the contours of American schooling in a distinct way. In the era of Jefferson, Black and Native peoples on Turtle Island posed a mighty problem for the shapers of the new republic.[4] They were an existential threat. And in his writings, Jefferson aimed to tackle that threat through rhetorical moves that would frame the nation and its schools for years to come.

Those who celebrate Jefferson have struggled to reconcile the seemingly irreconcilable ideas that he put forth into the world: On the one hand, he is viewed as the esteemed father of the Declaration of Independence, the champion of the Bill of Rights and the liberties we hold dear. On the other hand, he held enslaved people as property, and his ideas and policies were crucial in establishing the dogma of Black and Native inferiority. For many people in the United States, faced with the contradiction of Jefferson as a paragon of rational thought who also believed in the inhumanity of Black and Native peoples, Jefferson the erudite intellectual has seemingly won out. In our collective consciousness, the ways Jefferson grievously harmed Black and Native people don't *really* matter—he still gets to be the "Sage of Monticello," representing the zenith of gentlemanly intellect, statesmanship, creativity, and genteel society.

The pedestal of the U.S. presidency is widely understood to represent leadership, moral fortitude, and strength of will. That's why people love to tell kids they could grow up to be president someday if they work hard enough. But even among presidents, Thomas Jefferson is considered exceptional for his intelligence. In 2006, Dean Keith Simonton, distinguished professor of psychology at UC Davis, published a peer-reviewed journal article purporting to determine the IQ of forty-two American presidents. Simonton declared Jefferson to be the second-most intelligent president, after John Quincy Adams.[5] At a 1962 dinner honoring Nobel Prize winners, John F. Kennedy quipped, "I think this is the most extraordinary collection of talent, of human knowledge, that has ever been gathered together at the White House, with the possible exception of when Thomas Jefferson dined alone. Someone once said that Thomas Jefferson was a gentleman of thirty-two who could calculate an eclipse, survey an estate, tie an artery, plan an edifice, try a cause, break a horse, and dance the minuet."[6]

Jefferson retains a powerful image in the American consciousness, still lauded not only as the progenitor of our democracy but also as an emblem of intellectual excellence. However, two of Jefferson's key interventions in our country laid the groundwork for anti-Black and anti-Native ways of viewing the world, both inside schools and beyond their corridors.

Notes on the State of Virginia is the only full-length book Jefferson ever authored. In a definitive edited version of the text, historian William Peden called it the "best single statement of Jefferson's principles, the best reflection of his wide-ranging tastes and talents. It is, in short, an American classic," "unique in American literary history," and "probably the most important scientific and political book written by an American before 1785."[7] While the Declaration of Independence is certainly the document for which Jefferson is best known, the *Notes* were his magnum opus. The text is massive in scope, with twenty-three chapters addressing topics vast in their scale and variety. Jefferson wrote of Virginia's waterways, its mountain ranges, its militias, its legal system, its fiscal system of income and expenses.

And he wrote of its people.

Historian Arica L. Coleman has posited that the *Notes* "may well contain the most disparaging remarks regarding people of African descent ever written."[8] When I first read these words, I was startled, thinking immediately of all the hateful and vulgar words I have seen deployed against Black people. The more I thought about it, though, the more I had to concede that Coleman may be right. Jefferson's writings are cloaked in civility and the artful turn of phrase; the aptitude for language that has made him a beloved cultural figure obscures the true violence of what he is saying. Jefferson described Black people's faces as having an "eternal monotony, which reigns in the countenances, that immovable veil of black which covers all the emotions of the other race."[9]

He continues:

> They secrete less by the kidnies, and more by the glands of the skin, which gives them a very strong and disagreeable odour. This greater degree of transpiration renders them more tolerant of heat, and less so of cold, than the whites . . . They seem to require less sleep. A black after hard labour through the day, will be induced by the slightest amusements to sit up till midnight, or later, though knowing he must be out with the first dawn of the morning. They are at least as brave, and more adventuresome. But this may perhaps proceed from a want of fore-thought, which prevents their seeing a danger till it be present. When present, they do not go through it with more coolness or steadiness than the whites. They are more ardent after their female: but love seems with them to be more an eager desire, than a tender delicate mixture of sentiment and sensation. Their griefs are transient. Those numberless afflictions, which render it doubtful whether heaven has given life to us in mercy or in wrath, are less felt, and sooner forgotten with them. In general, their existence appears to participate more of sensation than reflection. To this must be ascribed their disposition to sleep when abstracted from their diversions, and unemployed in labour. An animal whose body is at rest, and who does not reflect, must be disposed to sleep of course. Comparing them by their faculties of memory, reason, and imagination, it appears to me, that in memory they are equal to the whites; in reason much inferior, as I think one could scarcely be found capable of tracing and comprehending the investigations of Euclid; and that in imagination they are dull, tasteless, and anomalous.[10]

Such ideas would be hurtful enough if they were merely bigoted perspectives coming from an idly opining individual. But the *Notes* represent something on a much grander scale. Jefferson was a son of the Enlightenment, a period characterized by efforts to systematically describe the order of the observable world. The work reflected his character as someone prone to obsessive enumeration, botanical experiments, meteorological observations, and dutiful record keeping.[11] He viewed naming, numbering, sorting, and categorizing as natural strengths to which he was called in life.[12] *Notes on the State of Virginia* was not only a treatise espousing Jefferson's political opinions. It was his attempt to organize the world.

In the *Notes,* Jefferson chastises himself and his peers for the fact that "though for a century and a half we have had under our eyes the races of black and of red men, they have never yet been viewed by us as subjects of natural history." He argues that such study is imperative. Shortly thereafter, he introduces his plan for a system of education to best serve the nation: Every county in Virginia should be divided into school districts. Each year, an expert would choose a brilliant boy whose parents were poor and send him forward for further schooling, to be paid for collectively. "By this means twenty of the best geniuses will be raked from the rubbish annually," Jefferson explained.[13]

In a sense, then, *Notes on the State of Virginia* may be the first book in the United States about race and education. For one of the most influential figures in U.S. history, writing one of the most influential texts in U.S. history, matters of race and matters of schooling were inseparable. Establishing the order of these two things—the hierarchy of Man and the way he should be educated—would be crucial to the foundation of his righteous republic. Jefferson's legacy makes it plain that we can never understand the history of schooling in this country without understanding the history of race and racism, and we can't truly understand the history of race and racism without understanding the history of schooling.

One of the defenses mounted on behalf of Jefferson's writing is that he was a "man of his time"—that, like all of us, he was shaped by the social norms of his era and could not be expected to have diverged from them.[14] But we should also consider the converse: the ways that Jefferson has shaped our collective consciousness. "In the years after the Revolution the speculations of Thomas Jefferson were of great importance because so many people read and reacted to them," argues historian Winthrop Jordan. "His remarks about Negroes in the only book he ever wrote were more widely read, in all probability, than any others until the mid-nineteenth century."[15]

And Jefferson's *Notes* raised some controversy even in his era. In 1784, having decided that the work might be of general enough interest that he should have it printed, he requested feedback from his close colleague Charles Thomson, secretary of the Continental Congress. Thomson wrote him an extensive set of comments in reply, and Jefferson was impressed enough by Thomson's editorial contributions that he included some of them as an appendix in the published version. In one section of the *Notes,* Jefferson argued that his generation of American slavers were kinder than the Roman slavers of antiquity.[16] Thomson recommended that these tales of the Romans were "not worthy a place here—I would therefore propose to expunge them and a great part of p. 70—because many people encourage & comfort themselves in keeping slaves because they do not treat them as bad as others have done."[17] Further, Thomson wrote, "Though I am much pleased with the dissertation on the difference between the Whites and blacks & am inclined to think the latter a race lower in the scale of being, yet for that very reason & because such an opinion might seem to justify slavery I should be inclined to leave it out."[18] In response, Jefferson made some strategic edits, such as the addition of this passage conceding that even if Black people were intellectually inferior by our very nature, at least we were bighearted: "Whether further observation will or will not verify the conjecture that Nature has been less bountiful to them in the endowments of the head, I believe that in those of the heart she will be found to have done them equal justice."[19] Despite Thomson's prescient warning that Jefferson's words could be read in apparent contradiction to his avowed claim of hating slavery—which he called a "moral and political depravity"—the section on Black inferiority remained.[20]

Jefferson's daily livelihood required him to engage in the casual dehumanization of the Black people who were his property; he calculated the costs and yields of his investments as coolly as someone today might comment on the resale value of an old car. In a 1792 letter responding to an Englishman inquiring about the cost of agriculture in the United States, Jefferson wrote, "Suppose a negro man of 25 years of age costs 75 sterling: he has an equal chance to live 30 years according to Buffon's table; so that you lose your principal in 30 years." Later, he notes, "I have observed that our families of negroes double in about 25 years, which is an increase of the capital, invested in them, of 4 per cent over and above keeping up the original number."[21] In a 1794 letter, he wrote of his frustrations with growing potatoes, and his ongoing faith that the endeavor could be successful because his neighbors had grown them well. "The first step towards the recovery of our lands is to find substitutes for corn and bacon. I count on potatoes, clover and sheep. The two former to feed every animal on the farm except my negroes, and the latter to feed them, diversified with rations of salted fish and molasses, both of them wholesome, agreeable and cheap articles of food."[22]

Every animal on the farm except my negroes.

Jefferson's reputation as a man of reason was so widespread that, a decade later, one man would try to refute him on his own terms. Benjamin Banneker was a Black mathematician, astronomical observer, and surveyor who would later earn acclaim for helping to establish the borders of the District of Columbia. He wrote to Jefferson in 1791. "I suppose it is a truth too well attested to you, to need a proof here," wrote Banneker, "that we are a race of Beings who have long laboured under the abuse and censure of the world, that we have long been looked upon with an eye of contempt, and that we have long been considered rather as brutish than human, and Scarcely capable of mental endowments." Despite Jefferson's own role in reinforcing these ideas, Banneker appealed to the idea that Jefferson might be "far less inflexible in Sentiments of this nature, than many others":

> Now Sir if this is founded in truth, I apprehend you will readily embrace every opportunity to eradicate that train of absurd and false ideas and oppinions which so generally prevails with respect to us, and that your Sentiments are concurrent with mine, which are that one universal Father hath given being to us all, and that he hath not only made us all of one flesh, but that he hath also without partiality afforded us all

> the Same Sensations, and endued us all with the same faculties, and that however variable we may be in Society or religion, however diversifyed in Situation or colour, we are all of the Same Family, and Stand in the Same relation to him.[23]

Banneker went on to remind Jefferson of his own professed ideals, noting that there was once a time when British imperial rule had reduced Jefferson and his peers to a status of servitude. Surely the freedom they now enjoyed, Banneker reasoned, was a divine blessing. Turning Jefferson's own words against him, Banneker drove home the point of Jefferson's obvious hypocrisy. "But Sir how pitiable is it to reflect, that suppose you were so fully convinced of the benevolence of the Father of mankind, and of his equal and impartial distribution of those rights and privileges which he had conferred upon them, that you should at the Same time counteract his mercies, in detaining by fraud and violence so numerous a part of my brethren under groaning captivity and cruel oppression, that you should at the Same time be found guilty of that most criminal act, which you professedly detested in others, with respect to yourselves."[24]

Black people were not the only Others subject to Jefferson's analysis in the *Notes.* As Arica Coleman writes, Jefferson approached the topic of Virginia Indians with two now familiar archetypal lenses: the "vanishing Indian" and the "noble savage."[25] The Indian, he wrote, would always choose death over surrender, "endures tortures with a firmness unknown." This was a "barbarous people," among whom "force is law." They were disappearing in Virginia, he asserted, though Jefferson firmly disputed the idea that White people might play a role in this fact. "Spirituous liquors, the small-pox, war, and an abridgment of territory, to a people who lived principally on the spontaneous productions of nature, had committed terrible havock among them, which generation, under the obstacles opposed to it among them, was not likely to make good. That the lands of this country were taken from them by conquest, is not so general a truth as is supposed." As Coleman points out, Jefferson's treatment of Black and Native peoples in the *Notes* created a paradigm that would prove fateful. "Jefferson used these 'inequalities' [between Black, White, and Native peoples] in the most egregious passage in his *Notes* to establish two distinct policies regarding African American and American Indian peoples that persist to this day. The policy simply entailed the forced exclusion of the former and the forced inclusion of the latter."[26] As we will come to see, "forced inclusion" in the Jeffersonian frame would amount to nothing less than genocide.

Ideology of Extinction

In school, many of us learn about the idea of "Manifest Destiny": the notion that the United States has a moral charge, ordained by God, to expand its borders from sea to shining sea. While the phrase was first used in 1845, two decades after his death, Thomas Jefferson laid the philosophical groundwork for Manifest Destiny. Through Jefferson's lens, the people who were the original occupants of the land were a type of creature he and his contemporaries came to define as a "Savage," with particular qualities different from his own, "normal" civilized human qualities.[27] The Jeffersonian framework would come to define the national mandate toward America's first nations for generations, well beyond his death in 1826.

As the nation's first secretary of state, Jefferson was a close adviser to President George Washington, and together they were charged with ensuring the success of the new republic. That meant dealing straightaway with the "Indian problem." As historian David Wallace Adams writes in *Education for Extinction,* during this period "no question was more pressing for the new national government than that of deciding the future status of Indians. The policy issue could be reduced to this fact: Indians possessed the land, and whites wanted the land. . . . The very survival of the republic demanded that Indians be dispossessed of the land."[28]

In 1792, Jefferson, ever inventive, called upon an idea that would provide one easy solution to this dilemma: the "Doctrine of Discovery." The Doctrine of Discovery was the idea that in the act of "discovering a new land" (in other words, arriving in a non-European place where Indigenous people already lived), White settlers instantly gained full legal, governmental, political, and commercial rights over the people living there, without the necessity of their knowledge or consent.[29] Whatever European country "discovered" Native land had an unimpeachable right to that land.[30] This basic premise, that European intervention—no matter how violent—was for the good of the Natives to save them from their own barbarism, would become a familiar refrain in the era of Jefferson and beyond. The Doctrine of Discovery was what made its more familiar cousin, Manifest Destiny, possible.[31]

Jefferson had what Anthony F. C. Wallace referred to as "a kind of mordant fascination with the image of the Indians as a conquered and dying race."[32] It was this stereotype—the vision of the noble savage—that enabled Jefferson's firm belief in the Doctrine of Discovery. From *Dances with Wolves* to *Avatar*, the United States has long required the mythological image of the noble savage as the basis for its very sense of self and nationhood.[33] The figure of the noble savage is unmarred by the flaws and cynicisms of the modern world, living a life that is simpler, closer to ancient tradition, and more "pure," and therefore both backwards and desirable, primitive and admirable. As this way of life is by definition irreconcilable with civilization, the noble savage is tragically doomed.[34] Through the refracting prism of the noble savage trope, White America defines itself against the backdrop of an Other, desiring at once the unfettered consumption and total annihilation of that Other. *I want it / I want to be it / That's not me / I hate it*—seemingly contradictory impulses seethe just beneath the surface of the national consciousness all at once.[35] In Jefferson's view, the decimation of Native peoples was a tragedy, with every quality that that word implies: romantic, noble, and inevitable. The disappearance was destiny, fait accompli.[36]

Jefferson drew upon the noble savage image in a story he told in the *Notes*. Jefferson devotes a passage to "Logan's Lament," a noted speech said to have been delivered by Logan, a Cayuga-Mingo leader,[37] in 1774. As Jefferson tells the story, Logan was a "friend of the whites" whose family was defeated in a wrongful attack, but he refused to surrender. Instead, he issued a speech in which he declared, "Logan never felt fear. He will not turn on his heel to save his life. Who is there to mourn for Logan?—Not one."[38]

The *Notes* framed "Logan's Lament" as a fable, concretizing the image of the noble savage that would provide a foundation for the Doctrine of Discovery years later. In Jefferson's telling, Logan was the ideal Indian—deeply good, a friend of the Whites, driven to risk his life for noble principles, and ultimately fated to disappear.[39] Through the story of Logan, Jefferson sowed the seeds of the story we are told in school about explorers, pioneers, and progress—a larger American myth that legitimizes genocide as the necessary cost of national thriving and the march of civilization.[40]

Jefferson himself played a key role in crafting the ideologies of his day. It's notable that the Declaration of Independence, the document that has most endeared Jefferson to the American imagination, ends with a list of twenty-seven grievances lodged against King George. The closer is this accusation: "He has excited domestic insurrections amongst us, and has endeavored to bring on the inhabitants of our frontiers, the merciless Indian Savages whose known rule of warfare, is an undistinguished destruction of all ages, sexes, and conditions."[41]

Jefferson's vision of the republic was one that explicitly required Native disappearance. Total elimination was inevitable; the question of whether it would happen through military action or civilizing projects was a matter of expediency. He wrote in the *Notes* about the role he believed institutions of education could play. His own alma mater, the College of William & Mary, had as part of its statutes the purpose of "teach[ing] the Indian boys to read, and write, and vulgar Arithmetick . . . to teach them thoroughly the Catechism and the Principles of the Christian Religion."[42] He argued that as soon as the legislature could take up the matter, a portion of the school should maintain "a perpetual mission among the Indian tribes" and return to the task of teaching them Christian ways.

The Founding Father's assertion of the Doctrine of Discovery was cemented by the Supreme Court in 1823.[43] During this period, as the United States set its sights more firmly on westward expansion, Jefferson recorded his opinion that Native people in the West were the most savage of all, "living under no law but that of nature, subsisting and covering themselves with the flesh and skins of wild beasts."[44] Two decades after the Louisiana Purchase and a few years before the passage of the Indian Removal Act, the stage was set for the unfettered pursuit of Manifest Destiny—which required a renewed conviction that the people occupying the lands of the West were not people at all.[45]

Jefferson wrote to John Adams in 1812 that although some Native people might join civilized life, over time "the backward will yield, and be thrown further back. These will relapse into barbarism and misery, lose numbers by war and want, and we shall be obliged to drive them, with the beasts of the forest into the stony mountains."[46] The imperative to conquer the "backward" on a path toward conquering the West was central to Jefferson's agenda as president—perhaps most visibly in the Louisiana Purchase and the Lewis and Clark expedition. With the Doctrine of Discovery laid forth as groundwork, Jefferson understood clearly the way that the Louisiana Purchase could serve as a pivot point for his dream of American expansion. "This speck which now appears as an almost invisible point in the horizon," he wrote in 1802, "is the embryo of a tornado which will burst on the countries on both shores of the Atlantic and involve in its effects their highest destinies."[47]

Meriwether Lewis and William Clark, both officers in the U.S. Army, were tasked by the president with the work of setting forth upon the western lands and determining the state of Indian affairs. Since their expedition ended over two centuries ago, Lewis and Clark have been memorialized as heroes, noble pioneers who set out at great personal risk to pursue the honorable work of bringing Manifest Destiny closer to reality. Multiple postage stamps have portrayed them as bold, statuesque men, looking out courageously across the lands that await them. *National Geographic Kids* offers teaching resources emphasizing the challenge and adventure of the journey, the bad weather, the friendship of Sacagawea, and the positive impact of the expedition. The publisher Scholastic offers a variety of teaching resources on the topic as well, including an activity guide that calls it "one of the greatest adventures in American history"[48] as well as books prominently featuring Lewis and Clark standing with impressive posture, Sacagawea at their side pointing at things.

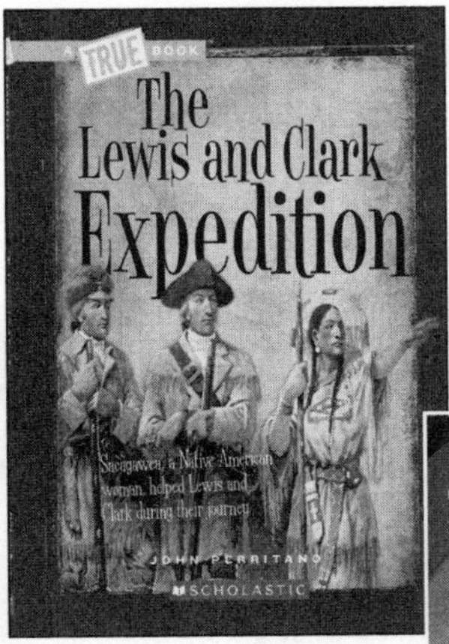

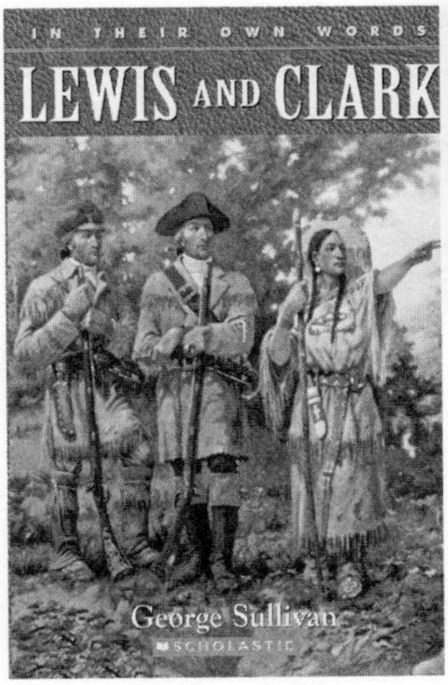

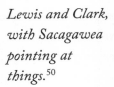

Lewis and Clark, with Sacagawea pointing at things.[50]

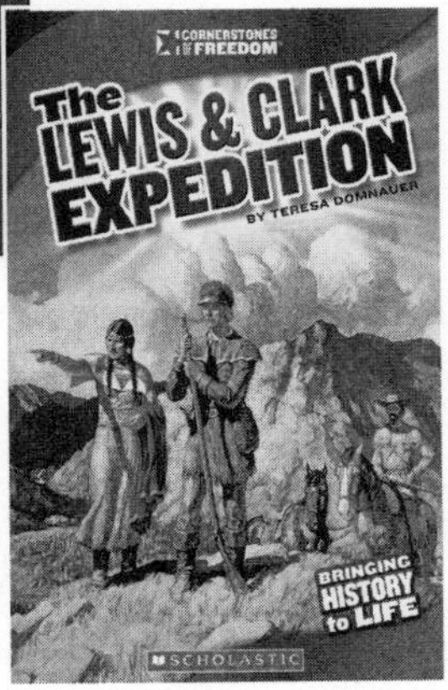

Much as Jefferson invoked the story of Logan to tell the story of a very specific kind of "good Indian" (friendly, honorable, and doomed), the story of Sacagawea has been mythologized over time in a way that legitimizes the narrative of United States expansion and the ideologies underpinning it.[49] This version of Sacagawea's life story exemplifies how narratives about Native people are historicized in our classrooms in ways that ultimately serve a settler colonial fantasy. Across the United States, students in elementary school classrooms learn about "how the Native Americans lived." Kids might learn about hunting and gathering, fishing, subsistence farming, or other traditional lifeways. They might, as was common in my elementary school, be asked to build a tepee or wigwam or longhouse out of felt or brown paper bags or popsicle sticks. They might take a field trip to a local museum and view moccasins or deerskin breechcloths.

These assignments construct a Native world that exists exclusively in the past tense: how the Native Americans *lived.* In this version of reality, Jefferson's prophesied future of total Indigenous disappearance has come to pass. The teacher might even take time to remark on how sad this is. This vision of the lands on which we live—in which the total elimination of Native peoples is viewed as complete, a sad but necessary component of the inevitable march of progress toward the establishment of America the Beautiful, Land That I Love—is a hallmark of *settler colonialism.*

Many of us first learn of a "colony" as an outpost of citizens who live under the authority of a faraway empire that extracts resources from the colony to enrich itself. For example, when Jamaica was a colony of England from 1655 until 1962, the British established hundreds of sugar plantations to grow cane that was exported for English sale and consumption. When Mexico was a colony of Spain from 1521 to 1821, the Spanish crown extracted literal tons of silver from the nation to fill its coffers. These practices are known as *expropriative* colonialism, or sometimes *external* or *exploitation* colonialism: the colonial authority expropriates resources from the land and its people.

Settler colonialism, on the other hand, seeks the complete elimination of the original inhabitants of the land. Simultaneously, it constructs a new society atop the old one. Kanaka Maoli scholar, poet, and political activist Haunani-Kay Trask described this concept in her writings about the American occupation of Hawaiʻi, which leaves the Indigenous people of the archipelago displaced under the hand of "a colonial power whose every law, policy, cultural institution, and collective behavior entrench foreign ways of life in our land and on our people," fighting for survival and sovereignty in "a society in which the indigenous culture and people have been murdered, suppressed, or marginalized for the benefit of settlers. . . . By definition, conquest is an extermination."[51] As anthropologist Patrick Wolfe put it, "Settler colonialism destroys to replace."[52]

Understanding settler colonialism challenges the most basic foundations of everything children in the United States are taught, from the first moment they learn that there is such a thing called "the United States"—because understanding settler colonialism means understanding the nation-state to be neither legitimate, nor natural, nor fundamentally good. Understanding settler colonialism means understanding the land on which we live, work, play, and raise children as land that was violently seized from the people who were in relation to it as mother and kin, land subjected to everyday consumption through the normalization of genocide. As Trask points out, merely talking about "civil rights" within this reality is woefully insufficient, since the supposed basis of those rights—individualistic civil society enshrined in a Constitution that is itself a settler document—offers no recognition of Indigenous peoples and their ties to the lands and waters. "Our daily existence in the modern world," she writes, "is thus best described not as a struggle for civil rights but as a struggle against our planned disappearance."[53]

In recent years, social justice advocates seeking to bring a more critical lens to the history of the United States have attempted to acknowledge the reality of settler colonialism by offering the urge to "decolonize" as a necessary counterpart. We are called to "decolonize our classrooms," "decolonize our curriculum," or "decolonize our bookshelves." As education scholars Eve Tuck (Unangax̂) and K. Wayne Yang have written, such easy use of the word "decolonize" is harmful in that it "domesticates decolonization," obscuring the fact that "decolonization is not a metaphor." Instead, they argue, true decolonization should involve *actual* unsettling, as colonization requires ongoing violence. "This violence is not temporally contained in the arrival of the settler but is reasserted each day of occupation."[54] As a result, every day that the project of "the United States"—a genocidal project at its core—persists, and every small way that this project is legitimized, celebrated, or normalized, constitutes an act of violence. Settler colonialism justifies the necessity of this violence by casting the original inhabitants of the land as savages; it requires racialization in order to assign itself a moral center. "The settler positions himself as both superior and normal; the settler is natural, whereas the Indigenous inhabitant and the chattel slave are unnatural, even supernatural," write Tuck and Yang.[55]

Thomas Jefferson's contribution to this ideological architecture is titanic in proportion. Using his gift for rhetoric, his widely circulated writings, and his role as statesman, he asserted that Black people and Native people had ingrained, fundamental, intractable inferiorities to White people, and upon this basis their subordination was necessary for the thriving of the United States. Beyond the continued deification of Jefferson himself, the ideas he laid forth in his long and prolific life enjoy continued currency—including in our ideas about schools and what purpose they ought to serve.

Schools serve as sites of political and ideological reproduction in society. Schools are the places where we project our collective fears, desires, aspirations, and insecurities. Schools are a mirror, reflecting the demands and tensions of the era in which they find themselves. Schools are where the nation-state tries to prove what it is and manifest what it wants to be. This basic fact has been the uniting thread throughout the history of schooling in the United States, the link that connects the schools of the eighteenth century with the schools of today.

I'll give you an example. On September 2, 1958, President Dwight D. Eisenhower signed the National Defense Education Act, or NDEA—less than a year after a basketball-sized aluminum sphere had changed the world forever. The Soviet Union's successful launch of Sputnik 1, the first satellite crafted by human hands, sent the United States into a tailspin, spurring despair and panic.[56] Sputnik circled Earth once every ninety-six minutes, emitting beeps that could be perceived through radio signals like small, inescapable taunts. NBC called it "the sound that will forever separate the old from the new."[57] Amid this new front in the Cold War, the very survival of the nation appeared to be at stake. How could this have happened? How could the global power of the United States, assumed to be unassailable and graced by God, be threatened by Soviet dominance? In the search for an institution first to blame and then, accordingly, to reform, military and research enterprises somehow escaped the critical view of the public. Instead, one explanation rose to prominence: the nation's schools had failed. The furor around the Space Race was deemed an educational crisis.[58]

In a Gallup poll, 71 percent of those surveyed agreed with the statement that "if we are to compete with Russia, high school students in this country must be required to work much harder than they do now."[59] In a 1959 press conference, Eisenhower told journalists that he was "astonished" to speak to scientists who told him that shoring up the nation's educational institutions was an "absolute necessity."[60] The

NDEA, authored by Senator J. Lister Hill and Representative Carl A. Elliott, declared that the nation was in the midst of an "educational emergency" and that the purpose of the legislation was to "insure trained manpower of sufficient quality and quantity to meet the national defense needs of the United States."[61] The NDEA authorized $70 million annually to strengthen high school instruction in science, math, and "modern foreign language" (Latin nerds need not apply); established "national defense fellowships" to expand graduate education; provided for new testing regimes "to identify students with outstanding aptitudes and ability"; funded new language institutes at colleges and universities where students would also learn about cultural and geographic history; and provided new grants for experimenting with the use of TV, radio, and film for educational purposes.[62] The NDEA authorized almost $300 million in low-interest federal student loans over the course of four years, making it the first such investment—equivalent to about $3.1 billion today.[63] The loans came with a hitch, though: every student loan beneficiary was required to take an oath of "true faith and allegiance to the United States of America" and sign an affidavit swearing that they did not "believe in, and [are] not a member of and [do] not support any organization that believes in or teaches, the overthrow of the United States Government."[64] Each of these provisions was to support a central goal: "the security of the Nation [which] requires the fullest development of the mental resources and technical skills of its young men and women."[65]

So if we were to ask ourselves about the purpose of schools in 1958, one clear answer would be: *the purpose of schools is to win the Cold War and ensure the defeat of Communism at home, abroad, and in space.* In 1978 or 1998, the answer would surely have been different, and so too would it vary across geography and political ideology. "What we have wanted from schooling has changed dramatically over time," writes historian Patricia Albjerg Graham, who refers to these ever changing demands as "shifting assignments given to schools," from teaching citizenship to solving social problems to providing preparation for employment.[66]

At this point in the book, we know that the United States relies upon what I have referred to as the Race Machine to operationalize an obsession with sorting humans into racialized categories and maintaining the arbitrary boundaries of those categories. We also know that Thomas Jefferson and many of his contemporaries, influential shapers of the American democratic project, believed in the subhuman savagery of Black and Native individuals and that they consequently built a social framework that established Black, Native, and White peoples as fundamentally different kinds of creatures. So you might assume that if schools hold up a mirror to society and if, as Graham argues, that mirror shifts over time, the mirror would also vary based on the different desires the country has for Black people and Native people. And you'd be right.

In the next three chapters, we'll look at the historical ways that our society has answered that deceptively simple question—"what is the purpose of schools?"—differently for different peoples. As schools have served as the instrument for the United States to build and maintain the society it wants, schools have been instrumental in reinforcing the respective roles that men like Jefferson envisioned for its inhabitants. Although, as we have just discussed, the purposes of school metamorphose over time, there are some consistent threads in our history that linger into the future. We have to understand these in order to understand what we call "racial inequality" in schools at present.[67] For White students, schools have been intended to provide unified leadership for a unified nation. For Black students, schools have been aimed at establishing a class of subservient laborers. And for Native students, schools have been designed to normalize that vision which Jefferson painted as inevitable: total disappearance.

CHAPTER 2

Making Citizens: Schools for White People

Here's the thing about White people: they didn't always exist.

Human beings with light-colored skin, descended from the nations of Europe, have existed for ages, of course. But the cohesive union into a group called White people—a union that required the conceptual flattening of people who looked different, spoke different languages, practiced different faiths, and ate different food—happened over time. Although, as Du Bois noted, the twentieth century would come to be defined by the color line, it is also true that the precise coordinates of that line have shifted more than once.[1]

In her book *The History of White People,* historian Nell Irvin Painter recounts the twisting, turning path by which a group of culturally disparate peoples have come to be viewed as a coherent collective body. For early observers of the United States, such as Jefferson and Alexis de Tocqueville, "White" meant "English."[2] In the many decades since then, the criteria for who gets to be White have been expanded in fits and starts, and in each instance only after great reluctance and the irrefutable onslaught of new immigrant groups. "A notion of freedom lies at the core of the American idea of whiteness," writes Painter, and we can mark changing notions of Whiteness over time by the freedoms permitted or denied to the many subgroups that we now take for granted as "White."[3]

In the nineteenth century, for instance, Irish Catholic people were not yet White. The state of New York kept laws on the books until 1821 denying Catholic people citizenship eligibility unless they would renounce allegiance to the Pope.[4] Around this time, celebrated writer Ralph Waldo Emerson wrote that "it cannot be maintained by any candid person that the African race have ever occupied or do promise ever to occupy any very high place in the human family. Their present condition is the strongest proof that they cannot. The Irish cannot; the American Indian cannot; the Chinese cannot. Before the energy of the Caucasian race all the other races have quailed and done obeisance."[5] From the 1830s to the 1850s, mobs and rioters burned down Irish Catholic churches and residences across the Northeast and, in at least one case, tarred and feathered a priest and almost burned him to death.[6]

After the Civil War, things would change. Between 1880 and 1920, a new wave of over twenty million immigrants would arrive in the United States, the majority of them from eastern and southern Europe.[7] Suddenly, in the face of these newcomers—bringing with them new physical appearances, faith practices, languages, and foods—German and Irish immigrants and their children became the "old" immigrants, in a process that Painter refers to as a "great enlargement of American whiteness."[8] They were no longer a foreign scourge; they got promoted to being White.

Francis Amasa Walker was one social commentator who made the order of things very plain. Born into an elite Boston family and the son of a congressman, Walker was a lauded economist and statistician as well as a Civil War veteran, director of the 1870 census, and ultimately president of the Massachusetts Institute of Technology *and* the American Statistical Association *and* the American Economic Association. In an 1896 issue of *The Atlantic,* Walker sounded the alarm about the newcomers in an article titled "Restriction of Immigration," in which he argued that "the immigrant of today is so widely different from that which existed regarding the immigrant of thirty or fifty years ago."

These *new* immigrants, Walker argued, were of inherently inferior stock, unfit for participation in American life. "The entrance into our political, social, and industrial life of such vast masses of peasantry, degraded below our utmost conceptions, is a matter which no intelligent patriot can look upon without the gravest apprehension and alarm," he warned. "These people have no history behind them which is of a nature to give encouragement. They have none of the inherited instincts and tendencies which made it comparatively easy to deal with the immigration of the olden time." If the United States wanted to help Europe, Walker argued, the nation could do so by serving as a shining example of economic success and self-sufficiency—not by "allowing its city slums and its vast stagnant reservoirs of degraded peasantry to be drained off upon our soil."[9]

Around the same time, Theodore Roosevelt expressed his anxieties about what he called "warfare of the cradle"—the danger that, as new immigrants bore more children, the "higher races" were at risk of "losing their nobler traits and from being overwhelmed by the lower races."[10] By "lower races," Roosevelt was referring to a panoply of people we would now consider White. Roosevelt's lifelong friend, the writer Owen Wister, recalled "race suicide" as being a phrase as closely associated with the president as the more familiar "speak softly and carry a big stick." Wister, who used the family nickname "Dan," wrote of Roosevelt:

> That power to go to the pith of any matter manifested itself in various ways, and quite often. His very phrases were compact instances of it: *Speak softly and carry a big stick; race suicide.* These, with many like them, are still remembered after a quarter of a century, because they hit the truth at a blow. Some of the papers found race suicide amusing, and ridiculed it. "But my dear Dan," he remarked, "they seem unable to see that it's simply a question of the multiplication table. If all our nice friends in Beacon Street, and Newport, and Fifth Avenue, and Philadelphia, have one child, or no child at all, while all the Finnegans, Hooligans, Antonios, Mandelbaums and Rabinskis have eight, or nine, or ten—it's simply a question of the multiplication table. How are you going to get away from it?"[11]

In a 1921 essay for *Good Housekeeping* magazine titled "Whose Country Is This?" Calvin Coolidge wondered aloud how to incorporate these new "aliens." Although Coolidge conceded that immigration could be good for the country, this was only the case insofar as immigrants were assimilable, and he lamented that "our country must cease to be regarded as a dumping ground."[12] How could a new melting pot of White culture, morals, and spirit be achieved? As the boundaries of Whiteness shifted and stretched, political and civic leaders saw schools as an essential site of possibility. Through the transformation of their children, the Irish and Germans and Italians and Czechs could become *American*—could become White.

In fact, although it was kicked into overdrive during the massive immigration wave of the early twentieth century, the idea that schools could create a united White citizenry dates back much earlier. The laws that we might consider the very first legislation governing education in the United States date back to the Massachusetts Bay Colony, where the Puritans who had shown up in the 1600s were very concerned about the wayward ways of unschooled children. The Massachusetts School Law of 1642 declared that every town must appoint men to manage "learning, and labor," and that these men were charged with keeping track of children's "ability to read and understand the principles of religion and the capital laws of the country."[13] A few years later, this statute was accompanied by a piece of legislation that has my personal favorite name among the entire history of education law: the Old Deluder Satan Law. Aside from its dramatic title (which comes from its opening line: "It being one chief project of that old deluder, Satan, to keep men from the knowledge of the Scriptures . . ."), the law is renowned for being the first in the United States to declare that schools should be established and supported collectively by members of a township, rather than the previously more common system of privately paid tutors or masters who took on apprentices.[14]

For the Puritans, these early efforts at creating and maintaining a system of compulsory education had little to do with some of the purposes of school we might hold up as noble today—helping children achieve their dreams or pursue their goals, for instance. Rather, the Massachusetts School Laws were intended to create good participants in the shared project of building a colonial society. As historian Joel Spring writes, "Education was considered essential to maintaining religious piety and social stability. The purpose of teaching reading and writing was to ensure not only that individuals read the Bible and religious tracts, but also that they became good workers and obeyed the laws of the community."[15] *The New-England Primer*, which became a widely used schoolbook for the White children of the colonies, made the duties of its young readers plain in the texts they were required to memorize and recite. Writer Paul Leicester Ford, who edited a reprint of the book in 1897, proclaimed that, by a conservative estimate, the *Primer* had sold three million copies over a 150-year period.[16] The text began with this declaration:

> Now the Child being entred in his Letters and Spelling, let him learn these and such like Sentences by Heart, whereby he will be both instructed in his Duty, and encouraged in his Learning.
>
> *The Dutiful Child's Promises,*
> *I will fear GOD, and honour the KING.*
> *I will honour my Father and Mother.*
> *I will Obey my Superiours.*
> *I will Submit to my Elders,*
> *I will Love my Friends.*[17]

For the Puritans, instructing their children to be good citizens meant teaching them duty and obedience above all. A century later, in the eyes of the men who were attempting to build a new republic, that wasn't going to fly.

In 1778, Thomas Jefferson's "Bill for the More General Diffusion of Knowledge" painted a different picture of what it meant to prepare the White citizenry through schooling. It would be best for everyone, Jefferson argued, if the individuals "whom nature hath endowed with genius and virtue, should be rendered by liberal education worthy to receive, and able to guard the sacred deposit of the rights and liberties of their fellow citizens, and that they should be called to that charge without regard to wealth, birth or other accidental condition or circumstance." Jefferson's law laid out a system in which those eligible to vote in Virginia (White male landowners) would choose a group of people to establish and oversee schools across the commonwealth. "All the free children, male and female," Jefferson wrote, would be allowed to attend these schools free for three years and would learn reading, writing, arithmetic, and the histories of the United States, England, and ancient Greece and Rome. The elected officials were to visit each school annually to examine the pupils and select students "of the best and most promising genius and disposition" to receive additional schooling. This system of "the most diligent examination and enquiry" to determine the cream of the crop would continue at each level of schooling until finally those students "of the best learning and most hopeful genius and disposition" would go on to the College of William & Mary, where they would also receive free tuition, room, and board.[18] The bill failed, but, as Spring argues, the basic ideological premise of Jefferson's proposal persists into our time. "The details of Jefferson's plan are not as important as the idea, which has become ingrained in American social thought, that schooling is the best means of identifying democratic leadership."[19]

One Country, One Language, One Flag

Jefferson's vision was an attempt to answer a question that was as yet unresolved in the early days of the new republic: How was democracy supposed to work, and what role were schools to play in preparing (White) people to participate in and maintain that democracy? For Noah Webster, sometimes called the "Schoolmaster of America," this was a question about the very character of the nation itself.[20] "The mode of Education and the arts taught to youth, have, in every nation, been adapted to its particular stage of society or local circumstances," wrote Webster in a 1790 essay, "On the Education of Youth in America."[21] In ancient Greece, Webster reasoned, schools taught martial skills and courage. In Persia, youth were raised to regulate and maintain a vast empire. So too, Webster reasoned, must the fledgling United States establish schools to serve the state's flourishing. "Our constitutions of civil government are not yet firmly established," he went on.

"Our national character is not yet formed; and it is an object of vast magnitude that systems of Education should be adopted and pursued which may not only diffuse a knowledge of the sciences, but may implant, in the minds of the American youth, the principles of virtue and of liberty; and inspire them with just and liberal ideas of government, and with an inviolable attachment to their own country."[22]

As far as Webster was concerned, the education of his era wasn't cutting it. First of all, too much time was being spent studying dead languages instead of English, a problem Webster called an "absurdity" and a waste of time, remarking that "life is short, and every hour should be employed to good purposes." Webster was also not a fan of the books being used in schools, which focused too much on the histories of ancient Greece and Rome or Britain. "Every child in America should be acquainted with his own country," he argued. "As soon as he opens his lips, he should rehearse the history of his own country; he should lisp the praise of liberty, and of those illustrious heroes and statesmen who have wrought a revolution in her favor."[23]

Webster's concerns were more than philosophical—they were demographic. In 1790, the year he wrote his essay, the United States was already experiencing the plurality of cultures and national origins that would later be subsumed under the general umbrella of Whiteness. Citizens of English origin now made up only 61 percent of the population and were now living alongside arrivals from Scotland, Ireland, Germany, the Netherlands, France, and Sweden.[24] Webster and his contemporaries were trying to build this thing called the United States, an entity that would be cohesive, strong, with a sense of patriotic selfhood and nationalistic pride. And Webster was determined to publish something that would use the commonality of language as a tool for creating commonality of national character and political purpose—which is how he went down in history as the guy whose name is synonymous with the dictionary. His *Grammatical Institute of the English Language* was a three-volume text that Webster hoped would "diffuse a uniformity and purity of language" as a means to "promote the honor and prosperity" of this "infant empire."[25] In another work, *The American Spelling Book,* Webster even created a "federal catechism," a riff on the inclusion of religious catechisms in texts like *The New-England Primer.* It included passages such as these for students to memorize:

> Q. What are the faults of despotic governments?
> A. In a despotic government, a whole nation is at the disposal of one person. If this person the prince, is of a cruel or tyrannical disposition, he may abuse his subjects, take away their lives, their property or their liberty.
>
> . . .
>
> Q. Is there another and better form of government than any of these?
> A. There is. A REPRESENTATIVE REPUBLIC in which the people freely choose deputies to make laws for them, is much the best form of government hitherto invented.
>
> . . .
>
> Q. It is not unjust that all should be bound to obey a law, when all do not consent to it?
> A. Every thing is JUST in government which is NECESSARY to the PUBLIC GOOD. It is impossible to bring all men to think alike on all subjects, so that if we wait for all opinions to be alike respecting laws, we shall have no laws at all.[26]

Webster's writing was a reaction to the already percolating problem of the schoolhouse being a battleground over the terms of citizenship, inclusion, and the boundaries of Whiteness. For instance, German immigrants as early as the 1740s had caused great consternation with their resistance to assimilation into dominant Anglo society, leading Benjamin Franklin to complain that if the already established Pennsylvanians didn't learn German, then true-blooded Americans like himself would now be forced to "live as in a foreign country."[27] Legislators attempted to ban German-language printing presses and books, and local leaders proposed "a common education of English and German youth at the same schools, [where] acquaintances and connections will be formed . . . the English language and a conformity of manners, will be acquired, and they may be taught to feel the meaning and exult in the enjoyment of liberty, a home and social endearments." The local Germans were not so keen on the idea, arguing that the whole project was based on a disparaging image of German culture.[28]

This question—of whether and how non-Anglo European cultures could be reflected in schooling—would resurface a century later, amid the fervor of anti–Irish Catholic sentiment. Throughout the 1830s, Irish Catholic residents of New York City operated their own schools, criticizing state-funded schools for their use of textbooks containing sentiments that were disparaging to Catholics, for using Bibles that they viewed as heretical, and for employing teachers who disrespected Catholic children. In 1840, Governor William Seward, concerned that Irish children educated separately (or not at all) were in danger both of illiteracy and of the failure to assimilate, suggested that the state sponsor "the establishment of schools in which they may be instructed by teachers speaking the same language with themselves and professing the same faith," thereby "qualifying their children for the high responsibilities of citizenship." After all, Seward wrote to a friend, "no system of education could answer the ends of a republic but one which secures the education of all."[29]

As it turned out, Seward's Anglo Protestant constituents did not see it that way. They accused him of "sapping the foundations of liberty," "plotting the ruin of the state," and imperiling the children of the nation by subjecting them to the sins and temptations of "Popery." Defending himself, Seward wrote that his initiative was not something he proposed "because I want [children] to be Catholics but because I want them to become good citizens." Emboldened, Catholic leaders submitted a petition requesting a portion of local public school funds to operate their own schools.[30]

Public opinion on both sides was escalating, and by the evening of the New York City municipal election, tensions had surged to physical fighting. Pro-Catholic and anti-Catholic factions met in the streets, and a bloody brawl between them grew to what local reports claimed was a mob of ten thousand fighters and onlookers. By nine o'clock at night, the anti-Catholic group—calling itself the "Spartans"—had broken into private homes, a hotel, and eventually the residence of St. Patrick's Cathedral, smashing windows and furniture and throwing rocks.[31] After it was all over, some of the press blamed the anti-Catholic violence on the Catholics themselves and their demand for school funding, "which has greatly exasperated our citizens."[32] Similar events took place in Philadelphia in 1843, after the school board ruled that Catholic students could read their own Bible. In the ensuing conflict, thirteen people died and a Catholic church was incinerated.[33]

If ideological differences regarding the purpose of schooling could so viciously rend the republic, the pressure would revert to schools to eliminate these differences as efficiently and peacefully as possible. This was the belief of Horace Mann, often known as the father of the common school movement. The age of the common school would end the piecemeal educational systems scattered across the country and replace them with the antecedent of the modern public school: consistent, state-funded and state-managed, and open to White children from all class backgrounds.

Mann was the first secretary of the Massachusetts State Board of Education before being elected to Congress. Troubled by what he saw as inevitable social strife arising from class and cultural conflicts in a diverse nation, Mann viewed the common school as a necessary alternative to political violence. For Mann, the "common" in *common school* meant more than class accessibility. It also meant a common moral, ideological, and political curriculum in support of a unified citizenry.[34] As historian Carl Kaestle points out, the idea of the common school put forth by Mann and his contemporaries reveals some pretty obvious self-contradictions if you scratch beneath the surface. In their view, "political education consisted of stressing common beliefs and glorifying the exercise of intelligence in a republic, while urging respect for laws and downplaying the very issues upon which citizens might exercise their intelligence."[35] Free speech was good in theory, but not if it threatened social stability. The ideal citizen should demonstrate independent thinking, but not in ways that would inspire disorder. He would be, as Kaestle describes, "constructive, on occasion critical, but always cautious and respectful."[36] Unity and social cohesion would be the keys to bringing the Founding Fathers' dream of a republic of intelligent White citizens to life, and schools would provide.

This was all well and good . . . until those *new* immigrants came along. In 1880, about 38,000 people immigrated from eastern and southern European countries to the United States. By 1890, that number had more than quadrupled, to almost 160,000. By 1900, *that* number had more than doubled.[37] Between 1900 and 1915, over fifteen million immigrants arrived, roughly matching the number of immigrants who had come to the United States in the previous four decades combined.[38] This era is much romanticized in our popular culture—Ellis Island and the Statue of Liberty; grandparents from the old country arriving with a pocket full of dreams; the cheerful "melting pot" from which we derive the glorious fiction of being "a nation of immigrants."[39]

But for the immigrants themselves, the men who deemed themselves guardians of democracy—and the unity that was seen as a prerequisite for that democracy—didn't exactly roll out the red carpet. Just as it seemed that the previously troublesome Irish and German immigrants were moving into the American mainstream, the newcomers created yet another crisis at the boundaries of Whiteness.

Ellwood Cubberley, an influential scholar of education and dean of the Stanford Graduate School of Education from 1917 to 1933, described the challenge as he saw it in a 1909 book titled *Changing Conceptions of Education.* "The willingness, good nature, and executive qualities of the Irish, the intellectual thoroughness of the German, the respect for law and order of the English, and the thrift of the Scandinavian have been good additions to our life," Cubberley wrote.[40] The new immigrants, in Cubberley's view, had no such redeeming qualities, and were clustered in "groups or settlements" upon arrival where they continued to maintain "their national manners, customs, and observances." In order to move forward, Cubberley argued, these groups should be broken up, "to assimilate and amalgamate these people as a part of our American race, and to implant in their children, so far as can be done, the Anglo-Saxon conception of righteousness, law and order, and popular government, and to awaken in them a reverence for our democratic institutions and for those things in our national life which we as a people hold to be of abiding worth."[41]

In the South, the newcomers were reminded that they were not yet White through their attempts to navigate the racial order. In the small town of Sumrall, Mississippi, in 1907, Joseph and Josephine Frier—two Italian children—attempted to enroll in their local White public school. When they arrived on their first day, the principal suspended them, pending a ruling from the school superintendent regarding whether they were indeed White. A local Sicilian shoemaker, Frank Scaglioni, led efforts to intervene on their behalf, and the superintendent decided in the children's favor. They returned to classes for the remainder of the week. On Friday, Scaglioni was dragged from his bed in the middle of the night, taken to the woods, viciously beaten and whipped, and abandoned. The children and their families fled the town the following Monday.[42]

"We soon got the idea that 'Italian' meant something inferior, and a barrier was erected between children of Italian origin and their parents," wrote educator Leonard Covello in his memoir, *The Heart Is the Teacher.* Covello and his friends, like generations of immigrants for years to come, would hide the food that their parents packed for them to avoid being mocked by their peers—the very same cheese and salami sandwiches that are now considered as American as apple pie.[43] "This was the accepted process of Americanization," wrote Covello. "We were becoming Americans by learning how to be ashamed of our parents."[44] It wasn't just about learning English. If these newcomers were to blend seamlessly into the fabric of the American project—if they were to become White—they needed to eat a certain way, to raise their children a certain way. This would be the key to national harmony, and once again schools were the place to make it happen. If you visit an average American public school today, you are likely to witness a number of social innovations that arose during this period. These everyday features, which we take for granted as part of the fabric of life in schools, are hallmarks of the generations-long project of using schools to create a sense of national cohesion and a unified White citizenry.

From the Pledge to the Playground

I vividly remember the night before my first day of kindergarten, drifting off to sleep next to my mother in the bed I shared with her and my brother. As I was fading away, she spoke to me quietly, letting me know what to expect when the school bus took me away. "And you'll say something called the Pledge of Allegiance," she whispered. "I pledge allegiance, to the flag . . ."

What does it mean to pledge allegiance to the flag, and to the republic for which it stands? Despite the vaguely militaristic and expressly nationalistic trappings of this practice, the pledge, which was written by Francis Bellamy in 1892, did not make its debut on a military base, in the halls of Congress, or at citizenship ceremonies. It was born for the place where it now most famously lives—the American school.

The first version of the pledge was created by George Balch, a former Civil War captain who found himself, in the 1880s, decrying what he saw as a decline in patriotism as the shared cause of maintaining the union faded into the background and the wave of new immigrants he referred to as "human scum" began arriving on the shores of the United States. "As time went on and the stirring events of the war passed into history, the exuberance of patriotic ardor became less and less," he lamented.[45] In his postwar career as a New York City school auditor, Balch saw an opportunity for a corrective. He wrote a simple pledge designed for school recitation, in honor of the first Flag Day celebration in 1885. "I give my heart and my hand to my country," declared the Balch Salute. "One country, one language, one flag."[46]

The Balch Salute spread in popularity but soon would be eclipsed by the version penned by Bellamy, who decried the first version as "too juvenile" and abstract, disconnected from real historical meaning.[47] Bellamy, a former pastor, was a brand-new employee at a popular magazine for children called *The Youth's Companion*. At the time when Bellamy came on board, *The Youth's Companion* was already engaged in an effort to spread the good news of patriotism to its young readers: the magazine advertised small, affordable flags that children could purchase for home or school and it sponsored an essay contest on the importance of flag raising.

Bellamy was tasked with an important job: planning activities for the 1892 celebrations that would commemorate the quadricentennial of Columbus's arrival in the Americas. Bellamy designed a program of speeches, celebrations, salutes, and pledges that he envisioned would be enacted simultaneously in every public school across the land, and he lobbied fiercely to gain support for the plan. He found cheerleaders in everyone from Grover Cleveland to John Palmer of the Grand Army of the Republic, who loved the idea. "It will impress all these pupils that they've got a country," declared Palmer. "The school is . . . the only thing that represents the nation to millions."[48] President Benjamin Harrison was in support of the effort, reflecting his belief that the schoolhouse was "the place for education in intelligent patriotism and citizenship."[49]

A little less than a month before he would ultimately write the pledge, Bellamy gave a speech to the annual meeting of the National Education Association on the theme "Americanism in the public schools." It was imperative, he told the assembled educators, for "children of foreign parentage" to see and salute the flag so as to receive a "daily object lesson in patriotism for the land of their adoption." Through the children, the flag would smooth the schisms that might otherwise divide the land. "The flag," asserted Bellamy, "has as great a potency to Americanize the alien child as it has to lead regiments to death."[50]

As the printing deadline approached for the issue of *The Youth's Companion* that would give schools the needed directions for the celebration, the magazine's leaders arranged the necessary content—an original song, a poem, a public address—but at the eleventh hour were still in need of a flag salute, something "of more dignity" than the popular Balch version.[51] Bellamy was tasked with the job. Under the wire, after many scribbles and revisions, he came up with a pledge that he thought adequately expressed not only loyalty but "the *reason* for loyalty." *I pledge allegiance to my Flag and to the Republic for which it stands—one Nation indivisible—with Liberty and Justice for all.*[52]

When the day of celebration came and schools led their celebratory exercises across the country, Bellamy himself attended one in Malden, Massachusetts. Speaking to the gathered audience, he made it clear that although Columbus's voyage was funded by Spain, the glory of America had little to do with people from such southern European countries. The United States, he reminded everyone, "was built purely of Anglo-Saxon stuff. Those mighty men of the Lord that settled Massachusetts, the clean Quakers of Pennsylvania, the cavalier stock that established itself on the James—these were the true makers of America." Had Spanish-controlled territories lingered and expanded in the United States, Bellamy argued, "then all this continent would have wallowed on in the dirty ignorance and superstition and barbarism which have characterized all the colonies of Spain." Not one for subtlety, Bellamy drove the point home further in case anyone had fallen asleep: "America is not due to the enterprise of Spain. If we have anything worth celebrating here, we are to remember it was in spite of Spain."[53] America was a White nation, Bellamy reminded everyone, and not all Europeans were White—only the "clean" ones. He had made this clear in other writing, as well: "The hard, inescapable fact is that men are not born equal."[54]

After the festivities had passed, *The Youth's Companion* published a commentary—unsigned, but likely written by Bellamy himself—lauding the success of the Columbus Day pageantry. The day had been "more marked by seriousness and unanimity, than any other single day in the last quarter of a century." The key word here, of course, was "unanimity." The celebration, and particularly the pledge that Bellamy had devised, had accomplished its goal of turning the schoolhouse into a place that affirmed the cohesion of an increasingly diverse nation-state. After all, the author asserted, "the common education of the citizen in the common duties of citizenship is the function of the state." The flag was to forever serve as a reminder that "the distinctive principles of true Americanism will not perish so long as free, public education endures," and the celebration "impressed powerfully upon the youth that we are a nation." As more new immigrants would continue to arrive in the coming decades, Bellamy and his supporters felt that they had instilled the perfect tool to bring unified nationalism into the daily routines of the classroom. No need to worry about the loyalties of these children and their families if they began each day with their hands over their hearts saluting the flag.

Other quotidian elements of the schoolhouse could be marshaled toward the project of Americanization as well. The children, impressionable and malleable, could serve willingly or unwillingly as the vanguard of assimilation in their households—even through their diets.

In 1890, the New England Kitchen was founded. It was bankrolled by Pauline Agassiz Shaw (daughter of Louis Agassiz, whom we'll meet later)[55] to serve as a "food depot," offering ready-to-eat foods to Boston's growing population of low-income immigrants in a year when over a third of the city's residents had been born in another country.[56] The project was overseen by a local chemist, Ellen Swallow Richards, who had been the first woman admitted to MIT and later would be the first woman to teach there. The two women set up shop in the North End, home to Irish and, increasingly, Italian immigrants. Similar public kitchens were soon opened in settlement houses in Chicago and Philadelphia.[57] Shaw believed that a proper diet could contribute to morality, health, and temperance among the poor, but after a few years Richards considered their efforts unsuccessful, because some of their charges knew how to eat more cheaply than what the New England Kitchen could offer, while others simply did "not care for clean wholesome food." By and large, their neighbors did not appreciate the offerings of pea soup, creamed codfish, and oatmeal mush.[58] Indeed, some of the would-be beneficiaries recognized that the kitchen was an attempt to assimilate them, such as the Irish boy who rejected the food with the remark, "You can't make a Yankee of me that way!"[59] Richards's co-crusader, Mary H. Abel, lamented that the immigrants were "incorrigible" and wondered aloud at how a shared diet, much like Bellamy's vision for a shared salute, could work to bring newcomers into the fold of Whiteness. More and more, Abel observed, people in big cities were veering away from dishes that needed time and a modicum of skill. "What are the national dishes of Americans?" she asked.[60] It didn't seem to occur to them that the very same immigrants whose food habits they called "depraved" could teach them a thing or two about flavor.[61] The spices, garlic, onions, and other aromatics used by these groups were seen as smelly and disgusting.[62]

No—there had to be a better approach, the women concluded. If the impoverished masses would not *choose* to eat their nutritious food, perhaps they should begin with people in institutional spaces who didn't have much choice in what they ate: people in asylums, hospitals, and schools. Indeed, even as the New England Kitchen was floundering overall, it was successfully selling lunches to Boston public schools and reaching five thousand students.[63] Schools, they reasoned, would be the way: a place not only to model, but to *teach* the science of how to eat well and manage a household efficiently.[64] And thus, "home economics" was born.

Richards, with her background in science, believed that this work was about more than short-term health or charity—it was the path toward human progress; she and other burgeoning home economics enthusiasts referred to poor dietary habits as "sins."[65] In 1904, Richards would attempt unsuccessfully to popularize the term "euthenics," which she defined as the science of improving society through controlling the environment (a corollary to "eugenics," the idea of improving society through selective breeding).[66] Home economics, according to Richards, was "nothing less than an effort to save our social fabric from what seems inevitable disintegration."[67]

Inspired to find like-minded evangelists, Richards founded an annual conference that paved the way for the creation of the American Home Economics Association. In 1912, the AHEA established a legislative subcommittee to bring its vision to a national scale.[68] By 1917, Congress was deliberating over the Smith-Hughes Act, which would promote and fund vocational and technical training and home economics. AHEA leadership called upon members to write their representatives in support, and as the bill was debated on Capitol Hill, congressmen painted a dire picture of where the country was headed in the absence of home economics. "Without this knowledge thousands of homes will be wrecked, thousands of lives ruined," said Vermont senator Carroll S. Page. Without this necessary training, "crime, disease, divorce, and race suicide" would continue their ascent.[69] The act funded the expansion of home economics courses in public schools nationwide, as well as college courses to train the teachers and supervisors needed for that expansion.[70] By 1921, two-thirds of major school systems required seventh- and eighth-grade girls to enroll in the course.[71]

With the rise of home economics came the rise of school lunch, bringing Abel and Richards's vision to scale. These efforts were seen as a means to narrow the cultural chasm between new immigrants and White Americans.[72] Through scientifically engineered and quintessentially American foods, immigrant children would assimilate, and bring the impact of their new identity home to the rest of the family. "An Italian girl who has had lessons in cooking at the public school," explained social reformer Jane Addams in *Ladies' Home Journal,* "will help her mother to connect the entire family with American food and household habits."[73]

Even kindergarten, that most precious of school institutions, can trace its ubiquity to the project of creating a unified White citizenry. The earliest advocates for kindergarten saw its potential to teach children to socialize, to work with companions, and to not be self-centered.[74] But with the rapid demographic changes of the 1880s and the 1890s came a new purpose for kindergarten: elevating the new immigrants into worthiness for assimilative citizenship. As historian Marvin Lazerson has written, social reformers believed that "the kindergarten was more akin to the settlement house than to the school"; it was less a place for children to begin learning academic foundations and more a mechanism to assist their families in "melting" into their new country.[75]

In an essay titled "The Kindergarten: An Uplifting Social Influence in the Home and the District" published in *The Kindergarten Review* in 1903, magazine editor Richard Watson Gilder made the case plain. New York, he argued, faced particular social challenges because of its surge in immigration. "Other American cities have to do with alien populations, but we more than any other. . . . We are trying to Americanize this great mass in the best sense of the word."[76] Given this challenge, the kindergarten offered an important opportunity. "You cannot catch your citizen too early in order to make him a good citizen," wrote Gilder. "The kindergarten age marks our earliest opportunity to catch the little Russian, the little Italian, the little German, Pole, Syrian, and the rest and begin to make good American citizens of them."[77]

This calling—"making good American citizens"—was understood to have a moral element; the newcomers were understood to be not only poor but also immoral, subject to the whims of ignorance and vice. Through the ministry of their children, they could become good, but only through early intervention. Otherwise the children would remain, as they were characterized by social reformer Mary Mann (wife of Horace Mann), "little savages" and "pests of the street," dragging society into chaos.[78]

Then there was the matter of recess. Social reformers saw the designation of formal times and spaces for play as another essential tool for building a cohesive national American character amid rapid social change. Organized play in schools, and the playgrounds on which it takes place, was popularized during the "playground movement" of the late nineteenth and early twentieth centuries.[79] When the Playground Association of America had its first conference in Chicago in 1907, the headlining speeches included topics such as "Relation of Play to Juvenile Delinquency" and "Play as Training in Citizenship," as well as a talk by Jane Addams on "Public Recreation and Social Morality."[80] Playground reformers summarized their beliefs in the "Playground National Song": *"While playing we learn our duties / We owe to one and all, / For with fair play and square deal, too, we are ready for our country's call."*[81]

Henry Stoddard Curtis, a child psychologist who became the playground director for New York City's public schools and later the city playground supervisor in Washington, D.C., was a leader in the movement. In his book *Education Through Play,* Curtis explained why play was serious business: "Play is always, I fancy, the most effective teacher of that kind of good comradeship that makes for political and social success."[82] As Curtis saw it, play was essential to teaching individuals the kind of self-sacrifice required for a functional republic, and such play required designated space:

> A person who thinks only of himself and his own welfare is a bad citizen. A person who always conceives of himself as a member of a larger whole to which his loyalty is due is a good citizen. . . . But the boy who is playing a game on a vacant lot

> does not acquire this spirit, for the reason that the scrub team has no permanent organization, no captain, and no future.[83]

If children were taught how to play games formally, in a designated space and with clearly transmitted rules, Curtis argued, "after six weeks, they did not know whether they were Jews or Italians."[84] The playground was "a junior republic" and "the most perfect democracy," preparing children for leadership and participation in civil society.[85] He felt that play was also important for children who were not immigrants, because, without it, they were destined to weaken from generation to generation and ultimately become fragile and sterile. Citing eugenicist doctor Havelock Ellis, Curtis argued that too much focus on indoor life was leading to lowered birth rates among "civilized" peoples, and if this trend was not corrected, "we shall soon become a nation of immigrants at the mercy of the ideals of South Europe."[86] Like Teddy Roosevelt, Curtis feared that "degeneracy of the race" was an ever present threat.

By the mid-twentieth century, these social innovations, which are now fixtures of schools—the Pledge of Allegiance, the cafeteria, the playground—had done their job.[87] As the twentieth century marched on, the social fabric of the nation was rocked first by World War II and then by the civil rights movement; each of these periods offered this diverse group of immigrants new figures of Others against whom they could define themselves as having a cohesive White identity. Toni Morrison described this process of "othering" as the "most enduring and efficient rite of passage into American culture. . . . Only when the lesson of racial estrangement is learned is assimilation complete."[88] With the help of schools, those who had been contemptible "aliens" could now partake of the fruits of American prosperity, like the benefits of the New Deal and eventually suburban homeownership. Historian Matthew Frye Jacobson refers to this as the end of "probationary whiteness." Having proved their mettle through social participation in schools and its associated institutions, those once considered dirty and unwelcome "were now remade and granted the scientific stamp of authenticity as the unitary Caucasian race—an earlier era's Celts, Slavs,

Hebrews, Iberics, and Saracens, among others, had become the Caucasians so familiar to our own visual economy and racial lexicon."[89]

Throughout these decades of consternation and debate about how schools could make immigrants into White people, the great thinkers and political leaders had not much to say about Black or Native people, who, it was understood, would *not* be participating in the project of democracy. Schools for them, then, would serve a different purpose.

CHAPTER 3

Saviorism and Social Control: Schools for Black People

Generations before the standoff at Central High School in Little Rock would captivate the nation and long before we watched the tiny figure of Ruby Bridges being escorted by federal marshals into her elementary school, it was clear that the "othering" Toni Morrison described, the "racial estrangement," had a home in the institution of schooling. We should understand public schools not only as a reflection of anti-Black ideology, but as sites fundamental to the creation, formalization, and reification of that ideology.

Consider, for instance, the African School, founded by free Black people in Boston in 1798.[1] The school was run independently until 1812, when the Boston public school system annexed it and began the formal practice of assigning all Black school-age children who enrolled in the district to that particular school. By 1846, Black parents had become concerned that this practice was leading to an inferior subsystem within the system. Fifty years before *Plessy v. Ferguson* and over a century before *Brown v. Board of Education,* the parents argued in a petition that separate was inherently unequal. "Where a small and despised class are shut out from the common benefit of any public institutions of learning and confined to separate schools," they wrote, "few or none [of those on the school committee] interest themselves about the schools . . . the teachers and students are soon considered and of course become an inferior class."[2]

The parents requested that the Boston Primary School Committee allow their children to enroll in whichever school was closest to where they lived. In a testimony before the committee, one representative called upon the very same spirit of social togetherness and fellowship that would drive the assimilation efforts described in the previous section. Merely offering an education to Black children in a segregated system, he argued, would deny them the opportunity to be fully participating members of civil society. Rather, each child should have "the right to be mingled in, and crumbled up with, the mass of society in which he lives." Indeed, he argued, this was the *most* important aspect of schooling, over and above academic influence: "It is the humanizing, socializing influence of the school system, which is its most important feature."[3]

In response, the school committee issued a clear decision: although Black children in Massachusetts were entitled access to free public schools, it was against natural law that they should do so in the company of White children. This was not simply a matter of skin color, they argued: "It is one of *races,* not of colors, merely. The distinction is one which the All-wise Creator has seen fit to establish; and it is founded deep in the physical, mental, and moral natures of the two races. No legislation, no social customs, can efface this distinction."[4] Allowing White and Black students to attend school together, according to the committee, would harm both groups.

Recall that this was occurring in 1846—*after* the political battles to do away with separate German schools, and around the same time as the fights over Irish schools. Separate schools for those students were understood to be bad, as it prevented them from passing into dominant culture and participating as loyal citizens of the republic. Separate schools for Black people, on the other hand, were understood to be good—a reflection of God's will for the natural order and the structural representation of separate standing in society.

These children were not meant to be participants in the republic, according to the prevailing logic, and should not be educated as such. Preparation for leadership, citizenship, and assimilation into the cohesive body politic that defines the American republic has *not* historically been the purpose of schools for Black people—because that body politic has been understood to be White, as the ideal of American citizenship has been understood to be White. For Black people in the

United States, schools have had a different purpose: civilization. With civilization comes its underlying ethos, *saviorism,* and its underlying purpose, social control.

Education for Black people, like education for all people, has happened in infinite ways and spaces, some of which are most profound when they have happened outside of formal settings. Enslaved people teaching one another to read, children learning songs and jump-rope games from their peers, families passing cherished recipes from generation to generation: these are all forms of education, the human enterprise of teaching and learning through social interaction. But if we are to understand the history of *schooling* for Black people as an institutional practice, our story takes root in the first mass effort to create formal learning structures for Black people in the United States: Reconstruction.[5]

The story of schools for Black people in Reconstruction is a complicated one, because it involves Black people seeking self-determination through schools and White people seeking a "civilizing" instrument of social control through those same schools. In the American South in the years following Emancipation, formerly enslaved Black people were strong advocates not only for their own education, but for universal public schools. As W. E. B. Du Bois wrote in his classic work *Black Reconstruction in America,* "Public education for all at public expense, was, in the South, a Negro idea," as establishing mass public education—for anyone—in the South prior to Reconstruction had not been a social priority.[6] In the 1850s, nearly one in five White men in the South was unable to read.[7] As newly freed Black people fought fervently for schools, their work inspired fear and contempt, as education was perceived as a barrier to continuing an extractive labor relationship. Du Bois explained that every Black person who was educated represented "labor lost," and too much teaching "encouraged directly or indirectly, insolence to employers. 'Schooling,' felt the South, 'ruins a nigger.'"[8] Even many Northerners who identified as progressive allies to freedpeople were often unwilling to extend their philanthropic spirit beyond basics like food and clothing, as they found the premise of educating Black people to be a discomfiting one.[9] But eventually, the efforts to offer schooling to formerly enslaved Black people would become one of the largest mass expansions of the public schooling project in American history.

From the early part of the Civil War through 1870, more than fifty religious and secular organizations were engaged in schooling the Black people of the South[10]—first, the Black people referred to as "contraband," who through escape or military participation found themselves in the care of the Union Army; later, the masses freed by the Emancipation Proclamation. By July 1870, over 3,500 teachers were involved in this effort.[11]

These teachers were not uniform in their motivations nor in their principles. Some came from a missionary tradition, from religious organizations that saw educating freedmen as a necessary step on the way to saving their souls. Others, inspired by the tradition of abolitionist William Lloyd Garrison, believed that the new schooling efforts should be nonsectarian and non-evangelical.[12] But the majority of these teachers, who were either White reformers from the North or local White women recruited in the South, were united by the same basic premise: the task of *civilization*. In their view, Black people's ways were wild, untamed, and backwards, and the job of the schoolmarm was to bring them closer to the White man's way of life.

Compared to some of their contemporaries, these teachers' views were "progressive" in that they did not profess Black people to be *innately* backwards or beyond redemption—only savage and barbarous as a result of their savage and barbarous circumstances, but nevertheless eligible to be "saved" through benevolent efforts. "The instruction most needed by the blacks was not in the knowledge of school books, but in that which should lead them to appreciate the advantages of civilized life," wrote the Boston Educational Commission for Freedmen in its first annual report.[13] John W. Alvord, who served as the general superintendent of education for the Freedmen's Bureau, wrote that education was necessary to uplift the moral character of the formerly enslaved. "With it they will at once start upward in all character. Without it they will as quickly sink into the depravities of ignorance and vice; free to be what they please, and in the presence only of bad example, they will be carried away with every species of evil."[14]

Despite their avowed dedication to the cause, Unitarian ministers

William Gannett and Edward Everett Hale wrote with caution that observers should not too readily believe the sunny reports of effective Negro education coming from the South in the 1860s, which they called "very exaggerated." They conceded that freed Black people could certainly develop those mental abilities that were "in close connection with the outward senses," such as memorization. However, Gannett and Hale wrote, they were "deficient in the more ideal operations, which require reflection and reasoning."[15] An 1864 questionnaire of representatives overseeing Negro education efforts reflected similar ideas. "They have great aptness for language, music and the imitative arts," said some superintendents. "Perhaps they will prove deficient in logic and the mathematics," said others.[16]

John William De Forest, a Union captain born in Connecticut who was an assistant commissioner of the Freedmen's Bureau in South Carolina, wrote that the desire for education was "the most hopeful sign" for the future of Black people in the United States. But on the question of Black intelligence, De Forest wrote that it was a pointless one. The Black children he observed in school, he believed, "could not compare with the Caucasian youngster of ten or twelve," a fact De Forest attributed to a lack of a "refined home influence," "advanced ideas from the daily converse of [the] family," and "ancestral intelligence, trained through generations of study." De Forest put it clearly: "I am convinced that the Negro as he is, no matter how educated, is not the mental equal of the European." Whether Black people were humans at all, according to De Forest, was "quite another question and of so little practical importance. . . . Human or not, there he is in our midst, millions strong; and if he is not educated mentally and morally, he will make us trouble."[17]

Indeed, some leaders charged with overseeing efforts at Negro education felt it tactically necessary to assure the public that their teachers were *not* trying to promote the idea that Black and White people were equal. To do so, they feared, would alienate local White citizens and therefore put the whole operation at risk. G. L. Eberhart, who was appointed to oversee educational efforts in Georgia, wrote with great concern of one teacher who had incited fury among the locals when she told a White person that "the negroes are as good as that white person," which Eberhart called "entirely unnecessary." Eberhart felt that "we can not therefore expect to excite any thing but ill feelings and disrespect among the white people here, if we run too far beyond what they deem the limits of prudence and propriety."[18] In Mississippi, superintendent Joseph Warren wrote reassuringly in a report to a superior that there was no need to worry about his teachers, as "I have not known a single case of association with the colored people on the ground of social equality."[19]

To an extent, their fears were motivated by the real threat of violence. Schools for Black people were burned and threatened, their educators condemned as "nigger teachers."[20] Despite this danger, some of the teachers persisted doggedly, impressed by the progress they saw possible in their pupils. Cornelia Hancock, a Quaker nurse during the Civil War and teacher during Reconstruction, wrote in one letter to her niece: "I have been teaching in school this week and you would be astonished at the little blacks. They know so much. They are very much smarter than the children of the people in our neighborhood who dislike them so much."[21]

For the majority of Reconstruction, most teachers were "Yankees," White Northerners typically from Massachusetts, New York, or Ohio, most often unmarried women.[22] In describing the ideal teaching candidate, the New England Freedmen's Aid Society (tellingly, using female pronouns) said that she ought to be able to see the spirit and mission of Jesus in her pupils, and "she should feel also the importance of the work in relation to our country. . . . She will need all these motives of religion and patriotism to sustain her in her duties."[23] She also would need to have "high moral character, purity of heart and mind . . . and dignified propriety of manner." The *Boston Recorder*, warning against the risks of sending non-evangelical teachers into the South, said that religion was a fundamental tenet of successfully educating the freedmen: "When this is ignored, or set at naught, the most effective instrumentality for their civilization is set aside."[24]

In addition to the archetypal "Yankee schoolmarm," some White leaders born in the South participated in Reconstruction education efforts, if they could overcome the Northern-led missionary leaders who often saw them as either ignorant and uneducated themselves or too loyal to the Confederacy to safely be allowed access to Black students. But given the desperate need for teachers, even avowedly progressive supervisors were willing to look the other way. Laura Matilda Towne, an abolitionist from Philadelphia, described observing a school led by two teachers who were "in the war undoubted rebels. Indeed, we hear that they whip the children in their school and make them call them 'Massa' and 'Missus,' as in the old time." Nevertheless, Towne wrote, she was still responsible for these teachers, so rather than fire them, "I did my duty by them as agreeably as I could."[25] Other school founders had previously owned slaves.[26] One White teacher in Virginia, applying for state funds to open a freedmen's school, wrote that education was a way to determine whether Black people were indeed "people or entirely of animal creation, as they have always been considered and treated."[27]

Anthony Toomer Porter was another such local leader. Porter was a son of the South who saw the work of schooling freedmen as an extension of his prior calling as a minister, and he characterized the institution of slavery as "the greatest missionary work ever done by man. Not five hundred thousand naked African savages were brought over to America before the trade was stopped, and had they remained in Africa, if they had not been eaten by the king of Dahomey, their descendants would be naked African savages still. . . . I love the African race, and think they are the most wonderful people (taking all their history) of the present day, and yet, I believe they are an inferior type of men, and the mass of them will be hewers of wood and drawers of water till the end of time—at the least, to the end of many generations. Do for them as we will, a black man will never be a white one."[28]

Porter believed that if Southerners did not make an effort to lead Reconstruction schooling efforts, formerly enslaved people would come to look upon Northerners as their "deliverers." He therefore traveled across the country to raise funds for a freedmen's school in South Carolina.[29] Meanwhile, in Georgia, avowed Confederate sympathizer James R. Smith believed that many in the North were determined to "degrade," "destroy," and "oppress" the South—and also that he was called by God "to this work . . . of educating the African."[30] William Hauser, who also ran a freedmen's school in Georgia, wrote that the "hundreds of bright eyed, smart little darkies" he observed around him "must become educated and useful citizens of the country, or they will relapse into barbarism, and become a curse to themselves and the country."[31]

Propriety and Civility

The textbooks created for newly freed Black people were accordingly designed to counter any threat of such a relapse into barbarism. Books like *The Freedman's Third Reader,* published by the Boston-based American Tract Society, laid bare the kinds of curricular priorities that reformers viewed as essential for Black learners. Alongside basic phonics and stories from the Bible and American history, the text contained parables and short stories designed to provide Black people with moral instruction about their role in the world.

A lesson titled "Love to Enemies" reminds readers of God's desire that we love and forgive those who have trespassed against us, using the biblical story of Stephen, who prayed for the wicked as they stoned him to death.[32] "Life of Paul Cuffe" tells the story of the Massachusetts freedman in a way that emphasizes Cuffe's "prudence and industry" and Christianity, the latter of which "lent the brightest charm to his manhood, and became the most important feature of his character."[33] A passage about Toussaint L'Ouverture, leader of the Haitian Revolution, describes his years of enslavement as "days of quiet domestic joy." (In reality, conditions of Haitian enslavement were deplorable, marked by ceaseless work, hunger, and beatings; estimates suggest that as many as one-third of Africans who arrived in the Caribbean and were forced into enslavement died within a year.[34]) L'Ouverture, we learn, "was sedate in manner, and exceedingly patient, being possessed of an evenness of temper which scarcely any thing seemed capable of disturbing."[35] In his fight for freedom, according to the *Reader,* L'Ouverture "had no feelings of revenge to gratify, but was the same amiable and charitable person as ever."[36] (His famous proclamation of 1793, in which L'Ouverture declared, "I have undertaken vengeance," doesn't get a mention.) Like Stephen, he always forgave those who had wronged him or treated him cruelly. We learn that once he attained a position of leadership, "the first use which he made of his power was to establish order and discipline among the blacks. To this they readily submitted"; and as governor, he "only noticed with favor the modest, the quiet, the diligent soldier and citizen."[37] The message to newly freed Black Americans about what makes for a prosperous nation is clear: through L'Ouverture's leadership, "a nation of freedmen had been created out of negro slaves; and their leader had succeeded in teaching them that virtue, order, industry, and necessary self-restraint, were, under God, the only and sufficient guaranty of civil and social liberty."[38]

"Virtue, order, industry, and necessary self-restraint" were traits equally emphasized in *The Freedman's Book,* edited by abolitionist writer Lydia Maria Child. *The Freedmen's Book* included poems and passages by William Lloyd Garrison, Frederick Douglass, and Phillis Wheatley, alongside biographical sketches of people like John Brown and Benjamin Banneker written by Child herself. Incredibly, Child's account of John Brown conveniently omits any mention of rebellion, instead recounting a story of how he paused on his way to the gallows to kiss a small Black child because it's what Jesus would have done. (The details of *why* he was going to the gallows are not included.)[39] At the end of the volume, Child included an essay titled "Advice from an Old Friend." Addressing Black readers directly, Child described herself as someone with "great sympathy for you, my brethren and sisters, and I have tried to do what I could to help you to freedom." Accordingly, Child offers what she believes to be the keys to Black thriving post-Emancipation:

> You can do a vast amount of good to people in various parts of the world, and through successive generations, by simply being sober, industrious, and honest. There are still many slaves in Brazil and in the Spanish possessions. If you are vicious, lazy, and careless, their masters will excuse themselves for continuing to hold them in bondage, by saying: "Look at the freedmen of the United States! What idle vagabonds they are! How dirty their cabins are! How slovenly their dress!

> That proves that negroes cannot take care of themselves, that they are not fit to be free." . . . Your manners will have a great effect in producing an impression to your advantage or disadvantage. Be always respectful and polite toward your associates, and toward those who have been in the habit of considering you an inferior race. It is one of the best ways to prove that you are not inferior.[40]

Child goes on to describe the importance of Black people maintaining propriety in all things: keeping clothes clean and "nicely patched" to "indicate that the wearer is neat and economical," using whitewash and strategic floral planting to "make the poorest cabin look beautiful" in order to cheer up neighbors and offer "an advertisement, easily read by all men, that the people who live there are not lazy, slovenly, or vulgar."[41] She implored freedpeople to work hard, be "temperate in your habits," save money, and donate some of it to charitable causes.

"If your former masters and mistresses are in trouble, show them every kindness in your power, whether they have treated you kindly or not," she urged. "Remember the words of the blessed Jesus: 'Do good to them that hate you, and pray for them which despitefully use you and persecute you.'"[42] Child encouraged readers to go work for these former masters if they were kindly enough, but also emphasized that freedpeople should react with forgiveness and charity regardless of any mistreatment they might receive, and to never cheat their employers or break promises to them. If the employers tried to sexually assault Black women, "teach them that freed women not only have the legal power to protect themselves from such degradation, but also that they have pride of character. If in fits of passion, they abuse your children as they formerly did, never revenge it by any injury to them or their property."[43] In the Child moral curriculum, there was no indignity so harmful, no violence so obscene that a Black person should not receive it with grace. And if the abuse continued, Child exhorted her readers, they ought to take it up with the local legal system. What if the local legal system was inhospitable to Black people? Child had a plan for this, too: write your senator! "If you are so unlucky as to live where the men in authority, whether civil or military, are still disposed to treat the colored people as slaves, let the most intelligent among you draw up a statement of your grievances and send it to some of your firm friends in Congress."[44] No matter what, rising up in righteous anger or retribution should never be an option. Be patient, she insisted. Freedom might not feel as great as formerly enslaved people had imagined—at least not right away—but, she swore, "year by year, if you respect yourselves, you will be more and more respected by white men."[45]

Throughout her life, Child proved herself a loyal servant to the abolitionist cause. She served on the executive board of the American Anti-Slavery Society, edited Harriet Jacobs's memoir, and became Jacobs's close friend. She had written an appeal to the Massachusetts legislature declaring the Fugitive Slave Act to be "utterly wicked" and arguing that it was the duty of good people to disobey it, and is believed to have offered safe harbor to enslaved people evading its reach.[46]

Yet Child's insistence in her writings on using the platform of educational endeavors to convince emancipated Black people that they should never give in to the human feelings of fury, vengefulness, or even plain frustration—despite generations of captivity, forced labor, sexual assault, family separation, and routine torture—place her within a long legacy of White women educators recruited by the state into the project of taming and controlling Black people through ostensibly charitable acts. Scholars have referred to this legacy through the image of the "White Lady Bountiful," an archetype prevalent in teaching and other "caring professions" such as social work.[47] "The image of 'Lady Bountiful' is particular[ly] salient in terms of the teacher or colonial governess who was seen as having a unique duty to bring civilization to the 'uncivilized,'" writes education scholar Helen Harper.[48] This figure serves as the "mother-teacher in the service of the empire," acting as the "mediating agent" between colonizer and colonized, working in service of one while earning the trust of the other through her acts of selflessness.

"The white lady teacher is charged, implicitly, with colonizing her 'native' students and molding them into good citizens of the republic," writes Erica Meiners.[49] "White women were viewed as essential to the survival and development of the nation and the dissemination of particular ideologies," their minds "less likely to be occupied by worldly issues" than those of men.[50]

The image of the White Lady Bountiful lives on, Meiners argues, in popular media representations of teachers who have come to save the day (think Michelle Pfeiffer in *Dangerous Minds* or Hilary Swank in *Freedom Writers*), as well as in the unquestioned assumptions about what kinds of people—what kinds of bodies—are well suited to the teaching profession.[51] Through this frame, not only being non-White but also being too masculine, too queer, or too overtly political are all seen as antithetical to being the ideal teacher. The image of the White Lady Bountiful is reflected in the demographics of the nation's public school teaching force, which is 77 percent female and 80 percent White, even though only about 46 percent of public school students are White.[52] Describing the contemporary implications of the White Lady Bountiful image, teacher educators Sherry Marx and Julie Pennington describe the quotidian ways in which "good" White female pre-service teachers enacted racist ideologies in teacher pre-service programs. The teachers they worked with "judged their tutees as living lives full of deficits in everything from home environments and culture to intelligence and civility, [while] these same young women described themselves in terms of benevolent, naturally occurring personal assets that would, without question, benefit the lives of any children with whom they worked."[53] The teachers saw their work, by extension, as a noble act of charity.

Today, efforts to create a teacher workforce that reflects the identities of the children in the classroom are often stymied by what observers lament is a "pipeline problem"—simply not enough Black people have the desire or qualifications to enter the classroom. This claim was prevalent during Reconstruction as well. Presented with the possibility of recruiting some Black teachers for the freedmen education effort, some superintendents lamented that qualified Black educators simply did not exist. In Florida, C. Thurston Chase derided potential Black teachers as " 'medicine men' who are said to hold mighty incantations for the benefit of their patients over the 'hind leg of a frog.' "[54] Such scorn toward traditional conjure practices was a source of cultural conflict and division. One reader of *Southern Workman*, the magazine of the Hampton Institute, described these beliefs and practices as common among, by their estimate, at least 75 percent of freed Black people, a mark of their savage immorality.[55]

Eberhart, the Georgia superintendent, had similar complaints about Black teachers' "total" lack of potential. "Although there is much to commend in the Negroes, under the difficulties which they labor, I am becoming daily more impressed with their total unfitness to assist in the moral and mental elevation of their own race."[56] Those Black teachers who, through whatever means, had acquired the education that would make them qualified to teach were sometimes dismissed from consideration because they did not live up to the standards of piety and patriotism established by the White-led aid societies—because they smoked, used curse words, or were not sufficiently religious.[57]

Nevertheless, some organizations hired Black teachers out of necessity—often because White teachers could not find a place to live or could not earn the trust of the local residents. Allowing newly freed Black people to be trained as teachers also provided them a pathway toward deeper, more meaningful involvement in the Reconstruction project . . . and it didn't hurt that they could be paid less.[58] Toward the end of the Reconstruction period, Black teachers came to represent the majority of teachers in Black schools in some areas.[59] But accounts remained of their White colleagues refusing to sit and eat with them or live alongside them in missionary-run dormitories.[60] Elias Hill, who was born into slavery, served as a schoolmaster during Reconstruction. In 1871, he was dragged from his home by the Ku Klux Klan in the middle of the night, beaten with a horsewhip, and accused of burning local White-owned buildings and instructing Black men to "ravish all the White women." In congressional testimony, Hill proclaimed that the experience had driven him to want to leave the United States for Liberia. "We do not believe it possible, from the past history and present aspect of affairs, for our people to live in this country peaceably, and to educate and elevate their children to that degree which they desire."[61]

Charlotte Forten, a Black woman poet born free in Philadelphia to a well-regarded abolitionist family, was optimistic as she made her way south to teach the newly freed people. In her journals, she described her White colleague Laura Matilda Towne teaching the pupils the popular song of John Brown and describing him as a "brave old man who had died for them." Forten, thinking it "well that they should know what one of their own color could do for his race," told the students about Toussaint L'Ouverture, just as Lydia Maria Child had. But in telling this story, Forten aspired to something different from the aim to civilize. "I long to inspire them with courage and ambition (of a noble sort), and high purposes," she wrote.[62] Her experience in the Sea Islands inspired her to be angry at the ways that her students and their families, whom despite her relative privileges she considered "mine own people," had been denied opportunities to live into their full personhood. "And one's indignation increases against those who, North as well as South, taunt the colored race with inferiority while they themselves use every means in their power to crush and degrade them, denying them every right and privilege, closing against them every avenue of elevation and improvement. Were they, under such circumstances, intellectual and refined, they would certainly be vastly superior to any other race that ever existed."[63]

If Black teachers like Charlotte Forten were to be produced en masse, they needed an institution to train them. But early visions of Black teacher credentialing focused less on Forten's ideas about courage, ambition, and high purposes. Consider, for instance, the Hampton Normal and Agricultural Institute, founded in 1868 by Civil War general Samuel Chapman Armstrong and championed by its illustrious alumnus Booker T. Washington. Armstrong created a school that in many ways was ideologically opposed to the freedom dreams of the newly emancipated, one that was meant to maintain the familiar social system of the South rather than to upend it.[64]

Though Hampton later became a technical school, it was conceived as a teacher training school, where teachers would first learn how to do manual labor and then learn to teach Black children how to do manual labor. Armstrong believed that Black self-governance was dangerous, that Black people should "let politics severely alone" and were "not capable of self-government," and that the "votes of Negroes . . . marshalled by cunning knavery are dangerous to the country in proportion to their numbers."

He assigned aspiring teachers at Hampton to till the ground and plow fields, reinforcing the idea that this was their natural role in the social order. Courses in classics were not allowed, as they were seen to encourage "vanity." The school's vice principal observed that "the dull plodder at Hampton is the real leader of his people toward better things."

Armstrong agreed, stating that "the plodding ones make good teachers." Armstrong had been raised in Hawai'i, where his father was a missionary, and he saw parallels between the Native Hawaiians he encountered growing up and the Black people of the United States. Both, he argued, were lazy, barbaric savages, incapable of judgment or planning, and morally underdeveloped. Schools, therefore, would be the places to remedy this immorality and to ensure that Black people understood their place in society—particularly because he saw cheap Black labor as necessary if the South were ever to recover economically from the war.[65] Visiting Hampton's summer conference, W. E. B. Du Bois proclaimed that Hampton's curriculum was teaching "young men not to hitch their wagons to a star, but to a mule . . . that the great duty of a minister is to teach his flock to raise a good dinner; and . . . around all and in all, there is an insistence on the practical in a manner and tone that would make Socrates an idiot and Jesus Christ a crank. . . . I am wondering and anxiously wondering, just what picture of the world and life your students are getting."[66]

For Black people, then, early projects in mass schooling were complicated. While newly emancipated individuals sought to use educational spaces to pursue their freedom dreams, White-led philanthropic institutions, under the sympathetic guise of "charity," shaped a vision of how Black people could participate in "civilization"—through schooling designed to keep them docile, manageable as laborers, and sufficiently satisfied at the lowest rungs of social hierarchy given their presumed savagery. *Civilization* meant *control.* Be industrious. Be grateful. Don't be angry.

The fight between civilization and perceived barbarism also shaped White leaders' design of schools for Native people. But, in line with the narrative of inevitable annihilation, schools for Native people took on the colonial presumption that the Indian was doomed to disappear—and played their part accordingly.

CHAPTER 4

Disappearance by Design: Schools for Native People

When he died in 1906, William Torrey Harris could draw his final breath with the confidence of a man who has indisputably made his mark on the world. Not only had he served as the superintendent of schools in the newly bustling metropolis of St. Louis—a role in which he helped establish one of the first kindergartens in the United States—and become one of the most well-known educational theorists in the country, he had also founded the nation's first journal of philosophy, and even invented a predecessor of the Dewey decimal system. And in the professional role he would play for the longest period of his life, he served as the United States Commissioner of Education, holding the post for seventeen years under the oversight of four presidents.[1]

When Harris spoke, his words carried weight. So it was at the 1883 conference of the Indian Rights Association when he described what he saw as the "stages" of Native people's steps toward civilization. "He is at the tribal stage," Harris told the assembled men. If the Indian could get past that stage, he would arrive at the "village community" stage, which would be followed by feudalism, a stage which, according to Harris, no one except White people had been blessed enough to achieve.[2]

As Harris saw it, these various uncivilized peoples might eventually progress by the will of nature through these stages, just as his European forebears had. But, he mused, might there be a way to speed up the process? Did White people have to wait for Native people to evolve, which could presumably take centuries? No, he reasoned—they could bring to them the light of civilization with the tool he knew best: the instrument of schooling. "In the light of Christian civilization we say there is a method of rapid progress. Education has become of great potency in our hands," he announced, "and we believe that we can now vicariously save them very much that the white race has had to go through. . . . We can help you out of these things. We can help you to avoid the imperfect stages that follow them on the way to our level. Give us your children and we will educate them in the kindergarten and in the schools."[3]

In Harris's testimonial, we find an answer inflected with a word that should be familiar by now: *civilization.* But whereas the school as civilizing institution in the lives of Black people served primarily to reinforce a socially subordinate position and provide assurance that Black people would not rise up in violent retribution against their former enslavers, the vision of school for Native people offered a different kind of existential threat: the premise of total disappearance. To be civilized, in this instance, was to be eradicated. This was not a fringe obsession of some mercenary cowboys "settling" the West, but was in fact the orthodox and explicitly stated policy of the United States government in the nineteenth century, still standing on the foundation of the Doctrine of Discovery established by Jefferson.

But how best to eradicate Native people? Like so many policies, it was seen as a matter of dollars and cents. Consider the 1881 report of the United States Board of Indian Commissioners:

> As a savage we cannot tolerate [the Indian] any more than as a half-civilized parasite, wanderer, or vagabond. The only alternative left is to fit him by education for civilized life. The Indian, though a simple child of nature with mental faculties dwarfed and shriveled, while groping his way for generations in the darkness of barbarism, already sees the importance of education. . . . The nation learned by costly experience that "it was cheaper to feed than to fight the Indian," and the same common sense teaches "it is cheaper to teach than to feed them." . . . If the common school is the glory and boast of our American civilization, why not extend its blessings to the

> 50,000 benighted children of the red men of our country, that they too may share its benefits and speedily emerge from the ignorance of centuries?[4]

Government leaders embarked upon a new effort, firm in their belief that schooling would unlock the most efficient means of total cultural eradication, of helping the "Indian" become "absorbed and assimilated with his pale brethren," to quote the board.[5] And the point about this approach being cheap could not be hammered home enough. Despite the fact that the United States was in the midst of the Gilded Age and experiencing rapid economic growth—a period itself fueled by imperialism and violent displacement[6]—the idea that the country could save money by schooling Indians rather than endeavoring to kill them recurred again and again.

"We are told that it costs little less than a million of dollars to kill an Indian in war. It costs about one hundred and fifty dollars a year to educate one at Hampton or Carlisle," wrote Carl Schurz, who was secretary of the interior (and thereby charged with managing Indian affairs) from 1877 to 1881.[7] "If the education of Indian children saves the country only one small Indian war in the future, it will save money enough to sustain ten schools like Carlisle, with three hundred pupils each, for ten years. To make a liberal appropriation for such a purpose would, therefore, not only be a philanthropic act, but also the truest and wisest economy."[8]

This proposed path to "civilization" was not optional. The political leaders tasked with managing Indian policy made it very clear that there was only one alternative, and that was utter destruction. "Extermination or civilization," declared Schurz. "Speedy entrance into the pale of American civilization, or absolute extinction," echoed Lucius Lamar, who was secretary of the interior a few years after Schurz. Hiram Price, Commissioner of Indian Affairs, put it this way: "Savage and civilized life cannot live and prosper on the same ground. One of the two must die."[9]

The rub was that "civilization" itself, as construed by these leaders of statecraft, *was* a form of extermination. In this worldview, as famed Kiowa novelist N. Scott Momaday has written, "the Indian is not a man; he is an inferior creature who can become a man only if his natural identity is destroyed."[10] The vision of men like Schurz was that the Indian would become Indian no longer, indistinguishable from White settlers in language, beliefs, work habits, customs, and attitudes. It was, to use historian David Wallace Adams's phrase, "education for extinction." *Civilization* was a code word for the total erasure of Indigenous peoples from the face of the land. *Civilization* meant genocide. The war of the United States against Native peoples had not ended; it was simply conscripting a different type of soldier.

Merrill Gates, an educator who would go on to be president of Rutgers and Amherst Colleges and later chair of the Board of Indian Commissioners, made it plain in 1891. "We do believe in a standing army; but it should be an army of Christian school-teachers! That is the army that is going to win the victory. We are going to conquer barbarism; but we are going to do it by getting at the barbarians one by one. We are going to do it by that conquest of the individual man, woman, and child which leads to the truest civilization. We are going to conquer the Indians by a standing army of school-teachers armed with ideas, winning victories by industrial training, and by the gospel of love and the gospel of work."[11]

The Army and Its Soldiers

The U.S. government was clear in its designs. But then there was the matter of execution. How ought the Indians to be educated? Efforts to run day schools where Native children would benefit from the "army" and the fruits of its labors were met with a minor logistical challenge: many Native parents recognized the schooling efforts for what they were and did not actually want their children to participate in an institution designed explicitly to eradicate their culture. "They oppose every effort made to civilize them, and will not permit their children to be taught in school and oppose very decidedly any missionary work among them. They adhere tenaciously to their old customs and religion," wrote Indian agent George L. Davenport in his annual report. He went on to lament that "it has been out of the power of the teacher to do much on account of the parents of the children refusing to let them attend the school. Every effort has been made to induce them but to no purpose; the children run away as soon as the teacher shows them a book. The Indians scare the children by telling them if they attend school they will be taken from their homes and made soldiers."[12]

If Native children would not show up for school, what could be done? The answer came from a man whose name would become notorious, for reasons that will soon become clear: General Richard Henry Pratt. Pratt's ideas about military discipline, corporal punishment, and school operating procedures became models for Indian boarding schools across the nation, shaping the fabric of Native educational experiences ever since.

Although he would go on to have greater influence on Native schooling than perhaps any other single individual in the United States, Pratt did not begin his career in education. He was a brigadier general of the army and a Civil War veteran. In the 1860s and 1870s, he participated in battles against Native nations across the Great Plains, including the Southern Cheyenne, Comanche, Kiowa, and Arapaho peoples, forcibly displacing them. In 1875, Pratt was charged with supervising an imprisoned group of Native men who were to be transported to St. Augustine, Florida, to be held at Fort Marion.[13] Pratt's appointment to this position, what he did with it, and the long-term consequences and cultural impact of what happened at Fort Marion would change tens of thousands of lives and define the state purpose of Indian schooling for generations to come.

The men headed to Fort Marion were no ordinary prisoners. They had been identified as ringleaders, chiefs, and esteemed warriors who had proven especially resistant in the battles that had erupted across the plains as the U.S. Army tried to seize western lands and hunted as many valuable bison as they could see. They were leaders among their peoples, and military strategists believed that removing them would quell resistance.[14] Some were accused of attacking White civilians or troops, while others were simply considered "turbulent, disobedient, agitators and stirrers up of bad feelings, and otherwise troublesome."[15]

The road to St. Augustine was physically and spiritually trying. Crowds of White onlookers gathered around the railroad stations, attempting to catch a glimpse of the imprisoned men. At least two of the captives attempted suicide. Gray Beard, who had been a chief among the Southern Cheyenne, first tried to hang himself before being found by two other men and stopped. Later, as Pratt toured the train car with his six-year-old daughter, Gray Beard confronted him directly, telling Pratt that he had but one child—a daughter of about the same age. How would Pratt like it, Gray Beard asked, if he were to be chained up and stolen away many miles from his daughter? "His voice trembled with deepest emotion," wrote Pratt in his memoir. "It was a hard question."[16] Later, Gray Beard jumped from a train window and was shot by guards. Captured again and brought back to the train, he declared that he had wanted to die from the moment he was taken from home. He passed away shortly thereafter.[17]

Fort Marion sat against the oceanfront, with a central courtyard of about one hundred square feet. The courtyard was surrounded by the spaces that would serve as cells, each of which had a small grated window facing the interior. Before the summer was over, some of the prisoners—facing confinement, oppressive heat, and humidity—died, and those who witnessed their deaths were overcome with despondency.[18]

Pratt had received no clear guidelines for his time at Fort Marion. He had been tasked with transporting the captives, who were to be held indefinitely, and nothing specific beyond that. Earlier in his life, Pratt had led the Black soldiers of the Tenth Cavalry—the Buffalo Soldiers—many of whom had formerly been enslaved. Through this experience, Pratt had become convinced—counter to the beliefs of many of his contemporaries—that "savages" were not completely irredeemable. Given the structure of military life and access to the White man's civilization, he reasoned, Black people had gone from being beasts to being men. Why not make the same attempt with the Indians?[19] And thus his famous, blood-chilling maxim was born: "Kill the Indian. Save the man."

Pratt's first step was to have the leg irons removed from the captives. Next, he had their hair cut, and he distributed old army uniforms for them not only to wear but to maintain as though they were soldiers. Trousers had to be creased and buttons had to be shiny. Sensing a public relations opportunity, Pratt called in photographers to ensure that he had photos of the captives before and after the haircuts to serve as later proof of their transformation into civilized beings.[20] Pratt then wrote to the commanding officer at nearby St. Francis Barracks with an unusual request: he was going to organize a subset of the younger captives into a military "company with sergeants and corporals." He needed some old guns from St. Francis so that he could "use the Indians to *guard themselves*."[21]

In his classic work *Discipline and Punish: The Birth of the Prison*, French theorist and philosopher Michel Foucault writes about the concept of the "panopticon,"[22] a prison model in which a guard sits at the center and is able to see the captives at all times and from all possible directions. "The major effect of the Panopticon," according to Foucault, is to "induce in the inmate a state of conscious and permanent visibility that assures the automatic functioning of power."[23] Once a person is in a situation where they have lost total control of the space they occupy, where someone *might* be watching them at all times but one can never actually be sure, the condition of incarceration is fully internalized. In other words, you don't actually need guards watching every person every second of every day if, through a regime of constant surveillance, the person thinks the guard *might* be watching them. When that state is achieved, the guard is essentially inside the person's head. At that stage, Foucault writes, those imprisoned are "caught up in a power situation of which they are themselves the bearers."[24] Carter G. Woodson put it this way:

> When you control a man's thinking you do not have to worry about his actions. You do not have to tell him not to stand here or go yonder. He will find his "proper place" and will stay in it. You do not need to send him to the back door. He will go without being told. In fact, if there is no back door, he will cut one for his special benefit. His education makes it necessary.[25]

Under Pratt's surveillance, in a state of total captivity a world away from lands that sustained them, and offered a modicum of relative "freedom" (the ability to walk around the courtyard rather than be confined in cells) in exchange for the performance Pratt demanded, the prisoners became hostages forced to participate in the maintenance of their own imprisonment. They were prisoner and prison guard at the same time.[26]

Convinced that he had started the group on the path from savagery into manhood, Pratt next sought ways to introduce them into White culture by creating connections with the world of St. Augustine beyond the walls of the fort. He took the men on fishing and swimming excursions, and on these trips encouraged them to collect the seedpods that washed up on the beach and polish them for local souvenir shops, a task for which they could earn ten cents per polished pod. After a year, Pratt began hiring them out as day laborers and created individual savings accounts based on whatever earnings they could accrue picking oranges or handling baggage at the train station.

Pratt also invited local tourists to visit the prison. In this way he met Sarah Mather, a retired teacher. Mather had been a member of the first graduating class from Mount Holyoke College and had gone on to operate an industrial training school for Black girls. Mather asked Pratt if she could "educate [the] wild Indians."[27] With that, the final piece of the puzzle was in place at Fort Marion. Mather and Pratt recruited several additional White women to volunteer, and soon the prison that was also a military base had become a schoolhouse.

Mather had an illustrious friend who lived nearby—none other than Harriet Beecher Stowe, the author of *Uncle Tom's Cabin.* Mather invited Stowe to visit her classes at the prison. Stowe published multiple accounts of her time with the men of St. Augustine. She wrote first of seeing them on the St. Johns River as they initially arrived from Fort Leavenworth, in Kansas. "They were looked upon in their transit with the mingled fear and curiosity with which one regards dangerous wild beasts," she wrote in *The Christian Union* in 1877. "Gloomy, scowling, dressed in wild and savage habiliments, painted in weird colors, their hair adorned, they seemed more like grim goblins than human beings." Referring to Gray Beard, she wrote: "One of the number on the transit threw himself from the cars into the palmettos, and was shot as would be a tiger escaped from a menagerie."[28] Two years later,

Stowe described, she had a very different perception of the same men when she visited them under Mather's tutelage. No longer were they animals in her eyes. Now they were "neat, compact, trim, with well-brushed boots and nicely kept clothing . . . docile and eager."[29] A week later, in another dispatch to *The Christian Union,* Stowe implored readers to learn from Pratt's lessons and consider how to propagate his work further across the country. "We have tried fighting and killing the Indians, and gained little by it. We have tried feeding them as paupers in their savage state, and the result has been dishonest contractors, and invitation and provocation to war. Suppose we try education?"[30]

Each morning, the men were awoken via bugle and called to a chapel. Thereafter they would attend classes focused on English language, spelling, and grammar, taught using phonetic drills and copybooks focused on penmanship. They completed reading primers, and memorized scripture and Christian hymns. Through this "experiment," as he characterized it, Pratt converted Fort Marion into a space that blurred the lines between school, military, and prison. Or, to think of it differently, he created the idea of the Indian school as a space defined by the traits of both the military and the prison.

As all human beings do in trying circumstances that are not of their making, the people held at Fort Marion engaged in strategies of resistance and adaptation. As historian Brad Lookingbill puts it, "In the prison house of education, adult learners remained calculating, savvy, and agile."[31] The prisoners at Fort Marion forged relationships across tribal lines. Many of them made art documenting their lives before capture, the trip to St. Augustine, and their daily experiences in and around the fort.[32] Several attempted escape.

Despite these acts of resistance, within a few years Pratt was satisfied that he had achieved his goal and pleased with his efforts at turning Indians into men. He believed that, through the civilizing efforts of his school-military-prison, many of the leaders who had previously been so "turbulent" and "disobedient" now posed no threat to expansionist goals of the United States. Wouhhunnih, who also used the name Roman Nose, had been praised for his skills as a hunter among his Cheyenne people growing up. He was an accomplished warrior, fighting his first battle against the Pawnee at thirteen and in his older years claiming the scalps of nine enemies.[33] In 1880, when he wrote of his life, he seemed to have been transformed, speaking warmly of his time in St. Augustine. "[Pratt] can show to us our hearts properly and he is anxious to make Indian men do right and guide them in the right way and he taught them all about the good ways of the whites. We promise to listen to Capt. R.H. Pratt to what is said. . . . Capt. Pratt showed us ABC and now we understand these letters. We did not know how to spell anything. It is not bad we stayed in prison three years there."[34]

Surely, Pratt reasoned, now that they were men and not savages, there was little point in keeping the men at Fort Marion? He wrote to his superiors multiple times, asking that the older captives be released and that the younger ones who had especially taken to schooling be permitted to seek further education so that they could go back among their own people and be effective missionaries for White culture. In 1878, his request was finally granted.[35] But despite Pratt's assurances that the former warriors were completely changed into model students, the state colleges he contacted all rebuffed his appeals that they be admitted. Finally, Pratt received an invitation from someone who shared his evangelical zeal for using school to transform savages into civilized people: Samuel Chapman Armstrong, who had founded Hampton to address what he saw as the barbarism endemic to Black people. Though he admitted some trepidation about the idea, Armstrong joked in a letter to a Hampton trustee that it would all be fine since the Native people, once "terrible cutthroats," were "now said to be tamed. . . . Now and then they will try to scalp a darky but their war hatchets won't make much impression on him."[36]

Aside from his belief in the calling of civilization, Armstrong had another incentive: congressionally appropriated funds dedicated to enrolling Indian children in "special schools." Soon, Hampton had approval to enroll fifty more Native students in addition to those who had arrived from Florida. Armstrong set about constructing a new building for their arrival and dispatched Pratt to the western states to seek out additional students. Just as had been the practice in Florida, when Pratt brought the new recruits back to Hampton, they immediately had their "before" photographs taken to serve as useful marketing tools. "Be sure and have them bring their wild barbarous things" to show off in the pictures, Armstrong instructed. "This will show whence we started."[37]

Things were running along smoothly. Through his never-ending fundraising efforts, Armstrong secured four hundred acres of land for "an Indian school to be a branch of Hampton," and told Pratt that he wanted him to run it. But Pratt was restless at Hampton, and demurred. "I went with him and looked the farm over," he wrote in his memoir, "but without sympathy for the General's purposes. I pointed out that the woods were full of degraded Negros, left there by the army after the war, that the remoteness from the observation of our best people was a fatal drawback, and would still be using Indian education to further the segregating and reserving process, and I could not undertake it."[38] In his view, the conditions that had made his work successful in St. Augustine were absent. Pratt saw both the "degraded Negros" and the lack of "our best people"—trusty Christian White women like Mather, Ladies Bountiful who could be relied upon to provide instruction not only in letters but in American tenets of individualism and thrift—as a threat to his primary goal of making the Indian indistinguishable from the White man. To do that, he reasoned, he would need his own school, and he would need to have access to pupils much earlier in life.

Pratt decided to appeal directly to Carl Schurz, secretary of the interior. He did so by implicitly reminding Schurz of the role schools had played in assimilating his own people, the Germans. "I said, 'You yourself, sir, are one of the very best examples of what we ought to do with the Indians. You immigrated to America as an individual to escape oppression in your own country. . . . It would have been impossible for you to have accomplished your elevation if, when you came to this country, you had been reservated in any of the solid German communities we have permitted to grow up in some sections of America.'"[39] Pratt pleaded for Schurz to give him oversight of the abandoned Carlisle Barracks in Pennsylvania, decommissioned since the Civil War, where he could "prove it is easy to give Indian youth the English language, education, and industries."[40] And so the Carlisle Indian Industrial School was born.

Carlisle opened in 1879 and would remain open until 1918; across this period, the school would enroll over ten thousand students from a vast array of tribal nations. When Pratt ventured west to recruit the first pupils, he began with eighty-two, focusing his efforts on Lakota youth at the behest of the U.S. government. George Armstrong Custer's defeat at the Battle of the Greasy Grass (known in U.S. history books as Little Bighorn) was a recent memory, and the War Department reckoned that having children enrolled in a school in far-off Pennsylvania would render them effective hostages who would deter any serious attempts at resistance on the part of their families.[41] Not long after, they were joined by the children of several hundred Chiricahua Apache families that had been taken as prisoners of war after a battle in the Southwest. While their parents were incarcerated in Alabama and Florida, the children were sent to Carlisle.[42]

In this manner, the school was able to serve its role as a tool of Manifest Destiny in two ways: by eradicating the tribal identities of the young people taken there; and by directly supporting the national land-grab agenda, holding the children hostage as a means to subdue those who would rise up in resistance.

Indeed, despite his new enthusiasm for the civilizing power of education, Pratt was still a military man through and through. In 1880, he requested an additional military officer to assist him. When he received a denial, with the critique that army officers were best suited for the army and not for the schoolhouse, he wrote an indignant letter to President Rutherford B. Hayes. "I am at this time, 'fighting' a greater number of 'the enemies of civilization,' than the whole of my regiment put together, and I know further that I am fighting them with a thousand times more hopes of success. . . . Here a Lieutenant struggles to evolve order out of the chaos of fourteen different Indian languages! Civilization out of savagery! Industry and thrift out of laziness! Education out of ignorance! Cleanliness out of filth!"[43]

Embarking on this war, Pratt called upon a reliable weapon. He could use the same formula that had served him so effectively at Fort Marion: displacement to an unknown environment followed by relentless military discipline. Except now, instead of using these tactics on adults who had been leaders and rebels in their respective tribes, he had children as his targets. The boys were given school uniforms and boots that made them resemble small soldiers, dark blue with red braids across the shoulder and stripes for those designated as "officers." The girls received Victorian-style dresses and navy cloaks lined in red. The children were assigned new names, which were affixed to the back of their shirts. They received army rations to eat; they marched and practiced drills in military formation.

And as they had been at Fort Marion, the students were sent away from the school for periods of time to engage in menial labor for the surrounding White communities, a signature innovation of Pratt's that became known as the "outing" program.[44] Pratt began by placing the boys as farmhands and the girls as domestic laborers, and later expanded the program to factories and other industrial trade work.[45] Students who were disobedient might be locked in the guardhouse, have their food withheld, or be beaten.[46] Letters to and from family members were carefully screened—and sometimes published in the school's paper for all to read if they contained some element of shame that Pratt deemed instructive.[47]

The Man Is Always Watching

The panopticon was alive and well at Carlisle, represented by a bizarre character: "The Man-on-the-band-stand." Every week, students at Carlisle could receive copies of the school's newspaper, *The Indian Helper*. And each week, on the second-page masthead, the paper declared: "the *Indian Helper* is PRINTED by Indian boys, but EDITED by The-Man-on-the-band-stand, who is NOT an Indian."[48] As historian Jacqueline Fear-Segal has articulated, the Man-on-the-band-stand was a weird amalgamation uniting "characteristics of God, Uncle Sam, and grandfather with those of prison officer, spy, and dirty old man." The bandstand was a real, visible location, at the center of the school grounds. The Man was most likely the nom de plume of the paper's editor and printer, Marianna Burgess, but she was also intentionally embodying the imposing and powerful figure of Pratt himself. "The Band-stand commands the whole situation [at Carlisle]," wrote the Man. "From it he can see all the quarters, the printing office, the chapel, the grounds, everything and everybody, all the girls and boys on the walks, at the window, everywhere. Nothing escapes the Man-on-the-Band-stand."[49]

Other times, the Man described himself as some sort of "elf"[50] or supernatural being, suggesting he had the ability to watch the students even when they were away from the school working as laborers. "It is not safe to predict that one day his vision may not extend much farther," said the Man ominously. "Already he sees into the homes of the boys and girls who go out upon the farms; and—but let us wait until that 'someday' comes."[51] A poem written by a Carlisle teacher and printed in *The Indian Helper* began with the question: "Who is that Man-on-the-Band-stand?" The poem closes with a disturbing quatrain:

You see it's no secret, but yet, it were well
To have an eye out for the elf.
Have care what you tell, or else you may find,
The Man-on-the-stand is yourself.[52]

The incredibly discomfiting figure of the Man sent a clear message to students: *You are being watched, all the time*. And like the prisoner-guard-student-soldiers of Fort Marion, the students at Carlisle were encouraged to internalize the eye of the panopticon, monitoring themselves and one another for deviant behavior.

All of this was in service of Pratt's central belief, which he summarized in a famous speech he delivered in 1892: "A great general has said that the only good Indian is a dead one. . . . In a sense, I agree with the sentiment, but only in this: that all the Indian there is in the race should be dead. Kill the Indian in him, and save the man." Pratt went on to argue that, although slavery was "horrible," it had also served as "the greatest blessing that ever came to the Negro race," because it brought Black people "from cannibalism in darkest Africa to citizenship in free and enlightened America." ("Not full, not complete citizenship," he conceded, "but possible.") The time had come, he reasoned, to extend the same "blessing" to Native people. He argued that Indians did not have to be savages forever, but had only remained in this state because White people had irresponsibly left them to their own devices. Now the country had reached an impasse where these lingering barbarians occupied "more space than they are entitled to either by numbers or worth." His efforts at Carlisle, he declared proudly, would "end this vexed question" once and for all. "Carlisle," he explained, "has always planted treason to the tribe and loyalty to the nation at large."[53]

Pratt's central belief was the guiding light of the pedagogical approach at the school. At one Carlisle commencement, a reverend invited as a guest speaker declared that those students graduating could now declare victory against their inner barbarism. "The Indian is dead in you. . . . Let all that is Indian within you die! . . . You cannot become truly American citizens, industrious, intelligent, cultured, civilized until the Indian within you is dead."[54]

Luther Standing Bear[55] was one of the first students to arrive at Carlisle, from the group of Lakota youth in Pratt's first round of recruits. He recalled his early days at the school:

> When I went East to Carlisle School, I thought I was going there to die. . . . I could think of white people wanting little Lakota for no other reason than to kill them, but I thought here is my chance to prove that I can die bravely. . . . We expected something terrible would happen. We held our blankets between our teeth, because our hands were both busy hanging to the seats [of the train], so frightened were we. . . . The big boys began to tell us little fellows that the white people were taking us over to the place where the sun rises, where they would dump us over the edge of the earth.[56]

Upon arrival at the building, Standing Bear waited with his peers as, one by one, boys were removed from the room and returned with short hair. When his own hair was cut, he said that "it hurt my feelings to such an extent that the tears came into my eyes. . . . The fact is that we were to be transformed, and short hair being the mark of gentility with the white man, he put upon us the mark."[57]

One boy, determined to maintain some sense of agency if his hair was to be cut against his will, changed the terms of the event. When Pratt was gone on another recruiting trip, the young man steadfastly refused to let his hair be cut. Pratt's wife, left in charge of the school, decided to wait for her husband to return to determine what should be done with the rebellious youth. She was awakened later that night by dramatic cries of grief coming from the barracks: the young man had gotten out of bed and walked out onto the parade grounds to make a public ceremony of cutting his own hair, as the other children watched and wailed in mourning.[58]

Students resisted the regime at Carlisle in myriad other ways. Many of them communicated not only in their spoken tribal languages, but in Plains Sign Talk, a form of sign language that had been widely used by groups such as the Kiowa, Cheyenne, and Lakota to communicate with one another for trade and other intertribal relations.[59] Ernest White Thunder, one of the first eighty-two students to arrive at Carlisle and the son of Chief White Thunder of the Lakota, engaged in ongoing resistance. He first refused to write, then attempted to hide out on a train heading west, then finally went on a two-month hunger strike that ultimately resulted in his death.[60]

As had been the case at Fort Marion, over time many Carlisle students internalized the messages they had received about their culture: that since it was forbidden, it must be inferior. A seven-year-old girl named Nellie Robertson wrote Pratt a letter in 1881, apologizing in a confessional that she had committed the sin of speaking her own language:

> Dear Sir Capt. Pratt: I write this letter with much sorrow to tell you that I have spoken one Indian word. I will tell you how it happened: yesterday evening in the dining-hall Alice Wynn talked to me in Sioux, and before I knew what I was saying I found that I had spoken one word, and I felt so sorry that I could not eat my supper, and I could not forget that Indian word, and while I was sitting at the table the tears rolled down my cheeks. I tried very hard to speak only English.[61]

Pratt, wishing to use Nellie's despair as an example for the other students, published the letter in *The Indian Helper.*

In 1879, Pratt's old student Wouhhunnih (or Roman Nose) visited Carlisle and praised Pratt's continuation of the experiences in St. Augustine. He described what he saw:

> It looked like wild Indian people who had learned nothing but just play every day and night and punishing each other and fighting with sticks and hurting their bodies. But Capt. Pratt threw away old Indian clothes and he gave them new white man's clothes and assisted them very patiently to make the boys and girls of different tribes go one way that is the right way the white man's way. Now we are following the white man's way and endeavoring to get [an] education and do something useful and teach the red man [to] avoid temptation. First I did not know anything about the white man's ways. I am very happy now that I can be useful, polite, and love God.[62]

Pratt was a pitchman, and a successful one; his efforts at Carlisle ultimately drove national policy. By 1891, attendance at boarding schools became compulsory for Native youth through a statute in an annual appropriation bill.[63] By 1902, following the example of Carlisle, a total of twenty-five off-reservation boarding schools had been opened, from Michigan to Montana, California to Colorado.[64] Some estimate that, by 1900, 75 percent of Native children were enrolled in boarding schools.[65] As with the early days of schools for freedpeople, the majority of their teachers were White women, seen as the most fitting conduits of good moral instruction. These teachers, as Quechua political scientist Sandy Grande describes, "enacted a full-scale program of colonization," serving at once as schoolteachers, missionaries, and proselytizers of a White middle-class ethos.[66]

Parents who refused to allow schools to take their children could face harsh punishment, including arrest and imprisonment. One federal agent noted that "it became necessary to visit the camps unexpectedly with a detachment of police, and seize such children as were proper and take them away to school, willing or unwilling. Some hurried their children off to the mountains or hid them away in camp, and the police had to chase and capture them like so many wild rabbits."[67] In Arizona, a detachment of troops was sent into the Hopi village of Oraibi to try to force resistant parents to enroll their children. They were met with barricades, but ultimately arrested a group of nineteen parents and sent them to the military prison at Alcatraz.[68] Undeterred, many in Oraibi continued their resistance, until they were forced at gunpoint to relinquish their children to school. According to one teacher's account, "Men, women and children were dragged almost naked from their beds and houses. Under the eyes and the guns of the invaders they were allowed to put on a few articles of clothing" before caregivers were forced to march with children on their backs down to the school building. It was cold that day, and they marched through the ice and snow.[69] A Diné parent achingly described the experience of seeing the children seized: "It has been with us like a tree dropping its leaves. . . . They fall one by one to the ground until finally the wind sweeps them away and they are gone forever. . . . The parents of those children who were taken away are crying for them. I had a boy who was taken from this school to Grand Junction. The tears come to our eyes whenever we think of them. I do not know whether my boy is alive or not."[70]

General Thomas Jefferson Morgan, Commissioner of Indian Affairs, wrote with disgust and contempt of this parental resistance, and of the lack of government support for armed forces that could be sent to more forcibly round up the children. He was furious that "people who, for the most part speak no English, live in squalor and degradation, make little progress from year to year, who are a perpetual source of expense to the Government and a constant menace to thousands of their white neighbors, a hindrance to civilization and a clog on our progress—have any right to forcibly keep their children out of school to grow up like themselves, a race of barbarians and semisavages."[71] The ultimate goal of education, in Morgan's view, was "the disintegration of the tribes, and not their segregation." He believed that such efforts should be extended as quickly as possible, through "whatever steps are necessary," because education "is the Indians [sic] only salvation. . . . Without it they are doomed either to destruction or hopeless degradation."[72] This perspective was legally bolstered in 1896 through a decision known as the Browning Ruling, in which Commissioner of Indian Affairs Daniel Browning declared that Native parents, understood to be wards of the government—in other words, functionally children themselves—did not even have the right to choose where their children would go to school. Though the rule mandating boarding school attendance would later be annulled in the letter of the law, forced enrollment continued to occur for decades into the twentieth century.[73]

Pratt would remain at the head of Carlisle until 1904, as the policy of the U.S. government was shifting toward increased emphasis on the reservation system. Federal leadership had shifted toward indefinitely colonizing Native people on parcels of land "of limited extent and well-defined boundaries."[74] This was counter to Pratt's ideology—after all, if Indians were separated from the influence of benevolent White people, how could they ever assimilate into Whiteness? Amid his public denouncements of these new approaches, Pratt was pushed out of the school he had founded—but the effects of his social invention remain.

Citizenship for Some, Civilization for Others

A few times over the years, when invited to give talks to public school teachers, I have shared Pratt's speech. *Kill the Indian in him, and save the man.* When I have asked the assembled groups if anyone had heard of him or the speech, very few hands have gone up. After reading, I have asked these groups if anything about Pratt's words felt familiar. Invariably, uncomfortable nods proliferated around the room. The historical context might have been new to the teachers, but the rhetoric was one they knew intimately.

Civilization. Helping. Benevolence. The gift of another, better way of life. These ideas feel painfully resonant for many contemporary teachers because, while Pratt's bluntness may feel like a historic relic, the basic premise of his beliefs is easily recognizable in schools today—

the idea that students of color come from a degraded and inferior home culture, and the way we save them, the way we *help* them succeed, is by bringing them as far away from that home culture as possible. Acting as the proverbial White Lady Bountiful (whether or not the individual is either White or a Lady), the figure of the American teacher is the figure of civilization, tasked with casting out the barbarism reflected in the child's language practices, modes of dress, and general selfhood. For Black and Native children, this has historically been the purpose of schools—not to prepare them for leadership within the body politic, but to elevate their natural savagery to some basic level of "civilization" and ensure that that civilization is tempered by docility and obedience.

When she was eight years old, in 1884, the renowned Dakota writer and activist Zitkála-Šá was taken from her mother by missionaries and enrolled in the Indiana Manual Labor Institute. Writing of her period at the boarding school, she said this: "I remember how, from morning till evening, many specimens of civilized peoples visited the Indian school. . . . In this fashion many have passed idly through the Indian schools during the last decade, afterward to boast of their charity to the North American Indian. But few there are who have paused to question whether real life or long-lasting death lies beneath this semblance of civilization."[75]

Zitkála-Šá's question is a provocative one for us to consider today: Beneath the veneer of charity, do we find life or death? How can an institution be considered benevolent if its "goodness" is predicated on the denial of personhood?

We've talked about how some of the founding thinkers of the United States perceived Black and Native people, and about the historic purpose of schools in enacting the racial hierarchies through which this country was forged. In the next three parts of the book, we will dive deeper into the *how* of these hierarchies. We'll talk about three pillars of American racism that are cultivated in our schools: the gospel of *intellectual inferiority;* the regime of *discipline and punishment;* and the structure of *economic subjugation.*

First let's talk about *intellectual inferiority:* the taken-for-granted idea that Black and Native people are inherently unintelligent.

PART II

DEFECTIVE STRAINS

I believe that nobody now regards the maxim "that all men are born equal," as any thing more than a convenient hypothesis or an extravagant declamation. For the reverse is true—that all men are born unequal in personal powers and in those essential circumstances, of time, parentage, country, fortune. The least knowledge of the natural history of man adds another important particular to these; namely, what class of men he belongs to—European, Moor, Tartar, African? Because Nature has plainly assigned different degrees of intellect to these different races, and the barriers between are insurmountable.

—RALPH WALDO EMERSON[1]

The test movement came to this country some twenty-five or thirty years ago accompanied by one of the most glorious fallacies in the history of science, namely, that tests measured native intelligence purely and simply without regard to training or schooling. I hope nobody believes that now.

—CARL BRIGHAM, CREATOR OF THE SAT[2]

A few years back and they told me Black
means a hole where other folks
got brain/it was like the cells in the heads
of Black children was out to every hour on the hour naps

—JUNE JORDAN, "A POEM ABOUT INTELLIGENCE FOR MY BROTHERS AND SISTERS"[3]

CHAPTER 5

The Gospel of Intellectual Inferiority

I came of age as an educator during the height of what we might call the "achievement gap frenzy." I was trained to understand that to be a good teacher was to close the gap, and to close the gap was to assess students as frequently as possible, to analyze the results with a fine-tooth comb, and to "own the data"—to understand it as an extension of yourself and your worth, and as a metric of whether your students would have access to the American Dream or be hopelessly doomed. Michelle Rhee was a celebrity; standardized testing was fast, frequent, and furious; and everyone was supposed to have a "data wall" at the front of the classroom where students could track their progress on little erasable marker dots scattered across a laminated handmade poster (causing motivation or despair, who's to say). Teachers I knew debated over the best pre-test treat to get the kids' neurons firing: peppermints were a tried-and-true popular choice based on some article someone read one time, but I favored clementines and granola bars, offering myself the little reassurance that at least I wasn't giving my kids candy at 8:30 A.M.

This was some years ago, but I'm pretty sure we're not out of the throes of this frenzy yet. For many Americans, from national experts to casual observers, any mention of the words "race" and "education" in proximity immediately elicits concern about *the achievement gap.* This is presumed to be the central problem of the education system in our country, conveniently quantifiable and plainly visible: The Minorities Are Doing Badly.[1] How badly, and how do we know? Very badly, we are told, and we know because of test scores. Consider the National Assessment of Educational Progress, the congressionally mandated national assessment sometimes referred to as "the nation's report card." Every two years, NAEP assesses public and private school students in grades four, eight, and twelve in a variety of subject areas, with results on a scale of 500 points. On the reading exam in 2019, the gap between Black eighth-grade students' average scores and those of White students was 28 points; for Native students this gap was 24 points.[2] In mathematics, the gap between Black eighth graders and their White peers was 32 points; for Native students it was 30 points.[3]

As far as countless books, talks, newspaper articles, water cooler conversations, and policy discussions are concerned, this is pretty much where the discourse ends. There's an achievement gap, and we need to close it. But such conversations are more or less pointless if we don't understand a deeper truth: that the entire regime of standardized testing reflects the unspoken assumption in American culture that Black people and Native people are inherently less intelligent or intellectually capable than White people. This belief is a widespread part of American ideology, one that more often than not goes unobserved and unquestioned.

Philosopher Derrick Darby and educational historian John L. Rury refer to this ideology as it pertains to Black people specifically as "the color of mind." They argue that any discussion about achievement gaps is inextricable from this underlying assumption. "Instead of measuring skull sizes," they write, "modern Americans look to social and economic status, opportunity gaps, and related factors to explain variation in academic achievement." Using test scores as evidence, they argue, Americans go on to assume that White people are superior to Black people, and therefore that "whites should dominate blacks or enjoy a more favorable allotment of societal benefits and burdens."[4]

Some critics have alleged that the presumption of Black inferiority was even baked into the court case widely viewed as a crowning achievement of American racial progress—the Supreme Court's *Brown v. Board of Education* decision in 1954. After all, as legal scholar Derrick Bell points out, the framing of the decision (and the NAACP strategy that led to it) was not based on an argument that Black children had been denied something they were fairly owed; it was based on an argument that all-Black schooling spaces were tacitly understood to be inferior. Bell, a civil rights attorney, told the story of two Black school leaders in rural Mississippi who wanted his help getting their all-Black community school reopened after the all-White school board had it shut down as a means of cruel intimidation. "Sadly unaware of the value of a black school in a small community, I told them that our crusade was not to save segregated schools but to eliminate them," Bell wrote.[5] Later, sitting in what felt like his thousandth school desegregation hearing, Bell found himself wondering if pursuing desegregation for its own sake had been a mistake. "Why was I trying to get these children admitted to schools where they were not wanted?" he asked himself.[6] The idea that majority-Black schooling spaces had no value had shaped a set of legal strategies that would define a generation of civil rights battles.

With gratitude to Darby and Rury, who draw on ample historical evidence to argue that this assumption of Black intellectual inferiority is built into the system of American thought, I argue that the same historical record demonstrates the presumed innate intellectual inferiority of Native people as well, and that understanding these presumptions side by side is essential to drawing a fuller portrait of what Americans think "intelligence" even is. In the present, these ideas about intelligence shape the educational lives of Black and Native youth at every level, from debates about the achievement gap to the structure of special education and gifted education.

Researchers have documented the ways that students' racial identities can drive teachers' expectations of them and their sense of responsibility for student success.[7] In a 1986 study comparing teacher expectations at majority-Native and majority-White schools in Alaska, the teachers at White schools were nearly twice as likely to agree that their students' abilities were the same as or higher than those of other students nationally. When asked whether the majority of their students were capable of getting good grades, only 62 percent of the teachers in majority-Native schools said yes; only 40 percent agreed with the statement that their students could achieve at or above national norms. The authors of the study note that many of these teachers were quick to explicitly argue that these beliefs did *not* represent "low expectations," but simply "realistic evaluations." This defensiveness is paradoxical: what does the phrase "low expectations" mean if not "I do not believe that my students can achieve what other students are capable of"? These outcomes are troubling when we consider the precise nature of what teachers were being asked—not: *Is it likely, in this unfair and cruel world, that your students will achieve all they might dream of in their educational lives?* They were asked, rather: *Do you think they could do it? Could* they achieve as well as their peers across the country? *Could* they get good grades? Presented with these findings, Native leaders in the area disagreed with the idea that these expectations were so benign. One Iñupiaq leader told the researchers: "I always knew the teachers thought that. I was just surprised that they would come out and admit it."[8]

We can also think about the gospel of intellectual inferiority by thinking about its converse: the notion of giftedness. If you believe that a certain proportion of children in our society are "gifted and talented"—born, through the magic of happenstance, with innate abilities that notably surpass those of their peers—it stands to reason that such gifts should be equally and randomly distributed across the population. But in the United States, accounting for their differing share of the population, White children are 1.7 times as likely to be enrolled in gifted and talented programs as are Native children. They are more than twice as likely to be enrolled in such programs as are Black children. If you break down this disproportion state by state, it gets even more jaw-dropping. In Nevada, for instance, White children are almost 6 times as likely as Black children to be enrolled in gifted and talented programs. In Ohio, they're about 5.5 times as likely. In Wyoming, they are more than 10 times as likely to be deemed "gifted" as their Native counterparts are. In South Dakota, they are *24* times as likely.[9] In recent years, educators and scholars have started to raise more alarm bells about these disparities as they pertain to students of color generally, but discussion about the underrepresentation of Native students in particular has remained limited—amounting to tacit acceptance.[10]

Some people might read these kinds of statistics and shrug them off with what might appear to be the most obvious rejoinder: *Maybe, you know, all groups of children aren't equally "gifted."* The gospel of intellectual inferiority tells us that this is a perfectly logical—indeed, maybe the *most* logical—explanation. After all, these are scientific assessments, right? Free of bias? If they happen to find that some students are smarter than others, they can be held no more to blame than the tape measure that finds me to be shorter than most of my friends.[11]

Except evidence suggests that these kinds of assessments are anything but objective. Researchers have found that schools with more Black teachers or a Black principal have greater numbers of Black students enrolled in gifted programs—suggesting that the biases, assumptions, and predispositions of the educators doing the evaluating could have as much to do with rates of student enrollments as do the actual abilities of the kids being evaluated.[12] And, of course, notions of "giftedness" are anything but culturally neutral.

In 1994, a researcher at the Santa Fe Indian School conducted a study exploring the ways that tribal members in the surrounding Keresan Pueblo community defined what it meant to be "gifted." For these local leaders, an individual having "gifts" was deemed notable only insofar as they used those gifts to serve others—a contrast to the popular Western notion of genius as highly individualized, even to the point where being abusive or cruel to others is an unavoidable part of the package. These elders spoke of *A' dzii ayama' guunu,* the concept of the heart or giving from the heart, as a valued domain of giftedness. *A' dzii ayama' guunu* encompasses qualities such as endurance, drive, generosity, empathy, self-sacrifice, and conviction. The leaders also valued other forms of giftedness that overlapped with a mainstream White perspective—skills such as linguistic ability, the ability to recall information and use reasoning to apply that information in ingenious ways, and psychomotor abilities needed to create art. But these skills were understood to be inherent in *all* people, not a select ordained few, and they were understood to be valuable only to the extent that they reflected an individual's desire to contribute to the well-being of the community.[13] In observing the 560 students enrolled in the school, the researcher noted that many of them clearly possessed these qualities. But not one of them had been officially identified as "gifted."

In her classic essay "Land as Pedagogy," Michi Saagiig Nishnaabeg scholar and artist Leanne Betasamosake Simpson describes a similar collective notion of intelligence within Nishnaabeg pedagogy: since meaning, knowledge, and wisdom can only be derived through shared context and teaching, intelligence cannot possibly be "an individual's property to own; once an individual has carried a particular teaching around to the point where they can easily embody that teaching, they, then, also become responsible for sharing it according to the ethics and protocols of the system."[14] I'm reminded of the June Jordan poem quoted at the beginning of this part of the book, in which the speaker describes someone who is allegedly a genius but "never did nothing for nobody in particular," "and he never made nobody a cup of tea / in his whole brilliant life!"[15] What good, we might ask, is self-serving "genius"? Is a gift not defined as such by the fact that it is shared?[16]

The gospel of intellectual inferiority is normalized within our educational systems, but its implications extend far beyond school walls. In 2021, *The Washington Post* reported that after the NFL agreed in a class action settlement to pay out millions of dollars to former players diagnosed with dementia and other cognitive challenges stemming from football-induced brain damage, the firm the league hired to manage settlement payouts attempted to pay Black players less money based on the use of "racial normative adjustments." They assessed the impact of brain damage using a lower baseline, reflecting the presumed inferiority of these players' normal brain function. In dollars and cents, Black brains were worth less.[17]

These beliefs draw the outlines of what we believe is possible in classrooms across the United States—how we think about notions such as intelligence, giftedness, deservingness, and the goals of a good education. In a 1984 survey of over one thousand researchers and experts focused on education and psychology, 45 percent reported a belief that Black-White differences in IQ tests were at least partially due to genetic causes.[18] And similar attitudes persist in more recent surveys of non-specialists. In the 2018 General Social Survey—funded by the National Science Foundation and considered one of the most informative and reliable surveys of American opinion—respondents were asked about the causes of Black-White racial disparities in jobs, income, and housing. More than one in three of those who responded said it was because Black people don't have "motivation or will power," and about one in twelve of those who responded said it was because Black people "have less in-born ability to learn." Respondents were also asked to "consider a person who believes that Blacks are genetically inferior. . . . If such a person wanted to make a speech in your community claiming that Blacks are inferior, should he be allowed to speak, or not?" and "Should such a person be allowed to teach in a college or university, or not?" Almost half of those who responded said yes, let him speak, and about one-third said yes, let him teach.[19]

Let that one sit for a moment before we move on. A sizable number of Americans responded that *if a professor believes Black people are genetically inferior*, that is *totally fine* and does not disqualify them from teaching at a college or university. This prompts me to wonder, in a country with a glut of people earning PhDs and not enough academic jobs to offer those graduates, what this hypothetical racist professor could have to offer that is so irreplaceable. What might they be teaching that is valuable enough to outweigh an insidious belief that would presumably inflect not only the content of their classes, but the way they treated their students? Are they teaching alchemy? *What could be so great as to outweigh this obviously disqualifying characteristic?* This question keeps me up at night.

The great thing about the General Social Survey is its consistency: the questions are asked in the same way every time it is administered, allowing meaningful comparison. But this also presents a challenge in how we interpret the results. In 1986, the year I was born, about one in five of those who responded said that differences in Black-White outcomes exist because "most Blacks have less in-born ability to learn."[20] Does the drop to one in twelve represent a radical shift in the public consciousness? Or simply a shift in what people believe it's acceptable to say aloud? Sociologist Eduardo Bonilla-Silva has argued that "because the normative climate in the post–civil rights era has made illegitimate the public expression of racially based feelings and viewpoints, surveys on racial attitudes have become like multiple-choice exams in which respondents work hard to choose the 'right' answers (i.e., those that fit public norms)."[21] While it's possible that beliefs about genetic inferiority have changed, so too have the *norms* about whether it's acceptable to express those beliefs explicitly. Either way, one in twelve remains alarmingly high.

And let's be honest—how much can we say norms about the permissibility of the gospel of intellectual inferiority have evolved when, like clockwork, we are collectively subjected to the periodic resurgence of "debates" about the role of racialized biological determinism in intelligence? Those advocating for the view that maybe, just maybe, human beings' ability to learn is a heritable trait that varies based on race or ethnicity, when inevitably accused of being racist, throw up their hands in wide-eyed defense, proclaiming their innocence. "I'm not racist!" they reassure us. "I'm just saying . . . maybe . . . in the name of scientific inquiry . . . shouldn't we at least *consider*? For *science*? I'm just asking, *what if*?"

The best known of these intrepid pioneers of scientific inquiry is Charles Murray, who co-authored *The Bell Curve* in 1994 alongside Richard Herrnstein (who died the year the book was published). The book argued that racial differences in intelligence are mostly innate, rendering social programs pointless. It was a *New York Times* bestseller, and despite countless critics in the intervening years assailing the book not only for its repugnant moral implications but also for its flawed statistical analysis, Murray retains relevance. In 2020, Murray published a new book with a mainstream publisher, *Human Diversity: The Biology of Gender, Race, and Class,* in which he argues that "raw race differences in genetic material related to cognitive repertoires" (which he defines as "personality, abilities, and social behavior") "are common, not exceptional."[22]

Andrew Sullivan—former editor of *The New Republic* and thereafter affiliated with various mainstream press outlets such as *Time, The Atlantic, New York* magazine, and *The Daily Beast*—has become another standard-bearer of the gospel of intellectual inferiority. Sullivan gave early credibility to *The Bell Curve,* publishing excerpts from it in *The New Republic.* Thereafter, on his blog and on Twitter, Sullivan has reveled not only in his unapologetic belief in racialized genetic inferiority, but also in the furor (and attention) he can generate by leaning into it. "It seems to be in my nature," he mused in 2011, "a querulous, insistent curiosity that sometimes relishes the hostility it often provokes."[23] In these missives, Sullivan adeptly uses a blogger's characteristic blend of wonkish curiosity and informality. In a 2013 post, he wrote:

> We remain the same species, just as a poodle and a beagle are of the same species. But poodles, in general, are smarter than beagles, and beagles have a much better sense of smell. . . . It would be deeply strange if Homo sapiens were the only species on earth that did not adapt to different climates, diseases, landscapes, and experiences over hundreds of millennia. We see such adaptation happening very quickly in the animal kingdom. Our skin color alone—clearly a genetic adaptation to climate—is, well, right in front of one's nose.[24]

It is therefore anti-intellectual, in Sullivan's view, not to ask essential questions like "what IQ means, how great the cultural and environmental impact can be (very considerable), [and] whether such tests should guide public policy at all." To avoid these questions, he contends, is tantamount to "denying empirical reality."[25] Sullivan's erudite writing style and reputation as an intellectual may lend him a degree of credibility in the public eye. He is not tied to any particular ideology, he insists, other than the ideology of free expression—handily occluding the fact that mere openness to the possibility that some humans are inherently racially inferior is, itself, a radically ideological position.

In 2020, a *New York Times* media analyst wrote an essay titled "I'm Still Reading Andrew Sullivan. But I Can't Defend Him," as though this represents a meaningful concession. The author laments: "I wish Mr. Sullivan would accept that the project of trying to link the biological fiction of race with the science of genetics ought, in fact, to be over." Sullivan doesn't seem to share in this lament. Once again, I find myself wondering: *What could be so great as to outweigh this obviously disqualifying characteristic?*[26]

The simplest explanation is that it's not actually disqualifying. There are lots of great writers who write wonderful blogs who *don't* have a legacy of legitimizing the gospel of intellectual inferiority. Yet even as a changing culture introspects hand-wringingly about the supposed marginalization of people like Andrew Sullivan and Charles Murray, the material reality of their continued doing-just-fine-ness belies this supposed moral dilemma.

As I slogged through writing this part of the book, it seemed like I could not go a month without seeing another tweet or article or blog post that made use of Sullivan-style *I'm-just-saying-what-if*-ism, nudging the window of acceptable public discourse like a toddler testing boundaries by throwing a toy and looking at you sideways to see if they can get away with it. As evolutionary theorist Stephen Jay Gould once wrote, "The same bad arguments recur every few years with a predictable and depressing regularity. No sooner do we debunk one version than the next chapter of the same bad text emerges to ephemeral prominence."[27] Geneticist Kathryn Paige Harden, profiled in *The New Yorker*, put it more directly: "There's a new white dude in every generation who gets famous talking about this."[28]

Gould went on to suggest that the eternal return of the gospel of intellectual inferiority reflects a cycle of social conflict, drawing people in during times of austerity:

> Resurgences of biological determinism correlate with episodes of political retrenchment, particularly with campaigns for reduced government spending on social programs, or at times of fear among ruling elites, when disadvantaged groups sow serious social unrest or even threaten to usurp power. What argument against social change could be more chillingly effective than the claim that established orders, with some groups on top and others at the bottom, exist as an accurate reflection of the innate and unchangeable intellectual capacities of people so ranked? Why struggle and spend to raise the unboostable IQ of races or social classes at the bottom of the economic ladder?[29]

I think Gould is correct—pundits turn to the gospel of intellectual inferiority because it is more soothing to believe that people experiencing the cruel end of an unequal society are simply living out their ill-fated lot in life. But I think there is another reason for the staying power of these ideas (always presented as though they are new, creative, innovative, and cutting-edge, despite being more or less a restatement of the last cycle).

The reason is that they sell.

These ideas bring acclaim to their proselytizers because they give voice to something that feels deliciously taboo for many Americans, something roiling just beneath the surface of polite discourse even if most people would never say it aloud. And that which is taboo, desired but unspoken, makes money. Put simply, claiming that White people might just inherently be smarter turns out to be a great way to sell books.

At least, Josiah Clark Nott bragged as much back in 1847. Nott, an anthropologist and surgeon who co-founded the Medical College of Alabama, gloated about how his scientific career was bustling thanks to the popularity of his area of study, which he referred to as "niggerology." Nott wrote to Samuel George Morton, "My Niggerology, so far from harming me at home, has made me a greater man than I ever expected to be—I am the big gun of the profession here."[30]

To better understand the gospel of intellectual inferiority, its origins, how it came to be taken-for-granted fact in the minds of many people in the United States, and how it settled into our schools, let's go back to Nott's time and learn more about what men of science had to say about brains back in his day.

Noble Men of Science

Part of why today's pervasive *I'm-just-saying-what-if*-ism eugenics-lite discourse is so ironic is that we have been here before, and this area of inquiry has left its imprint in some less than obvious places—the census, for instance.

Josiah Clark Nott was part of the "American School," a group of influential scientists who used their European training to establish a new and reputable intellectual tradition on this side of the Atlantic, and their ideas set the stage for scholarly paradigms in both medicine and anthropology.[31] One of Nott's beliefs was that since White and Black people were different species, their offspring would, like some other interspecies hybrids, be smaller, weaker, less fertile, or have shorter lifespans—much as a mule, the product of a horse and a donkey, is generally unable to reproduce. (The word "mulatto" is derived from sixteenth-century Spanish and Portuguese words meaning "young mule.")[32]

Nott made this argument in an 1843 medical journal article titled "The Mulatto a Hybrid—Probable Extermination of the Two Races if the Whites and Blacks Are Allowed to Intermarry." The only trouble, Nott felt, was that he was short on robust statistical evidence to support this theory. "I hope I have said enough to make apparent the paramount importance of negro statistics," he wrote in a letter a few years later.[33] Such hard data, he argued, was needed to determine "if the longevity and physical perfection of the mixed race is below that of either of the pure races."[34]

In 1850, as Congress deliberated over the nature of that year's census, Nott found a champion in Kentucky senator Joseph Underwood. In debating what questions should and should not be included on the census—particularly in discussion with his fellow Southerners, who believed that the fewer questions asked about enslaved people, the better—Underwood explained that Nott was in need of evidence. "The gentleman in conversation with me said that he believed that a certain class of colored people had fewer children than a certain other class; and he believed that the average duration of the lives of the darker class was longer than that of the lighter colored class, or mixed," Underwood told his peers. "And it was for the purpose of ascertaining the physiological fact, that he wanted the inquiry made."[35]

Other things that Nott wanted to know, such as how many children in an enslaved household had died, never made it onto the census. But on the matter of the new "mulatto" option, he eventually won the day.[36] In the 1870 census, instructions to enumerators highlighted that this information was essential for science. "The column [of Color] is always to be filled. Be particularly careful in reporting the class mulatto. The word is here generic, and includes quadroons, octoroons, and all persons having any perceptible trace of African blood. Important scientific results depend upon the correct determination of this class in schedules 1 and 2."[37] (The category would remain on the census until 1900, when former census superintendent Robert Porter complained that the subcategories attempting to determine precisely how much "Black blood" someone had were "of little value," "misleading," and too complicated for enumerators.)[38]

Nott's assertions about the importance of measuring the feeble and inferior mulatto admixture was influential in other ways. In 1896, Frederick Hoffman—a statistician at the Prudential Life Insurance Company—published a 330-page report, *Race Traits and Tendencies of the American Negro,* to which the American Economic Association gamely dedicated two full issues of its official journal. Hoffman was far from a marginal quack; over the course of his life he was a respected statistician and advocate for public health who co-founded the American Lung Association and the American Cancer Society and was one of the first researchers to observe a link between cancer and tobacco.[39] In *Race Traits,* he turned to another important social problem and presented what he believed to be definitive results.

Sadly, Hoffman determined that the "so-called education" Black people had received since Emancipation was not "genuine" but "a mere varnish of questionable value." Meanwhile, as per Nott's theory about race-mixing creating an inferior line of stock, Black people as a whole were experiencing "a decrease in vital force by reason of the infusion of white blood." Hoffman determined that while "mulattoes" might resemble White people "in the least important physical characteristics" (i.e., skin color or hair texture), "in the more important, that is in the vital and moral characteristics, it [the mulatto] is inferior even to the pure black."[40] The bottom line, Hoffman concluded, was that Black people were uninsurable because they were doomed to "excessive mortality." Not a matter of racism, of course—simply the numbers. For his employers at Prudential, he had done an excellent job.[41] In any case, his findings were in line with a policy the company had put in place in 1881, paying out one-third less to Black policyholders than to White ones, though Black folks would have to pay the same premiums; the Metropolitan Life Insurance Company (now

MetLife) had followed suit.[42] But now they had more data to support their discrimination.

Two of Nott's dear contemporaries in the American School had left their own cultural mark. First there was Samuel George Morton, a man who in his obituary was referred to as probably the American scientist with the most esteemed reputation among scholars in the entire world[43] and who earned that reputation by collecting about a thousand human skulls over the course of his career—especially the skulls of Native people. His first published study of human skulls and their sizes, *Crania Americana,* represented Morton's dutiful efforts to painstakingly measure the capacity of his collected skulls as evidence that different racial groups not only represented different species, but could be ordered in a hierarchy with the size of their skulls serving as indisputable proof.

"In their mental character," Morton wrote, Native people were "averse to cultivation, and slow in acquiring knowledge; restless, revengeful, and fond of war, and wholly destitute of maritime adventure."[44] They were "warlike, cruel, and unforgiving. They turn with aversion from the restraints of civilised life, and have made but trifling progress in mental culture or the useful arts."[45] They were prone to infanticide if their children were born weak, and capable of withstanding fatigue, hunger, thirst, and cold in the pursuit of either game or revenge. This obsession with revenge was "sleepless and bloody" and paired with cautiousness and cunning. Indians rarely showed happiness or joy, and would not laugh unless "stimulated by intoxicating drinks," which in turn would spur "extravagant mirth and brutal ferocity"; and "the stoicism with which he bears every variety of bodily suffering" should be considered "extraordinary."[46] They were not in the habit of conceptualizing the past or the future, nor could they functionally understand numbers, leading them to give their lands away without comprehending what they were doing, which Morton cited as the chief cause of "misunderstandings" regarding land and treaties.[47]

All of these traits and more were evident, Morton asserted, not only through the testimony of careful observers but through the indisputable fact of the skulls. No detail escaped his notice: "From the parietal protuberances there is a slightly curved slope to the vertex, producing a conical, or rather a wedge-shaped outline." Or: "What has been said of the bony orbits obtains with surprising uniformity: thus the superior margin is but slightly curved, while the inferior may be compared to an inverted arch."[48]

Today, Morton's observations come across as both incredibly precise and more or less random.[49] Yet his work was widely influential and accepted orthodoxy. For decades, his skull collection sat in public view at the Penn Museum (affiliated with the University of Pennsylvania), where, until its removal in 2020, it was used as a teaching aid more than almost any other collection.[50]

Louis Agassiz was the other member of the American School whose impact on science and culture casts a long shadow. Agassiz, like his peers, was hugely influential. An extrovert who happily courted attention, fans, and controversy, he published over four hundred books and articles, taught at Harvard and founded the university's Museum of Comparative Zoology, and regularly made the front page of *The New York Times*.[51] He became an adherent of the doctrine of polygeny—the idea that people of different racial groups do not share a common ancestor, but rather are different species—after meeting a Black person for the first time in Philadelphia. He described his impressions to his mother in an 1846 letter:

> It was in Philadelphia that I first found myself in prolonged contact with negroes; all the domestics in my hotel were men of color. . . . I experienced pity at the sight of this degraded and degenerate race, and their lot inspired compassion in me in thinking that they are really men. Nonetheless, it is impossible for me to reprocess the feeling that they are not of the same blood as us. In seeing their black faces with their thick lips and grimacing teeth, the wool on their head, their bent knees, their elongated hands, their large curved nails, and especially the livid color of the palm of their hands, I could not take my eyes off their face in order to tell them to stay far away. And when they advanced that hideous hand towards

> my plate in order to serve me, I wished I were able to depart in order to eat a piece of bread elsewhere, rather than dine with such service.[52]

Agassiz published his arguments for polygeny in an 1850 issue of *The Christian Examiner.* In a historic early example of *I'm-just-saying-what-if*-ism, he was scandalized by the suggestion that his arguments might be used in support of slavery: "Naturalists have a right to consider the questions growing out of men's physical relations as merely scientific questions," he argued, "and to investigate them without reference to either politics or religion." Did his work implicitly justify human bondage? He parried. "Is that a fair objection to a philosophical investigation? . . . Let those who feel themselves called upon to regulate human society, see what they can do with the results. It is for us to examine into the characters of different races, to ascertain their physical peculiarities, their natural developments."[53]

Agassiz closed his essay with the suggestion that attempting to educate Black people, Native people, or any other "colored races" would be a futile enterprise "in consequence of their primitive difference." It would be best, he reasoned, to be "guided by a full consciousness of the real difference existing between us and them, and a desire to foster those dispositions that are eminently marked in them, rather than by treating them on terms of equality."[54]

It bears repeating: Nott, Morton, and Agassiz were not fringe characters peddling their cockamamie theories to a few scattered devotees. They were influential thinkers who used their institutional authority to lend these ideas credibility. Looking back, it's easy to write them off, but doing so dismisses the real legitimacy they were granted in their time. From a contemporary vantage point, we tend to selectively call the beliefs of the past *pseudoscience* when they make us uncomfortable, rather than confronting the reality that they were once considered *orthodox* science and reflecting on what that should mean for us now. We would never call the early efforts of Galileo, da Vinci, or Newton "pseudoscience," even though we understand some of their axioms to have been wrong. In calling something "pseudoscience," we disavow the ideas of these men of an earlier age as being retrograde and distant.

This *was* science, and to many people it still is. How do we reckon with that fact?[55] These men were well respected, well liked, and influential, and they held positions of material and social power—and accordingly, their ideas became orthodoxy across various sectors of American society.

Consider the words of Estelle Reel, who held the title of Superintendent of Indian Schools from 1898 to 1910. Echoing the biological arguments of the American School, Reel worried that intermarriage between White and Native people would lead to "more or less a state of degeneracy among the offspring."[56] In a 1900 newspaper interview, Reel explained her beliefs matter-of-factly:

> Allowing for exceptional cases, the Indian child is of lower physical organization than the white child of corresponding age. His forearms are smaller and his fingers and hands less flexible; the very structure of his bones and muscles will not permit so wide a variety of manual movements as are customary among Caucasian children, and his very instincts and modes of thought are adjusted to this imperfect manual development. In like manner his face is without that complete development of nerve and muscle which gives character to expressive features; his face seems stolid because it is without free expression, and at the same time his mind remains measurably stolid because of the very absence of mechanism for its own expression.[57]

Reel set out to develop what she called the "Uniform Course of Study," a standard curriculum to be used in all federally run Indian schools and designed to meet the needs of what she believed to be the intellectually inferior Indian child. The work was intended to follow the model of what Booker T. Washington had created at Tuskegee, which Reel visited in 1906.[58] The curriculum covered gardening, harness-making, farm chores, baking, laundering, and other practical skills. A 1902 *American Education* profile of Reel explained that the course of study focused only on basic concepts in literacy and arithmetic and was "not intended to take the pupils beyond elementary principles."[59] Reel, the profile went on to explain, "thinks that industrial training should have the foremost place in Indian education, believing it to be the foundation upon which the government's desire for the improvement of the Indian is built."[60]

From the scientific endeavors of Samuel George Morton to their practical application in the work of Estelle Reel, by the beginning of the progressive era the stage was set for the gospel of intellectual inferiority to thrive. To quote legal scholar and sociologist Dorothy Roberts, "Science is the most effective tool for giving claims about human difference the stamp of legitimacy," and some of the country's most esteemed early scientists did so with great enthusiasm. "What we call racial pseudoscience today," Roberts continues, "was considered the vanguard of scientific progress at the time it was practiced, and those who practiced it were admired by the scientific community and the public as pioneering geniuses."[61] American interest in "perfecting" society through scientific inquiry was poised to bloom into the dawn of a new era. Accordingly, schooling was about to be transformed with the arrival of a technological innovation, one that would lend another stroke of scientific legitimacy to the ongoing project of White supremacy: the IQ test.

CHAPTER 6

A Nation for the Fittest: Endless Measurement and the Architects of Progress

During the progressive era—the period roughly defined by the first two decades of the twentieth century—reformers of all stripes saw it as their mission to use the new ideas, technologies, and capital available to them in ways they believed would strategically improve society. There were economic reforms, such as the creation of the Federal Reserve and the adoption of the income tax. In politics, the Seventeenth Amendment allowed voters to directly elect senators for the first time, and suffragettes were campaigning for women to be able to participate in elections.[1] The explosive growth of cities and the massive waves of European immigration were reshaping the tenor of the social world, and progressive reformers saw it as their duty to tackle the crises attending these changes; collective efforts such as the temperance movement and the settlement house movement grew accordingly. Unions and labor movement leaders organized for higher wages and safer working conditions. Women like Jane Addams, Ida B. Wells, Emma Goldman, and Mary Harris "Mother" Jones made names for themselves as writers, activists, political leaders, and voices of moral urgency.

Amid it all, there was another type of "progress" that captured the cultural imagination: eugenics. Charles Davenport, one of the movement's leaders in the United States, defined the term simply as "the science of the improvement of the human race by better breeding." From the eugenicist's point of view, Davenport explained, "man is an organism—an animal; and the laws of improvement of corn and of race horses hold true for him also. Unless people accept this simple truth and let it influence marriage selection human progress will cease."[2] Davenport lamented that while "the human babies born each year constitute the world's most valuable crop," only a small percentage of them would be "fully effective" in "forming a united, altruistic, God-serving, law-abiding, effective, and productive nation."[3] *Progress,* from a hereditarian perspective, would require American society to apply to itself the same laws of careful science that had been used to create cheaper cars and hardier crops.

Davenport, a proud descendant of a wealthy New England family with Puritan roots, founded the Eugenics Record Office in 1910 with the financial support of the Carnegie, Rockefeller, and Harriman families. The purpose of the ERO was to produce massive "pedigree" charts that responsible young people could use to inform their decisions in courtship, marriage, and reproduction. Through the ERO and his writings, Davenport set about to educate the public on what he viewed as the simple heritability of everything from literary and mathematical ability to shiftlessness and pauperism. And while voluntary selective marriage was all well and good, Davenport argued that it was not enough: the state was also obliged to assist in the project of human betterment by institutionalizing, castrating, or executing people whose genes were deemed too dangerous for propagation.[4]

Davenport's ideas were enthusiastically received, just as those of his scientific forebears Nott, Morton, and Agassiz had been. His book *Heredity in Relation to Eugenics* became a popular college textbook; he was elected to the National Academy of Sciences and invited to serve on the board of several influential scientific journals.[5] He would go on to be a leader in the American Eugenics Society, which took on such popular education efforts as traveling exhibitions for museums and PTA conventions, offering cash awards to pastors delivering the best eugenics-themed sermon, and the signature innovation of the "Fitter Families Contests." These competitions, held at state fairs, allowed families to enter and be evaluated by experts (such as a psychologist, a dentist, a historian, a pediatrician) and win prizes alongside the livestock for being the "best crop."[6]

Eugenics classes were offered at colleges and universities around the country, sometimes in biology or zoology departments—and sometimes in education.[7] At the University of Virginia's Curry School of Education, for instance, one of the department's very first faculty members, William Heck, taught a class on "Evolution, Heredity, and Education." A 1916 volume of *Eugenical News* listed Heck's course alongside others taught at ninety institutions across the country.[8] Courses in eugenics were found at every Ivy League school except for Brown, at state schools from the University of Washington to the University of Maine and everywhere in between, and at liberal arts schools like Beloit and Swarthmore.[9]

The urgency of "better breeding" was becoming firmly entrenched in the imagination of the nation's elites. But if there was one lesson to be gleaned from the progressive era's industrial efficiencies, it was this: there could be no progress without measurement. The first order of business in the project of uplifting the most "fully effective" individuals, then, was to develop reliable tools for assessing and sorting the unfit masses.[10] A new crop of scientific innovators was more than happy to meet this need, and the systems they invented would affect schooling for a century to come.

In the 1890s, French psychologist Alfred Binet was directing a lab at the prestigious Sorbonne. Binet was interested in the measurement of intelligence, which he believed would be a crucial step in elevating his still young discipline.[11] Following in the dutiful footsteps of his predecessors, he traveled about the country measuring children's skulls. But after several years of this, Binet was frustrated by an issue with his findings: there seemed to be no correlation whatsoever between the students' skull sizes and teacher reports of their capabilities. Could it be that . . . skull size was *not* a great way to measure intellectual capacity? By 1904, he was seeking alternatives, and an opportunity presented itself: the minister of public education in France was searching for a way to identify students who were struggling in their classroom and needed additional intervention. Binet developed a battery of tasks for children to complete, from counting coins to choosing which face was "prettier" among a set.[12]

In examining his findings, Binet noticed a relationship between the results of children he called "young normals, and subnormals much older," which suggested to him that all children were following the same developmental sequence at different rates. This was an appealing idea, one that synced well with other prevailing notions of "progress"—that the human species, and human societies, began at a "primitive" state and proceeded step-by-step toward the elevated state of civilization. Accordingly, he revised his examinations into a set of tasks arranged by whether they could be completed by a child of three, five, seven, and so on, and created a scale in which the number of tasks done correctly would be counted and the child assigned a "mental age."[13] Binet then subtracted mental age from chronological age to produce a number that in turn could be used to determine whether the child qualified for special assistance from the state. A few years later, another psychologist argued that division was a better mechanism for calculation than subtraction, and Binet revised his scheme. Voilà: the *intelligence quotient.*[14]

As the test grew in visibility and popularity, Binet made two things clear: that it should be used by trained professionals to identify children who needed extra assistance, and that it was the job of educators to then meet "their character and their aptitudes."[15] Intelligence, in his view, was *not* a fixed quantity, nor was it easy to measure. Binet also emphasized that *no* reading or writing tasks should be required for his tests, since this would not measure students' innate abilities so much as the effectiveness of their teachers. "We give him nothing to read, nothing to write, and submit him to no test in which he might succeed by means of rote learning," thereby determining the child's abilities free from "the trammels of the school."[16]

Two decades earlier and four thousand miles away, a boy in Indiana named Lewis M. Terman had taken part in another form of intelligence testing. When Terman was a child, a phrenologist visited his family farm and felt the bumps on everyone's head. "When my turn came to be examined," Terman recalled, "he predicted great things of me."[17] Terman was hooked, and by 1905 he had earned a PhD in psychology. After a brief time as a high school principal, he became a professor of educational psychology at Stanford University's school of education. In short order, Terman took to a task he believed could revolutionize schooling: adapting Binet's exam for universal use. He published a new guide, *The Measurement of Intelligence,* intended to be accessible to principals, teachers, social workers, physicians, and concerned parents. In the introduction, Stanford Graduate School of Education dean Ellwood Cubberley praised the volume and its many uses—beyond the limited applications Binet had envisioned. "Questions relating to the choice of studies, vocational guidance, schoolroom procedure, the grading of pupils, promotional schemes, the study of the retardation of children in the schools, juvenile delinquency, and the proper handling of subnormals on the one hand and gifted children on the other—all alike acquire new meaning and significance when viewed in the light of the measurement of intelligence as outlined in this volume."[18]

And with that, the Stanford-Binet scale was born, its name paying homage to Terman's institutional home and Binet's original work—despite being in direct contradiction to Binet's insistence that his scales were not suited to measuring anything innate that we could call "intelligence."[19] Since Terman published the Stanford-Binet guide in 1916, it has been revised only four times and it remains a widely used assessment tool. The fifth and most recent edition was published in 2003; the first edition to be published without direct oversight from Terman himself came out only in 1986.

In his 1916 version, Terman made an argument for the importance of testing as many children as possible to avoid "wasting energy in the vain attempt to hold mentally slow and defective children up to a level of progress which is normal to the average child."[20] Mass testing, he wrote, was for the broader social good, facilitating early identification of those who were unfit and a drain on society so that they could be handled accordingly. Intelligence testing would be able to "bring tens of thousands of these high-grade defectives under the surveillance and protection of society. This will ultimately result in curtailing the reproduction of feeble-mindedness and in the elimination of an enormous amount of crime, pauperism, and industrial inefficiency."[21] Without such tests, Terman argued, we could never really know how to run schools effectively, because we could never know the true causes of educational attainment. "Is genius more common among children of the educated classes than among the children of the ignorant and poor? Are the inferior races really inferior, or are they merely unfortunate in their opportunity to learn? Only intelligence tests can answer these questions and grade the raw material with which education works," he insisted. "Without them we can never distinguish the results of our educational efforts with a given child from the influence of the child's original endowment."[22] Some examples of the things examinees were asked to do, in order of the difficulty assigned to them by Terman:

- Answer the question "Are you a little boy or a little girl?"
- Name the correct uses of a chair, a horse, a fork, a doll, a pencil, and a table.
- Explain what you do if it is raining on your way to school, if you realize that your house is on fire, or if you are going somewhere and miss your train. [*Unsatisfactory answers for these questions include, respectively, "Stay at home," "Stay with your friends," and "Run and try to catch it."*]
- Explain the difference between a fly and a butterfly, a stone and an egg, and wood and glass.
- Let us suppose that your baseball has been lost in this round field. You have no idea what part of the field it is in. You don't know what direction it came from, how it got there, or with what force it came. All you know is that the ball is lost somewhere in the field. Now, take this pencil and mark out a path to show me how you would hunt for the ball so as to be sure to not miss it. Begin at the gate and show me what path you would take.
- Answer the question "What's the thing for you to do if a playmate hits you without meaning to do it?" [*Unsatisfactory answers include "Tell them not to do it again" and "He'd say 'excuse me' and I'd say 'thank you.'"*]

There were also questions under the category of "detecting absurdities," in which the examinee had to explain "what is foolish" about sentences such as:

> A man said: "I know a road from my house to the city which is downhill all the way to the city and downhill all the way back home."

and

> An engineer said that the more cars he had on his train the faster he could go.[23]

And so on and so on, dozens of questions and tasks. These questions seem more arbitrary, inflected by cultural assumptions, or outright bizarre than an objective measure of someone's fixed and innate abilities. But Terman believed they could meet any number of useful social purposes. Business owners, he suggested, could "employ a psychologist to examine applicants for positions and to weed out the unfit." Philanthropists could use the tests to stop wasting money on initiatives that only gave unfit people more opportunities to pass along their genes. "When charity organizations help the feeble-minded to float along in the social and industrial world, and to produce and rear children after their kind, a doubtful service is rendered. A little psychological research would aid the united charities of any city to direct their expenditures into more profitable channels than would otherwise be possible."[24]

Terman's work was a natural fit for the zeitgeist of his time: a relatively accessible and (he insisted) rigorously scientific, objective tool that would aid in the progress of American society by efficiently separating the unfit from the fit. But to achieve his dream of administering intelligence tests across broad swaths of the country's students, something extraordinary would have to happen: America went to war.

Testing Scales Up

In 1917, the field of psychology was struggling. The discipline was still relatively new; many researchers did not view psychology as a truly rigorous "hard" scientific endeavor. After a survey of the profession, one commentator concluded that "psychology, after 25 years of growth, does not stand very high on the honor roll among other academic subjects."[25] The previous year, the nation's first ever professor of psychology had lamented: "We are doing a larger quantity of work than any other nation and work of equal value. But our accomplishment falls far below what it might be and should be," which he blamed on lack of financial support and effective recruitment of new psychologists.[26] How would the field lift itself from the doldrums?

Across the Atlantic Ocean lay the answer. World War I was raging, and hundreds of thousands of soldiers had already lost their lives. Where most saw only strife, sacrifice, and tragedy, Robert M. Yerkes, a Harvard professor and the new president of the American Psychological Association, saw opportunity. What Yerkes needed, in his view, was an opportunity to gather the kind of large-scale, objective, indisputable data that would earn legitimacy for the field. Where better to turn than the U.S. Army? When war broke out, Yerkes organized the Committee on Methods of Psychological Examining of Recruits and looped in a group of experts—including Terman, whose recent publication of the Stanford-Binet scale brought name recognition.

With that, the Army Alpha and Beta tests were born and administered to over 1.7 million individuals—the first real standardized tests. The testing, as the team pitched it to the army, would create the kind of efficient sorting mechanism Terman had dreamed of: "a) To aid in segregating and eliminating the mentally incompetent, b) To classify men according to their mental ability, c) To assist in selecting competent men for responsible positions." Yet the unprecedentedly massive scale of data collection would, of course, be insufficient if nobody knew about it. Yerkes and his team worked hard to publicize their efforts in books and articles that would capture the popular imagination. And it worked. Before the war, said one specialist, "the average intelligent layman probably had little confidence in the value or the use of mental tests. After the War, he believed that psychologists had devised a simple and relatively perfect method of measuring intelligence." Mission accomplished.[27]

Except that the Army Alpha and Beta test items were neither simple nor perfect. A cursory look at them makes it evident how absurd it is to claim they could measure pure "intelligence" independently of social or cultural background. Considering that many of the military recruits were Black men from the South or recent European immigrants—both groups that had few opportunities for formal schooling, and whose cultural repertoires vastly differed from those of the men making the tests—it would be hard to deem them "unintelligent" for not knowing answers to questions such as:

> Ensilage is a term used in: fishing / athletics / farming / hunting
> The Pierce Arrow car is made in: Buffalo / Detroit / Toledo / Flint
> Becky Sharp appears in: Vanity Fair / Romola / The [sic] Christmas Carol / Henry IV[28]

> If your load of coal gets stuck in the mud, what should you do?
> Leave it there
> Get more horses or men to pull it out
> Throw off the load[29]

If you don't know the answer to any of these questions because they fall outside your relevant schema of life experiences, congratulations! You now have something in common with me and with countless other "unintelligent" World War I recruits, the sharecropper from Mississippi or the recent arrival from Sicily who had never heard of the novel *Vanity Fair.* (In which Becky Sharp is apparently the protagonist. I guessed, incorrectly, that she was an actress. I need to brush up on my nineteenth-century British war fiction.) If my load of coal gets stuck in the mud, I'm totally screwed.

Of course, unlike those men, I—and likely you—at least have the advantage of having taken a multiple-choice test before. They would have done no such thing, so even the format of the examination would have been an alien experience. But the tests were a rousing success, especially for Lewis Terman's rising star. Based on the Army Alpha efforts, he would finally get his wish. In the wake of the widely publicized success, the National Research Council was awarded $25,000 from the Rockefeller family to develop a National Intelligence Test under Terman's leadership.[30] Thus the United States moved another step closer to the public school standardized testing regime that we take for granted today.

The new intelligence exams were adapted from the Army Alpha and Beta tests, designed to be administered in a half hour each to students in third through eighth grade and again upon entering high school. The instructions assured that "any intelligent teacher who can control his class should be able, after brief instruction and practice, to administer the National Intelligence Tests in a reasonably satisfactory manner, and to obtain reliable results."[31] Once the tests were developed, they were sold to schools and districts through the privately owned World Book Company, launching another tradition in American testing—private companies selling testing materials to public schools for profit.

The first part of the National Intelligence Tests comprised basic math problems: *If a man gets $2.50 a day, what will he be paid for six days' work? One quart of ice cream is enough for 5 persons. How many quarts of ice cream are needed for 25 persons?*

After that, some of the questions began to reflect Terman's beliefs that "intelligence" was inextricable from a particular moral view of the universe.

> Write on each dotted line one word to make the sentence sound sensible and right.
>
> Poverty cannot .... a man .... is intelligent and .... hard.
>
> A man should learn to .... his anger.
>
> In each row draw a line under each of the two words that tell what the thing always has.
>
> Idiocy (crime foolishness poverty stupidity tuberculosis)
>
> Crime (death lawlessness punishment theft wrong)[32]

As with the Army Alpha and Beta tests, several questions on the National Intelligence Tests reflected experiences that certainly would not have been universal among all children in 1920.

The highest price per bushel is usually paid for: corn / oats / turnips / wheat

Among Robin Hood's men was: Allen Breck / Natty Bumppo / Galahad / Friar Tuck

Despite these quirks, Terman used the results of the National Intelligence Tests to make far-reaching claims about children's innate abilities—especially children he deemed "gifted," in whom he held a particular interest. In his lengthy analysis "Mental and Physical Traits of a Thousand Gifted Children," Terman organized his findings by "racial stock" and concluded that almost three-quarters of gifted children were descended from English, German, Scotch, Irish, or French families, whereas 0.4 percent (so, about four children in Terman's sample) were descended from Black or Native families.[33] Familiarity with the test itself might lead us to wonder if the other Black and Native children in the sample were indeed not "gifted" or had maybe just never read *Robin Hood*, but Terman reported his results with the utmost confidence.

In a 1922 report, *Intelligence Tests and School Reorganization*, Terman went on to argue that schools should be structured into distinct tracks based on the results of such testing. "Intelligence tests have 1) demonstrated more convincingly the extent of individual differences and 2) made it possible to classify children more accurately on the basis of native ability. . . . It is the conviction of the writer that, ideally, provision should be made for five groups of children: the very superior, the superior, the average, the inferior, and the very inferior. We may refer to these as classes for the 'gifted,' 'bright,' 'average,' 'slow,' and 'special' pupils." The lowest of these groups, Terman argued, didn't really need to go "beyond the fourth or fifth grade."[34] Decades later, the tracks Terman envisioned have remained a resilient feature of schooling despite the massive criticism the practice has received. In 2009, 71 percent of fourth-grade reading teachers surveyed said that they divided students into groups based on ability; in 2011, 76 percent of eighth-grade math teachers said the same.[35]

In Terman's own time, researchers continued to draw sweeping conclusions based on the new testing technology. Scholars analyzing

Native people later in the 1920s and 1930s, for instance, combined IQ testing with analyses of blood quantum to determine that "the intelligence of mixed bloods, as tested [was] superior to that of full bloods but inferior to that of Whites,"[36] that "the scores show a definite negative correlation between degree of Indian blood and intelligence score,"[37] and that "school education has only slight effect on intelligence . . . [and] it is more influenced by degree of white blood."[38]

As lasting as Terman's legacy has been, the biggest test was yet to come—the one that would linger into our present, spurring never-ending debates about fairness, merit, racial difference, and ability. It would be created by Carl Brigham, a Massachusetts-born soldier who had worked as an assistant to Yerkes in administering the Army Alpha and Beta tests. In a 1923 book, Brigham—by then a psychology professor at Princeton—would publish the definitive book on their findings, *A Study of American Intelligence.* The outcomes were clear, Brigham argued. "Our results showing the marked intellectual inferiority of the negro are corroborated by practically all of the investigators who have used psychological tests on white and negro groups."[39] There was one hitch in this finding that Brigham had to address: the fact that Black people born in the North, where there was relatively greater educational and social equality, did better on the tests. Was this not evidence that the test was a measure of opportunity, not innate intellectual abilities? Far from it, said Brigham. While he conceded that educational opportunity and social conditions indeed made some difference, he argued that this was a selection effect—the more intelligent Negro, he reasoned, was more likely to move North, and more likely to have some "white blood."[40]

In his capacity as a Princeton professor, Brigham saw a new opportunity: to ensure that only the best and brightest filled the hallowed halls of the university, why not use a modified version of the army tests for admissions? He developed a new edition and administered it to Princeton students to test it out, then gave it to applicants seeking admission to Cooper Union in New York City. He renamed this latest version the Scholastic Aptitude Test, or SAT.[41] Thanks to Brigham's connections in higher education and the military, its rollout was quick: on June 23, 1926, over eight thousand high school students took the test, and their scores were directly reported to the universities of their choosing. Soon West Point and the U.S. Naval Academy agreed to use Brigham's test for all their applicants.

Brigham believed that "American intelligence is declining, and will proceed with an accelerating rate as the racial admixture becomes more and more extensive."[42] Indeed, Brigham initially saw his SAT as a crucial tool in proving what he saw as inherent facts of biology. But within a few years, that began to change.

"The more I work in this field," Brigham wrote in a 1929 letter to fellow eugenicist Charles Davenport, "the more I am convinced that psychologists have sinned greatly in sliding easy from the name of the test to the function or trait measured." In other words, just calling something an "intelligence test" was enough to convince the public that intelligence was in fact being measured, regardless of what the exam actually involved. In this way, he was concerned, such testing amounted to "psycho-phrenology,"[43] using numbers and statistics to cover up what was in essence nothing more scientific than feeling bumps on skulls.

Despite ongoing claims of objectivity, scholars have since documented the many ways that the modern SAT continues to be shaped by the biases of the human beings who create the test. For example, analysts William C. Kidder and Jay Rosner found a troubling pattern in their research on over 100,000 test takers who completed the SAT in the late 1990s: when the test's annual "experimental" questions—a selection of items included each year on a trial basis, to be analyzed and potentially included in future iterations of the test—resulted in Black students doing better than White students, the questions were thrown out. The logic, guided by the unquestioned gospel of intellectual inferiority, was that if Black students performed better on an item, the question must be inherently flawed. Questions White students did better on, however, were included without hesitation. Kidder and Rosner call this "covert racial gerrymandering in favor of Whites."[44]

Ultimately, Brigham would aggressively disavow the very work that came to define his legacy. In 1930, he wrote that, under scrutiny, his own early theorization "with its entire hypothetical superstructure of racial differences collapses completely."[45] Using intelligence testing to compare racial groups was a futile exercise, he argued, and "one of the most pretentious of these comparative racial studies—the writer's own—was without foundation."[46] The push toward national standardized intelligence testing, Brigham came to believe, had been "accompanied by one of the most glorious fallacies in the history of science, namely, that tests measured native intelligence purely and simply without regard to training and schooling. I hope nobody believes that now."[47]

Well, Carl . . . lots of people do.

Race and IQ: The "Debate" That Never Dies

The early history of standardized testing involves men who believed ardently in racial hierarchies and went to great lengths to systematize, and to reproduce, them as broadly as possible. These eugenicists were loud and proud. In the decades since the civil rights movement, we've seen recurrent waves of their philosophical descendants. But their ideological descendants are not so comfortable waving the "race purity" flag, and so they make curious efforts to perpetuate the ideas of their predecessors while insisting that they are *not* racist. Throughout the 1970s, the new acolytes of the gospel of intellectual inferiority took on a visible presence in public space, this time under the auspices of a "debate" over IQ.

Consider the 1969 *Harvard Educational Review* article by Berkeley professor Arthur Jensen, "How Much Can We Boost IQ and Scholastic Achievement?"[48] In his essay, Jensen criticized "popular textbooks of psychology and education" in which the role of genetic factors in determining IQ had been "belittled, obscured, or denigrated," an omission Jensen called "ostrich-like."[49] In reviewing a variety of interventions aimed at increasing educational equity, he determined that most of them were ineffective in raising children's IQs, and therefore should be more closely scrutinized as societal investments.

Jensen insisted he was not a racist—just another guy asking questions. To *not* ask whether disparities in education and employment might be attributable to IQ differences between racial groups would "represent a danger to free inquiry."[50] In his own examination of the evidence, Jensen observed that it was "a not unreasonable hypothesis that genetic factors are strongly implicated in the average Negro-white intelligence difference."[51] Further, in a unique twist on the old "race suicide" fears we talked about in chapter 2, Jensen warned that *Black* people should be concerned about the way birth rate trends were going. Negro middle- and upper-class families and Negro women married to professional workers were experiencing declining birth rates, while welfare was encouraging unmarried, unskilled Black women to have children. Should these trends continue, he suggested, Black people could face "genetic enslavement" if "unaided by eugenic foresight," and if someone didn't step in quickly, such a failure "may well be viewed by future generations as our society's greatest injustice to Negro Americans."[52]

Rather than being dismissed out of hand as unethical and morally repugnant, Jensen's article sparked a wave of spirited debate. Three years later, the respected education journal *Phi Delta Kappan* invited William Shockley to weigh in as part of a special issue. Shockley was not an education scholar, nor a psychologist or even a biologist—he was a physicist, albeit a Nobel Prize–winning one whose research had been instrumental in the development of Silicon Valley. But by the late 1960s, Shockley had strayed far from his area of expertise to weigh in on an issue that he believed to be crucial to the continued thriving of American society. In a statement at the 1967 meeting of the National Academy of Sciences, Shockley had raised fears that the nation was moving against what he saw as potentially beneficial policies—such as unforced sterilization—due to public ignorance, which he viewed as "undemocratic" and "totalitarian." "The lesson to be learned from Nazi history," he told the academy, "is the value of free speech, not that eugenics is intolerable."[53] Once again, free speech and self-styled courageous resistance were uplifted as the benchmark of a good and just society, over and above other presumably important principles such as reproductive agency.[54]

Shockley urged further study of the matter, insisting that he did so in the spirit of "a visitor to a sick friend who strongly urges a diagnosis that seeks to expose all significant ailments." To get things started, he offered his own new analytic measure: a "social capacity index" based on a variety of factors, from the likelihood of enrolling in law school to rates of narcotic addiction. And—act surprised—Black people, by Shockley's estimation, were not doing so well in his new dataset.[55] The best course of action, in his view, was to configure adoption programs to place Negro babies in an "improved environment" and see what their outcomes would be, an effort he assured the Academy would be both inexpensive and humanitarian.[56] Take Black children from their genetically inferior homes, place them among worthier families, and see what happens. For science.

And now the *Phi Delta Kappan* wanted to hear *more* from Shockley—who, it bears repeating, was a physicist being invited to publish in an education journal. In their introduction to his article, the editors sneered at the suggestion that Shockley's ideas did not deserve a platform.

> When we invited one prominent sociologist to respond to Mr. Shockley's paper, he promptly refused, arguing first that Mr. Shockley is not qualified to write on this topic, then that his notions on heredity and race are "wrongheaded" and "obscene." The implication was that wrongheaded and obscene theories should be suppressed, or at least denied a prominent forum.[57]

Undeterred, and eager to prove that they were more than happy to serve as a prominent forum for the wrongheaded and obscene, the editors argued that Shockley's questions were "fundamental to enlightened education policy." As for the essay itself, Shockley's contribution to the *Phi Delta Kappan* was titled "Dysgenics, Geneticity, Raceology: A Challenge to the Intellectual Responsibility of Educators." Shockley argued that social welfare programs might be inadvertently promoting "dysgenics—retrogressive evolution through the disproportionate reproduction of the genetically disadvantaged."[58] And if dysgenics were allowed to proceed unchecked, Shockley predicted that the consequences could lead to . . . nuclear holocaust.

"With the advent of nuclear weapons," he wrote, "man has in effect reached the point of no return in the necessity to continue his intellectual evolution. Unless his collective mental ability can enable him reliably to predict consequences of his actions, it is possible that he may provoke his own extinction." How exactly this would happen Shockley does not make clear, but he assured readers that we should genuinely consider the possibility of "a nuclear holocaust as a consequence of advancing weapons technology combined with a dysgenic decline in national foresight."[59]

Visible racial differences, Shockley wrote, were evolution's way of letting us know who had a diminished social capacity. "Nature has color-coded groups of individuals so that statistically reliable predictions of their adaptability to intellectually rewarding and effective lives can easily be made and profitably be used by the pragmatic man in the street."[60] But! Of course, Shockley reassured readers that he was *not* racist. "Studies like mine . . . are not racist. They are motivated by concern for the feelings of all involved—not by fear and hate."[61] Which was why he was in favor of a *voluntary* eugenics program, with paid incentives:

> Bonuses would be offered for sterilization. Payers of income tax would get nothing. Bonuses for all others, regardless of sex, race, or welfare status, would depend on best scientific estimates of hereditary factors in disadvantages such as diabetes, epilepsy, heroin addiction, arthritis, etc. At a bonus rate of $1,000 for each point below 100 I.Q., $30,000 put in trust for a 70 I.Q. moron potentially capable of producing 20 children might return $250,000 to taxpayers in reduced costs of mental retardation care.[62]

As Stephen Jay Gould pointed out, Shockley's insistence on his good intentions, and the claim that those unwilling to ask the important questions were somehow backwards anti-intellectuals, is part of a historical pattern. "Determinists have often invoked the traditional prestige of science as objective knowledge, free from social and political taint," wrote Gould. "They portray themselves as purveyors of harsh truth and their opponents as sentimentalists, ideologues, and wishful thinkers." In this way, defenders of the gospel of intellectual inferiority attempt to "make nature herself an accomplice in the crime of political inequality."[63]

Meanwhile, as Shockley openly fantasized about sterilization programs, they were already happening.

In 1972, Choctaw and Cherokee physician Connie Uri was hearing troubling stories from Native women telling her that they had received hysterectomies under duress, or without knowingly consenting to the irreversible surgery. Eventually, the pattern became so glaring that Uri contacted her senator to demand an investigation. The inquiry found that health service officials were not complying with informed consent standards, and in some cases sterilizations had been performed on women under twenty-one, which was unlawful.[64] After further investigation, Uri came to the conclusion that at least a quarter of Native women between fifteen and forty-four years old in the United States may have undergone sterilizations because they were believed to be too unintelligent to use other methods of birth control.[65]

Medically unnecessary and uninformed sterilizations of Black women were also widespread during the 1970s. The practice of teaching hospitals performing such hysterectomies on Black women, both for resident "practice" and for the financial incentives of Medicaid reimbursements, was so common that these operations were referred to as "Mississippi appendectomies." Fannie Lou Hamer, the legendary organizer and civil rights leader, spoke publicly about going to the hospital to have a small uterine tumor removed and undergoing a complete hysterectomy without her prior knowledge or consent.[66]

And it wasn't just happening in the South. In Boston and New York City teaching hospitals, Black women were routinely given unnecessary hysterectomies without their knowledge or consent, simply so that medical residents could have a learning experience. Sometimes the surgeries were omitted from their medical records. The doctors who performed these procedures offered a familiar rationale: the mothers and their children were a drain on society, they were immoral, they were unintelligent.[67]

A 2022 report from the National Women's Law Center found that thirty-one states and Washington, D.C., have laws that still permit sterilization without an individual's consent, many of them specifically targeting disabled people.[68] In 2013, investigative reporting revealed that women incarcerated in California were being coerced by medical professionals into being irreversibly sterilized without authorization. James Heinrich, the physician who oversaw the operations, told investigators that his efforts saved the state money "compared to what you save in welfare paying for these unwanted children—as they procreated more."[69]

So, as it turns out, Shockley got his way.

CHAPTER 7

Whose Knowledge?

Whose knowledge becomes school knowledge? Whose interests are served by the knowledge that becomes the school curriculum?

—LINDA M. MCNEIL[1]

It's easy for us to look back more than a century later and laugh at old standardized tests. It's okay—they are, after all, pretty silly. I've often shown them to my students and we've done just that. Like this image from the Army Beta test:[2]

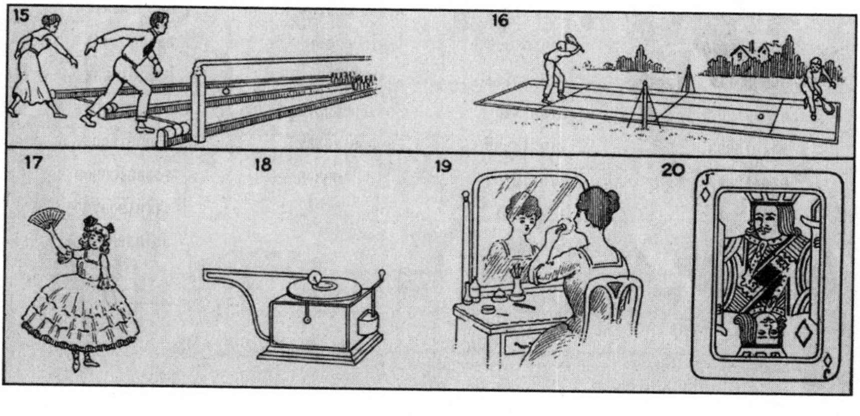

In image number 18, the phonograph is missing a piece. If you have never seen this type of phonograph, you know that getting this question wrong reflects your life experience as a person living in the contemporary era. It has nothing to do with your innate intellectual abilities, nor should it govern your lot in life. Displaced as we are from the world in these pictures by the yawning gap of time, we understand easily how someone who was a sharecropper living in a cabin or a recent immigrant from a place where there are no tennis nets might fail this test. We know that these are arbitrary cultural artifacts.

But as silly as it seems, we continue to do the same thing to students today: we pay huge corporations a ton of public money for tests based on arbitrary standards of innate human capability, and attach incredibly high stakes to those tests. Then, to add insult to injury, we face repeated musing aloud as to whether all this data collectively means that some groups of people might just be genetically inferior, under the guise of "just asking!!!" innocent questions. All this happens without acknowledging that the people who first developed these testing regimes and their attendant ideas of intelligence outwardly and unabashedly believed Black and Native people were not full human beings.

Even if we are no longer measuring skulls, write Derrick Darby and John L. Rury, "the conclusions we draw today about differences in intelligence, character, and conduct between blacks and whites often resemble those of the past."[3] The reality is that innocent "scientific curiosity" about IQ and race is inherently difficult to dissociate from the project of eugenics. Pretending that the ideas undergirding scientific racism are relegated to distant history can "raise serious questions about how we remember—and forget—eugenics," writes historian Alexandra Minna Stern. "By drawing a fairly stark line between an ugly and benighted chapter of pseudoscience in which misguided authorities were ensnared by Nazi-inspired ideas of racial hygiene and a much savvier and sagacious present in which such mistakes will not be repeated," well-meaning critics "can create a specious sense of security, even hubris."[4]

There is nothing "past" about eugenicist ideas. But there is a more fundamental problem as well: IQ testing and standardized testing, even if they *were* decoupled from high-stakes outcomes (like losing school funding or being forced to undergo sterilization), are based on extremely narrow ideas of intelligence, and their use benefits from the fact that most people don't understand them very well.

In the present edition of Terman's exam, now known as the Stanford-Binet Intelligence Scales, the authors caution against interpreting IQ findings without considering contextual factors. "Avoid overinterpretation of SB5 [Stanford-Binet fifth edition] results," they write in the guide accompanying the test. "The results of intellectual assessments such as the SB5 should never be interpreted in isolation. The examiner should consider the context of the evaluation, environmental conditions of testing, examinee behavior and moods during the administration, and possible disabilities and linguistic or cultural factors. . . . The use of scores without good contextual understanding may lead to inappropriate and unethical decisions."[5] This warning appears in a large gray box labeled CAUTION in bold, all-caps text. Given some of the discourse around IQ, one has to wonder whether most people have considered this warning.

Terman's impact lingers. The current version of the test includes "classic items," which have been included "to provide consistency across editions."[6] Some things have changed. The test no longer bears its cringey previous logos: a bell curve and an image of the globe with calipers measuring it.

In 1960, the Stanford-Binet test was adorned with these two logos: calipers measuring the world and a bell curve.

The current test includes a number of items under the category "knowledge," which require the individual being tested to be familiar with situations, objects, or experiences that are by no means universal. For instance, an illustration of a letter shows a stamp placed in the center rather than at the corner. Can't identify where it's supposed to go? Zero points. In another, a rooster sits in a nest. Can't identify why this is "silly or impossible"? Zero points. Another illustration shows a plane on a runway, its engines inverted. An air traffic controller with protective headphones stands in front of it, arms raised. If you don't catch the issue with the engines, zero points. If you say, "The man is going to get run over," zero points.[7] While this set of "knowledge" items represents only one component of the Stanford-Binet, it stands in contrast to the public perception that IQ tests measure something innate and therefore immune to cultural or experiential influence. Some studies have shown that contrary to the assumption that it is static across the lifespan, someone's IQ *can* change significantly over time—it's not actually an immovable measure of inherent ability.[8] And even as many within the field of educational psychology increasingly admit that tests like this are regressive, biased, and irrelevant, they remain in use in school districts across the country; one psychologist told an education journalist that "the field is mired in the past in 100-year-old technology that people think is good because it's been used for so long, not because it really works."[9]

Here's another example. From 2014 to 2020,[10] some private preschools in New York City used the Admission Assessment for Beginning Learners as part of their admissions process. The AABL was designed for children as young as four to take independently on an iPad, with no assistance or support from an adult. On the website of the company that produced the AABL, you and your child could watch a short video together to help prepare them for the experience.[11] In the section on verbal reasoning, the sample question shows a family of cartoon owls standing in front of their very nice single-family home.

"Mama and Papa Owl are taking the children to the zoo," coos the voice-over. "Touch the best way for them to get to the zoo!" Should they take the red wagon? That's a popular choice for families to haul

little ones around the zoo, isn't it? Or the bicycle? Should they take the motorbike, which families around the world use as a fast and affordable way to get around? Should they be going to the zoo at all, seeing as they are owls? Is that a thing owls do?

If you notice the little bus stop sign to the left of the family, you will know that they are waiting for the bus, and you will officially be less confused than I was the first time I watched this video. If you are a four-year-old in a place that does not have reliable public transit or you have never waited for a bus, too bad for you.

"While the score report is only one element of a child's application," reads a statement on the website of the private Horace Mann School, "it is the only piece of the application that is consistent and objective for our applicants, who come from many schools and many different backgrounds and include children who do not come to us from formalized preschool settings."[12] The presumption is that the AABL test is "objective," that it measures something innate, and that this is important enough to help determine whether a child is worthy of attending a preschool that costs $64,000 a year (!).

In his book *The Testing Charade,* developmental psychologist and assessment expert Daniel Koretz argues that "many of the people with their hands on the levers in education don't understand what tests are and what they can and can't do. Many think that testing is simpler and more straightforward than it is. A good example was a claim by George W. Bush when NCLB [No Child Left Behind Act] was being debated. 'A reading comprehension test is a reading comprehension test. And a math test in the fourth grade—there's not many ways you can foul up a test. It's pretty easy to "norm" scores.' Not one of these three assertions is remotely correct."[13] Testing is complex; it represents an inherently limited attempt to take a snapshot of a slice of knowledge at a point in time.

As with any snapshot, this picture is subject to distortion. If the unchecked assumption about test scores is that they reflect an accurate and simple image of reality, what happens when the picture omits Native people altogether? In reports of educational statistics, it's common to see an asterisk in lieu of results for Native students—which means "not enough data." In this realm, knowledge doesn't "count" unless it's based on a massive enough sample size to be statistically significant—deemed the only form of significance worth discussing—such that these data reports can serve as yet another route toward disappearance. Native peoples' absence passes as unremarkable. "The absence of data on Native American students reinforces our invisibility, where our presence is hidden by the ever-present 'asterisk,' and further marginalizes Native people," write the editors of the book *Beyond the Asterisk*. In their view, this seemingly passive omission is in fact an intentional act, serving as "an active 'writing out' of the story" of education discourse.[14] As Diné education scholar Amanda Tachine explains, this "writing out" creates an endless feedback loop of invisibility. Where there is only an asterisk, there is nothing worthy of further discussion. The asterisk "justifies exclusion from research studies because of low numbers. . . . These types of exclusionary measures signify 'statistical extermination,' which are formulas sanctioned by the federal government that quantify the validation of the removal of Indigenous existence and presence."[15] Through the logic of testing, if Native people are not countable, they do not count.

As anyone who has taught in the past two decades will tell you, the idea that standardized tests are the only measure worth talking about seeps into everyday life in the classroom. When I was a middle school science teacher, I tried to design my lessons and classroom environment with research-based best practices for science instruction and using methods for getting kids excited about science. As much as possible with my limited budget and time (as the only science teacher across three grade levels), I worked to develop inquiry-based, collaborative, lab-oriented lessons. This was what research supported, it was what my students found fun, and it was what I knew from professional scientists was most likely to prepare students for careers in science if they chose to pursue that path.

That was all fine and good, until test time. The state science test had no performance evaluation, no collaborative activities, no lab component. Students would have to sit at their desks and answer rote multiple-choice questions about random facts. One of the standards, I recall vividly, required students to identify the difference between a pinnate leaf and a palmate leaf. You can take a moment to put this book down and look it up if you'd like to know the difference. Indeed, so could my students, outside the testing environment. But their ability to recall this random fact during test time had very high stakes, and so I came in on Saturdays to make chart paper posters with drawings of these two types of leaf. State rules allowed us to have such "instructional materials" hung on the walls as long as we posted them a certain number of days before testing began. Of course, since my students would be taking the test in their homerooms, I had to make multiple such posters and give them to my colleagues to hang on *their* walls. Chart paper was too expensive for me, so my district-assigned instructional coach stole some from her office on the low for me to use and stayed late in the evening to help me make the posters. Both of us understood that, for my students, doing badly on this test could have consequences that would literally shape the rest of their lives, and as inane as I thought the questions were, I couldn't take any risks.

Years later, I still run into former students at the store, while walking my dog, or while going for a run. They are grown-ups, some with kids of their own. They tell me how much they loved my class, how they enjoyed using a microscope and going to the aquarium and taking care of the gecko that was our class pet. The details they were required to memorize out of context for rapid recall in an artificially constructed setting don't seem to rank among their memories of what made school matter for them.

I remember a story that Nicole Begay, a learning and literacy specialist at Arizona State University, shared over lunch with a group of friends and collaborators. She told us about being in a special education meeting, reviewing the progress of a young boy from her rural Diné community. As the gathered experts delineated one deficit after another, she thought about all the remarkable things the young boy knew how to do. "You mean to tell me that this child, who can shear and break down an entire sheep on his own, doesn't know *anything*? Anything? He knows so much!"[16]

What if we had a more expansive notion of the miracles of human creativity and cognition, one that wasn't poisoned by the fetid waters of White supremacy? Because, of course, there is more than one way to think about human giftedness, as the elders of the Keresan Pueblo suggest. *A' dzii ayama' guunu*—giving from the heart. Alas, some of the most vitriolic fights in contemporary public education are over this very question: what constitutes knowledge worth knowing?

This is one of the reasons that the battle over race and racism in schools is so incendiary. Part of the gospel of intellectual inferiority is the assumption that only White people's knowledge is worth knowing—indeed, that only White people's knowledge *counts* as knowledge at all.

Though the modern iteration of this conflict has risen most visibly to public consciousness in the form of battles over what I might call lowercase "critical race theory," the fight is actually much older than that.[17] For instance, in 1977 the state of Montana passed a law requiring teachers on or near reservations to complete six hours of coursework in Native American studies. Before the law was ultimately taken off the books, it *infuriated* local White teachers, such as the two who wrote this letter to their senator:

> We believe this law is in violation of our rights both as Montana residents and as United States citizens. . . . The present white guilt complex concerning Indians is no more edifying than the past "dirty savage" stereotype of the 19th century. An

> appreciation for Indian culture *should not, nor cannot* be legislated. Why stop at Indian Studies? How about Mexican Studies? . . . Problems arising because Montana Indians feel their culture is being slighted are not in keeping with the 14th amendment and clearly take away our rights if we are forced to learn about them to keep our jobs.[18]

If we have to learn about Native American studies, where does it stop? *Mexican studies?* Chaos!

In an August 2021 hearing on education, Wisconsin state representative Chuck Wichgers submitted testimony in favor of a bill preventing "critical race theory" from being taught in schools, including an addendum of terms that, if used in lessons, would be considered a violation of the law. The list of eighty-nine words and phrases included "colorism," "equity," "land acknowledgment," "racial prejudice," and "Whiteness."[19] The incredible feat of Wichgers's list is that it ensures that students can continue to study White *people*—presumably Thomas Jefferson and Christopher Columbus[20] will still be A-okay—but the phenomenon of White*ness* itself has to remain invisible and unspoken in order to continue humming along genially in the background.

In a way, Wichgers's list, and the work of his contemporaries seething as they try to ban "critical race theory," represents a rather sad limit of the imagination. And that limitation is violent, because it sees no paths for other ways of knowing to exist. It requires their total elimination—the destruction of our *epistemologies.*

Epistemologies are theories of knowing—what knowledge is, how we construct it, where it comes from, and what "counts" as *knowing* something. If we understand that settler colonialism "destroys to replace," it makes sense that this would require the destruction of one system of knowledge, one philosophy of what it means to *know,* to learn, to understand, with another.[21] For White supremacy to thrive, for America to attain its ideal of "progress," the complete eradication of Black and Native ways of knowing is required. We can also think of this as an extension of Jefferson's Doctrine of Discovery: when children enter school, their minds are seen as "new lands" to be shaped according to the social, cultural, and political conventions of their teachers, without any acknowledgment of the funds of knowledge they enter with or recognition of the value and beauty of that prior knowledge.[22]

Intelligence testing as part of the gospel of intellectual inferiority, therefore, is devastating not only because it reinforces the idea that we are stupid. Moreover, it does so by relying on a violent system of knowledge that requires the eradication of all other forms of wisdom and creativity. As Patricia Hill Collins has written, "Epistemology points to the ways in which power relations shape who is believed and why."[23] Epistemology, therefore, is far from an arcane academic concept; it makes up our daily understanding of what is knowable, how we know it, and what kinds of bodies can be considered sources of credible knowledge—indeed, of "intelligence."

As political scientist and critical Indigenous theorist Sandy Grande writes in her landmark book *Red Pedagogy*, White supremacist epistemology is highly individualized. Through this worldview, "success and individual worth are measured by abstract and impersonal standards of excellence whereby students are aware of being in direct competition with each other"; and "children and the reservoirs of local knowledge with which they come to school are not perceived as sufficient or valid foundations of real or universal knowledge."[24] The gospel of intellectual inferiority not only harms Black and Native children individually—propagating the idea that our children are lesser, are incapable—but harms *all* children in this deeper, more fundamental, even spiritual way, by denying all of us forms of knowledge that celebrate the wisdoms of our ancestors, that encourage us to be in good relation to the more-than-human world, to our kin, to our souls and the souls of others.

The gospel of intellectual inferiority denies us access, for instance, to ideas of Native science, which Tewa ethnobotanist Gregory Cajete describes as "born of a lived and storied participation with a natural landscape and reality" that requires one to "be open to the roles of sensation, perception, imagination, emotion, symbols, and spirit" in knowledge-making.[25] It denies us ways of thinking about data collection and measurement like those developed by the United States Indigenous Data Sovereignty Network, governed by principles of caring and fairness: for example, the idea that "those working with Indigenous data have a responsibility to share how those data are used to support Indigenous Peoples' self-determination and collective benefit," or that "any value created from Indigenous data should benefit Indigenous communities in an equitable manner and contribute to Indigenous aspirations for wellbeing."[26] We miss out on the opportunity to practice what Potawatomi scientist Robin Wall Kimmerer calls "heart-driven science," with its orientation of mutual responsibility and listening rather than mere classification.[27]

So much heart-driven inquiry awaits us if we make space for it—so many other epistemologies. My own position of inquiry has been forever transformed by thinkers like Black queer feminist writer Audre Lorde, who wrote: "The white fathers told us: I think, therefore I am. The black goddess within each of us—the poet—whispers in our dreams: I feel, therefore I can be free."[28] Indeed, a great deal of Black feminist epistemology recenters the roles of feelings, intuition, and observed wisdom as critical forms of knowledge. As Patricia Hill Collins describes, Black feminist epistemology has four central components: 1) lived experience as a criterion of meaning, 2) the use of dialogue, 3) the ethic of personal accountability, and 4) the ethic of caring.[29]

We might look to the example of Septima Clark and her adult education Citizenship Schools of the 1960s, which reconfigured the notion of school from being outside the community to being inside and among, specifically designed to develop critical tools for collective liberation, and—most important—to challenge the orthodox understanding of who is a student and who is a teacher.[30] In these schools, students were evaluated not only on their ability to read and write, but also on their community activities, such as helping neighbors or attending meetings.[31] Clark's cousin Bernice Robinson, who taught in one such school, recalled telling students, "I'm not a teacher. And we are going to learn together."[32] This approach stands against the highly hierarchized setting of most formal schools (characterized by grades, tracks, and firm teacher/student boundaries) and draws from the tradition of insurgent communal learning among enslaved people a few generations prior. Enslaved people gathered on Sundays when masters were at church or met before dawn and after dark to teach and learn together; those who could not read would sometimes memorize scraps of conversation or spelled-out words and then repeat them to literate loved ones to transcribe.[33]

Black studies scholar Katherine McKittrick writes that *wonder* and *curiosity* are powerful places from which to begin the work of learning, and they are as rigorous as any other starting point. "Within black studies and anticolonial studies," writes McKittrick, "one can observe an ongoing method of gathering multifariously textured tales, narratives, fictions, whispers, songs, grooves."[34] The "logic of knowing-to-prove," as she terms it—the drive to argue, to compete, to prove yourself the smartest by defeating your perceived enemies in a battle of intellectual will—will never be as sustainable as curiosity. "Wonder is study. Curiosity is attentive."[35]

As psychologist Douglas Medin and education scholar Megan Bang (Ojibwe and Italian) point out, children in schooling spaces already have to learn how to navigate among multiple competing epistemologies—whether or not educators choose to acknowledge them. For instance, in one study, Medin and Bang asked Native middle school students to look at images of animals, plants, water, the sun, rocks, and artifacts. They then asked the students to classify what a science teacher would consider to be "alive" and what an elder would say is "alive." "Generally, the students answered differently for each context, saying, for example, that an elder but not a science teacher would say that rocks and water are alive."[36] It is important, then, for educators to take the time to recognize the epistemological resources[37] young people bring to school, to go beyond "celebrating" them through the lens of feel-good multicultural diversity narratives, and to actually value them as legitimate points of origin for inquiry.[38]

The problem is not that Black and Native children perform poorly on tests, such that we have to get them to do as well as White children. Nor is the problem only that the tests are unfair, or that the consequences attached to them too dire. The problem is that the regime of standardized testing that has become so central to our system of public education, and more fundamentally *the assumptions about intelligence* that undergird that regime, are offshoots of a philosophy of knowledge that was *explicitly* eugenicist, that categorically excluded the possibility that such a thing as Black or Native intelligence could possibly exist, and that promulgates itself through the delegitimization and destruction of any other forms of epistemology. To make matters worse, the gospel of intellectual inferiority provides justification for the violent control and discipline of Black and Native children. Because you can't truly *teach* a sub-intelligent creature, can you? Faced with such a beastly thing, there is only ever control. More on that next.

PART III

HANDS CLASPED

This part of the book contains descriptions of abuse and harm against children and youth, as well as suicide.

I've come to view the privatization and commodification of the body as one of the greatest affronts to sovereignty, compelling not only materialist analyses but also those that account for the immaterial—the soul, the spirit, and especially the sacred.

—SANDY GRANDE, *RED PEDAGOGY*[1]

The police department in Rochester, N.Y., released body-camera footage on Sunday that showed a 9-year-old girl being handcuffed and pepper-sprayed by police officers who had responded to a family disturbance call. During the incident, which occurred Friday afternoon, officers restrained the girl, pushing her into the snow in order to handcuff her, while she screamed repeatedly for her father, the footage showed. At one point, an officer said, "You're acting like a child." She responded, "I am a child."

—NICOLE HONG, *THE NEW YORK TIMES*, JANUARY 31, 2021[2]

the voice shot out, a stray bullet / of accusation. stop, police. /
our jog became sprint. / how could you blame us? . . . when the
officer caught me / my grape pop tumbled to the crabgrass, /
spilled like piss. my fear / or the fear i now evoked /
when the officer caught me / i cried

—NATE MARSHALL, "WHEN THE OFFICER CAUGHT ME"[3]

CHAPTER 8

Carceral Logics

The spring of my third year as a middle school teacher, I was told by a colleague that there was a field trip coming up, arranged through a special program.

It was a field trip to the Cook County Jail.

The students would meet with corrections officers and incarcerated people, and would be warned of the dire consequences of a life of crime. I was told that it was a great success year after year.

I hesitated. The colleagues organizing this trip were extremely experienced educators I respected a great deal; one of them was a Black woman. But I felt uncomfortable with the entire premise. Why should we spend instructional time to take our students (virtually all of whom were Black; a couple were Latine) to jail? What were they to gain from this experience? The basic idea seemed to be that they would be "scared straight"—that seeing the punishments that awaited them if they broke the law would deter them from doing so.

The thing was, I didn't believe that people, even thirteen- and fourteen-year-olds, break the law for lack of information. I didn't believe that taking the students to Cook County Jail would tell them anything they didn't already know, and I worried that it would send them a very specific message about our expectations for them. With limited time and funding, we only got to take a couple of field trips a year. I didn't think this should be one of them.

As my colleague talked to me about the trip, I was caught up with memories of my own time in middle school, in another part of the city, when my class took a field trip to the courthouse. I remembered setting off the metal detector because I had a foil gum wrapper in my pocket, and how terrified I was when I was pulled aside by the guards at the entrance. I remembered how I had felt many years earlier when I learned that my own father had gone to jail, the sinking feeling in the pit of my stomach.

I could not think of one educationally valuable, beneficial, or caring thing that could come from this field trip. But in an effort to be respectful of my colleagues and of whatever the students' parents might want—after all, maybe I, the green, inexperienced teacher, was the one out of touch here—I devised an alternative field trip. On the same day, I would take a group to the Gene Siskel Film Center downtown to see a free screening of a new documentary about high school poetry slams. It would be open to anyone, even the students outside my homeroom. That way, everyone could choose which trip they wanted to attend. Movie or jail.

When the appointed day came, half of us found ourselves barreling down Lake Shore Drive on the big yellow bus headed back to school. The weather was warm, which is an instant morale booster in Chicago. Everyone was abuzz, talking about their favorite parts of the film, musing out loud that they wanted to put in more work on their own poetry, or planning to find out if the high school of their dreams had a poetry club or slam team. Being responsible for the kids outside of the building always turned me into a bundle of nerves. I would spend every moment away from school obsessively counting on my fingers, tracking the students with my eyes like they were wandering ducklings while also trying to make sure they had some age-appropriate opportunities for independence. My goals were to make sure everyone had fun, make sure everyone was safe and accounted for, and get us back to the building on time. Today I was on track to hit all three marks. So, all around, I was feeling pretty pleased.

When we made it back to room 219, it was almost time for dismissal. But half my class was missing—they hadn't yet made it back from the other trip. No big deal. Those that were present focused on packing their bags and getting ready to go.

A few minutes before the bell rang, the door opened. It was the rest of my class, and they bore with them the air of a funeral procession. Simone[1] rushed over to me, and before I could speak, she was hugging me, her head on my shoulder. "Ms. Ewing," she said. "I'm so glad to see you."

"I'm glad to see you, too!" I said. "Are you okay?" I looked over her shoulder. Deyanna, a usually cheerful girl with a long brushed-out ponytail and an affinity for colorful keychains and necklaces to complement her bright glasses, sat at her desk. She was quietly crying to herself as she gathered her things to go home. I moved toward her desk and leaned down, trying to comfort her without embarrassing her.

"My daddy is in there," she said, almost whispering. "I don't like thinking about the fact that my daddy is in there."

Next to her, Josiah sat stone-faced, not moving. Josiah loved reading, which he did a lot of, and hated homework, which he did virtually none of. He had been in my classes since he was eleven, and as we had gotten to know each other, he had matured into one of my most helpful and thoughtful students even as other adults in the building seemed irritated with him most of the time. Now he was staring into the distance, refusing to make eye contact with me or anyone. I asked him if he was okay, and he nodded without speaking. His father, I would learn later, had been incarcerated after attempting to rob a grocery store. As of this writing, he is scheduled to be released in 2079. Josiah was named after him. If you search online for Josiah's name, his father's listing in the Illinois Department of Corrections is the first thing that comes up.

I barely knew what to do. The bell was ringing and I had to let everyone go or they would miss pickups and buses. But half my students were shell-shocked. I comforted those I could amid the end-of-day chaos, then let them go. When they were gone, I sat in my chair, stunned.

My colleague came in. The trip had gone well, I heard. The jail was very scary. The students hadn't been sequestered from the men; they had to walk past the cells to get to the room where an officer would give them a speech. As they walked, some of the men yelled warnings and cautions. Others yelled threats, including graphic threats of sexual assault. I was too shocked, too sad, too caught off guard to ask what I should have asked, what I regret not asking all these years later: *Why did we allow this to happen when our job is to keep them safe?*

The day my students went to jail was one day of a long, slow, tedious, and consistent message that Black and Native students have received, loud and clear, for generations. *Your lot in life is to be controlled. You need to be controlled, because you are bad. You are bad not because of what you have* done, *but because of who you* are. *You were born bad. In order for the rest of this great country to work as it is supposed to, we have to use every tool of discipline and punishment at our disposal to make sure you don't ruin things for the nice people.*

Schools have been extraordinarily effective as one of these punitive tools, as a place where young people are made to practice their life's destiny of being an object of control and discipline, and where daily machinations—tiny, seemingly innocent practices—are brought to bear to make this way of things seem not only normal, but necessary.

This story of Black and Native children's bodies being made into sites of corporeal control and harsh punishment is a long one, as old as the nation.

They say that Hannah Ocuish, for instance, didn't understand that she was about to be hanged. In the days before her execution, she played with the children who visited her, and seemed unconcerned during her trial. "Children and servants should be early taught to read," preached the reverend when the appointed day came—December 20, 1786. "This is an advantage which the children in a family generally enjoy. But are not our servants, my brethren, too long forgotten?" He lamented the ignorance of Hannah—perhaps it was this ignorance, her inability to access moral education, that had led her here. Her mother, after all, was a member of the Pequot Nation. In some accounts, her father is reported to have been Black.[2]

The reverend, Henry Channing, wrote that Hannah's mind "wanted to be properly instructed, and her disposition to be corrected." She had been accused of murdering a little girl, hitting her on the head with a stone after the girl had taken some strawberries from her. They said that Hannah waited until the girl was going to school and jumped out at her, killing her. There were no witnesses.[3] Hannah was twelve years old; though her exact birth date is hard to confirm, to this day she is considered to be the youngest person in the history of the United States to be sentenced to death and executed.[4]

No one saw George Stinney commit murder, either. Nor was there any physical evidence. His trial had no witnesses called; the only information presented was the account of the police officers who said George had confessed to them that he had killed two little White girls in his mill town of Alcolu, South Carolina, in 1944.[5] George was not allowed to see his parents, who had been driven out of town by a lynch mob. Fifteen hundred spectators assembled to watch the jury deliver their verdict after deliberating for less than ten minutes.[6] When the governor was petitioned for clemency, he declined, with a statement that George had raped the corpse of one of the girls—despite the fact that a postmortem examination did not indicate that either of them had been sexually assaulted.[7] George weighed ninety-five pounds, and when the time came for the state to end his life, his body was too small for the restraints of the electric chair.[8] He was fourteen.

While the stories of Hannah and George are extreme, the manner in which they were treated—like adults, and like criminals—has persisted in the lives of Black and Native youth. Historically, one of the social functions of schooling has been to discipline and punish Black and Native children—to repress in them a presumed proclivity for immorality and violence, to sanction them for the safety of society at large, and then to socialize them to be accustomed to surveillance and control so that they can be effectively policed as adults.

From Pipeline to Nexus to Carceral Logics

The "school-to-prison pipeline" is a term familiar to many people even outside the field of education, and in the last two decades it has broken through from the worlds of research and activism into mainstream conversation and public concern. And it's no wonder, as the phrase does a striking job of naming something intuitive: that both schools and prisons seem to be sites of extreme racial disproportionality, and that a number of features of some school buildings—from metal detectors to police—seem designed to funnel a subset of students toward incarceration.

Policy analysts Johanna Wald and Daniel J. Losen, who used the phrase in writing before many others, described the pipeline as "a journey through school that becomes increasingly punitive and isolating for its travelers." Students face poor instruction, high-stakes testing, and repeated suspension "before dropping or getting pushed out of school altogether. Without a safety net, the likelihood that these same youths will wind up arrested and incarcerated increases sharply."[9]

While the idea of the "pipeline" is illustrative, some scholars and activists have taken to using a different phrase: the school-prison *nexus*. The word comes from the Latin *nectere*, "to bind," and scholars like Erica Meiners have suggested this phrase in order to capture the ways that schools and prisons are bound together, wrapped around one another like the strands of a spider's silk. These bonds, writes Meiners, are "a web of intertwined, punitive threads," a set of relationships that is "historic, systemic, and multifaceted."[10]

Within the school-prison nexus, the logics of the prison are used on certain young people *whether or not* they are actually ever arrested and incarcerated. These are the spoken and unspoken rules of social engagement. Whose body requires control and discipline, and why? What are the acceptable ways to address perceived misbehavior? Which children are presumed to be innocent, and which are treated like adults? As Meiners reminds us, it is not simply a matter of "how our schools' physical structures resemble prisons—metal detectors or school uniforms—but also the tentacles in *policies, practices, and informal knowledges* that support, naturalize, and extend relationships between incarceration and schools."[11] We see the school-prison nexus reflected in commonly stated assumptions. *We need police in schools to keep us safe. If a child is misbehaving, send them out of the room so the others who really* want *to learn can focus.*

Decisions made in classrooms and principals' offices often make use of *carceral logic*—literally, the logic of the prison.[12] Quietly, the rules of a society that is addicted to arresting and punishing people are mapped onto the everyday functions of the school building. In her extensive writings on the prison-industrial complex, abolitionist writer Mariame Kaba offers us some examples of carceral logics: If we dispose of people by locking them away, it will prevent, reduce, or transform the harms of our society.[13] Surveillance, containment, and punishment are the most effective ways to keep our communities safe.[14] For society to function, we need to control potentially unruly people by using weapons, fear, and acquiescence to authority. Some individuals are inherently "dangerous people," a trait which is innate and permanent.[15]

Carceral logics work in tandem with one another. In "A Jailbreak of the Imagination," an essay co-authored with Menominee writer and organizer Kelly Hayes, Kaba writes that when observers are confronted "with historical evidence that policing and incarceration have always been grounded in anti-Blackness, Native erasure, and protection of property," they will often admit that this is bad before insisting that nothing is to be done about it, because if the "dangerous people" are not locked away, we will all be in danger.[16] Like a car stuck on ice, we find ourselves unable to escape these logics, spinning our tires uselessly and endlessly.

The fact that Black and Native people—branded the "dangerous people"—will suffer is considered insufficient motivation for us to try something else. Carceral logics cloud our imaginations; they keep us from asking questions or exploring other possibilities for how we might pursue other methods to find safety and address the forever problem of humans harming other humans. They keep us from turning to other ideas that actually might be easier, cheaper, more obvious, or more effective. As Kaba and Hayes write, "We live in a society that has been locked into a false sense of inevitability."[17]

If you think about it, our easy reliance on carceral logics in schools is especially sad. After all, shouldn't schools—allegedly places dedicated to learning, nurturing, and understanding child development—be the first place where it occurs to us to address problems through care, compassion, and gentle inquiry rather than through punishment and containment?

To the contrary, Black and Native people have been criminalized—labeled "dangerous people"—in schooling spaces throughout history. Like a perpetual motion machine, this allows carceral logics to sustain themselves: school becomes the place where they are routinized and made acceptable beyond questioning at an early age, impressing upon both children and the adults charged with caring for them that this is the *only* way things can possibly work. That normalization is cast upon the rest of our society, which in turn fails to condemn everyday acts of punishment and disposal enacted against children because these acts are seen as inevitable necessities. To quote anthropologist Damien Sojoyner, "There is nothing normal about a prison. . . . There is serious work that has to be done to make these processes *seem* normal," and schools, Sojoyner argues, have "been at the forefront of ushering in the prison regime."[18]

As sociologist Carla Shedd has written, the "routines and rituals" created by carceral logics—everything from interacting with police officers in schools to strict uniform codes of conduct—become integral to the way a school functions, and can ultimately undermine the ostensibly educational purpose of the school building by making students feel unsafe.[19] One high school student, Dewayne, described his feelings to Shedd in an interview:

> [My school] feels like a prison, to tell you the truth. 'Cuz you have to stay in the classroom, use the bathroom when they tell us, eat lunch when they tell us, it's like a jail. . . . That's why kids act bad. They feel like they trapped in here.[20]

Dewayne's observation echoes a point made by Foucault in his classic *Discipline and Punish: The Birth of the Prison,* which you'll remember from chapter 4. Through practices like those Dewayne describes, the human being becomes less a spirit animated by agency and more a "body as object and target of power," a thing to be "manipulated, shaped, trained, which obeys [and] responds."[21] In his everyday interactions in the building, Dewayne is reminded that his body is not his own. Necessary human functions like eating and using the bathroom can only be conducted with the approval and surveillance of those in a position of authority.

Through these efforts, students are transformed into what Foucault calls "docile bodies"—bodies that can be "subjected, used, transformed, and improved" in ways that are endorsed by those in power. This process requires "uninterrupted, constant coercion, supervising the processes of the activity rather than its result"—think of students completing meaningless busywork where the quality of the outcome is of no consequence, only the fact that they are sitting still and doing it—"and is exercised according to a codification that partitions as closely as possible time, space, movement."[22]

Foucault's description calls to mind the work of Estelle Reel, the Superintendent of Indian Schools we met in chapter 5. In the Uniform Course of Study, her curriculum for Native schooling, Reel drew attention not only to the matter of what Indian children should learn, but to the precise details of bodily, spatial, and temporal control that should attend their lessons at all times. Children tasked with learning sewing must always use a thimble and never be permitted to make knots in the thread. "See to it that all sit in an erect position, never resting any part of the arm on the desk," Reel wrote, alongside directions for "marching, breathing, [and] calisthenics." As K. Tsianina Lomawaima puts it, these details were intended to be "a blueprint for total control of Indian people—mental, physical, and moral—in excruciating detail."[23]

From within the space of the school, such regimes of discipline can become so routine that they escape notice by those who are accustomed to them. "Disciplinary power," writes Foucault, "is exercised through its invisibility; at the same time it imposes on those whom it subjects a principle of compulsory visibility. In discipline, it is the subjects who have to be seen. Their visibility assures the hold of the power that is exercised over them."[24] The expansion of technological tools for surveillance has broadened the reach of such compulsory visibility. In 2020, during the COVID-19 pandemic, a Colorado art teacher saw a toy gun in the home of twelve-year-old Isaiah Elliott during a virtual learning session. The gun was neon green with an orange tip and the words ZOMBIE HUNTER printed on one side. Without contacting Isaiah's parents, the principal called the police, dispatching the sheriff's department to his home and leaving Isaiah in tears. He was suspended for five days.[25] Isaiah's parents told reporters that they were unaware their son's virtual class was being recorded, and that the school district first refused to show them a copy of the recording to see what had occurred. Once they did view the video, it showed Isaiah idly picking up the toy gun and moving it from one side of the couch to the other, not realizing that it was visible on screen.[26]

"If [the teacher's] main concern was his safety, a two-minute phone call to me or my husband could easily have alleviated this whole situation to where I told them it was fake," said Isaiah's mother.[27] His father said that he was afraid for his son's life—a reasonable fear given that police being called to a home where they have been told a young Black boy has a gun could have ended in a tragic loss.

There are other ways a student's body can be "manipulated, shaped, and trained" toward the goal of docility. In 2013, principal Sally Hadden of Loleta Elementary School in California was accused by the ACLU of a wide variety of physical and psychological assaults against Native students. On one occasion, she grabbed a student by the ear and pinched, commenting, "See how red it's getting?" On another, she called the sheriff on a student for sitting outside his classroom on a bench because he was upset about something and did not want to go inside. Hadden and other members of the school staff hit students, grabbed their faces, and pushed them into their seats, sometimes in view of other adults. Wiyot students had their hair touched by teachers without their consent, and were forced to drink spoiled milk in the cafeteria. They were kicked, and hit with a notepad and clipboard so hard it made an audible "crack." Native students at Loleta were routinely suspended for infractions such as talking in class or getting up to sharpen a pencil.[28]

That last tactic—suspension—is perhaps the aspect of the school-prison nexus that has captured the most public attention. It's worth taking a moment to think deeply about suspension and expulsion, which experts in this area of research refer to collectively as "school exclusion"—any action or policy that removes the student from the learning environment for the purpose of punishment. We often think about school exclusion in terms of what it *does* to students. We know that school exclusion is associated with lower academic achievement, higher future rates of misbehavior, and a higher likelihood of dropping out.[29] But what does school exclusion *tell* students? What does it mean to exclude a student from the learning environment? What does it mean for the excluded students themselves, and what does it mean for the other students who are watching?

School exclusion is, fundamentally, a strategy of disappearance.

In a 2003 conversation about prisons, Angela Davis described incarceration as "the punitive solution to a whole range of social problems that are not being addressed by the institutions that could make people's lives better. So instead of building housing, throw the homeless in prison. Instead of developing the educational system, throw people who are illiterate into prison. . . . You know, get rid of them. They are considered to be dispensable populations. So the prison becomes a way of disappearing people and disappearing the social problems associated with those people."[30] The phenomenon that Davis describes here—of disappearance—occurs in a sort of microcosm within schools in the form of school exclusion. If students are "bad"—unruly, inconvenient, a reminder of social problems that seem impossible to solve—simply get rid of them. Put them out in the hallway, suspend them, expel them. Throw them away and the problem is solved for the moment. And that is good enough.

As you'll recall from Part I, disappearance has long been considered the inevitable fate of Native people who stand in the way of American progress. For Native students who experience school exclusion, therefore, *disappearance* has multiple valences. Sending them away allows them to conveniently disappear. When they drop out of high school or are incarcerated, they disappear.[31] And in our conversations about the school-prison nexus, these students are often disappeared again. Despite incidents like the Loleta case, Native students have largely been excluded from scholarly conversations about school discipline and policing, even though they are suspended, expelled, and arrested at disproportionate rates. Black students are almost four times as likely to receive out-of-school suspensions as their White peers. Native students are nearly twice as likely.[32] In Montana, an ACLU study found that "Native American students lost nearly six times the amount of instruction as white students and were arrested more than six times as often," while "Black students lost nearly three times more days than white students."[33] Native students are also more likely to be incarcerated than Asian American, Latine, and White students combined.[34] Analysis by the Lakota People's Law Project has found that, in twenty-six states, Native youth are disproportionately placed in secure confinement, and in South Dakota, Alaska, North Dakota, and Montana, "Native youth account for anywhere from 29 to 42 percent of youth in secure confinement."[35]

In the Loleta case, students and attorneys alleged that Principal Hadden regularly suspended Wiyot students for infractions that earned no punishment when White students did them—things like shooting rubber bands, talking back to teachers, throwing a pencil, or hanging for too long on a basketball rim. One seven-year-old Native student at Loleta had been suspended an estimated *eleven* times. Once was for breaking crayons. As sociologist Nancy Heitzeg has pointed out, these kinds of purportedly disruptive behaviors are more likely to be medicalized or attributed to mental illness or socioemotional needs when White students (especially middle-class White students) do them:

> In highly publicized cases of extreme white violence such as mass shootings, there are often immediate appeals to the medical model to explain the deviance as "sickness." Although the most serious of white criminals do indeed face serious criminal charges, it is the medical model that is called on to "understand" them. They are not totally "bad"—they are "sick." Someone should have or could have helped them before it was too late.[36]

In contrast, at Loleta, the school secretary referred to the kids as a "bunch of wild Indians." One teacher physically shoved a student into a chair to force them to sit; when a parent reported the incident to Hadden, she remarked that "some kids need that."

Some kids need that. In my days as a teacher, I heard variations on this phrase a lot. Generally it was used to explain why children were being asked to sit in silence, or sit in isolation, or be subjected to a set of draconian rules that the adults around them would never be able to follow themselves. In the United States, statistically, *some kids* are disproportionately Black and Native. And they are in trouble. Or, more accurately, in the eyes of their schools and American society, they *are* trouble. They are a puzzle: what are the best means to contend with a nation of Black and Indigenous people, ungovernable and unruly?

In schools, discipline and punishment enable us to kill two savage birds with one stone. The treatment endured by young people like Hadden's students is traumatic and dehumanizing. But just as important, this treatment prepares Black and Native youth for lives as disciplined and punished adults—as docile bodies. Schools work to normalize the idea that we should accept external control exerted upon our bodily autonomy. Further, schools normalize the idea in the minds of White people that such control is necessary. In the present, adultification, sexual abuse, corporal punishment, zero tolerance, social control, surveillance, and school exclusion are all ways that discipline and violence continue to be central to schooling regimes, under the paternalistic guise of protecting beasts from their own uncontrollable instincts. But these contemporary social trends have much deeper historical roots.

CHAPTER 9

To Resist Is to Be Criminal

The white man had concluded that the only way to save Indians was to destroy them, that the last great Indian war should be waged against children. They were coming for the children.

—DAVID WALLACE ADAMS[1]

The great lie is that civilization is good for us.

—TERRANCE LAFROMBOISE, QUOTING JOHN TRUDELL[2]

On the last stretch of my first year of college :) In the photo posted on Instagram, Brendon Galbreath sits in the grass, looking directly into the camera. He is dressed comfortably in jeans, a gray pair of Chuck Taylors, and a black T-shirt. A few stray acne scars are scattered across his forehead and chin, a signpost of his youth. Around his neck hangs a pendant of a turtle, a Blackfoot symbol of creation, patience, wisdom, and longevity reflected in the phrase *Iikakimat mookakiit*—"Be wise and persevere."[3]

In another photo, he grins alongside a group of friends, wearing a shirt that says STRONG RESILIENT INDIGENOUS. "When Brendon was born . . . he created a lot of good things for our family," his older brother Terrance Lafromboise told an interviewer.[4] "And his spirit shined, you know, since he was little . . . and that's kind of who he was. He was always filling space. He was consistently an ear for somebody, or wisdom for another, or jokes for somebody else. He was an all-around empathetic person, to his friends, his family. Ever since he was a tiny little baby. You could feel his presence."

Brendon had enrolled at UCLA with hopes for a career in medicine. It made sense—his mother had been in nursing school when she was pregnant with him, and Brendon was born into a family of healers. He was serious about it, too, joining the Indians Into Medicine program at the University of North Dakota beginning in seventh grade. Brendon shined in school, taking on a breathtaking array of activities: he ran track, did speech and debate, was a member of a poetry club and a human rights club, served in student government, traveled to Washington, D.C., on an exchange program—where he met Michelle Obama—and graduated as salutatorian, sharing the title with three of his friends. At UCLA, he grew in his understanding of himself, including coming into his identity as a leader in the campus LGBTQ community. "He kind of got out of his shell and was able to be more outspoken and able to make connections with new people and just kind of blossom really," said his high school friend Hailie Henderson.[5] Brendon's queerness, like so much else in his life, became a gift of healing and learning. "He fought to have a place in the world," said another friend, Jolee Bullshoe. "I hope to meet people where they're at because of who Brendon was—he inspires me to be more inclusive, he inspires me to be more kind-hearted and easygoing with people."[6]

In 2020, Brendon lost his grandmother, who had been instrumental in raising him, to COVID.[7] He left UCLA for Missoula, Montana, intending to spend time there grieving her, comforting his mother, and staying closer to family. He got a job at AT&T in Missoula and contemplated whether he should change his major to engineering when he headed back to college in the fall. He lived with his cat, Midnight.

In the early morning of August 12, 2021, Terrance was awoken by a pounding on the door. He was told that Brendon had died of a self-inflicted gunshot wound after an encounter with the Missoula Police Department. Brendon had been admitted to the hospital after the incident, but no one in his family was notified until he had already passed away. When Brendon's parents arrived at the hospital, his body was already gone, taken to a crime lab.

For Terrance, his mother, Eva, and the rest of Brendon's family, the tragedy of losing someone they loved escalated quickly into a new kind of nightmare. As far as Terrance and Eva could tell, their need for closure, their longing to have even the most basic factual understanding of what had happened to Brendon, was of no urgency for the police. For over seven months, they called the Missoula police and asked the same questions: Could they see an autopsy report? Could they see bodycam footage? "We couldn't even get a conversation," Terrance told me. "We couldn't even get a conversation . . . 'It's under investigation, and that takes time.' And that's all we got . . . It felt like they were just getting tired of us calling. They would just say, 'Leave us your information. Oop, we already have it! We'll call you!' "[8]

In the midst of being rebuffed over and over, Terrance and his mother started to question their grip on reality. Were they somehow bad people for calling and calling and calling? Were they wrong to ask these questions? "At the most vulnerable time in our life," Terrance told me, "we weren't validated. It was like they thought we were lying." When Terrance and I spoke, months after the inquest where he finally got to see the bodycam footage, he told me that his mother was just starting to regain flashes of memory from that time; to cope with the overwhelming anxiety, grief, and uncertainty, she had been dissociating, her mind blocking everything out for her own survival.[9]

Getting the runaround from the police was painful. But it didn't feel unexpected. Montana has long been scarred by anti-Indigenous violence. Terrance wondered if Brendon's car had been targeted because he had rez plates. Their mother had warned them about the police when they were growing up. "They're gonna look at your long hair and they're gonna think 'troublemaker.' They're gonna look at your brown skin and mark you." The boys had been raised to understand that there were certain towns where, as Native people, they should never go alone. When they played other teams in basketball, the parents called them racial slurs from the sidelines. The police, Terrance had come to believe, "only care about their crew. Their brotherhood. It's a good ol' boys system."[10]

In April 2022, Brendon's family was finally permitted to watch the video of their beloved—son, brother, friend, healer—losing his life.

Investigators determined that, after a car chase, two weapons had discharged within a split second of each other. Brendon had fired a weapon. Then, so did Officer Garrett Brown. Both of them were targeting the same person. It was the self-inflicted gunshot that ended Brendon's life. He was twenty-one years old.[11]

For Terrance, a trained social worker, the video presented infinite questions, a cascade of alternate realities that sent him spiraling. When he was pulled over, Brendon was polite, deferential, obedient—and, Terrance felt, glassy-eyed and distressed. What if the officer had intervened differently? In Terrance's view, the officer "didn't know how to help somebody who was in a crisis, and it showed in his ability to communicate with said person . . . his ability to just fire at somebody like that." Or a different possibility: Terrance finds himself wishing Brendon had been arrested. "I would rather my brother been in jail," he tells me, "and you and I would not even have this conversation." One detail that Officer Brown presented in his testimony pains Terrance to this day. Brown told the assembled jury that when he first saw Brendon driving—when he slowed at a stop sign and did not come to a complete stop before turning—his first instinct was to leave it alone. Go back to the precinct.

"You could have just went on your day," Terrance says. "And my brother would have still been here."

In the months since the video was released, Terrance has worked to stop blaming himself, to move past the period of torment when it felt like no one in power cared about Brendon, his life, or his death. He has come to see what he calls a "nuanced" relationship between Brendon's mental health, the deep history of racism in Montana, intergenerational legacies—among Native people and among White Montanans raised to hate them—and the moment Brendon was pulled over. He is convinced by the forensic evidence; when I ask him if he believes that Brendon died by suicide, not at the hand of Garrett Brown, he answers quickly and unequivocally that he does.[12]

"But the crisis," he tells me, "was created through the interaction between my brother and the police officer." For Native communities, Terrance believes, police do not bring safety. "I feel like they're just creating pockets of chaos in our communities."[13]

For years, activists have spoken up about the potential for traffic stops, mental health crises, and mundane everyday interactions with the police to turn into deadly encounters. But even as more and more people across the United States have become aware of the epidemic of police-involved shootings, data on when, how, and where they happen remains unreliable and undercounted.[14] What we do know from figures published by the Centers for Disease Control and Prevention suggests that Native people are killed by police at a rate higher than *any* other racial or ethnic group in the country. The CDC reports that 2.9 deaths by "legal intervention" per million Native people is the annual average; some other sources suggest that the rate may be as much as twice that high.[15] The stories sound familiar: Jason Pero, we are told, lunged at an officer with a knife. He was fourteen years old.[16] Renee Davis, a pregnant mother of three who was both Black and Muckleshoot, was killed by police after her partner alerted them that she was in the midst of a mental health crisis.[17] Loreal Tsingine was shot by an officer five times when she waved a pair of scissors at him.[18]

When Zachary Bearheels went missing on his way home to Oklahoma, his mother called the police to make a report and to inform them that he had bipolar disorder and schizophrenia. When they found him at a convenience store, the officers put him on the phone with her. "I heard him say, 'Mama, mama,'" she said. The police handcuffed Bearheels and put him into the back of a police cruiser; when he tried to get out of the car, they Tasered him and dragged him across the parking lot by his hair. He was pronounced dead on arrival at the local hospital.[19]

Paul Castaway was shot and killed by officers after his mother called the police to report that he was having a dangerous mental health crisis. "He wasn't a danger to anybody but himself," said his brother, Gabriel Black Elk. It was not Gabriel's first experience with this kind of devastating loss; his cousin was killed by police in 2012 while holding a wrench. Another cousin was shot by tribal police for allegedly resisting arrest.[20]

We have talked about the omission of Native people from school data reports as a form of erasure, continuing the settler colonial legacy of disappearance. In the media, the lack of attention cast on Native deaths at the hands of police serves the same function; in one analysis of news articles published from 2014 to 2016—a time of heightened public awareness about police violence—researchers found that lethal police encounters involving Native people were severely underreported in the news. Even when they were reported, they were unlikely to find much resonance in high-circulation publications outside of local outlets and Native-focused news sites such as *Indian Country Today*.[21] Part of the problem is that Native issues are underreported generally: one analysis found that stories about Native people make up 0.6 percent of popular news stories, despite Native people comprising almost five times that proportion of the U.S. population.[22]

Lakota journalist Tim Giago has argued that there is something more nefarious at play in police opinions of Native lives. Historically, the brutal murder of Native people was deemed acceptable and "left unpunished because after all, they were only killing Indians. Did some of this frontier mentality leak into the minds of present day law enforcement officers?" Giago asks.[23] Settler colonialism requires disappearance, which in turn requires dehumanization; dehumanization requires "savages," and savages require complete and unequivocal social control. As Salish and Kootenai sociologist Luana Ross describes in her book *Inventing the Savage,* the criminal legal system as it pertains to Native people is "a system that imposes on indigenous populations cradle-to-grave control designed to obliterate worldview, political independence, and economic control. To resist is to be criminal, risking the wrath of multiple state law enforcement agencies. In the Americas, this exploitation has been the backbone of a colonial relationship now hundreds of years old yet still vigorous."[24]

As Ross describes, the construction of criminality as quintessentially Native and Indigeneity as quintessentially criminal goes back a long way. Today, a stunning number of Native youth find themselves entangled in a system of harsh penalties and cruel treatment—due, in part, to the legacy of a crime that took place in 1881 and the settler belief that Native people cannot independently manage harms done within Native communities.

From the onset of colonization, Native people were understood to be lawless and to require the imposition of order by White settlers, or else they would turn to uncontrolled primitive violence.[25] The Commissioner of Indian Affairs established a distinct system of laws, courts, and punishments intended to govern Native peoples; rather than leaving them to determine their own sovereign systems of laws or even making them subject to the laws of the (stolen) land, the Court of Indian Offenses dictated that Native people be subject to specific prohibitions and consequences. Offenses included "immorality," intoxication, destroying property (ignoring the fact that destroying the belongings of the deceased was a customary mourning practice in many tribes), any dancing that was "intended and calculated to stimulate the warlike passions of the young warriors of the tribes," and the practices of medicine people. Medicine people in particular were seen as a threat for the risks of "preventing the attendance of the children at the public schools, using their conjurers' arts to prevent the people from abandoning their heathenish rites and customs."[26]

When Native communities did try to resolve wrongs using their own internal systems, White leaders deemed these resolutions unacceptable. In 1881, the Lakota man Crow Dog shot and killed another Lakota man, Spotted Tail, during a dispute. Spotted Tail was a tribal leader who had supervisory power over the police on the Rosebud reservation.[27] Under Brulé law, Crow Dog and his family were called upon to pay restitution to the victim's family, which they did, thus concluding the matter in their eyes. But the federal attorney for the Dakota Territory, upon learning of the outcome, was horrified by the lack of retributive punishment and charged Crow Dog with murder.[28] Crow Dog petitioned the U.S. Supreme Court, which determined that according to an 1868 treaty affording the Lakota the right to manage the punishment of serious crimes, the United States government did not have the jurisdiction to punish him if his crime was against another Native.

Public fury over the case from White observers—why wasn't Crow Dog punished more harshly?—drove Congress to pass the Major Crimes Act of 1885, giving federal courts unilateral jurisdiction over "major crimes" when they were committed by Native people—taking away sovereign tribal nations' right to manage crimes such as murder, arson, burglary, and larceny.[29] One congressional representative, urging passage of the law, declared: "I do not believe that we shall ever succeed in civilizing the Indian race until we teach them regard for law and show them that they are not only responsible to the law but amenable to its penalties."[30] The outrage, of course, ignored the fact that Crow Dog *had* been brought forth for judgment, and met the terms of that judgment under Lakota law.[31]

Notably, this rule only goes one way; the Supreme Court ruled in 1978 that tribal courts do *not* have any criminal jurisdiction over non-Native individuals who commit crimes on tribal lands.[32] Native people can be multiply criminalized and punished, but cannot reciprocally enact the rule of law as they see fit. As Dian Million (Tanana Athabascan) writes, this creates a "double bind" wherein "U.S. law 'polices,' but does not protect, Native communities."[33] This leads Vine Deloria Jr. to ask: "If, Indians reasoned, justice is for society's benefit, why isn't our justice accepted?"[34]

Under the logic that Native people are inherently more violent and also unfit to carry out the call of justice, the law leaves us with a system that enables discriminatory sentencing. At present, the Major Crimes Act effectively allows Native people who have committed crimes to face sentencing both by tribal courts *and* the federal government, leaving them doubly punished. Federal criminal sentences are generally longer than state sentences and often include mandatory minimums, such that the law—rooted in a fundamental belief in Native lawlessness—has the effect of automatically creating a system of sentencing disparities. As one South Dakota judge noted in his sentencing of a Native man convicted of drunk driving in 2000:

> Congress has seen fit to impose altogether different penalties on Native Americans. . . . Thus, a person of German or Norwegian descent driving under the influence in Aberdeen, SD, would not face nearly the same penalties as a Native American driving on one of the reservations in South Dakota. Why Congress would have done this is beyond me. . . . Again, I do not understand the logic of any of this. It is, if nothing else,

> unfair and discriminatory. It is certainly not "equal justice under the law." But it is the law and my job is to follow constitutional laws as enacted by Congress.[35]

So what does the Major Crimes Act—an arcane two-tiered system created by Congress after a nineteenth-century murder—have to do with the lives of Native young people today?

Well, as is the case with adults, any Native youth offender who commits one of the "major crimes" on the list is rerouted into federal jurisdiction. Remember, this includes offenses like robbery or larceny (the theft of personal property), acts that wouldn't ordinarily be charged as federal crimes. As a result, almost *one in five* youth arrested by federal entities is Native, despite Native youth representing less than 2 percent of the overall population of young people in the country.[36] That is a disparity of jaw-dropping proportions.

And being routed into the federal jurisdiction makes a difference. The federal legal system, unlike state juvenile justice systems, often lacks judges and prosecutors who are specially trained to work with young people. Young people incarcerated in federal facilities are also unlikely to have access to educational programs and other initiatives that would be found in a juvenile facility.[37] For those Native youth charged with crimes that don't land them in the federal system, disparities are still drastic. They are more likely than their non-Native peers to be petitioned to state courts for status offenses (actions that are considered a crime only because of the offender's age, such as truancy or drinking alcohol). When convicted, they are less likely to be placed on probation, and more likely to be incarcerated.[38] In one juvenile facility, a 2003 court investigation revealed, a young girl from the Pine Ridge Reservation was "held in a secure unit within the facility for almost two years, during which time she was placed in four-point restraints while spread-eagled on a cement slab for hours at a time, kept in isolation for days and even weeks, and pepper-sprayed numerous times. . . . The facility also instituted a rule that penalized Native youth for speaking in their Native language, and several were placed on lockdown status for speaking Lakota to each other."[39]

Punishing young people for speaking their own language . . . reminds us of a form of control historically practiced in schools, doesn't it? Policies like this situate Native youth as enemies of the state not because they've committed any one act of subversion, but based on their very being; it is their Indigeneity itself that is seen as inherently criminal. Such policies are reminiscent of the nineteenth-century Code of Indian Offenses—also known as the "Civilization Regulations," because they were established as part of an explicit strategy of assimilation and disappearance.[40] These laws banned Indigenous peoples from hosting dances or feasts and prohibited the practices of medicine men and healers.[41] Subsequently, laws would ban other everyday practices of Native joy, culture, and tradition that were seen as hindrances to becoming "civilized" and effectively disappearing into the fog of Whiteness: wearing long hair, dressing traditionally, face painting.[42] These practices, wrote one official, were not protected as a matter of normal civil liberties. They were an impediment to "salvation," "a badge of servitude to savage ways and traditions which are effectual barriers to the uplifting of the race."[43]

These prohibitions represented an attempt to erase and destroy Indigenous culture *through control of the body.* By marking the Native body as an "object and target of power," the laws stripped Native people of the basic agency and personal autonomy that is so central to personhood, reconfiguring them into subhuman vessels for state control and discipline. They attempted to prevent Native youth from inheriting the practices of their ancestors, in the hopes of destroying Indigeneity itself by interrupting the movement of love and custom from the old to the young that had persisted for countless generations. Practices like traditional dance or wearing long hair were not fully protected under the law until the American Indian Religious Freedom Act was passed in 1978.[44]

By their very existence, Native people represent a challenge to the legitimacy of the land theft that provided the basis for this republic. Characterizing Native people as savage, as dangerous enemies of the state, is a neat way to address this problem. In her book *Red Scare: The State's Indigenous Terrorist,* Lenape scholar Joanne Barker argues that these representations are supported by the public because they hearken back to the notion of what she calls "the Murderable Indian." The

Murderable Indian is murderable because their life inherently threatens American peace and prosperity; their savagery leaves the state with no choice but to use "counterterrorist, military, police, and vigilante responses to contain, punish, and deter."[45] The state needs to mark Native people as criminal not only because they serve as a reminder of the nation's past harms, but also because they represent the possibility of a future and present where other forms of relation are possible. In order to maintain a legitimate claim to being able to dehumanize, displace, and murder Native people, the state must maintain the fiction that no other way of being can exist.[46] Native children and all that they embody—the promise of a sovereign future—are a particular hindrance. As Sabina Vaught, Bryan McKinley Jones Brayboy (Lumbee), and Jeremiah Chin write:

> In empire, with its scarcity, its reliance on forms of death, and its obsession with insecure self-defense, Native children are a beautiful threat. In their very existence, they are refusal, as they make futures, as they signal that Indianness has not only not been broken or killed but is and will be self-determined.[47]

K-12 institutions often normalize the narrative of the Murderable Indian, especially through the figure of Christopher Columbus. As cultural theorist Sylvia Wynter writes in her landmark essay "1492: A New World View," Columbus's interpretation of the people he confronted in the "New World" was based on a set of ideas that were already established in the European worldview of his time: the Taino and Arawak peoples were "idolators," making them eligible for enslavement and land expropriation for the ultimate benefit of the state.[48] The basic framework of this idea lingers with us in classrooms from sea to shining sea: a cultural attachment to the breathless, awed, admiring narrative of "discovery" and "explorers."

When I was in fifth grade, we began our unit on "explorers" with an announcement from the teacher that she had hidden little baggies of M&M's around the room and we were to search every corner until we found them. We were just like the explorers! Having used candy to prompt our interest in this "Age of Exploration," the teacher then assigned each of us an "explorer" to learn more about. Mine was Bartolomeu Dias. I learned that he had bravely made it around the Cape of Good Hope, opening trade routes. I learned nothing about the role of Dias's home country of Portugal and its creation of the transatlantic slave trade, nor did I learn about Dias's own role in human trafficking.[49] Then—because, as this teacher told us, the purpose of all this "exploration" was to obtain spices—we were each assigned a spice to research and then prepare a dish using that spice to serve to the class. I was assigned dill. And that was it for the Age of Exploration: M&M's, brave men, and dill.[50]

I was in fifth grade a really long time ago. But this story is in line with what Western Shoshone historian Ned Blackhawk identifies as a broader narrative in which, consistently, "explorers are the protagonists. They are the drama's actors and subjects. They think and name, conquer and settle, govern and own . . . just as Native Americans remain absent or appear as hostile or passive objects awaiting discovery and domination. Indigenous absence has been a long tradition of American historical analysis."[51] Columbus remains a ubiquitous figure in our culture; in 2021, the *National Monument Audit* listed him as the third most represented individual in U.S. public monuments (after Abraham Lincoln and George Washington, but ahead of Martin Luther King Jr., John F. Kennedy, and Benjamin Franklin).[52]

In 2021, when my research team and I did an analysis of content labeled "Christopher Columbus" on the online teacher marketplace TPT (Teachers Pay Teachers), we turned up over 3,200 results.[53] About 46 percent of the lesson plans, activities, worksheets, and other materials introduced a neutral view of Columbus, often couched in the form of a "debate" or "let's learn both sides" perspective. These lessons included titles such as "Columbus Day Opinion Writing Unit—Hero or . . . Villain?" and "Christopher Columbus: Was He a Great Historical Figure?" About 32 percent were explicitly positive and celebratory. Fewer than 1 percent of the lessons we found were primarily critical, either centering an Indigenous view of Columbus or addressing his legacy of violence, colonization, and slavery.[54] Meanwhile, a search for "Indigenous Peoples Day" turns up about 750 lessons—a mere fraction of the content.

If you are a teacher and would like to teach a lesson on Columbus Day, and you believe that the most valuable thing you can offer your students is an opportunity to color in a grinning cartoon illustration of a childlike Columbus holding a telescope, then you're in luck.

Columbus's purpose in these materials is more mythological than factual; he's a kind of Santa Claus, an invented character that U.S. culture has determined collectively that children ought to know about, with little critical inquiry as to why or what national narrative this mythmaking perpetuates. In some cases, White supremacy in our country is perpetuated by lies of omission—by repressed memories, by willful ignorance. But in the case of Columbus, it becomes clear that "the deeper mnemonic issue with white majority settler nations such as the United States is not what we forget but how we remember, not just an 'un-knowing' but particular forms of knowing," as political scientist Kevin Bruyneel tells us.[55] Not much mention about how Columbus, after declaring Indigenous lands the rightful possession of the Spanish crown and Indigenous peoples to be idolators, kidnapped hundreds of people; and when about two hundred of them died upon arrival near Europe, he jettisoned their bodies into the water.[56] The genocide, the slavery—those things are footnotes, extras, optional. This matters because, as Wynter writes, the framing of our collective founding narratives sets the boundaries of our ability to see others as part of our own species, as being within the bounds of an *us,* as beings like ourselves deserving of kindness and altruism.[57] This is the national origin story the United States has adopted for itself.

One analysis of state-recommended California elementary school textbooks found that Native people were presented as violent aggressors in the state's colonial history, "a framing that is drastically out of alignment with the historical record as it is agreed upon by historians."[58] In 2016, a California fourth-grade teacher was celebrated by the local news for a "creative" assignment in which students were asked to think of the best place to establish a Spanish mission. They had to consider questions about geography and natural resources and, their teacher explained to the reporter, "they also had to look at the Native Americans to see if they were friendly and hard-working, or did they revolt?"[59]

Through this kind of everyday narrative, kids are taught that there are two kinds of Natives: the good ones (friendly and hardworking) and the bad ones (the ones who revolt). In reality, colonization in California was a regime wrought by brutal violence, torture, sexual exploitation, environmental devastation, and biological warfare against Native peoples. But textbooks tell a different story, referencing "California Indian rebellion and revolt" more than three times as often as they describe violence enacted by Spanish colonizers. Conversely, Spanish colonizers are represented as *victims* of violence more than three times as often as Native people.[60]

Native observers have long critiqued the persistent invisibility of Native people, histories, and perspectives in the mass media, perpetuating the myth of the vanishing Indian. The project Reclaiming Native Truth puts it plainly: "Native peoples are invisible to most Americans."[61] Schools play a huge part in perpetuating this disappearance. One report found that 87 percent of state history standards do not mention Native history after 1900. (Perhaps you've experienced this in your own schooling—the association of anything and everything Native people "did" with the past tense.) Twenty-seven states make no mention of a single Native person in their K-12 curriculum.[62]

These omissions don't happen by accident. They are part and parcel of what Bruyneel calls "settler memory," in which a settler society reproduces images and stories of dispossession while, at the same time, leaving out the parts that center Indigenous people within that story as political actors with agency, and eliding the ways our status as a settler society inflects political struggles, sovereignty, and identity in the contemporary world.[63] In the stories we receive in schools, the "pilgrims," "pioneers," and "explorers" are the ingenious heroes who built this country from nothingness to greatness. No genocide or land theft mentioned along the way to make the tale unpleasant.

In another study, researchers found that fourth- and fifth-grade social studies teachers used language that made Native resistance seem like a routine inconvenience to be quelled, rather than a valid response to the project of colonization. One teacher asked students to pretend they were English colonists planning their new society. "There must be adequate protection for the inhabitants from attack by hostile savages," she told the class, "but you will also have to oversee friendly trade with the natives to ensure their proper treatment. We want the Indians to help us and not be our enemies."[64] Compare this to, say, how the American Revolution is discussed in class. When Patrick Henry or the Sons of Liberty resist their colonizers, they are heroes. When Indigenous people do it, they are hostile savages.

These moments reveal what Tigua and Chicana feminist scholar Dolores Calderon calls "settler grammars in curriculum."[65] These are the narrative terms of engagement that we often take for granted, the structures that govern our language—generally without our even noticing it. Suddenly, you find yourself in a world where asking fourth graders to role-play people implicated in violent mass murder seems like a fun way to engage in project-based learning.

Settler grammars tell us that to be Indigenous is to be criminal, that Indigeneity is inherently a threat to state cohesion, and that the only way to manage the savage Indian is through violent control and repression. Those ideas are embedded in state surveillance and control of "lawless" Native people, in the veneration and normalization of settlers in our curriculum—and in the way Native youth are treated in schools. The old bans on long hair reverberate into the present day, making a child's hair a site of contestation when school officials deem it unruly and uncivilized, much as they did a century ago. As Bryan McKinley Jones Brayboy and Jeremiah Chin have written, the seemingly benign policies of the school building can turn state violence into a normal, everyday occurrence. They argue:

> School discipline, corporate exploitation, and police violence all are sanctioned by law in neutral tones, preserving a hierarchy of power that prioritizes whiteness and colonial interests, without having to mention either. Educators no longer follow the words of Richard Pratt, to "Kill the Indian, and Save the Man." Now the violence is masked in neutral tones of school dress codes that require "clean and neat" haircuts for boys, often leading to Black and Native students being singled out, disciplined, suspended, or even expelled for wearing their hair

> in ways that do not conform to white norms. . . . Scalping bounties and dress codes are different implementations of the same continuum of racialized, colonial violence through alienation. Forcing students out of schools is a means of control, reinforcing hierarchies of domination.[66]

The Military-School-Prison

These policies, once they are integrated into the everyday operations of schools, blend into the background as the "natural order of things."[67] And if you recall our discussion of the Carlisle Indian Industrial School, they should sound familiar. *Kill the Indian, save the man.* Native youth, according to Commissioner of Indian Affairs Thomas Jefferson Morgan, were individuals who were "naturally brutish and whose training has developed their anima and left their higher nature underdeveloped . . . and can be reached apparently in no other way than by corporal punishment, confinement, deprivation of privileges, or restriction of diet."[68]

It's important to stress that Carlisle was not an anomaly—it was a blueprint. It was a prison that became a school, and the hundreds of boarding schools constructed in its image—which operated well into the twentieth century—became places where bodily discipline, corporal control, and punishment were seen as vital to the schools' job of civilizing their Indians.[69]

Memoirs and personal accounts from those who attended the boarding schools constructed in the wake of Carlisle are legion, and carry countless different perspectives, voices, and experiences across tribes, geography, and generations. When we fail to account for the resistance, meaning-making, and kinship unearthed as part of the horrific legacy of Indian boarding school narratives, we miss an important part of the story. As K. Tsianina Lomawaima has described, children in boarding schools developed strategies for undermining the government agenda, from developing group solidarity to evade school rules to everyday forms of resistance such as hiding uncomfortable woolen uniform underwear behind the bushes after wearing it just long enough to pass inspection.[70]

These acts of resistance happened against the backdrop of what Lomawaima has referred to as "the battleground of the body."[71] War would be fought on the backs, literally, of Indian youth. A Kiowa woman who attended the Riverside School described the school uniforms as "awful clothes . . . I guess we got prison uniforms and didn't know it."[72] One Kiowa man recalls his first few moments at school—the moment his parents were gone, he was taken into a room where he was held down by two adults while a third cut his braid off.[73] No aspect of the body was too intimate to be free of surveillance: one boarding school alumna described a matron who would collect and dispose of the rags issued to menstruating students and used the task as an opportunity to carefully track their periods in school records.[74]

Another Riverside student characterized their time as "really a military regime," complete with drilling maneuvers and marching. "We marched everywhere, to the dining hall, to classes; everything we did was in military fashion. We were taught to make our beds in military fashion, you know, with square corners and sheets and blankets tucked in a special way. . . . On Sundays we had an inspection . . . just like the military."[75] The superintendent of the Phoenix Indian School outlined his view of the benefits of this approach: "Too much praise cannot be given to the merits of military organization, drill and routine in connection with the discipline of the school; every good end is obtained thereby." Phoenix, like most Indian schools, had a jail onsite where students could be held.[76] *The Native American*, the school's newspaper, described the students as hailing from places "where impulse or appetite takes the place of bugle call and military regulation," whereas the school offered "the forming of regular habit, that mother of self-control, which distinguishes civilization from savagery."[77]

In his memoir about growing up at the Pipestone Indian School, Chippewa activist Adam Fortunate Eagle describes one way the students were pushed toward the forming of regular habit: by having a bottle of cold water poured on their heads if they didn't promptly get out of bed with the 6:30 A.M. bell. Sometimes, the head of the school would use a bullwhip instead. "He puts the Coke bottle away, and when he walks down the hallway and we hear that bullwhip popping, we scramble out of bed. Any boy stupid enough to think he can sleep in makes his butt an easy target for that bullwhip."[78] Tellingly, a young man who frequently ran away from the Albuquerque Boarding School was described in a letter from the clerk to the superintendent as a "deserter." "Joseph Siow, age fourteen, a Laguna from Casa Blanca, deserted last night some time after the bed checks were taken. Joseph is a chronic run-a-way, he having deserted several times last year. . . . The last time he deserted it took us thirty days to get him back and . . . [the] sentence was one day in jail for each day's absence, but he was let out on good behavior in twenty days."[79]

The schools' hybrid prison-military character did not stop there. Students were given English names but could be referred to by an assigned number rather than by any name at all, and in some cases were assigned to be members of a "company" in the manner of a military unit.[80] "We were under strict discipline, we were never free," described Kiowa linguist Parker McKenzie.[81] Forced to stand at attention, "it was not unusual for the little ones' skins to appear blue from the cold. It was very sad to see 6, 7, and 8 year-olds being compelled to learn the rudiments of soldiery as early as 6:00 a.m."[82] Deviating from these expectations meant harsh punishment, as did the unforgivable offense of being caught speaking an Indigenous language. Student accounts include every inventively cruel form of abuse imaginable, from being forced to carry a stepladder on the shoulders for hours, to being forced to dress across perceived gender lines as a form of sexual humiliation, to being whipped, to being locked in a darkened closet, forced to eat rotten food, and then eat one's own vomit after throwing up, to being forced to wear a ball and chain.[83] One superintendent boasted: "The child is taught how to do a thing, when to do it, and to do it whether he wants to or not."[84]

Students who transgressed, a teacher at one school noted, were sent to the "dark room," which had only a four-inch window in the door and no other light.[85] Elaine Salinas (White Earth Ojibwe) moved to Wahpeton Indian School in 1956, when she was seven years old. Salinas lived on campus because her parents worked as a carpenter and a dormitory attendant, giving her a unique point of view:

> I'd stand in front of the school at the beginning of the year and watch the buses arrive: children from six to eighteen looked lonely and scared. School personnel herded them like cattle into showers and treated them for lice. The youngsters slept in large, cold dormitory rooms. At night, I heard little children and even older ones crying for their parents. . . . If a girl disobeyed a rule she'd have to wear a long, green dress as a signal to others that she had misbehaved, or she'd have her beautiful long hair cut short. A boy who disobeyed had to scrub the basement floor with toothbrushes; if he was defiant, he was sprayed with a fire hose. If he tried to run away, the police would track him down, the school superintendent would pick him up and make him run beside the car. The most severe punishment I witnessed was "the hot line." An eighteen-year-old boy had been allowed to attend a movie downtown and had come back late. The staff made the male students form two lines and gave them belts; the boy had to run the gauntlet and be whipped by his peers. That created a lot of hostility within the student body, which I think is what the staff intended.[86]

Failing to attend school, failing to send your child to school, and "deserting" from school could all be cited as criminal offenses.[87] One commissioner said that he would withhold rations from parents who did not give up their children, "and if that does not suffice, I will send their children anyway. Make it peremptory, and let them understand that I do not care and will not have any obstacles in the way of these children going."[88] If someone was located after having "gone AWOL" from the school, the police could be called in to bring them back, and intensified beatings would follow. "When they whip 'em some would half kill them," recalled one former student.[89] These threats were coupled with other dangers—smallpox, measles, influenza, whooping cough, pneumonia, contaminated drinking water, and inadequate plumbing all presented deadly threats to Native students.[90] Sexual violence served as another form of coercion, reminding students daily that their bodies were not their own. Berenice Levchuk, a Diné woman who attended Carlisle as a girl, recalls the terror that struck her and her classmates: "Intimidation and fear were very much present in our daily lives. . . . After a nine-year-old girl was raped in her dormitory bed during the night, we girls would be so scared that we would jump into each other's bed as soon as the lights went out. The sustained terror in our hearts further tested our endurance, as it was better to suffer with a full bladder and be safe than to walk through the dark, seemingly endless hallway to the bathroom. When we were older, we girls anguished each time we entered the classroom of a certain male teacher who stalked and molested girls."[91]

The line between the criminalization and punishment Native students faced *within* the confines of the school and their subjection to the same *outside* the school could be a blurry one. Ruth Underhill, who served as a U.S. supervisor of Indian education from 1942 to 1948, described boys being rounded up in trucks and "shackled together to prevent their jumping out. When they were once inside the school, scarcely a week passed without some group attempting to run away. . . . They were brought back by a Navaho [sic] policeman and, as punishment, were dressed for weeks in girls' clothes. In their free time, they had to carry heavy logs round and round the parade ground of the old fort as punishment."[92]

On the northern end of Turtle Island, the Truth and Reconciliation Commission on Canadian residential schools, which concluded its mandate in 2015, documented the deaths of over six thousand students, with the assumption that this is almost certainly a significant undercounting.[93] Meanwhile, in 2021, Deb Haaland—the first Native person to be secretary of the interior of the United States—ordered the first ever accounting of the boarding school system this side of the border, with a focus on identifying boarding school survivors who are living, as well as burial sites on the grounds of former schools. As of this writing, the investigation has identified fifty-three burial sites.[94]

By 1969, amid social turmoil as freedom struggles were erupting in Black, Native, Asian, and Latine communities, a congressional subcommittee turned its attention to the institution of the boarding school and the question of Native education more broadly. In *Indian Education: A National Tragedy—A National Challenge,* a group of senators from the Committee on Labor and Public Welfare issued a scathing indictment of the status quo that had been official government policy for generations, critiquing the state-led emphasis on pushing students to choose between Native identity and "complete assimilation into the dominant society."[95] The senators found the school environment to be "sterile, impersonal and rigid, with a major emphasis on discipline and punishment, which is deeply resented by the students," and characterized the family separation encouraged by boarding schools to be "traumatic and emotionally destructive."[96]

In 1972, Congress passed the Indian Education Act,[97] which authorized new funding for local education agencies to develop programs for Native youth, stipulating that grants would be partially assessed on whether they had been developed "in open consultation with parents of Indian children" and using "the best available talents and resources (including persons from the Indian community)." The Indian Self-Determination and Education Assistance Act followed in 1975, promising new pathways for educational sovereignty and tribal control over federal education funds. In 1978, the Indian Child Welfare Act noted that "an alarmingly high percentage of Indian families are broken up by the removal, often unwarranted, of their children from them by nontribal public and private agencies" and established minimum federal guidelines for such removal, declaring that Native children not be taken from parents' custody "unless returning the child to his parent or custodian would subject the child to a substantial and immediate danger."

The decline of the boarding school era has not meant the decline of the immeasurable trauma that still leaves bruises not just on survivors but on their families and loved ones as well. At the same time, the ideologies that governed the boarding school linger on: the idea of the Murderable Indian, images of Native people as inherently criminal, notions of Native children as savages in need of paternalistic civilization as a pathway to assimilation and eventual disappearance, and the assumption that the best way to bring it to them is through discipline, punishment, and bodily control.

Looking Like Trouble

"They just really stand out," the forty-five-year-old White parent told the 911 dispatcher in 2018. She said the two boys' behavior was "odd," that they were quiet and seemed different from the other members of the tour group at Colorado State University. Mohawk brothers Lloyd Skanahwati Gray and Thomas Kanewakeron Gray were seventeen and nineteen years old and had driven seven hours to take the campus tour. After the call, campus police arrived, pulled Lloyd and Thomas out of the group, patted them down, searched them, and asked them to show email proof that they had registered for the tour. They asked why the boys hadn't been more talkative when others on the tour tried to talk to them; they explained that they were shy. The police told them that others were concerned because they were quiet, and because they didn't have parents with them.[98]

For Lloyd and Thomas, the very comportment that might have been seen as desirable in other bodies—quietly listening; having the initiative to attend a college tour without an adult—was enough to mark them as criminal, turning a day that should have been about exploration and possibility into a reminder that there are consequences for being Native and not acting in precisely the way White onlookers demand of you, especially in an educational setting. Many scholars have documented the ways that Native students' perceived silence can be interpreted by White educators as a sign of disengagement, low cognitive ability, laziness, or disinterest.[99] Refracted through the lens of this parent's Whiteness, and her attendant comfort with policing who does and does not "belong" in a college space, these perceived deficits rose to the level of the unlawful, to the realm of the threatening. After being detained, Lloyd and Thomas missed the rest of the tour. "I am lucky my sons are both still alive," said their mother, Lorraine.[100] "My boys were publicly humiliated and told that their looks alone make them suspicious characters," she explained in a statement.[101] "They were trying to listen."[102]

If the criminalization of Native youth did not end with the boarding school era, neither did the assumption that their parents were unfit to raise them—a perceived failure also marked as criminal and requiring state intervention and punishment. In the United States, a little under 6 percent of children will experience foster care placement between the time they are born and the time they turn eighteen years old—about one in sixteen children. For Black children, that rate is about one in nine. For Native children, it's about one in seven.[103]

Are we to believe that Black and Native parents are just less capable caretakers? Black and Native families are more likely to be investigated for abuse and neglect than White families, and once investigated they're more likely to have their children placed in foster care.[104] One explanation for this phenomenon is obvious: poverty. Failure to provide food, adequate shelter, or medical care can all constitute neglect in the eyes of the law. But rather than make use of collective societal affluence to build social support structures that ensure that all families have these things, we turn to familial disruption. As political scientist Barbara J. Nelson has written, child abuse has been framed as a matter of individual families' "deviance" because that is easier than "considering the social-structural and social-psychological underpinnings of abuse and neglect."[105] Living in an apartment that lacks heat, is not large enough, or has roaches can all be grounds for the state to take children from their parents, even when simply addressing those issues would be less expensive *and* less traumatic than family separation.[106]

But that explanation—Black and Native parental neglect due to poverty—is not sufficient on its own. Because *within* the child welfare system, White children are less likely to be placed in foster care (as opposed to receiving in-home services), and their parents are less likely to have their parental rights terminated.[107]

In an NPR investigative report on Native children and the foster care system in South Dakota, tribal leaders alleged that what state social workers referred to as "neglect" could sometimes be cultural difference: having a large number of family members living together because of the value of intergenerational bonds, or leaving one refrigerator empty because another relative is storing and sharing food, could be grounds for declaring a parent unfit. One grandmother described having her grandchildren taken to a White foster home for a year and a half because their mother was accused of abusing prescription pills. The accusation turned out to be based on an unsubstantiated rumor, but despite several appeals, the children were returned only when the tribal council passed a formal resolution threatening to charge the state with kidnapping. The older children returned home wearing clothes that were a size smaller and having developed a new habit of hoarding food and hiding it beneath their pillows. When they heard a car pull up in front of the house, they would hide under their beds.[108]

They were coming for the children. Once again, the logic of elimination masks itself as benevolence.

CHAPTER 10

Absolute Obedience and Perfect Submission

When we treat Black children in schools as though they are there primarily to be controlled—not to learn, or grow, or be loved—we are carrying on a centuries-long tradition that has been central to the very definition of Blackness since the inception of slavery. Black people in this country arrived Mandinka and Mende, Ashanti and Fante.[1] They *became* "Black"—became members of a sociopolitical category that had no inherent meaning until it was thrust upon them—through the institution of slavery, which required them to be subhuman to facilitate their subjection.

There's a risk in thinking of enslavement only as a political status (the inability to participate in civic institutions) or an economic status (the lack of control over one's labor). We can't forget that, in order to function, slavery required brutal systems of physical control and torture. This was not an incidental idea but a constitutive one, a categorical one: to be Black was to be subject to control, full stop. By definition. In determining what constituted "reasonable punishment," in 1861 the Alabama Supreme Court determined that "absolute obedience, and subordination to the lawful authority of the master, are the duty of the slave," and therefore slaveholders could "employ so much force as may be reasonably necessary to secure that obedience."[2] Total obedience required total discipline.[3]

During the Civil War, when enslaved people fled north and were housed in Union camps, observers like nurse and teacher Cornelia Hancock took account of the marks of cruelty they bore. These people were considered not refugees, but "contraband"—property that had been seized from the enemy.[4] In an 1863 letter, Hancock described what she saw in one field hospital:

> There were two very fine looking slaves arrived here from Louisiana, one of them had his master's name branded on his forehead, and with him he brought all the instruments of torture that he wore at different times during 39 years of very hard slavery. I will try to send you a Photograph of him he wore an iron collar with 3 prongs standing up so he could not lay down his head; then a contrivance to render one leg entirely stiff and a chain clanking behind him with a bar weighing 50 lbs. This he wore and worked all the time hard. At night they hung a little bell upon the prongs above his head so that if he hid in any bushes it would tinkle and tell his whereabouts. The baton that was used to whip them he also had. It is so constructed that a little child could whip them till the blood streamed down their backs.[5]

Cruel physical punishment could be meted out with any number of justifications. Accounts of formerly enslaved people describe tactics so inventive in their sadism that they are physically sickening to consider: Beatings with whips, sticks, ax handles, rocks. Immobilizing people by handcuffing them, trussing them up like hogs, or burying them up to their necks in the ground. Pouring water laced with salt or red pepper into open wounds, or pouring hot wax over them.[6] As historian Anthony Gene Carey writes, the purpose of these punishments was not only to deter the individual from future misdeeds. Rather, their purpose was to instill fear in witnesses through trauma. "The mayhem worked to control bodies by imprinting minds; the horrors witnessed or stories heard were meant to be hard to shake."[7]

For enslaved women, the regime of bodily control included control over their reproductive capabilities and their ability to feed and care for their own children. As historian Stephanie E. Jones-Rogers has written, "The appropriation of their breast milk and the nutritive and maternal care they provided to white children" were central to the ways that enslaved women's bodies were treated as commodities.[8] The use of enslaved women as wet nurses was common—and to be effective, reliable wet nurses, these women had to be constantly conceiving and giving birth, creating another incentive for routine sexual assault.[9] The physical violence of such assault was multiplied by the spiritual violence of being robbed of the chance to nurture their own babies—who were, of course, not viewed as babies at all, but as property.

Physical force—public whippings, sexual assault, dogs dispatched to catch runaways, instruments of torture like those Hancock described—constituted one important form of enacting the "absolute obedience" described by the Alabama Supreme Court. But social structures were equally crucial to creating the web of control that characterized chattel slavery. The system required that a free Black body be deemed inherently a *criminal* body; it required the construction of a social world wherein a Black person resisting the total control thrust upon them was not only taboo or undesirable but illegal.

White children and Black children learned divergent early lessons about the role of control in their lives—whether one was suited to enact control or receive control. Frederick Law Olmsted, the celebrated architect and landscape designer who created Central Park, gave an account of observing a White girl interacting with an enslaved adult man. "I have seen a girl, twelve years old in a district where, in ten miles, the slave population was fifty to one of the free, stop an old man on the public road, demand to know where he was going, and by what authority, order him to face about and return to his plantation, and enforce her command with turbulent anger, when he hesitated, by threatening that she would have him well whipped if he did not instantly obey. . . . She instantly resumed the manner of a lovely child with me."[10] As Jones-Rogers points out, this child and others like her had a concrete understanding at an early age of the "pricelessness" of their Whiteness—the endowment of the power to enact ultimate control over another human being with no consequence and no cause other than capriciousness.

In the images of slavery that occupy the popular imagination, our narratives tend to focus on adults. But, in fact, about one in three enslaved people in the United States between 1830 and 1860 was a child under ten years old—an even more remarkable fact when we consider the rates of infant mortality.[11] For slavery to work, the idea of "Black child" had to be made impossible, a contradiction in terms.

Children in our society are considered innocents, afforded certain protections and concessions. Enslaved children were not afforded this protected status. For them, the state of work and bondage was, as historian Wilma King describes it, "the thief of the childhood."[12] One formerly enslaved man, Jacob Branch, said that as a child he and the other children around him began working "soon's us could toddle," and if it was freezing or hot outside, all the better—to "toughen us up."[13] By the time they were ten years old, enslaved children might be designated for a specific form of job: domestic service, laundry, caring for younger children, or caring for poultry or horses.[14] No legal protection guarded them from the sexual assault to which they were uniquely vulnerable.

In Mississippi, when an enslaved man was convicted for having "carnal knowledge of a female slave, under ten years of age," his conviction was overturned on appeal on the grounds that such a thing could categorically not be considered a crime.[15] When six-year-old Betty Gordon, an enslaved girl in Virginia, confided in her aunt that a local cemetery groundskeeper—an enslaved Black man named Ned—had locked her in the cemetery and raped her, it was discovered that he had done the same to a White girl, nine-year-old Eunice Thompson. Eunice had also witnessed Betty's assault and corroborated her story. When the state brought charges against Ned, it was for "an attempt to commit a rape on Eunice Thompson" and "violating the person of Betty Gordon." Although the two girls were subject to the same grievous harm, there was no provision under the law for what happened to Betty to be categorized as "rape."[16] As historian Crystal Lynn Webster argues, the result of these divergent racialized ideas about what childhood is and who counts as a child results in "the construction of American childhood [being] developed over time into a tool of racial oppression," by virtue of whom it includes and whom it excludes.[17] For Betty, the construct of childhood offered no protective factor. Instead, it was little more than a cruel joke.

In her brilliant account *No Mercy Here: Gender, Punishment, and the*

Making of Jim Crow Modernity, Sarah Haley demonstrates how the convict leasing system in particular served as an instrument of dehumanization not only for the Black men we often see in nauseating photos of chain gangs, but also for Black women—and Black children. After Emancipation, convict leasing became a way for Black people's bodies to remain legally in bondage, machines from which all fungible labor was to be extracted through the power of a racist criminal legal system. Incarcerated people—often convicted of crimes of poverty, such as vagrancy, or minor "immorality" charges, such as using profanity—had their labor contracted out to build railroads, work in sawmills, pick cotton on plantations, mine coal or iron, clear swamplands, or quarry rocks on the chain gang.[18] The conditions under which they worked were horrendous—reportedly often worse than slavery. The difference, as one representative to the American Prison Congress declared at its regular meeting in 1883, was simple: "Before the war, we owned the Negro. If a man had a good nigger, he could afford to take care of him; if he fell sick, he would get a doctor. He might even put gold plugs in his teeth; but these convicts—we don't own 'em—one dies—get another!"[19]

Black children were not spared; in this context, they were not considered children at all. Records show that, in 1900, Georgia's Milledgeville State Prison Farm, for instance, held young people like Mary Lou Fears, age fourteen; Bianca Ward, fifteen; Julius White, fourteen; and William F. Sherman, twelve.[20] A few hours away, in Atlanta, reports described a "13-year-old black girl wearing only two thin undergarments" being stockaded and whipped in a "bucking machine"—a pillory-like torture device that held a person still so that they could be beaten. After being assaulted, "the girl became hysterical . . . and said something unintelligible to the superintendent. He ordered her back into the chair," where she was beaten again for being "mean" and "fussing."[21] In North Carolina in 1884, the warden overseeing convict laborers constructing the state's railroads complained that all inmates, aged nine through seventy, had to cohabitate.[22] As historian David Oshinsky writes in his account of convict labor in Mississippi, *"Worse Than Slavery,"* by the 1880s not *one* person involved in the convict leasing system lived long enough to serve out a ten-year sentence, and throughout the decade an average of one in four of these laborers was a child or adolescent.[23] In Washington County, an eight-year-old Black boy was sent away for stealing some change from a dry goods store; in Vicksburg, a six-year-old Black girl was sent away for stealing a hat. When a Mississippi legislator proposed a juvenile reform school as an alternative, the bill failed, since "it was no use trying to reform a negro."[24] Once these children were sentenced, they were frequently targets of sexual assault, on top of the torments the adults faced—malaria, frostbite, dysentery, vicious beatings, and worse.[25]

When construction workers discovered in 2018 the unmarked remains of ninety-five Black convict laborers in the affluent suburb of Sugar Land, just outside Houston, the youngest among them was only fourteen years old.[26] In Florida, where 90 percent of the state prison population was Black, it was common for children between the ages of ten and sixteen to be leased out as laborers.[27] In Albany, Georgia, sixteen-year-old Carrie Williams and her neighbors Hattie Bishop—already employed as a home nurse despite being only eleven years old—and twelve-year-old Gladis Trumbick were sentenced to the chain gang for breaking a window and some flower pots near their homes.[28]

In *No Mercy Here*, Haley writes of a Black woman in Savannah, Georgia, sentenced to the chain gang in 1905 for the crime of shoplifting.[29] After reading this story, I turned to the newspaper archives to see if I could learn more—and stumbled upon a *different* awful story, one that remains hard for me to write about even as it feels imperative to do so: the story of Julia Grant.

Thirteen-year-old Julia Grant, also of Savannah, was arrested in 1903 for shoplifting pants from local stores. I first learned about Julia from a series of gruesome news articles; after being sentenced to the county farm for her crimes, she had been badly burned from the waist down. Doctors treating her wanted to use skin grafts, and article after article in the *Savannah Morning News* detailed their attempts to secure a donation. After a little more digging, here's what I could find about Julia: Living on the penal farm where she had been sentenced to hard labor, she fell ill and was sick for several days. While she was standing over a fire—for warmth? for comfort?—her skirts were caught in the flames. She ran out into the yard for help, but was grievously injured. For two days, she was in so much pain that she was "almost crazed"; only after that time had passed was she brought to the state infirmary.

With a bit more digging, I found other details about Julia's arrest. She had been caught with two others, Idell and Mamie, visiting four different stores and stealing multiple pairs of pants, which the newspaper remarked on as "strange."[30] She is referred to in reports as a woman, though she was only thirteen at the time she was apprehended; in her court records, it's noted that she was arrested "tho slow of wits."[31] Several weeks after being burned, Julia contracted pneumonia in the hospital, where she passed away.[32]

This is what the archive holds of Julia: she lived, she was a criminal, she was punished, she was hurt, she died. It took me the longest time to find out what had happened to Julia, *how* she had been hurt, because so much more ink was spilled telling and retelling the contours of her crimes and her suffering. Four articles about the attempted skin grafts, two about the crimes. One about the incident itself, in which she is referred to as "Emma Julia," no last name.

I think, as I have countless times in my life, about the words of poet Gwendolyn Brooks describing the young truants at the center of her poem "We Real Cool." "Instead of asking myself, 'Why aren't they in school?'" she once explained when introducing the poem, "I asked myself, 'I wonder how they feel about themselves.'"[33] The logic of punishment, of criminality, unfolds in the brutal omissions of the archive, in the calculus of what is recorded and what is forgotten—who is disappeared anew. How did Julia feel about herself? Where was she born? What did she want from the world? Who loved her? Who cried when she went away? Who grieved when she went away again?

The horrific conditions under which Black children lived in the convict leasing system was not some shameful secret unknown to common people. In states like Georgia, the government relied upon convict leasing as a labor source to build the railroads and paved highways that would aid the headlong leap toward modernity in the late nineteenth and early twentieth century. Trees were felled and iron was forged by the hands of unfree Black people, including children, in the name of progress. Writing in *The Atlanta Independent*, a Black columnist described the shame of seeing the captives "during any week day digging away, a half hundred Negroes in chains and stripes. We never pass them but that our sense of pride is made to trail in the dust."[34] And in a particularly visible form of convict leasing, Black women and girls were sometimes placed into domestic servitude within private households.[35]

Schooling the Un-Child

At the same time, popular culture defined a widespread representation of the subhuman Black child. As historian Robin Bernstein has written, "Representations of black children, in contrast [to White children] were increasingly and overwhelmingly evacuated of innocence . . . the black child was redefined as a nonchild—a 'pickaninny.' The pickaninny was an imagined, subhuman black juvenile who was typically depicted outdoors, merrily accepting (or even inviting) violence."[36] In songs, films, radio, and other popular media, the idea of the Black child as a creature, unlike *real* children and deserving of violence, casually prevailed.

In the modern era, the media has played a similar role—from "superpredators" to "crack babies," we are inundated with language and images suggesting that Black children are subhuman. I think often of a 2014 *ABC World News Tonight* interview with the child actress Quvenzhané Wallis. The interviewer, David Muir, asked Wallis, who had just been cast in a film adaptation of *Annie*, if she had watched the movie or stage play when she was a little girl. The eleven-year-old Wallis begins to answer, then stops herself and corrects him: "Well, I'm still a little girl."[37] What a stunning intervention for a child to have to make in the moment—the articulation of her own childhood. For the interviewer, to quote Black studies scholar Christina Sharpe, "the meaning of *child*, as it abuts blackness, falls . . . apart."[38]

These moments shape the contours of our classrooms, whether or not they are spoken aloud. In one study, researchers used software that tracked early childhood educators' eye movements. Participants were shown a six-minute video of preschoolers engaging in classroom activities and told, "We are interested in learning about how teachers detect challenging behaviors in the classroom. . . . Your job is to press the enter key on the external keypad every time you see a behavior that could become a potential challenge."[39] In fact, none of the children in the video were engaged in "challenging behaviors"; they were doing mundane preschool activities such as sitting around a small table and playing with toys. Primed by this expectation, though, the educators spent most of their time with their gaze resting on the Black boy in the video, expecting him to be "challenging."

I was eighteen years old, enrolled in my first year of college, when I started out at the first school I worked in. I assisted a first-grade teacher, which usually meant helping students with worksheets one-on-one or grading papers quietly in the corner while she talked on the phone. One day, as the students—all Black, as was the teacher—chatted among themselves, she grew frustrated with them for being what she perceived as too loud. She stood up from her desk and surveyed them angrily. "That's it!" she shouted. "That's it! Get up! Come on, now!" I looked around, confused as to what exactly was supposed to happen. The students knew, though.

One by one, they got up from their seats, stood next to their desks, and crouched down into a squat. They struggled to maintain the position of the physical punishment, crying or falling over. Terrified, I reported what I had seen to my supervisor. He sighed heavily, said he was hesitant to make too many waves, and would not escalate the report. I was reassigned unceremoniously out of the school.

What that teacher did is illegal in Chicago. But it is plenty legal elsewhere. Seventeen states allow corporal punishment in public schools.[40] While some school codes specify the manner in which physical punishment should be handled (e.g., the tool to use, such as a paddle, as well as the size of the paddle and the number of strikes), others are more broad. The Texas Education Code, for instance, allows "any other physical force used as a means of discipline" as permissible. One national analysis found that students in the United States can and do receive corporal punishment not only for more serious offenses such as fighting, but also for failing to be "docile bodies"—for being late, for violating the dress code, for talking back, for laughing too loudly in the hallway.[41]

Within the pool of states that have corporal punishment on the books, states with higher proportions of Black students are more likely to actually use it. Arizona, Colorado, Idaho, and Wyoming, for instance, all have extremely low reported rates of corporal punishment, whereas states like Alabama, Mississippi, and Louisiana are more likely to see the rule enacted. And within those states, racial disparities can soar. In some school districts across the southeastern United States, Black children are over five times more likely than White children to be physically punished in their public schools.[42] Notably, Mississippi is the state with both the largest proportion of Black students—47 percent[43]—and the highest rate of corporal punishment, with one in fourteen students experiencing state-sanctioned physical harm in public school.[44]

But the threat of physical punishment from without is not enough for the enactment of the truest "discipline." It has to be internalized.

When legal enslavement ended, legal and extralegal ways to enforce Black people's subhumanity did not end with it. In the years after the Civil War, Black people could be beaten or killed for refusing to step aside when a White person approached on the sidewalk or for addressing White people without sufficient deference; educated Black people could be made particular targets of such attacks because they were seen as "uppity." In Georgia, for instance, Ku Klux Klansmen murdered a Black man named Washington Eager for the crime of being able to read, and destroyed a teacher's library, challenging "any other nigger to have a book in his house."[45]

As cultural theorist Saidiya Hartman writes in her classic work *Scenes of Subjection,* "Freedom did not abolish the lash." In the years after slavery, the problem of Black liberty could be managed without literal masters or overseers, replaced by "*self-discipline* and *policing.* The whip was not to be abandoned; rather, it was to be internalized. The emphasis on correct training, proper spirit, and bent backs illuminated the invasive forms of discipline idealized as the self-fashioning of the moral and rational subject."[46]

Both of these forms of control—self-discipline and policing—have shown themselves throughout the past century to be powerful tools for the subjugation of Black children. These forces mirror each other: when we create systems that force people to assume they are always being policed and could be punished at any time, folks internalize that assumption until they turn the eye of surveillance on themselves and one another. Survival drives us to try to be "docile bodies" even when the threat of policing isn't immediately visible.[47] And teachers, willingly or unwillingly, can be conscripted into maintaining these systems of control.

In 2013, KIPP New Jersey, part of the well-known Knowledge Is Power Program, the largest charter school network in the United States, shared a resource video titled "How to Teach Your Class to Line Up" on its YouTube channel.[48] At the beginning of the video, a young teacher instructs an all-Black class of students who are perhaps seven or eight years old. "Hands by your sides! All eyes forward! Legs walking safely! Zip up those lips! Throw the key out the window!" The students mime throwing away an invisible key, then proceed silently into the hallway. A narrator then shares helpful tips for viewers, such as creating "tape spots"—designated points on the floor where each student is required to stand—and calling students "table by table, depending on which table is sitting up the straightest and the nicest." At this point, the narrator mimics what it means to sit up the "straightest and the nicest." Her back is ramrod straight to an extent that looks uncomfortable, and her grin is huge. The video goes on to show children's legs, all brown and all clad in matching uniforms, marching slowly down the hallway along a straight piece of electrical tape. If you see students who excel at marching quietly, the narrator says, you can reward them with "something awesome, like a cape that actually says 'Hallway Hero' . . . Another thing is a Hallway Soldier. We have Hallway Soldiers in our school all the time. They pretty much walk around with a soldier hat, and it lets us know that this scholar is always doing the right thing in the hallway." The video shows a teacher carefully placing a plastic pith helmet on a student's head.

In more recent years, some KIPP leaders have started to question whether their noted "no-excuses" approach is actually the best one and have pivoted away somewhat from the harsh disciplinary measures that made them famous.[49] But fame is hard to put back into Pandora's box—especially this level of fame. The network has been Oprah-level and CNN-level famous, attracting millions of dollars in donations.[50] However they may feel about it now, KIPP and programs like it attracted glowing praise across the country because their approach simply *felt* right to people. Hearing that Black children could get their test scores up, at the low, low cost of their bodily autonomy, was appealing. Folks were into it. It satisfied something that has felt natural and good for the nation-state since long before KIPP was a twinkle in its founders' eyes. In a *New York Times* opinion piece praising KIPP and suggesting that it should be a model for school success, columnist Bob Herbert began with this line: "The first thing you notice about the school is how quiet it is." Silence is seen as inherently virtuous and desirable. Not collaboration, not play, not engagement, not exploration. Silence. "You hardly hear a sound," Herbert writes approvingly.[51]

My husband shared a story with me of a group of colleagues presenting their findings on the academic success of a "no-excuses" school to a virtually all-White audience. The students were subject to strict disciplinary measures, from their everyday comportment to their dress code, and their academic outcomes were lauded.

A mentor of his, another Black man, raised his hand to ask a question of the assembled group. It was not a question about the data or the methods of the study. He asked something much more straightforward.

"Would any of you send your child to this school?"

There was awkward silence. His question revealed what had been unspoken in the room: that such schooling experiences, which many reasonable parents would deem unpleasant or even cruel (do *you* want to sit in absolute silence all day?), are assumed to be acceptable for Black children.

In fact, more than merely being deemed acceptable, such measures have been internalized by countless teachers, parents, principals, and onlookers as *necessary*. How else, the logic goes, are we to curtail the innate savagery of the Black child, a dangerous being if not reined in with force? In one study, a group of social psychologists found that participants rated Black children as less "innocent" overall than White children beginning at age ten, using questions such as "How much do _____ need care?" and "How much are _____ a danger to others?" The researchers also presented police officers with a hypothetical scenario of a crime and a photograph of an offender, a boy between age ten and seventeen. They found that the officers overestimated the age of the Black children in the photos by about 4.5 years.[52] Such effects are also mediated by colorism—darker-skinned Black students are more likely to be suspended than their lighter-skinned counterparts.[53] In another study, authors found that survey participants rated Black girls as seeming older than their stated age, more knowledgeable about adult topics, including sex, and more likely to take on adult roles and responsibilities than White girls.[54]

This phenomenon—projecting adultlike traits onto children[55]—is known as "adultification," and it contributes to the presumption of Black youth criminality. And although, within the frame of the school-prison nexus, we know that school can serve as a site of carceral logics even when students are not formally arrested, there remain many pathways through which schools lead students—and their parents—to the criminal legal system. In his book about Black education in Los Angeles, *First Strike,* anthropologist Damien Sojoyner describes sitting in a required all-school assembly while a school administrator casually informed students that if they were deemed truant, they would be incarcerated in juvenile detention and their parents would be charged by the prosecutor's office. Just to drive the lesson home, there would be a school field trip to the Los Padrinos Juvenile Hall early in the school year.[56]

But, recall again, the school-prison nexus does not require an actual prison. In her ethnography *Scripting the Moves,* a detailed account of classroom life at a no-excuses charter school, sociologist Joanne Golann details the student behavioral handbook from one KIPP school in Atlanta. "Losing focus," "fiddling w/tool or object," "losing place in book," and "making faces" are all listed as infractions, along with "any other potentially distracting *behavior exhibited unintentionally or without malicious intent.*"[57]

No wiggles are allowed here. No slouching comfortably, no gazing out the window, no daydreaming, no improvisation. No acknowledgment that the space to dream, to be a lone wanderer in one's own head, is not only integral to meaningful learning experiences but also a fundamental part of being alive, to which all children should have access. Daydreaming is a right, not a privilege.

Golann describes a similar practice at another school. After the first day of orientation, teachers met to review which students had committed transgressions such as "twirling around" or refusing to track the speaker with their eyes. The next day, these students were directed to sit not in seats but on the floor in a row in front of everyone, making a display of their badness.[58] Teachers were conscripted into enforcement; like police officers assigned arrest quotas,[59] they were reviewed based on "monthly performance metrics" and they could be penalized for not assigning as many detentions or recording as many infractions as their peers.[60]

Students could also be subject to a punishment known as "benching" or "porching." These children endured public isolation as punishment for their transgressions. Being benched or porched could include wearing your shirt inside out or wearing a yellow shirt all day—a scarlet letter so that everyone knew of your status—being forbidden from speaking to peers, and being made to eat lunch alone. Students who spoke to a benched friend could also be benched as punishment.[61] In school, a space intended to be social, these actions can amount to a form of psychological warfare. For Black students, such forms of discipline also tap into a preexisting set of cultural repertoires that define social isolation and control as necessary implements to maintain order, for the good of the group and the good of the deviant. *Some kids need that.*

A thriving industry of books, videos, and philosophies promises to give teachers the tools to manage undesirable bodily habits such as noise and movement. One popular mnemonic device is SLANT: Sit up, Listen, Ask questions if needed, Nod your head, Track the speaker. In a blog post, one KIPP teacher spelled out the details of how SLANT should look. Sitting up straight means that a student should "show good posture by having your back against the seat back," while tracking the speaker means "following the speaker with your eyes. When the speaker changes, all eyes follow the conversation."[62] Education scholar Chezare Warren wrote of the weight placed on SLANT at the predominantly Black KIPP middle school where he once worked: students did not start out with desks, but had to "earn" them by being silent, walking in straight lines, and "SLANTing."[63]

While sitting up in a chair and nodding to convey that you are actively listening can certainly be considered prosocial behaviors that signal participation in a community, the way they are enforced in some classrooms seems to overwhelm other needs, like creative intellectual engagement or childhood play. Do a video search for "teach like a champion techniques" (taken from Doug Lemov's book of the same title) or "SLANT classroom" and you'll see any number of students with their hands clasped tightly, reciting the word "track" as a group to signal that they are listening to the person who has been called on, eyes moving eerily in unison as they follow the teacher's movements around the room as if spectators watching a tennis volley.

After years of receiving criticism for his approach, in the 2021 edition of *Teach Like a Champion* Lemov addresses those who refer to these techniques as "carceral." The author characterizes his detractors as being a group of "selfish" people who only want to "exonerate themselves from responsibility" by using "self-serving calumny."[64] Besides, he says, "if we care about young people, if we believe their learning and their futures are important, we can't allow them to simply opt out of attending to learning."

Lemov's argument misses the fact that opting *in* to "attending to learning" looks a lot different when the students in question are White or wealthy. As low-income students of color are told that "college preparation" means learning how to walk in a straight line, keeping your shirt tucked in, repeating verbatim what your teacher just said aloud, or keeping your hands clasped, students at elite schools receive a very different message. For them, *independence, exploration,* and *collaboration* are the watchwords. In *The Best of the Best,* an ethnographic account of an elite private boarding school, Rubén A. Gaztambide-Fernández describes open-ended classroom seminars as central to the school's identity. In these seminars, teachers say very little, leaving room instead for students to participate in unstructured peer dialogue. The students he observed were encouraged to "engage in difficult conversations, to challenge one another's ideas, and to engage in lively discussions." One teacher said half-jokingly, "I don't actually teach the class, I have nothing to do with this. I just show up."[65] As Chezare Warren notes, "Suburban schools with predominantly White student populations would never require students to earn their desks, or expect students to sit, talk, dress, and even celebrate a classmate's success in the exact same way."[66]

I remember a moment as a teacher when I was in the hallway, having a conversation with a colleague. A student walked up to ask us a question. "Excuse me," he began politely. My colleague interrupted him. "Be quiet while adults are talking."

The person who said this was Black. Make no mistake about it—these practices are so commonplace that teachers of color can fall prey to them as much as anyone. And I believe that this particular person loved these children. If I had asked them, or anyone else in the building, what their dreams were for our students, they would have said they wanted the kids to be able to attend a great high school and a great college. Sometimes they even name-checked particular institutions—in some cases, institutions I had attended. I remember a coworker saying that if one of our students got into Northside College Prep, the elite public high school I graduated from, it would be "a dream come true." So in that moment—*Be quiet while adults are talking*—I found my mind flashing to memories of everyday life at Northside, filled with freewheeling class debates and easy banter. As our principal explained in one *Chicago Sun-Times* article, "We have very few rules; the challenge is to be responsible."[67] Music played between passing periods because bells and buzzers were seen as a harsh symbol of authoritarianism. Eating in class was seen as a humane necessity.

At the University of Chicago, where I went after high school, debate and discussion were viewed as the most central tenets of a good education. At Harvard, where I went to graduate school, students were encouraged to be independent innovators, bold leaders who defied conventional logic. At all of these schools, I knew firsthand, a student who learned to "be quiet while adults were talking" would be viewed as a pretty poor student. Why was it, then, that we—like many other schools serving Black students—were teaching kids to be obedient and disciplined subjects above all else, in the name of preparation for supposed future academic success? The crushing weight of social control stifles students from defining a pathway toward what they believe to be a good life. To make it in college, this logic goes, these students don't have to be creative or flexible, joyful or inventive. They have to be *civilized.*

Although we often focus on how Black boys are uniquely targeted by school discipline, the regime of discipline and punishment also distinctly affects Black girls, who are marked as criminal for engaging in everyday acts of adolescent defiance (or *perceived* defiance).[68] In Alabama, a high school student with diabetes who fell asleep during in-school suspension was physically assaulted by a school police officer—who slammed her face into a filing cabinet—and subsequently arrested. Terrified, she threw up in the squad car.[69] In Georgia, a six-year-old girl who threw a tantrum in class, hurling books, toys, and classroom furniture, was arrested and handcuffed.[70] In Chicago, students and teachers at the Noble Network of Charter Schools complained that menstruating students bled on themselves because of the schools' strict policy requiring them to be escorted to the bathroom.[71] In Michigan, a fifteen-year-old girl was jailed for failing to complete her homework during COVID-induced remote learning, a misstep that a judge ruled to be a violation of her probation after her previous offenses of fighting with her mother and stealing. Begging the judge for her release, the girl invoked the language of discipline that she hoped would be legible to the court: "I can control myself," she said. "I can be obedient."[72] And although trans students are often omitted altogether from discourse and research about racialized school punishment and discipline, one study of adult Black trans women found that one in six had reported being expelled from school in their earlier years or denied the opportunity to enroll altogether, because they were out as trans.[73]

Gender-based violence is intimately connected to the discipline Black and Native youth face inside and outside schools. When schools normalize violence against Black and Native girls, positioning them as disposable, it should be no surprise that they face the highest rates of sexual assault or that they are more likely to go missing without mass public outcry.[74] These experiences, in turn, make Black and Native girls especially susceptible to criminalization for survival behaviors such as running away, sex work, truancy, or curfew violations.[75] In *Inventing the Savage,* Luana Ross shares the story of Gloria Wells-Norlin, a Little Shell Chippewa doll maker who reflected on how anti-Indigenous stereotypes shaped her self-image before she was old enough to even fully understand them. "Many times, I would come home from school crying because some white kid had called me dirty names. I didn't know why nobody liked me, and a lot of times I'd come home and ask, 'Why do we have to be Indian? Why can't we be like other kids?' I was, in my mind, a squ*w slut before I ever knew what a slut was."[76]

Though Gloria's mother told her that her people were the rightful first stewards of the land, that wasn't enough. "A child of six is hardly capable of debating the wrongs dealt Native American people, so instead of being a debater I became a fighter. Nobody was going to call me any dirty names and get away with it. I'd teach them a thing or two. It didn't matter that I could get the tar knocked out of me. I had to stand up for what I thought was right." At fourteen, Gloria fled her home, where her father was abusing her. He told her that if she did not return, he would call the police and report her as a runaway. Terrified, she borrowed a car to drive home and was quickly jailed for driving without a license. While in jail, Gloria escaped an attempted molestation by one of the guards. The following Monday, she was taken to court—and charged with truancy for missing school.[77]

Stories like Gloria's represent a vicious cycle, one that continues when Black and Native girls grow up to be women who are viewed as unfit mothers because of their inherent inferiority, hypersexuality (represented by the slur Gloria used and the analogous stereotype for Black women, the "jezebel"), and savage criminality. As we discussed in chapter 6, Black and Native women share grim histories of being subjected to nonconsensual or coerced sterilizations.[78] Indeed, using federal funding to coerce sterilizations—including through threats that welfare benefits will be revoked—became illegal only after a lawsuit filed on behalf of two Black sisters, Mary Alice and Minnie Lee Relf, who were sterilized at age twelve and fourteen, respectively.[79]

In a painful essay about the similarities between Korryn Gaines and Loreal Tsingine—both young mothers shot to death by police officers in the same year—Kelly Hayes writes:

> As Black and Native women, any cultural safety that does exist was not constructed for us. But to proclaim we are ready to protect ourselves against racism, rape culture, and whatever ugliness might violate us, is seen as radical. . . . Black women are treated as socially disposable, and Native women are treated as socially irrelevant (or even nonexistent).[80]

For Loreal and Korryn, motherhood was far from sacrosanct. Their position as givers of life, as nurturers called to lovingly raise their children, was secondary in the eyes of the state to their position as Native and Black and therefore as criminal. In the words of Christina Sharpe, "*Mother* doesn't mean 'mother,' but 'felon' and 'defender' and/or 'birther of terror.' "[81]

Good Relations with Self

I have a memory from childhood day camp at my local park. I am around six years old. I'm crying—about something; who knows what. Two of the junior counselors, probably around twelve or thirteen years old, are comforting me. Their superior, a young adult, tells them to stop. "She just wants attention," she tells them.

"Well, why can't we give it to her?" one of the girls asks, her chin up. "Yeah," the other one chimes in, a note of defiance in her voice. "Why can't we give it to her?"

This moment lingers in my head, I think, because when two young people were told they shouldn't show me care, they spoke up to someone older and more powerful to ask a simple question. *Why not?* Why not lead with care? I had buried this memory, but it resurfaced in a conversation about this book, when historian Crystal Lynn Webster talked about her own experience teaching fourth graders. She asked aloud: "How do children fight to make themselves visible?" When children are told that their feelings, their hopes, their needs don't matter, how do they react? How do they fight to show that they do indeed *count*? "How is that also," Crystal added, "a political act of selfhood?"

Our schools are sites of punishment. As someone who strives to think, write, and speak through an abolitionist lens, I have heard plenty of variations on that familiar question: "Well, what should we have instead?" In a sense, racism, colonialism, and their attendant myths and ideologies deprive us of an important counterstory, a powerful one for any abolitionist to consider: there were once nations on this land that did not have prisons. In other words, the very thing we are told is impossible was once the prevailing reality. As Vine Deloria Jr. and Clifford M. Lytle wrote in *American Indians, American Justice,* judicial traditions before colonization differed from nation to nation, but generally reflected principles that today we might refer to as restorative justice. "The primary goal was simply to mediate the case to everyone's satisfaction. It was not to ascertain guilt and then bestow punishment upon the offender. Under Anglo-American notions of criminal jurisprudence, the objectives are to establish fault or guilt and then to punish. The sentencing goals of retribution, revenge, and deterrence and isolation of the offender are extremely important (though the system often pays much lip service to the concept of rehabilitation as well). Under the traditional Indian system the major objective was more to ensure restitution and compensation than retribution." Within this worldview, the goal was to find a form of restitution that would both address the harm that had been committed and allow the offending party to continue to live peaceably within the community.[82] Luana Ross describes the Diné legal system, for instance, as "one of horizontal justice," in which "there is no one authority that ascertains the truth . . . a system of restorative justice based on equality and participation, with a notion of justice that involves recuperating both the offender and victim." She goes on to quote Robert Yazzie, former chief justice of the Navajo Nation:

> That feeling of oneness with one's surroundings, and the reconciliation of the individual with everyone and everything else, is what allows an alternative to vertical justice to work. It rejects the process of convicting a person and throwing the

> keys away in favor of methods that use solidarity to restore good relations among people. Most importantly, it restores good relations with self.[83]

Dismantling the school-prison nexus requires more than the quick replacement of suspension policies with peace circles. It requires something immensely more difficult: a reevaluation of our knee-jerk reliance, as a culture, on punishment and exclusion. As Savannah Shange writes, even schools—and educators, including educators of color—that identify as "progressive" run the risk of conforming "with a notion of justice that is deeply compatible with the existing social order."[84]

The United States is a nation of vengeance, prone to retribution when we could pursue healing; drawn to reciprocal cruelty when we could choose restoration. Collectively, we find comfort in reacting with all our might to avenge a transgressor rather than dedicating creative energy toward asking much harder questions about the root of the transgression. And from the inception of the nation-state, the bodies of Black and Native children have been recipient vessels to that vengeance. To run a good country, the story goes, we need to control *those* children, *those* bodies. Perhaps it's foolish of me, but I do believe schools can be laboratories of the otherwise—places where we try new things, new ways of dealing with the harms we all inevitably enact upon one another. But such a change first requires a hard look at our addiction to discipline, and hard questions about what it would look like to restore good relations with self.

PART IV

SOMEBODY'S GOT TO MOW THE LAWN

Get the Indian out of the blanket and into trousers—
and trousers with a pocket in them, and with
a pocket that aches to be filled with dollars!

—MERRILL EDWARDS GATES[1]

Remember that you are to be industrious.
Freedom does not mean that you are not to work.

—MASSACHUSETTS SENATOR HENRY WILSON[2]

Racism enshrines the inequalities
that capitalism requires.

—JODI MELAMED[3]

CHAPTER 11

A Crooked Playing Field

At the beginning of this book, I asked you to reflect on what you see as the fundamental purpose of school. For many people—perhaps including you!—the answer is clear: education provides a pathway toward economic opportunity. More schooling, more money, better life chances. Simple enough equation.

But is education, as Horace Mann famously declared, the great equalizer? If the United States is, as we know it to be, a nation with a deep chasm between haves and have-nots, do schools play a role in smoothing that divide and allowing everyone the same access to wealth? If schooling does indeed pay dividends, does it do so equally for everybody—including for Black and Native people?

The problem is, in the United States, wealth inequality is a feature, not a bug. At its foundations, there is no American capitalism without slavery and settler colonialism. The accrual of wealth through capitalism was never meant for Black and Native people's participation, any more than cattle can "participate" in the work of a slaughterhouse. Rather, at the origins of the United States, capitalism held roles for Black and Native people that were purely extractive: Taking bodies. Taking babies. Taking land. While cheerleaders striving for an "inclusive" capitalist system can herald individual successes, we have to judge a system by its averages, not by its exceptions—those who happen to stand out as great athletes, artists, or entrepreneurs.

One important way to understand the average outcomes of Black and Native people under capitalism is by looking at wealth. In their landmark book *From Here to Equality*, William A. Darity Jr. and A. Kirsten Mullen make a powerful case for why they consider wealth to be "the best single indicator of the cumulative impact of white racism over time." Wealth, they argue, has a unique ability to confer advantage and buffer hardships:

> Wealthier families are far better positioned to finance elite independent school and college, access capital to start a business, finance expensive medical procedures, reside in higher amenity neighborhoods, exert political influence through campaign financing, purchase better counsel if confronted with an expensive legal system, leave a bequest, and/or withstand financial hardship resulting from any number of emergencies. . . . Wealth provides financial agency over one's life.[1]

The typical White family possesses eight times the wealth of the typical Black family.[2] Casual observers are quick to offer simple pathways to closing the wealth gap, often rooted in the need for Black people to change their behavior: "get it together," save more, create different family structures, or value school more highly. But exactly zero of these theories is borne out by the evidence. Black people don't actually save proportionally less than White families; being in a home with two married parents does not close the racial wealth gap; and studies consistently show that Black people highly value education—and invest in it accordingly.[3] But, tragically, those investments don't pay off equally across racial boundaries. White college students are more likely to have their college education paid for by grandparents or parents, and they receive more money: On average, White households contribute $73,500 to their children's college education. Black parents are less likely to have anything to contribute, and they pay just over $16,000 on average toward college costs.[4]

And after graduation? White families where the head of household has an undergraduate or postgraduate degree hold, at the median, *over three times as much wealth* as Black households with the *same* level of educational attainment; in fact a typical Black household headed by someone with a bachelor's degree has less wealth than a White family headed by someone who didn't finish high school.[5] Breaking it down by gender makes the disparity even more stark: Among those between the ages of twenty and twenty-nine, single White women with no bachelor's degree have a median wealth of $2,000. Single Black women *with* a bachelor's degree have a median net worth of *negative* $11,000. They're in the red.[6]

How can this be? How can education, supposedly an equal-access pathway to a prosperous life, fail so spectacularly to level the playing field?

One explanation is employment discrimination. In one study, a group of sociologists sent a group of 340 young men of different racial backgrounds to apply for real entry-level jobs across New York City, armed with fictional resumes reporting identical levels of education and work experience. They were even matched on other traits, such as their level of eye contact and the way they dressed. The Black study participants were half as likely as White participants with equal qualifications to hear back with an offer. When some of the role-players were given resumes that noted a criminal background, 17 percent of the White men *with* a criminal record got a callback, while 13 percent of the Black men *without* a criminal record got one.[7] Other "audit studies"—where researchers carefully craft a pretend applicant and send them out into the world, thus controlling for factors such as disparate levels of education or personal connections—have found that when all applicants have degrees from the same elite institutions, those with "Black-sounding" names on their resumes are less likely to get a callback.[8]

There's more to the story. Employment discrimination impacts a person's *income*—how much money they take home in their paycheck every month. But to truly understand economic inequality, we have to think about gaps in *wealth*—the assets a person has in the form of not only their income but their savings, home, and other things of material value, as well as the amount of debt they've accrued. And we have to think not only about how that one person is faring, but about how things are likely to pan out for their kids and grandkids.

To understand these disparities, consider the findings of economist Raj Chetty and his team, who have analyzed census records and anonymous tax data following the life outcomes of over twenty million Americans. They traced these individuals' fortunes from childhood through adulthood to understand their likelihood of climbing the economic ladder and fulfilling the American Dream of ending up better off than their parents' generation.[9] Chetty's research documents that intergenerational mobility in the United States has been stagnant for decades, that most Americans fare roughly the same economically as their parents, and that different regions have different average rates of economic mobility; the South, where the majority of Black Americans live, has comparatively worse levels of economic mobility.[10] When focusing their analysis on the specific outcomes of different racial groups, Chetty and his team have revealed even more striking findings: Black and Native children have much lower rates of upward mobility than children of other racial/ethnic groups.[11] The authors note that while other people of color may have lower *income,* their rate of *upward mobility* is comparable to that of White Americans, meaning that over time these income disparities are on track to shrink. To make matters worse, Black and Native kids have much higher rates of *downward mobility* than children from other racial/ethnic groups, meaning they are more likely to fare *worse* economically than their parents.

We can imagine these statistics as applied to a group of cars on a track. A car with a White family is zooming around at speed, and the driver has their foot on the accelerator so that their speed is increasing as time passes. The car with the average Latine family is moving at a slower speed, but they are accelerating, such that they will just about catch up with the White family eventually. The cars with the Black and Native families, meanwhile, are broken. They are moving at a low speed . . . *and* the gas pedal isn't working. They're not accelerating and, if these patterns continue, are not likely to catch up. And some of the cars are actually slowly braking, decreasing in speed *and* acceleration. "Reducing racial disparities," Chetty and his team write, "will require reducing *intergenerational* gaps—that is, disparities in children's outcomes conditional on parental income—for blacks and American Indians. Transient programs that do not affect intergenerational mobility, such as temporary cash transfers, are insufficient to reduce disparities because income distributions will eventually revert back to their steady states."[12] Giving the car a temporary boost in speed won't work—if you don't fix the accelerator, eventually it will fall behind again while everyone else is pulling away.

"Okay," you're thinking, "cool metaphor. How does this actually work in real life?" When we talk about accruing wealth in America, we often assume that the metaphorical gas pedal is related to things we control as individuals, including how you do in school. But it turns out there's a huge factor in wealth accrual that doesn't have much to do with any choice *you* make. And that factor is intergenerational wealth transfer. If your parents or your parents' parents have plenty to pass your way—a house or a down payment for one, contributions to your education, or a straight cash inheritance—good for you! If they do not have those things, your lot in life is likely to look rather different.

We might assume that intergenerational wealth transfer makes a difference only at the margin. Surely, you'd think, inheriting some cash might be a nice bonus for some people, but most of how you do in life is based on *your* effort. But it makes a much bigger difference than you might think. One analysis of wealth transfers conducted by the Federal Reserve estimated that the share of an individual's wealth attributable to intergenerational transfers is just over *half*.[13] And intergenerational wealth transfer can take several forms. Inheriting money when someone in your family passes away is one obvious example. One study, based on data from the 1990s, found that about one in four White families received money this way—about $145,000 on average. One in twenty Black families did the same, receiving about $42,000 on average.[14] Intergenerational wealth transfer can also come in the form of gifts and financial support from living relatives, a common practice at all income levels. Most people, whether rich or poor, help their family members out. But there's a big difference between "help" that comes in the form of a small loan for a car repair or assistance with school supplies and "help" that looks like a car, condo, or college degree. (Never mind that, for some people, help flows the other way—from children to parents.)[15]

Sociologist Thomas Shapiro has carefully documented how this plays out in practice for different groups of people. Shapiro set out to talk to many kinds of families—solidly middle-class folks as well as low-income folks across the country—and gather intimate stories about the ways that intergenerational wealth transfer has made a difference in their lives. As he points out, those who receive large-scale intergenerational wealth transfers don't just have more cash to spend on daily bills or fun leisure activities; they are often able to leverage these transfers into major life-transforming outcomes. When asked about parental contributions, one mother Shapiro interviewed, Briggette, rattled off examples, including those that had an impact on her children's education:

> They've given us money for the down payment on the house. . . . My parents paid the tuition for my daughter's school, because it's the Catholic school and they just wanted her to be educated for that. Let's see. Yeah, you name it, we get it. They paid our mortgage payment for two months, before my husband found his other job. They have set up trust funds for my children, for each of my children; so that when it's time for them to go to college, they will have money to do so.[16]

Another interviewee, Shauna, invested the money she received when her parents passed away. She described the many ways it was useful to her and her husband as they tried to provide a high quality of life for their children:

> And we did use some to move during law school. . . . We've used some to buy a computer. And I used some [for] one small school loan: two thousand dollars. And I paid that off. And I put a little money down on the car. I bought a baby crib, which was four hundred dollars. I took a trip to Russia. Oh, I cannot tell you how much peace it gives me, just to know that if something happened. . . . And that is my security blanket, because I have—you know, I have investments.[17]

Because Shauna has invested her inheritance—in education, in her child, and in interest-accruing financial accounts—it can continue to grow in value, serving as a "security blanket" for her. Having these savings for retirement rather than as an emergency rainy-day fund puts Shauna at an economic advantage. People of color generally have less retirement savings to draw on than White households to supplement their Social Security income.[18] As for those Social Security benefits, they are tied to your earnings from eligible work over the course of your life. This means that people who earn less income or earn their income from ineligible or unrecognized forms of work (i.e., via the gig economy or work done for cash in the informal economy) receive less to live on in their senior years. One analysis of over two million households found that White recipients of Social Security reported receiving $9,800 annually on average, while Black recipients averaged $7,900 and Native recipients averaged $7,600.[19]

Briggette's decision to buy a house mirrors the choice of countless Americans who have been told that investing in property is the path to prosperity both for you and for your children. For Black people, though, this gambit doesn't always pan out. The mere presence of Black people has long been seen as an unspoken proxy for poor neighborhood quality, leading to the widespread devaluation of homes in majority-Black neighborhoods. One national analysis found that even when comparing homes of similar quality in neighborhoods with similar amenities, houses in majority-Black neighborhoods were valued at 23 percent less, amounting to over $150 billion in cumulative lost value for those homeowners.[20] Nathan Connolly and Shani Mott, married Black professors, made national headlines in 2022 for this telling story: An appraiser and mortgage lender valued their home at $472,000. The couple then recruited a White colleague to pretend it was his home, borrowed family photos from White friends to hang on the walls, and removed all the books by Black authors from their shelves. A second appraiser then magically valued the home at $750,000.[21]

Biases about schools play a critical role in this widespread devaluation, as negative stereotypes about schools and neighborhoods feed one another in a malignant loop. "Good neighborhoods" are understood to be shaped by "good schools," and Black schools are understood to be *bad* schools. Researchers have found that both White and Latine parents are more likely to leave public schools for private or magnet schools as the percentage of Black students in their local schools increases.[22]

These structural patterns leave all of us making choices about where we live, where we send our children to school, or how we save money within a constrained set of circumstances—except that we can't always see the constraints, the differences that leave some people in a bind while others move freely through the market. For some of you reading the stories of Shauna and Briggette, the educational dividends emerging from relatives' financial gifts may sound mundane. Maybe it strikes a chord with ways your own family members have helped you out. Meanwhile, others of you probably have your mouths hanging open right now. That's because, as legal scholar Dorothy A. Brown has pointed out, those for whom inheritances are a casual part of life rarely talk about them openly. In her research, White interviewees "downplayed the inheritances and gifts they received, or the significance of graduating from college without debt because a family member paid their way."[23] Shapiro echoed this observation in his research on families who'd received significant intergenerational wealth transfers. Even after listing all the many forms of inheritance that have shaped their lives, almost within the same breath they would reassure him that they had in fact worked for everything they have, describing themselves "as self-made, conveniently forgetting that they inherited much of what they own."[24]

These families probably don't mean to be hypocritical; they simply don't see the contradiction between the hard-work narrative and the fact that, as Shapiro puts it, "what a family inherits cannot be earned." Their cognitive dissonance likely emerges from the fact that moral goodness and educational success are equated with hard, laborious effort. To be a good person is to work, and to accumulate wealth through that work. To be poor is to be lazy, and to be lazy is to be immoral. (Never mind disabled people, people who perform other forms of nonearning labor such as family care work, or people who simply believe that resting is just fine.)

As Brown notes, because these transfers within families are a well-kept secret, poorer families may not realize the extent of their prevalence, while wealthier families may simply assume that *everyone* enjoys such benefits, leading them to vastly underestimate how wide the racial wealth gap really is.[25] One group of social psychologists found that when they asked respondents to estimate how big the wealth gap was in 1963 and in 2016, they were off by 40 points and a whopping 80 points, respectively.[26]

Of course, the patterns Shapiro and Brown have documented may not describe every individual's life story. A Black or Native person might have extraordinary success and thrive economically, growing their wealth and surpassing the fortunes of their parents. A White individual might have hard luck and real struggle, falling on hard times and slipping to a lower rung on the economic ladder than their parents. I certainly know there are examples of both happening amid my family and friends. But again, when we're thinking about how society works, we have to look at trends, patterns, averages over time for the majority of people, rather than focus on exceptional anecdotal circumstances. "I do not begrudge an average family inheritance," writes Shapiro, "but I am concerned about how weakened public commitments to children, families, schools, and communities encourage people to use inheritances for private advantage."[27] And what does it mean if schools, the alleged great equalizer, are doing little to even the odds?

CHAPTER 12

Slavery, Settler Colonialism, and American Wealth

The wealth accumulation that allows many White families to have a pathway to prosperity and a cushion against disaster—the same wealth that blurs the effects of educational attainment on economic outcomes—is itself inextricable from the legacies of chattel slavery and settler colonialism.

When it was legal, slavery bolstered the economy even in states where it was not permitted. Financing the slave trade, selling the goods and services that supported it, insuring enslaved human "property," and hosting auctions were big business. Northern banks extended the lines of credit that slavers needed to purchase human beings and agricultural equipment. New England businessmen helped Southern rural planters negotiate the cotton market, serving as brokers and paid advisers.[1] New York Life, now the nation's third-largest insurer and a Fortune 500 company, sold hundreds of policies covering the value of enslaved people so slavers could recoup their worth in case they died doing hazardous work in mills, mines, or factories. In 1847, such policies accounted for a third of their business.[2] Aetna and US Life (now a subsidiary of AIG) did brisk business as well. Before becoming one of the nation's most influential investment banks (and ultimately collapsing in 2008), Lehman Brothers began as an Alabama cotton brokerage. The fortunes of J. P. Morgan, John Jacob Astor, Charles Lewis Tiffany (the jeweler), and Archibald Gracie III (of the family of Gracie Mansion, now the official residence of the mayor of New York City) all had ties to the booming cotton trade.[3]

Wealth and enslavement are not confined to the histories of a few individuals and families who enriched themselves off the backs of people who were viewed as property. Rather, the ascendance of the entire American economy was spurred by the institution of slavery. Human bodies were exploited to support all the moving pieces that make up a "modern" economy: credit, currency, and capital. The abolitionist Theodore Weld, writing in 1839, made this connection explicitly: "The laws of slave states make them property, equally with goats and swine; they are levied upon for debt in the same way; they are included in the same advertisements of public sales with cattle, swine, and asses. . . . They are bought and sold, and separated like cattle. . . . That slaveholders do not practically regard slaves as *human beings* is abundantly shown by their own voluntary testimony."[4] As historian Daina Ramey Berry writes, enslaved children therefore learned at an early age that they could be "bought, sold, transferred, deeded, gifted, raffled, compensated, insured, and executed."[5]

At the same time, the U.S. government engaged in what scholar of law and economics Douglas Allen has called "giving away an empire," using White citizens as proxies for rapid incursion into Native lands to establish a claim on the western half of the continent.[6] In textbooks and popular culture, the period of westward expansion in the nineteenth century is portrayed as a time of bold adventure, the settlers who set out into the vastness of dangerous unknown lands embodying the American spirit of tenacity and moxie, their enterprising spirit and willingness to take risks supported by a generous and forward-thinking government. In reality, this period saw an acceleration of the theft of land and natural resources that had tremendous social and economic impact on Indigenous peoples while enriching the settler nation.[7]

"It is a mercy to the red devils to exterminate them, and a saving of many white lives," wrote one California newspaper editorial. "Treaties are played out—there is only one kind of treaty that is effective—cold lead."[8] Notably, the California gold rush also inspired a convict leasing system that could send Native people into a life of forced labor. In 1850, California's Act for the Government and Protection of Indians decreed that "any Indian found loitering or strolling about" or "leading an immoral or profligate course of life" was subject to arrest in response to a citizen complaint, whereupon the court was required "to hire out such vagrant within twenty-four hours to the best bidder" for up to four months.[9]

The waves of massive land expropriation that transformed the continent in the nineteenth century required mundane acts of violence and theft at the hands of both military forces and everyday settlers. Native people forcefully marched from their homes left behind White neighbors who dismantled their houses literally brick by brick, stealing windows, doors, stone chimneys, wooden floorboards, and the planks of fences—or they just moved in, claiming the homes as their own.[10] Sometimes they didn't wait, prying the boards off elderly Native people's homes while they lived in them or plowing around their houses and fencing them in.[11] Settlers entered burial spaces, dug up the bodies of the deceased, and sold their skulls to people like Samuel George Morton, whom we discussed in chapter 5.[12] Native people who refused to comply with deportation orders could be thrown in prison, tortured, or driven off by arson.[13] One Choctaw man recalled being told by U.S. agents "that they would catch the children, tie their legs together like pigs, and haul them off in wagons."[14]

These two intimately linked structural events—slavery and land dispossession, which would indelibly shape the economic fortunes of Black and Native peoples for untold generations to come—were, on the flip side, extremely lucrative for White financiers as far away as New York, Boston, and London. As historian Claudio Saunt writes in his book *Unworthy Republic,* these captains of industry invested in Southern banks; supplied capital for purchasing enslaved people, mules, plows, and land; and sold bonds in the millions of dollars to scoop up the newly available land.[15] There was money to be made, money that would drive the opulence of the growing republic. All it required was the brutalization of people deemed savages, and a little bit of capital.

In 1887, the Dawes Act (or General Allotment Act) further facilitated land theft, in ways that impact Indigenous communities to this very day. The Dawes Act carved up land into parcels and allotted it to some Native households—an effort Theodore Roosevelt later characterized as a "mighty pulverizing engine" to break up collectivist tribal relationships, encouraging Native people to focus instead on the possession of private property.[16] It was intended, as historian Alaina E. Roberts writes, to "destroy tribal sovereignty, extended kinship ties, and Indigenous ideas about wealth and individualism."[17] The aim was to further the project of Native disappearance by parceling out something that didn't belong to the U.S. government and destroying Indigenous relationships to land.

Families did not receive these allotments right away—they were held "in trust," kept under the control of the U.S. government for twenty-five years. But that paternalistic relationship has not gone away—today, many lands that would otherwise be held by Native tribes and individuals are still held in "trust," along with any natural resources on that land and any wealth or income those natural resources might produce.[18] This arrangement limits the ability of Native people and tribes to leverage land as collateral and use property ownership as a means for wealth generation, limiting economic prosperity in turn.[19]

Today, the descendants of allotment recipients *do not retain the legal title to the land.* The federal government does. The property is not transferable. It cannot be sold, nor can it be used as collateral to finance home mortgages or business loans, which is a major hindrance to wealth generation.[20] One economic analysis suggested that if Native people and tribes had had full property rights over their allotments since the Dawes Act, and had been able to use them to fully participate in the market by buying and selling the land at will, the land would have an additional value as high as $4,765 per acre.[21] Even so, as Kelli Mosteller, former executive director of the Citizen Potawatomi Nation Cultural Heritage Center, has pointed out, at this point selling and redistributing the land for private benefit would be an unacceptable solution anyway—one that "disregards the cultural and spiritual values at the core of Native American tribal societies," such as collective governance, sustainable stewardship of land, and developing shared resources.[22]

The trust arrangement is rooted in the assumption that Native people are childlike or unintelligent, fundamentally incapable of managing their own financial affairs. Over decades, the U.S. government has leveraged that idea to fill its own coffers at the expense of Native people.

In the 1980s, a Blackfoot woman named Elouise Cobell uncovered the reality that the U.S. government was doing just that with Native people's funds held in trust—using the money for its own benefit, while the folks who were supposed to be able to rely on those funds suffered. Growing up in Montana, Cobell constantly heard from loved ones that they were unable to access their trust funds; her uncle lost his life after the Bureau of Indian Affairs denied and delayed his request for funds to seek medical care for an illness.[23] Another elder, trying to withdraw funds after a fire destroyed her log cabin home, was told by BIA agents that she wasn't "competent" to withdraw the funds she asked for; they gave her a fraction of her requested withdrawal, then told her later that her balance was now zero, without providing any ledger to prove it.[24] In Cobell's attempts to confront BIA agents and research basic facts about her own trust funds, she was constantly turned away as unintelligent; when she asked for a basic statement of how much money she held, she was told that there was no point in giving it to her because she would not be able to understand the accounting.[25] Enraged, Cobell went to school to become an accountant, and ultimately became the treasurer for the Blackfeet Nation. The stories didn't stop: erratic trust fund checks, missing checks, and a total lack of accounting or transparency were endemic. After talking with her peers in other tribal nations, Cobell uncovered evidence that the trust money was being redirected into a fund for general government use rather than paid out to the people whose lands had been taken.[26] "One administration after another treated the trusts as slush funds," she said. "It didn't matter to them that it was Indians' money."[27]

In 1996, Cobell became a lead plaintiff on a class action lawsuit against the U.S. government on behalf of hundreds of thousands of Native trust beneficiaries—one of the largest class action suits in the nation's history. They argued that the government had mismanaged and outright destroyed records and illegally diverted their trust funds for government use.[28] In 2009, the U.S. government finally settled with the plaintiffs in the amount of $3.4 billion—a victory Cobell called "bittersweet," as thousands of them had already passed away.[29] To the idea that such a large settlement would somehow hurt the U.S. economically, Cobell replied, "It's not your money and never was."[30]

Cobell herself died of cancer two years later, having spent years of her life in court battling the idea that Native people were not smart enough to manage their own money. Another plaintiff in the suit, James "Mad Dog" Kennerly, watched for decades in frustration as his lands, containing prosperous farms and multiple oil reserves, were leased by the government to non-Native tenants at rates far below fair-market value.[31] Each year, he received about $89 in return for the thousands of dollars' worth of oil drawn from the earth stolen from his ancestors.[32] Asked what his life might have been like if that money had not been stolen for years, Kennerly replied: "I'd have gone to school and become a lawyer and fought the goddamned BIA." Kennerly died hours before Cobell, having received none of the settlement money yet.

For people like Cobell, Kennerly, and countless others, the mismanaged trusts and stolen funds are about far more than lost income. The stolen money represents stolen agency, stolen possibility, and stolen autonomy.[33] Today, Native people experience poverty at rates higher than any other racial or ethnic group in the United States.[34] They also have the highest unemployment rate, which the Bureau of Labor Statistics has reported in its monthly job analysis only since January 2022.[35] At the beginning of the COVID-19 pandemic, Native unemployment was a towering 28.6 percent—exceeding the national unemployment rate during the Great Depression.[36] Lower rates of educational attainment, higher rates of disability, and greater residential distance from available jobs could all contribute.

But even when controlling for such factors—comparing Native individuals to White peers of the same age, gender, education, marital status, and location—Native people are still 31 percent less likely to be employed.[37] And despite increased public attention to wealth inequality in the past two decades, basic data about Native people's wealth is missing from the public record—denying us a critical opportunity to truly understand the ways that White supremacy has impacted Native economic well-being.[38] This massive data gap, partially attributable to limited sample sizes, further exemplifies how Native people are once again made invisible in data analysis, as we discussed in Part II. When public policy, public conversation, and public outrage are driven by data, having no data to specify your problem becomes tantamount to disappearance. Yet the data we do have paints a stark picture; one national survey from 2000 indicated that the median wealth for Native baby boomers was $5,700; the median wealth for the sample overall was $65,500.[39]

So yeah. Black and Native folks are struggling, and they're struggling in a country where being poor signals a lack of virtue. In the United States, poverty is considered a mark of immorality, proof enough that you deserve to suffer. I think of a dear friend, Diné scholar Amanda Tachine, and the interviews with Diné college students featured in her book *Native Presence and Sovereignty in College*. One young man shared his conversation with a peer, who asked him if he only received cast-off rubbish for Christmas. "I said, 'What?' She said, 'That is all you Natives deserve anyway, if you look back at the reservation, because I passed through there and it's just a piece of trash.'"[40]

Other students Tachine spoke with in her research were keenly aware of these stereotypes and the assumptions they felt others had of them. When asked how society views Native people, Chris responded, "Natives drink a lot, Natives fail, and all this stuff." Another student, Joy, shared an experience of overhearing White classmates saying that Native students "should just go back to their moccasin worlds and live back in their dirt homes. It makes no sense for them to be here. They're just getting everything for free." Not knowing how to intervene, feeling isolated and alone, Joy went back to her dormitory and cried. "Many think that Natives live off of the government—healthcare is free, education is free, homes are free, etc.," writes Tachine. "Yet, these are fictions that at their root attempt to problematize Native peoples as insufficient, overreliant on the government, and incapable of self-sufficiency: failures. Simply put, in this telling, Natives are lazy, wasteful, and a burden."[41]

These stereotypes are common. But poor Black people and poor Native people are not poor by accident. Our peoples have been poor because the United States needed us to be poor—needed to steal from us, needed to make that stealing morally permissible by belittling and dehumanizing us, needed to normalize and naturalize that poverty as a built-in fixture. Just as the project of empire required fundamentally unintelligent beings, wild savages in need of discipline, so too did it require beings permanently positioned on the bottom rungs of the economic hierarchy. And educational institutions, once again, have played a vital role in reinforcing this narrative and the structures beneath it.

Dispossession by Degrees: Universities and the Legacy of Theft

The nation's public universities are often viewed as an embodiment of the American ideal, a mechanism through which young people from any background can seek a better future through higher education. Some of those public universities have a special designation—they are known as "land grant institutions." In 1862, Congress passed the Morrill Land Grant College Act, offering up parcels of land to states that they could sell for the purposes of creating and funding universities. From the University of Maine to the University of California system, from Louisiana State University to North Dakota State University, fifty-two new institutions mushroomed into existence across the country.[42] These new universities were meant to churn out a new generation of "educated bureaucrats" to usher the country into an era of modernity, overseeing railroad expansion, agricultural innovation, manufacturing, and trade.[43] Economic analysis has suggested that the Morrill Act was transformative for the nation, creating a massive surge in human capital, leading to increases in university enrollment and GDP per capita, and allowing the United States to rise into the position of global superpower.[44]

But the land parceled out for the sake of U.S. economic ascendancy was Indigenous land. Almost eleven million acres of land from nearly 250 Native tribes and communities enabled the universities to garner over $22 million—equivalent to almost $500 million in our time.[45] And those universities have used that money to become bastions of economic opportunity for generation after generation of college students—the vast majority of them White. Despite the fact that these land grant institutions came into being only through the theft of

Indigenous land, Native students make up less than half a percentage point of the enrollment at the Morrill Act universities; these schools also have lower graduation rates among Native students than non-Morrill universities.[46]

The University of Minnesota emerged from one of the most violent and most profitable of these land cessions.[47] The land transfer occurred just months after a group of Dakota warriors, led by Taoyateduta (Little Crow), mounted a war effort against the European settlers whose numbers had increased from 6,000 to 180,000 over the course of a decade and who had driven the Dakota to starvation after failing to deliver food and supplies promised in exchange for land.[48] When they were defeated, Governor Alexander Ramsey called for the genocide of the Dakota, saying that they should be "exterminated" and that if any should "escape extinction, the wretched remnant must be driven beyond our borders."[49] It was amid this fervor that thirty-eight Dakota men were publicly hanged on the day after Christmas in 1862, in what remains the largest mass execution in the history of the United States.[50] Thirty-two days later, the state legislature approved the transfer of 120,000 acres of land to the university.[51] No university without land theft; no land theft without violence.

Of the many 1862 land grant institutions, Cornell University was able to leverage the sale of the stolen land for the highest return. By 1935, sales of Indigenous land had netted the institution a total of $5.7 million.[52] The class of 2021 at Cornell had 3,375 incoming students. Eleven of them—less than a third of a percentage point—were Native. In this sense, the Morrill Act created a form of direct wealth transfer: a bitter alchemy in which violent land seizure turned into institutional wealth for universities, which turned into individual and family wealth for generations of White students.

But as Bryan McKinley Jones Brayboy and Amanda Tachine write, this has amounted to more than simply economic injustice. The legacy of the Morrill Act generates a form of mythmaking and violent erasure, as Native students and educators are absent or invisible on the very campuses where "it was the lands of our ancestors (tied to the violent ways they were eliminated) that made so many of these institutions viable and whole."[53] There is a cruel irony to the idea that the very same universities whose success is predicated on the seizure of Indigenous land now laud themselves for being bastions of equity and opportunity, while failing to serve as such for Native young people descended from those who once stewarded that land. In addition to the institutional transfers of the Morrill Act, we also have to consider the individual-level effects of the Homestead Acts, which transferred millions of acres of tribal land to White settlers between 1862 and 1934. Estimates suggest that the number of living adults who are descended from Homestead Act beneficiaries could range from twenty million to as many as ninety-three million.[54]

In the past several decades, some universities have enacted a different kind of land grab for profit. These institutions present a public facade wherein educating the leaders of tomorrow is their primary focus. But their actions and investments more reflect those of a giant hedge fund—one that benefits from nonprofit status allowing them to pay few to no taxes. As urbanist and historian Davarian Baldwin writes, in many spaces across the United States, universities pursue relentless growth and real estate development, "and the lower-income neighborhoods and communities of color that stand in the immediate path of campus expansion, while in deep need of new investments, are left the most vulnerable. These residents face increased housing costs or even displacement amid university land developments."[55] Universities take and build and take and build, feeding an endless maw of new labs, fancy dorms, and faculty housing in order to construct a new version of old urban spaces: all the fanciest amenities, without any of the inconvenience of the people who used to be there. Baldwin calls the resulting conglomerates "UniverCities": these institutions, helmed by private boards of trustees often made up almost entirely of corporate leaders, make decisions that have a profound impact on public life, including "housing costs, labor conditions, and policing practices."[56] From Los Angeles to Baltimore, from Chicago to New York City, the pattern is the same: universities balloon into spaces once occupied by low-income people of color, transforming them for their own constituents while rendering them inaccessible to longtime residents, who make up minuscule proportions of the enrollment and are unable to weather rising rents. Meanwhile, many of these residents *are* invited into the "UniverCity" as low-wage workers, doing crucial work without which the institutions could not function while being underpaid and undersupported, and increasingly hired through third-party private contractors that prevent these jobs from being a pathway to economic thriving.

The landscape of American universities also benefits from the historical enslavement of Black people. As historian Craig Steven Wilder writes in his landmark work *Ebony & Ivy,* "The earliest American academies became rooted in the slave economies of the colonial world."[57] In the eighteenth century, the men who would become influential leaders of prestigious universities such as the University of Pennsylvania, Dartmouth, Columbia, and Brown eagerly drew upon the wealth and influence of the plantation class in the United States and the Caribbean.[58] When Dartmouth was founded, there were more enslaved people on campus than there were faculty, administrators, or trustees.[59] The first public university in the country, the University of North Carolina, was founded in part using twenty thousand acres of land donated by politician Benjamin Smith, who owned 221 enslaved people.[60] The relationship between slavery and America's new universities spanned state borders as well. Yale University received the donation of a plantation in Rhode Island, which it was then able to lease to various slaveholding tenants to generate revenue.[61] Under the leadership of President John Witherspoon, who believed that relationships with plantation owners could give the university a competitive edge over its peers, Princeton developed a symbiotic relationship with the slaveholding families of the South, intentionally courting them to benefit from their wealth while conferring a new kind of elite social status upon their sons.[62] In Virginia, Princeton alums would go on to found Liberty Hall—a predecessor of what would become Washington and Lee University—using the sale and lease of enslaved Black people to fund the endowment.[63]

As Wilder writes, the intimate tie between enslavement and the rise of prestigious universities was not an incidental consequence, but the result of a series of strategic acts: "Human slavery was the *precondition* for the rise of higher education in the Americas."[64] Enslaved people often undertook the essential and uncelebrated tasks necessary to keep burgeoning institutions of higher learning running: chopping wood, preparing meals, emptying chamber pots, and constructing academic buildings.[65] They could also be forced to endure cruel abuse in the guise of "jokes" and "pranks" at the hands of the young men set to inherit the reins of American aristocratic power. A historian of Williams College, writing about a Black man students paid to smash his head with wooden boards as entertainment, called him a "formidable battering ram" with a "phenomenally thick skull."[66]

Writing about the University of Virginia, historian Maurie McInnis has pointed out that life for enslaved people at the university could be even more unpredictable and dangerous than on a plantation, because their daily lives brought them into contact with any number of random White people who held their fate in their hands despite having fuzzier lines of authority and no clear economic investment in their survival. "Enslaved people were daily subject to the arbitrary actions of faculty, hotelkeepers, and students and the commands of these different groups were frequently contradictory, making navigating daily life fraught with peril." This danger was borne out for individuals like the ten-year-old girl brutally beaten by student Nathan B. Noland after he saw her chasing after a pigeon, or the twelve-year-old girl raped by students George H. Hardy, Armistead C. Eliason, and James E. Montandon.[67]

Routine violence also occurred at the top of the university hierarchy, as when the president of the University of Alabama whipped an enslaved man named Sam for his "insolence" in not receiving or measuring a scheduled coal delivery. Unlike the daily cruelties of plantation violence, this assault had the legitimacy of an institutional decision: the faculty had agreed on this punishment for Sam, and they ordered that the whipping be held under their observation. When it was over, the president felt that Sam was "not sufficiently humbled." And so, he "whipped him a second time, very severely," as the assembled faculty watched.[68]

Today, descendants of people like Sam are some of the least likely to benefit from the ascent of these institutions—even as others have built a path to institutional prosperity on the foundations of their flayed backs.

CHAPTER 13

A Place to Learn Your Place: Education and Racial Capitalism

The distribution of wealth in our country is deeply unequal, and institutions of higher education not only fail to remedy that inequality, they also have a hand in legitimizing it. But far before young people reach college age, they receive messages about capitalist hierarchy and their place in it. Schools are the place where we learn the ropes—we establish the rules for how our democracy is to function. For Black and Native children, schools are also a place where their ordained role within a capitalist society—sources of extraction—is taught, reinforced, and ultimately normalized.

I remember one of my teacher preparation classes, sitting in a hot classroom as we talked about racism and the history of tracking in public schools—generation after generation of Black, Native, and Latine students summarily prevented from pursuing college aspirations, relegated to inflexible "tracks" where they learned skills to prepare them for low-wage vocations or were counseled not to finish high school at all, regardless of their individual interests or abilities. Across the room from me, someone else in my program screwed up his face, silently announcing to the room that he was going to say something uncomfortable but necessary. "Look," he said. "At the end of the day, somebody's got to mow the lawn." His implication, of course, was that it's not just *somebody* who has to mow the lawn, but a very specific *type* of somebody, and that's just the way the world is, always has been, and always should be. (Never mind the fact that mowing the lawn, like all labor, deserves fair compensation and respect.)

Despite many years of scholarly critique aimed at countering old-school tracking, Black and Native students still disproportionately receive educational direction intended to prepare them for low-wage jobs in an economically stratified society. At the secondary level, they are less likely to be in college preparatory tracks than White students, and more likely to be in vocational tracks. Past studies have shown Native students to be the least likely among students of all racial groups to be enrolled in math and foreign language classes, and Black students are least likely to be in science classes.[1] Native students are less likely than students from any other racial or ethnic group to be eligible for an Advanced Placement math course, an opportunity that has positive effects on math achievement and the likelihood of enrolling in college but is available to you only if your high school offers the advanced math prerequisites, such as algebra II.[2]

Direct economic remedies that address the harms of the past—such as reparations, land repatriation, or affirmative action—are virulently resisted by the majority of White Americans. Even initiatives that are marked as forward-looking or intended to further racial equity can end up reinforcing socioeconomic stratification. For instance, some worry that attempts to welcome more diverse cadres of students into the broad, creative, problem-solving world of computer science are being transformed into a simplistic overemphasis on coding, leading to what a former National Science Foundation computer science education program director has referred to as "technical ghettos," where Black students trained in introductory-level coding academies are prepared for lower-paying IT help desk jobs while their White counterparts move into innovation-based start-ups.[3]

These persistent trends reflect what scholar Cedric J. Robinson termed "racial capitalism"—the idea that capitalism, as we know it, does not exist without racialized systems of harm, extraction, and exploitation.[4] Racial capitalism, in Robinson's formulation, is not a type of capitalism; rather, it represents the assertion that capitalism is inherently racialized. The rise of modern capitalism rests upon colonization and enslavement, dispossession, subjugation, and conquest—from

Ireland to Turtle Island, from Vietnam to Algeria. The architectures of violence that have driven the tides of wealth for centuries have necessitated systems of racial order, labeling Those People as savages who deserve what they get, whose destruction is warranted if it facilitates the flow of gold or oil or sugarcane. Capitalism rests on violence; violence rests on racial hierarchies that dehumanize the "Other." Schools, as purveyors of social ideology, handily stand in as the place where these ideas can be built, normalized, and reinforced.

Scholars have long argued that schools prepare students differently for their perceived place as workers or leaders in a capitalist social order.[5] Although highly structured, explicit forms of tracking have fallen somewhat out of favor, more recent research has detailed the subtler ways in which schools continue to reinforce the idea that *some students* are destined for a life of leadership and professional-class success, while others are destined for the lowest rung of the capitalist ladder in a process some scholars have called "de facto tracking."[6]

Some teachers will read this critique with alarm and guilt. Is teaching students in clusters, based on their learning needs, always bad? Not necessarily. Having students work in small groups tailored to specific instructional goals, and moving them between those groups as they master precise skills, has been shown to be effective.[7] But the goals have to be specific and the groups have to be flexible. In practice, this might look like pulling aside one group of students to work on phonemic awareness one day and a different group to work on word decoding another day—not vaguely assigning a broad swath of students to the "low reading group" where they are destined to remain all year.

Despite claims that tracking is the best way to ensure positive outcomes for all students by "going at their pace" or eventually allowing students who are behind to catch up to their peers, research has shown that tracking does not benefit overall student achievement; gains for "high achievers" are canceled out by losses for "low achievers," and at the high school level the two groups of students grow further and further apart as they go along.[8] Teachers of higher-tracked courses tend to use more challenging curricula, to have more experience and better reputations, and to use more engaging instructional strategies like open discussion and in-depth feedback.[9] In one study, researchers using a national analysis of racially diverse schools found that even when controlling for factors such as students' first-year grades and parents' level of education, Black students were underrepresented in advanced sophomore math classes, limiting their access to other advanced coursework that can, in some cases, count for post-secondary credit and would consequently make them competitive college applicants.[10]

So how do we explain these differences? For one thing, teacher expectations may play a role. One national analysis of 752 schools found that Black students were significantly more likely to be expected to seek higher education beyond high school when they had a Black teacher compared to a non-Black teacher.[11] In another study, 126 White teachers were asked to provide feedback on an essay supposedly written by a middle or high school student, but actually crafted by researchers and sown with obvious grammatical errors. Teachers in the study gave overly positive ratings when they thought the student writers were Black, suggesting they had lower expectations on average for these students to be successful or reach high standards—although notably, this finding only held when teachers were in schools with low levels of support, suggesting that an effective school environment could serve to counteract some of this bias.[12]

In another study, 152 high school counselors evaluated randomly assigned transcripts, created by researchers and labeled as belonging to either "Deja Jackson," "DeAndre Washington," "Hannah Douglas," or "Jake Connor." Even when their transcripts were identical to those of their peers, the "Deja Jackson" transcripts were least likely to be recommended for AP Calculus and "Deja" was rated by the counselors as being the least prepared for the course.[13] In another study in which math teachers were similarly given randomly labeled student work to review, they showed no bias in assessing whether the work was actually correct, but when asked to rate the students' mathematical ability, they rated Black students—particularly girls—as being less talented.[14] As Gloria Ladson-Billings has written, in the United States the study of mathematics is "a feared and revered subject" and many believe it "signals advanced thinking reserved only for the intelligentsia."[15]

The entrenchment of these assumptions means that many people uncritically view not only the quality of an individual, but also the quality of a school or district, through a racialized lens. And it doesn't help that school quality truly does benefit from the presence of wealth. "Good" schools are tautologically understood to be White schools, and schools perceived as good raise property value—establishing a tax base that, in turn, provides greater resources to those schools. Meanwhile, the legacy of policies such as the G.I. Bill and the influence of wealth inheritance provide White families with a leg up in accessing those good schools and good houses in the first instance. As Ira Katznelson documented in *When Affirmative Action Was White*, the G.I. Bill was all but useless in supporting homeownership for Black veterans facing redlining, segregation, and other discriminatory roadblocks to securing a mortgage.[16] And the G.I. Bill has also failed to help Native families en masse. Native people have the highest per capita military enlistment numbers of *any* racial or ethnic group in the United States.[17] But banks won't finance G.I. Bill–supported home loans for purchases made on tribal lands, excluding countless possible Native beneficiaries.[18] As Katznelson points out, missed chances at homeownership obviously compound over time."[19] But as many Americans are unaware of the role these policies and practices play in White wealth accumulation, such riches are interpreted merely as more evidence that White people have things because they are smarter, plan better, and work harder.

One important factor that can either magnify or challenge tracking in schools is parental advocacy. In *Despite the Best Intentions*, Amanda E. Lewis and John B. Diamond's study of how tracking and racial inequality persist even when parents and school leaders espouse the importance of diversity, the sociologists' interviews with White parents reveal assumptions about their children's inherent suitability for advanced work—coupled with a willingness to make a fuss if those assumptions are not met, and school administrators' willingness to respond to said fuss. When asked, "for the most part they described an uncomplicated, almost automatic placement in upper-level classes (honors and AP). These parents conveyed a sense of inevitability, as if they took for granted that their children would end up in these classes."[20] One parent described how her son was not placed in an honors biology class because the teacher felt that his reading scores "were just not to the standard she felt an incoming freshman with all the other honors classes [should have]." The parent then "fought" with the head of the school's science department, and ultimately "they were very flexible. Because I'm articulate enough to be able to say, 'Here, you know, let's look at all the facts.' "[21] Ultimately, this student's placement in an advanced science course—and all the benefits that came with it, from a higher GPA to improved social status and the assumption of "smartness" from others around him—had less to do with an assessment of his skills than with his mother's ability to be "articulate" in a way that was legible and deemed worthy of a response by school leadership. A Black math teacher who was interviewed by Lewis and Diamond expressed her frustration with the way these processes tended to play out: "Because the school allows the parents to make the final decision as to what level the kids are in, we have a lot of kids in honors who shouldn't be there. Good kids. Nice kids, and they do their homework every day but they shouldn't be in the honors track."[22]

In contrast, Indigenous families are often discouraged from engaging in school partnerships or speaking up to share wisdom regarding what's best for their children. What "counts" as family engagement for Native families is often based on the ongoing push toward assimilation, the need for compliance and obedience, or total exclusion. "Indigenous families and communities continue to be positioned into having to choose," according to education scholar Megan Bang and her co-authors, "between either participating as compliance officers for schools enacting settler-colonial agendas or being positioned as deficient, deviant, or uncaring."[23] Native parents who show up and demand that their child be placed in an honors track may be less likely to get their desired outcome; meanwhile, Indigenous parents are presumed not to care, even as more holistic ways of engaging with children's learning—such as a focus on learning through community, teaching respect for elders, cultivating connections to extended family, and encouraging good relations with the land and waters—tend to be less valued in schooling spaces.[24]

Indolence and Idleness

So far in this part of the book, we've talked about the ways that Black and Native people have been relegated to the bottom of the capitalist hierarchy in the United States, the ways that postsecondary institutions capitalize on economic exploitation while continuing to exclude Black and Native people, and the ways that K-12 schooling normalizes this status quo through tracking. But I think it's also important to take a step back and consider the ways that Black and Indigenous cultural practices were seen as a threat to racial capitalism in the early days of this country. Our very ways of being were a challenge to the hypervaluation of working to accrue capital.

In the early twentieth century, German sociologist and historian Max Weber published one of the most influential works of social science ever written: *The Protestant Ethic and the Spirit of Capitalism.* In it, Weber argued that the rise of Calvinist and Puritan beliefs ushered in a historically unique form of capitalism—one in which individuals aspired to make money not only to sustain themselves, but to fulfill a "philosophy of avarice," "the idea of a *duty* of the individual toward the increase of his capital, which is assumed as an end in itself."[25] Weber summarized the Yankees' capitalist spirit thusly:

> The *summum bonum* [highest good] of this ethic, the earning of more and more money, combined with the strict avoidance of all spontaneous enjoyment of life. . . . Man is dominated by the making of money, by acquisition as the ultimate purpose of his life. Economic acquisition is no longer subordinated to man as the means for the satisfaction of his material needs.

In Weber's view, this philosophy had ascended in American culture to a level of religious fervor, a worldview in which earning money is "an expression of virtue," the proof of a good and moral life worth living. "It is an obligation which the individual is supposed to feel and does feel towards the content of his professional activity, no matter in what it consists."[26] For many, the assumption that working as hard as possible, to earn as much money as possible, is unquestioned as an inherent good.

In particular, since the founding of the United States, the accrual of property as a special form of capital has been romanticized, reified, and uplifted as the mark of a good person who has lived life well. John Adams, in debating whether men without property should be allowed to vote, provocatively compared such men to children and (*gasp*) women. If you let people without property vote, you might as well grant suffrage to "lads from twelve to twenty-one," and "every man who has not a farthing, will demand an equal voice with any other."[27] Broke people voting! Utter chaos! Adams's protest reflected a long-standing idea, going back at least to seventeenth-century England, that anyone who hadn't succeeded in acquiring property was an unreliable, incompetent person who would be a danger to themselves and others if permitted to participate in civic life.[28] Therefore, writes J. Kameron Carter, "the religion of whiteness is the propertization of the earth."[29]

Within this rubric, practices among Black and Native people who had other ways of being have historically been condemned, dismissed, ridiculed, or forbidden. The Protestant work ethic and the spirit of capitalism require(d) one to work not for subsistence, but for accumulation; not for joy or satisfaction, but because to do anything *other* than work is a waste of a life; not for the support of others, but because accruing property is the mark of a worthwhile human being. In the past few years, the notion of "wellness" has superficially seemed to challenge this idea, urging notions of "rest" and "self-care" that look less like Audre Lorde's radical formulation and more like wanton consumption. Writer Fariha Róisín calls this the "wellness industrial complex," a world in which "whiteness and capitalism have co-opted wellness, relegating caring for oneself as a privilege when wellness should be for all."[30] If *wellness* can be an industry—if it can be appropriated by White cultural influencers who use it as a means of profit—then it's justifiable. But throughout history, Black and Native people's desire to rest, to work as a means of feeding themselves and their families rather than to endlessly accumulate, has been seen as a marker of their racial inferiority.

AFTER THE END OF slavery, social observers from various corners of the political realm expressed a shared fear. Their primary concern, over and above consideration of how Black people might be remunerated for centuries of forced labor, was the matter of *idleness.* Black people, they believed, had an inherent tendency to be lazy, overly satisfied with the bare minimum needed for subsistence, rather than driven to participate in the capitalist project of hoarding wealth. The notion of Negro idleness so motivated moral panic that one Pennsylvania gubernatorial candidate in 1866 ran an advertisement calling the Freedmen's Bureau "an agency to keep the Negro in idleness at the expense of the White man." The poster showed a caricature of a Black person at rest, legs crossed, looking up wistfully at the sky as a White man engages in the hard labor of chopping wood nearby. In the background, the columns of the U.S. Capitol are upheld by such sinful Negro diversions as candy, indolence, and a personal favorite of mine, pies.[31]

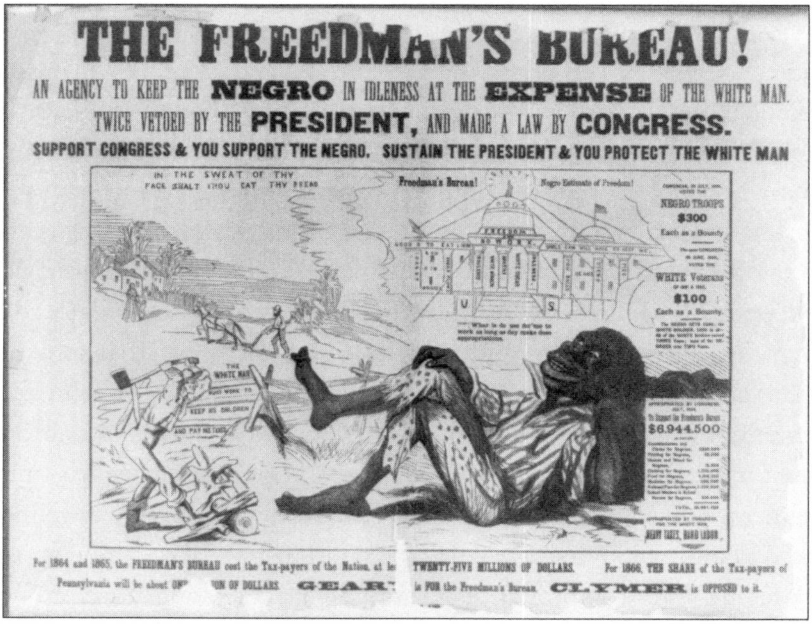

The matter of Black people at rest presented a moral and philosophical problem alongside an economic one. If Black people focused on simply growing and building what they needed, they might have idle time to rest and ideate—in other words, come up with dangerous, provocative political ideas and engage in rabble-rousing—and they would have little incentive to participate in exploitative economic schemes that also served as a means of social control. As one Kentucky newspaper put it, the ideal would be for formerly enslaved people to see themselves as "*free,* but free only to labor."[32]

As always, schooling was roped in as an effective way to ensure that Black people were complacent in the role assigned to them: unquestioning laborers, motivated by the promise of accumulation. Textbooks for freedpeople became one vehicle to tell them what they should and should not do with their new liberty. In *John Freeman and His Family,* a fictional tale about a wise formerly enslaved man, John Freeman counsels his family that freedom "is not to be let loose like the wild hogs in the woods, to root along in the bogs and just pick up a living as we can. No; we are to do just what free men do. You look round and you see every free man, black and white, works for a living. . . . He works in some 'spectable profession."[33] Lydia Maria Child, the author of *The Freedmen's Book,* discussed in chapter 3, offered what she considered to be the most useful advice for newly freed Black people. This included a transcription of an 1865 speech from a South Carolina judge to an assembled group of Black people: "Labor is the law of all. Your friends in the North appeal to you to help them in the great work they undertook to do for you. We want you to work with us. We want you to do it by working here in South Carolina, earning wages, taking care of your money, and making profit out of that money. Work on the plantation, if that is all you can do."[34] Clinton B. Fisk, who worked as a commissioner in the Freedmen's Bureau (and is the namesake of Fisk University), published a book called *Plain Counsels for Freedmen,* compiling sixteen lectures. Fisk included an illustration of "Peter Puff and Betty Simple," fools who were content to go out having fun and dancing "like a monkey," as a cautionary tale.

No fun allowed! Fisk urged Black people not to be satisfied by earning only the money they needed to eat or wearing just anything. "Do not attempt to live on the little jobs you may pick up about hotels and places of business. Do not be content with cold victuals, old clothes, and a blanket on the floor. Be a MAN. Earn money, and save it," wrote Fisk.[35] In another lecture on the subject of work—creatively titled "Work"—Fisk acknowledges that formerly enslaved people might not want to do all this extra stuff when they could be having fun

PETER PUFF AND BETTY SIMPLE.

like Peter and Betty, "because you have seen slaves working all their lives, and free people doing little or nothing. And I should not blame you if you should ask, 'What have we gained by freedom, if we are to work, work, work!'"[36] But, he counters, all noble characters share this one thing in common. "All the holy angels in heaven are very busy," Fisk reasons. God placed Adam and Eve into the Garden of Eden so that they might till the soil, Jesus was a carpenter, and even Abraham Lincoln "used the hoe, the ax, and the maul, cleared ground, and fenced it with the rails he had split." So too should formerly enslaved people see dignity in working for themselves and for pay. Idleness—the sin of *not* working—should be avoided at all costs. Idleness was temptation toward immorality, consignment to a fate literally worse than death. "Oh, my friends, it is a sad thing to see a child die . . . but I would rather every one of my children should die and be buried thus, than that they should be raised in idleness."[37]

The Freedman's Third Reader, another primer for emancipated students, drove these principles home in a chapter titled "Labor and Capital." After frontloading with some vocabulary words that might aid the reader in comprehension (like *ben-e-fit* and *des-ti-tute*), the chapter offers the idea that while "there must be labor"—a universal principle that applies to the "inferior animals as well as to man," down to the bee that "goes from flower to flower"—it's not sufficient to labor just enough to take care of your immediate needs. Rather, "there must be an accumulation of the results of labor, which is capital."[38] One testament to how essential this lesson was deemed to be is the fact that it's sandwiched between lesson 69, which is an account of how Joseph was sold into Egypt in the book of Genesis, and lesson 71, which is simply titled "Heaven." Understanding the naturally ordained obligation to labor toward accumulation was seen as equally essential to one's spiritual thriving.

Despite these exhortations, many newly emancipated Black people explicitly resisted the idea of growing cash crops rather than things they could eat. Growing a little bit of corn, raising a few hogs, and perhaps growing some cotton to enable other purchases was fine for most, though some detested the idea of growing cotton altogether: "If ole massa want to grow cotton," said one formerly enslaved man, "let him plant it himself."[39] A. Warren Kelsey, a representative sent to the South by Northern textile manufacturers to investigate the likely future of the cotton crop on which they so intensely relied, reported back that this economic freedom—including the freedom to *not* labor toward accumulation—was the dream of the Black Southerner, whose "sole ambition . . . appears to be to become the owner of a little piece of land, there to erect a humble home, and to dwell in peace and security at his own free will and pleasure."[40]

For White observers, this ambition was not enough. After all, *civilization* requires *accumulation.* Orra Langhorne, a White suffragette who was considered an advocate for Black education, published a critique in *Southern Workman* about the Black people she witnessed in Washington, D.C., whom she saw as making the unwise and sentimental choice of hanging on to those humble homes rather than using property as a form of investment. "The colored man cannot be made to see that he can sell his property for a sum that will bring him in quite a large income, and he can rent for $10.00 per month, a house that will suit him as well for a dwelling," she wrote. However, she predicted, such foolishness would die off as the children of formerly enslaved people assimilated into the capitalist ranks. "The old generation of Negroes is fast passing away. A new generation, born in freedom, *educated in the public schools of the city,* with very different tastes and habits from those of the old slaves, is rapidly taking their places. The children of the ex-slave, to whom the little cot, earned by the sweat of his brow, was a sacred place, will be able to count and appreciate at its true value, the interest on each dollar's worth of property. . . . The real estate dealer will soon have his way."[41]

As Langhorne saw it, schools would be the place where these children learned new "tastes and habits" and would usher the simple dreams of their parents, born in bondage, into a new future. Others, like General Nathaniel P. Banks, agreed. Banks established a Board of Education in Louisiana in March 1864 for the purpose of educating newly freed Black people—specifically and explicitly to be effective laborers. In reporting on the success of his efforts, he wrote with satisfaction that "the progress of both young and old, are gratifying and surprising, and it leaves no possible doubt whatever that the negro population not only can perform all that is required of the laboring population, but that they can make such rapid improvement as answers the expectations of the Government."[42] The new schools enrolled over 9,500 Black children, and the goal of the entire new education system, as he saw it, would be to provide "the elements of knowledge which give intelligence and greater value to labor."[43] Banks carefully designed the system toward this end. Many newly emancipated Black people were moving away from rural Louisiana and toward cities, seeking independent opportunities away from plantations—and creating a shortage of the laborers needed by the planter class. Banks issued a directive that land for the schools should be sought among "sites in plantation districts," creating an incentive for Black people to stay where they could be used for agriculture. Teachers were directed to provide only the most "rudimental instruction"—nothing that would prepare Black people for taking work above their station or lead them to question their place in the socioeconomic hierarchy—and children were allowed to attend school only until they turned twelve years old.[44]

Work or Starve: Inculcating the Love of Property

In Native people, too, White observers decried the great shortcoming of idleness. But in the case of Native people, encouraging a love of property and accumulation served another purpose toward building the ideal state. If they desired property and were willing to work to get it, and to enter into trade relations with White people, this economic relationship would both "civilize" them and create a point of leverage for the further seizure of Indigenous land. After all, how do you buy something from someone who doesn't believe it can be sold? As Julian Brave NoiseCat writes:

> While indigenous values, beliefs and practices are as diverse as indigenous people themselves, they find common roots in a relationship to land and water radically different from the notion of property. For indigenous people, land and water are regarded as sacred, living relatives, ancestors, places of origin or any combination of the above. . . . The people are of the land and the land is of the people. These kindred spirits are alive and inseparable.[45]

Native nations prior to colonization approached the land through the lens of stewardship rather than the European notion of ownership. Modes of stewardship varied in accordance with the diverse circumstances of the lands and waters; negotiating who would fish when, where, and how would look very different in the salmon-rich coastal waters of the Pacific Northwest than it might look in the freshwater streams hundreds of miles east. Indigenous people across Turtle Island negotiated among families to manage who would hunt, fish, grow crops across which lands, and they altered the environment through forest and water management.[46] After all, as Pawnee/Comanche legal scholar Kevin Gover reminds us, "Any Hopi farmer will tell you that corn doesn't just spring from the dry red earth of Arizona, even though it has grown there for thousands of years." Such bounty results from careful stewardship of the land and from agricultural wisdom at odds with "the image of the innocent primitive frolicking in an unblemished landscape." The truth lies between the myth of simply waiting for the earth to yield and the colonial European extreme of relentless extraction with no regard for consequence. Mother Earth, Gover says, "teaches us how we should live our lives—*don't take more than you need,* she chides . . . This is Indian thinking."[47]

This way of life was at odds with European and American notions of capitalist labor toward the accumulation of property as not only an inherent good but also the mark of worthy, civilized culture. Desire for property was seen as the defining hallmark of civilization, a sign that a human society had reached its zenith out of the depths of savagery. Early anthropologist Lewis Henry Morgan expressed this belief in his book *Ancient Society: Or Researches in the Lines of Human Progress from Savagery Through Barbarism to Civilization.* The idea of property, he wrote, had a "controlling influence" over the human brain. "Its dominance as a passion over all other passions marks the commencement of civilization. . . . A critical knowledge of the evolution of the idea of property would embody, in some respects, the most remarkable portion of the mental history of mankind."[48]

Viewed through this political ideology, there was something contemptible about Native peoples' collectivist ways of being. Richard Henry Pratt, the Carlisle founder you'll recall from Part I, referred to it as a form of "socialism."[49] William Torrey Harris, who would serve as the nation's Commissioner of Education under four U.S. presidents, complained that such beliefs would have to be overcome, that "we have to bring the Indian into that consciousness [of individualism]," toward an understanding that that collective, community-based identity was not the way toward either holy salvation or economic salvation. "A civilization that will help people to help themselves is what we want," said Harris. "Men are not saved by communities, by congregations, by peoples. They are saved individually."[50] Collectivity was also seen as a contributor to idleness in another arena: dancing and any cultural practices that brought Native people together for fellowship and joy when they could have been plowing a field. "The dances of the Indians held on the reservation by the older Indians are a hindrance to progress in that they induce idleness and take the Indians away from farm work."[51] White officials conceded that simply banning such gatherings would not stop them—only schooling could do that. "They will leave their homes and spend days at a dance when they should be on their farms attending to their crops or irrigating their fields. . . . Education is the only solution that occurs to this office. Arbitrary prohibition is not practicable to eliminate dances."[52] They made the same complaint about funerals, bemoaning the fact that Native people spent too much time hosting memorial feasts after the loss of a loved one, and that these feasts were too expensive.[53]

As long as Native people were living collectively, sharing resources in community, they would never be adequately driven to work toward accumulation. John Oberly, Commissioner of Indian Affairs, argued that "the Indian should be taught not only how to work, but also that it is his duty to work; for the degrading communism of the tribal-reservation system gives to the individual no incentive to labor, but puts a premium upon idleness and makes it fashionable. . . . And he must be imbued with the exalting egotism of American civilization, so that he will say 'I' instead of 'We,' and 'This is mine,' instead of 'This is ours.' "[54]

Fittingly, cultivating a desire for individualized property would hold a central role in the plans the U.S. government would undertake vis-à-vis Native people and their disappearance through assimilation. In his final year in the post, Secretary of the Interior Carl Schurz spelled out a strategy based in a love of work, property, and profit alongside education as pillars of an assimilationist approach. "To fit the Indians for their ultimate absorption in the great body of American citizenship, three things are suggested . . . 1. That they be taught to work by making work profitable and attractive to them. 2. That they be educated, especially the youth of both sexes. 3. That they be individualized in the possession of property."[55] This third point was critical for the assimilationist project so as to create incentives for Native people to want to sell their land. Surely, Schurz reasoned, when they held their land with a title, "they will feel more readily inclined to part with such of their lands as they cannot themselves cultivate," and in short order:

> The Indians, with their possessions, will cease to stand in the way of the "development of the country." The difficulty which has provoked so many encroachments and conflicts will then no longer exist. When the Indians are individual owners of real property, and as individuals enjoy the protection of the laws, their tribal cohesion will necessarily relax, and gradually disappear. They will have advanced an immense step in the direction of the "white man's way."[56]

While Schurz's plan highlighted the efficacy of schooling and capitalism as assimilationist strategies, others quickly realized that they could establish schooling *for* capitalism. Commissioner Oberly decreed that all schools for Native children should be "schools in which they will be instructed in the use of agricultural implements, the carpenter's saw and plane, the stonemason's trowel, the tailor's needle, and the shoemaker's awl."[57] In a congressional report, the superintendent of the Phoenix Indian Industrial Training School outlined his philosophy on the matter: "Indolence is the cankerworm of progress, so our pupils are taught to kill the worm."[58] Learning any academic subjects in the school—math, history, literacy, or geography—was seen as being valuable only insofar as it could support manual labor. In fact, literary teachers were required to visit industrial teachers to ensure that their teaching was in alignment. "We pride ourselves on being a working school," the superintendent wrote. "Working" in this view was not merely the technical skill needed to make bricks or build a barn; "working" entailed the social and psychological understanding of oneself as an individual laboring for accumulation, as well as contentment with one's place at the bottom of capitalist hierarchy.

Phoenix, like hundreds of other schools for Native children at the end of the nineteenth century and into the 1910s and 1920s, was also proud of having adopted the "outing" program invented by Richard Henry Pratt, whereby children were sent to work as live-in laborers for White families in nearby towns. In fact, the location of the Phoenix school—originally planned for another site, Fort McDowell—was selected precisely because citrus orchards were being developed nearby, and students could work there as cheap agricultural laborers. When the site was chosen, writers in a local newspaper crowed at the news, writing that "the establishment of this school will furnish cheap and efficient labor," leading farmers and fruit growers to begin requesting child workers to bring in the harvest before the school even opened.[59] Once the school was established, boys were hired out to agricultural work or to assist contractors in building new structures on campus; girls were sent to serve as domestics in nearby homes.[60] Eventually, such girls would come to live in the homes of their employers Monday through Friday, returning to the school only on weekends. For these children, "schooling" didn't mean being a student and working on the side. They were full-time laborers, fitting in the business of education on weekends if they happened to have time.[61] Learning to cook, clean, and mend clothes effectively was the top priority. Estelle Reel, the Superintendent of Indian Schools discussed earlier (who said that Native children's bones, muscles, and nerve development were weakened compared to those of White children), stressed that even if there was "no time for nothing else, housekeeping must be taught."[62] Sometimes White housewives, newly reliant on the Native girls working in their homes, wouldn't let them return to school at all.[63] In Kansas, the superintendent of the Haskell Institute admitted that those who hired the youth did not have "enough of the feeling that the Indians are human beings and are capable of being civilized."[64] As time went on, students across the western states were sent through the outing system to places farther and farther afield from school—to beet farms in Colorado, to railroad companies in California, to ranches, to power companies.[65]

The Summum Bonum

We've talked throughout this book about the ways that systems of schooling have been used to "civilize" Black and Native young people. In the United States, part of being "civilized" means that you should crave infinite accumulation. Remember Weber's words: the *summum bonum*, the highest good, is achieved through the earning of more and more money. Paradoxically, people in power in the United States have castigated Black and Native people historically for not wanting money badly enough, while in the present the very system that is supposed to promise equity of access—schooling—has done little to redress the wealth gaps that make it hard for folks to just cover their basic necessities. Black and Native people have been permitted to participate in the grand project of capitalist accumulation—as sources of extraction, keepers of bodies and lands from whom as much profit should be taken as possible.

And yet, as we consider this history, it doesn't feel like enough to demand that our people be given fairer access to wealth and all that it entails—educational opportunities, housing, medical care. I find myself wondering whether the models of history, the people criticized as being "indolent," might invite us to think differently about our relationship to work, and about the ways that schools prepare young people for work. What would it look like for schooling spaces to invite joyful, meaningful, purposeful labor, coupled with ample rest? Instead of schools being tracked, stratified, and partitioned in a way that mirrors our deeply unequal country, could they be models of an ethical relationship to work, preparing young people to build something different in years to come?

Perhaps I'm feeling dreamy and aspirational because, as this chapter draws to a close, we're now done talking about the three pillars of racial hierarchy. As we now conclude, it's time to get to one of *my* favorite forms of purposeful labor: the work of imagining something new. Onward we go.

CONCLUSION

Strands Together: Imagination, Liberation, and Braiding

Home's the place we head for in our sleep.
Boxcars stumbling north in dreams
don't wait for us. We catch them on the run.

—LOUISE ERDRICH, "INDIAN BOARDING SCHOOL: THE RUNAWAYS"[1]

Black and Indigenous folks are the most dangerous union to the stability of America.

—BOBBY JOE SMITH III[2]

We should expect that we will not be perfect with one another. We should embrace failure in the attempt toward intimacy. After all, isn't working together a move toward intimacy? Hasn't this always been a bit icky, scary, and awkward? Why do we expect each other to be perfectly formed political subjects when we have all been institutionalized to think badly of each other and ourselves? . . . It is lonely at the bottom of the heap. I want to be with other people. I want to talk with other people.

—CHRIS FINLEY, "BUILDING MAROON INTELLECTUAL COMMUNITIES"[3]

In this book, I have shared a lot of stories I believe are important for us to understand the world in which we find ourselves. Much of it is pretty discouraging. But, as Joanne Barker reminds us, it's not enough to engage in "merely retelling the state's permanence and the futility of everything we might do to change things."[4] When we do that—when we throw up our hands and pronounce that we're doomed—we abdicate our responsibility to those who come after us, to those who will look to us as ancestors. Further, we disrespect the struggles of those who came before us, who fought and laughed and wrote and built things—not because they believed they would win every battle in their lifetimes, but because they saw it as essential for *us*. They went through a whole lot of trouble to draw maps toward our freedom, to forge tools for us. They did so while they were locked up, while they were starving, while they felt like they had hit bottom on the well of their sorrows. Still, they were thinking of us. Who are we, then, to abandon these inheritances?

This final part of the book is the one I was looking forward to writing the most, and also the most challenging. It's the most challenging because some of you are expecting some conclusive reflection about hundreds of years of history, and some answers about how to correct course. I don't know if I can do that.

But it's also the most exciting for me to write! It brings me delight to think about the ways we can dedicate ourselves to a world that has space for everyone to thrive, to live in good relation to the lands and waters and to one another, to pursue joy. I am not so interested in being prescriptive about how we do this. Rather, I think about these spaces of possibility as being a little like the boxcars that legendary Chippewa writer Louise Erdrich describes in her poem "Indian Boarding School: The Runaways": routes for escape, places toward which we amble in our sleep even when we're not sure how to get there. We sprint forward in faith and in fear, knowing that what's ahead is uncertain—but what we have surely ain't working. We don't wait for the conditions of our flight to be perfect, and we know we might get hurt along the way, but we know that the journey is urgent.

Boxcars stumbling north in dreams / don't wait for us. We catch them on the run.

Black and Indigenous peoples have been harmed in so many ways by capitalism, and we continue to struggle toward notions of community care and abundance. So it's surprising how much the interaction between Black and Indigenous scholarship on the page has been defined by what I would consider the fundamental units of capitalism: competition, scarcity, binary logics (it's either *this* or *that*), and assertions that reality can be ordered along a concrete and hierarchical ladder. Scholars who have focused exclusively on the concept of anti-Blackness have not always sufficiently accounted for the ongoing violence of settler colonialism and genocide, while the "settler/native" dichotomy proposed by many scholars of settler colonialism does not account for the grotesque institution of chattel slavery. Some of that is due to the limitations of academic pontificating. But on a more fundamental level, we might think of these strained moments as forms of harm, in which two peoples aggrieved by White supremacy have, in an attempt to denote the boundaries of those grievances, failed to treat one another with an ethic of care.[5]

The fields of both Black studies and Indigenous studies have "made claims to exceptionalism that leave the two fields at an impasse," writes historian Justin Leroy. Yet a closer look at the history of the United States—and global imperialism and colonialism—lends us a more nuanced understanding of the ways our hurts are deeply entangled. "Slavery and settler colonialism share deep and overlapping histories," Leroy explains. Indeed, "even a casual engagement with the entanglements of black and indigenous history in the United States reveals that the claims of exceptionalism underlying so much black and indigenous critical theory cannot stand up to scrutiny."[6]

So how should we understand Black history and Indigenous history, Black struggle and Indigenous struggle, Black futures and Indigenous futures in relation to one another? It would be easy to just tell beautiful stories about all the ways Black and Indigenous people within this colonized state have helped each other, lived together, and loved one another. We can talk with pride about maroon communities, where enslaved Black people who ran away made spaces outside the bounds of captivity—often within and among Native people, forming new creole societies. I could talk here about how the city I'm from, Chicago, was born by the river when a Potawatomi woman and a Black man established a home along the water. I could talk about the ways the Black Panther Party and the American Indian Movement learned from, celebrated, and protested in solidarity with each other.[7] I could talk about the Black people who showed up at Standing Rock and the Indigenous people who took part in Black Lives Matter marches. Those stories are powerful and important.

But I think it's equally important to acknowledge the ways we have hurt one another—sometimes of our own volition, sometimes as instruments of the state. After all, as scholar George Lipsitz reminds us, throughout U.S. history "the power of whiteness [has] depended not only on white hegemony over separate racialized groups, but also on manipulating racial outsiders to fight against one another, to compete with each other for white approval, and to seek the rewards and privileges of whiteness for themselves at the expense of other racialized populations."[8] Black and Native people have been forced to fight for survival under the same regimes of terror, within which we have harmed one another in the ways humans living under duress will always do.[9] Black soldiers fought in the "Indian Wars," participating in the settler project of killing and displacing Native people. (These "Buffalo Soldiers" are often romanticized as heroes in contemporary Black culture, from the Bob Marley song to historical reenactments in which enthusiasts dress up in nineteenth-century uniforms.) Members of the Choctaw, Chickasaw, Creek, Cherokee, and Seminole Nations owned enslaved Africans. White officials referred to them as the "Five Civilized Tribes" and encouraged them to participate in slavery as a crucial element of that civilizing project. One government official wrote in an annual report: "I am clearly of the opinion that the rapid advancement of the Cherokees is owing in part to the fact of their being slaveholders, which has operated as an incentive to all industrial pursuits; and I believe, if every family of the wild roving tribes of Indians were to own a negro man and woman, who would teach them to cultivate the soil, and to properly prepare and cook their food . . . it would tend more to civilize them than any other plan that could be adopted."[10] Today, anti-

Blackness continues in Indian Country as it does elsewhere in the world, with particularly insidious implications for the rights and livelihoods of those descended from the thousands who were enslaved within the Five Tribes.[11] And anti-Indigeneity continues among Black people, who are susceptible to the same stereotypes about Native people found elsewhere in mainstream American culture—as well as the habit of rendering Native people altogether invisible, thus participating in settler memory.

These open wounds have reinforced the idea that Blackness and Indigeneity are somehow incompatible—an idea established by the policies of the settler state, from the Dawes Act to Virginia's 1924 Racial Integrity Act prohibiting interracial marriage, actions that prevented people from being legally recognized as both Black and Native.[12] This fiction still causes harm to Afro-Indigenous people, rendered invisible through a reductive framework that acts as though they don't or categorically *can't* exist.

It is important to know and understand this history. Only by facing our ugliest narratives of the past can we hope not to "move past them," but to surmount them. At the same time, it's worth thinking critically about how our presumed knowledge about one another is filtered through the ideology of a racist settler state. As historian Tiya Miles writes, moments of conflict that at first appear to be binary—Black vs. Native—can be "in fact triangular, holding in tension Indian experience, black experience, and an invisible, structuring white presence."[13] What does it look like to escape the bounds of this structure, to redefine the terms of our engagement?

I also believe that within our shared histories lies a deep and furious power, and that Black and Native co-accountability and co-conspiracy offer some of the most insurgent and revolutionary sites of possibility imaginable. We are two groups of people whose humanity is inherently contradictory to the White supremacist and settler colonialist machinations of this country. Our thriving was so threatening to the project of what would become the United States that the country had to invest in our total subjugation and destruction in order to forge itself. It follows, then, that our refusal not only to die but also to turn on one another—the refusal to accept the terms we have been handed to sow the seeds of our enmity—would be incendiary. In her accounting of the relational possibilities between Black and Native peoples, Tiffany Lethabo King describes the power of "a kind of co-witnessing that enables people not only to mirror back pain but also to implicate one another in our survival."[14] What would it mean to not only say, *You hurt me,* to not only say, *I see you, too, have been hurt,* but to say: *I see that my thriving happens alongside yours*? What would it mean to move together, as critical theorist and literary scholar Chad Infante calls us to do, not only in *coalition* but in *collusion*?[15]

I briefly mentioned *solidarity* earlier—the idea that we see ourselves in a union spurred by shared interests. I would like to offer that solidarity is not a declaration; it is a set of actions in a constant state of emergence. Solidarity doesn't happen just because you say it, nor is it a static state. Rather, solidarity lies in a set of ever unfolding decisions, made against the backdrop of a world committed to our destruction. "Solidarity is an uneasy, reserved, and unsettled matter that neither reconciles present grievances nor forecloses future conflict," write Eve Tuck and K. Wayne Yang.[16] Can we dedicate ourselves to navigating that unease, because the choice not to do so is perilous to our lives? To "be in solidarity" does not mean we have never harmed one another and never will; instead, it demands a continuous state of learning and change, of communication and failures and iteration after those failures. Solidarity, the fact of being in league with one another and committed to one another's survival and thriving, is not the place we begin; that commitment emerges from a more fundamental orientation toward two other principles: *collective struggle* and an *ethic of care.*[17]

Building power through collective struggle means that when we band together in groups of people who share many things in common—not everything, but many things—and we decide we want to work toward something, the very process of doing that is the practice of making the world we want to live in. In building the relationships we need to topple an unjust world, we are also strengthening the muscles we need to care for one another; we are stitching together microcosms of the world that will replace the one we have.

From the Black feminist tradition and the tradition of being an educator—someone charged with tending to the flourishing of young people—I have received the gift of believing it is essential to care for one another.[18] As told in the history we learn in schools and on television and in the news, the work of social transformation often sidelines narratives of care or omits them altogether. The world is changed, we are told, when the loudest people talk the most and fight the hardest and come up with the best ideas. And that, indeed, can be important work. But care work—asking basic questions like, *Has everyone been fed? Do people have a safe place to sleep? Is there safe and reliable childcare? Are we attending to everyone's health?*—not only provides the necessary conditions for all the other stuff to happen; it is *also* a form of stitching together microcosms of a more just and loving world.[19] Such a commitment is also woven through Indigenous feminist thought and writings. As Gina Starblanket (Cree/Saulteaux and French) explains, Indigenous movements toward resurgence, freedom, and autonomy are undergirded by Indigenous feminisms that call on us to attend to the ways we treat one another in our daily interactions. "Decolonization and liberation [are] incremental, dynamic, and ongoing processes that are constantly changing and comprise a multiplicity of everyday relations," she writes. There are, therefore, "transformative possibilities that exist within our relations with our family and friends and within our relations with ideas and knowledge, as well as within our relationship with ourselves."[20]

Collective struggle and an ethic of care, as lenses for approaching the question of our relationships to one another, invite us to set aside assumptions that *either* slavery and its afterlives *or* settler colonialism is the One Violence to Rule Them All, and instead to commit ourselves to dreaming. When we do that, we may find that there is more generative space than we know what to do with. I believe that Black and Indigenous peoples, working within and between communities, have the tools to *imagine, iterate,* and *build* radical new models for what teaching and learning can look like. I use the word "radical" here in a mindful way, gesturing toward its etymology, meaning "root"; I believe we can build pathways for teaching and learning—for education in all its forms, beyond schooling—that have deep roots in history, in ancestry, in ways of knowing and being that create conditions for thriving. We can *imagine:* we can look toward our most audacious dreams, toward our memories, toward the speculative and the wild, to think about what might be possible and what currently seems impossible but what we should strive for anyway. We can *iterate:* engaging in cycles of play, experimentation, trial, failure, reflective practice, and a willingness to say, *This might work!* and then being honest and communicative about how to do better when it doesn't. And we can *build.* As we commit ourselves to dismantling the structures that no longer serve us, we don't have to wait for anybody's permission—any state, any institution, any hierarchical system of power—to make the spaces and structures we want to see.

This implies that the modes in which we organize should be flexible and responsive to what we need in the moment. And so there are, and always will be, times when building intracommunity coalitions is necessary. Forming a reading group that is just for Indigenous people, or just Haudenosaunee people, or just Haudenosaunee educators, can be powerful in one moment. Starting a zine that publishes work by just Black people, or just Black folks of Haitian descent, or just Black folks of Haitian descent who have children in the New York City school system, can be radical in another moment. And across all of these spaces, thinking about how modes of teaching and learning might blossom to attend to intersecting identities—from class status to queerness, from disability to being undocumented—is necessary. Every coalition is not for every moment.

However, what broader coalitions rooted in collective care *do* make possible is the illumination of something unique about where we come from and where we could be going. Our points of intersection make our visions of a better life more robust and more honest insofar as we can strive to be accountable to one another. Mutual accountability is not a concession. It's not a limitation. Our crossroads—the places where our paths meet—are places of power. Here, I think of these words from a friend, interdisciplinary scholar and artist Ashon Crawley:

> Perhaps the way to think the relation of Blackness to Indigeneity is to think about what we have always done, been, and what we have available that allows us to think connection. To

> do as we always have done is to mark the fact that otherwise possibility is not tending toward a future that is to come but is the marking of the practices that we have and do and carry with care and love for one another against the imposition of settler colonial violence, the violence that is coarticulated with anti-Blackness to produce the modern crisis of racialization, the theft of ground and air, and the strangulation of life possibilities.[21]

I want to *think connection*, as Ashon calls us to do, by thinking about *what we have available*. One way to do that is by thinking about groundswells that are already surging beneath our feet. To think not only about "how we can change our schools" but rather about how schools as sites of struggle are central to incipient movements of social change that are already springing from the soil.

Schools for Us: Abolition and Land Back

Looking back on my time as a classroom teacher, I am struck by how many microlevel technocratic innovations we were told could be instrumental in transforming our young people's capacity to learn. This type of reading strategy, that type of desk arrangement, this fancy new software. These interventions might be helpful, but they are all for naught if we don't pay attention to the context in which schools sit, in which we are trying to get this tricky thing called *teaching and learning* to happen. Otherwise, it's a little bit like investigating the grain of the wood on the deck of the ship when the vessel is being tossed by the storm. We can't actually "tinker toward utopia," to use school reform scholars David Tyack and Larry Cuban's formulation.[22] Indeed, sometimes the pitiably small or entirely symbolic nature of such tinkering is itself a symptom of concession, a sign of defeat. As Nick Estes argues, changing the names of buildings or having a social justice book club is easy to do when it costs our institutions absolutely nothing: "Acts of apologies or so-called truth and reconciliation happen from the comfort of settler societies that have so thoroughly subjugated Native people through violence and genocide that they have no fear that symbolic acts change the socioeconomic or political realities of today," says Estes. "In other words, they don't challenge the colonial relation. In fact, they can be seen as a technology of colonial rule."[23]

So how can we stretch our imaginations to consider questions of love, justice, and flourishing at the same scale, with the same temerity, that the architects of this country had when they made schools into spaces of intellectual degradation, punishment, and economic subjugation? Put differently: Rather than asking how we can change *schools*, *students*, or *teachers*, how might we see the transformation of schools as part of the broader work of transforming society? How do we acknowledge schools as a mirror facing a world that mirrors right back, twin images bouncing recursively against each other forever and ever, and therefore requiring interventions that keep sight of the whole shebang? And how do we center Black and Indigenous children themselves—center their notions of self-concept, of history and ancestry, of play and joy, of communal dreaming, of wonderment—in our vision of a transformed world?

The enormity of these questions must not offer an excuse to do nothing or to throw up our hands when we see harms unfolding in the classroom—"It's just a reflection of the world outside. Nothing to be done in here." Rather, it's a call to think critically about how those harms emerge from the world and how they build a world in turn. If folks who call for social change don't see school spaces as central to the struggle, they're missing a big part of the picture. And if folks who call for transformed schools don't see that work as one stone amid a broader rushing river, they're missing a big part of the picture. I think (hope, pray) that a lot of teachers and principals may read this book and think, "Oh, there is so much I have to do to change the way things are done at my school." That would be lovely. But what I also hope you realize at this point is that the things that happen in schools are a broader reflection of the society we have all committed to making and participating in, and therefore it's incumbent upon all of us to think about how to change it from wherever we sit. As Savannah Shange writes, "If we take schools as one of the many organs of the state's anatomy, the cellular wall that separates it from the jailhouse and the social services office, the military bunker and the hospital ward becomes more porous, leaving us with far fewer problems that can be solved by 'students' and 'teachers.'"[24]

So what can we learn, for instance, from abolitionist movements central to the current iteration of the Black freedom struggle? Abolitionist writers and thinkers have made clear that the vision of abolition is as much about *building* as it is about *taking away.* As Mariame Kaba and Andrea J. Ritchie write, calls for dismantling carceral systems are also an index for a robust creative impulse, the imperative to *make* and *create:* "meeting basic needs that include housing, health care, access to care for disabled people, childcare, elder care, a basic guaranteed income, and accessible, sustainable living-wage jobs that enable people to prevent, escape, intervene in, and transform the conditions that make violence possible."[25] The critique is implicitly about divestiture and investiture at the same time. Abolition is "not just about prisons or even police, but the entire world they reflect and produce."[26] The problems you've read about in this book—the ways that Black and Indigenous young people have been controlled, surveilled, and belittled in schools, the ways they have been deemed incapable of sophisticated thought, the ways they've been dismissed as lazy and doomed to the bottom of capitalist hierarchy—those problems emerge from a carceral world, a world that constantly invests in punishment, policing, and criminalization. Building systems of teaching and learning that nourish and celebrate Indigenous and Black youth requires attention to the world that would slay us with a thousand cuts—the systems and structures we aim to tackle through an abolitionist lens. And abolitionists would be wise to attend to the major role schools have played in normalizing punitive culture from our earliest days, as well as, in the other direction, the abolitionist counterspaces that young people, educators, and community activists are building that have much to teach us.

Education scholar Bettina Love has written extensively about how this work can be centered in classrooms and in the everyday decisions of teachers. "Abolitionist teaching," she writes, "is the practice of working in solidarity with communities of color while drawing on the imagination, creativity, refusal, (re)membering, visionary thinking, healing, rebellious spirit, boldness, determination, and subversiveness of abolitionists to eradicate injustice in and outside of schools."[27] In his essay "Are We Ready for 'School' Abolition?" my friend and colleague David O. Stovall has taken this thinking a step further, arguing that school itself has to be abolished—because what we have defined as "school" in this country is "part and parcel of the larger projects of settler colonialism and white supremacy/racism."[28] In order to transform *education*—an endeavor that is expansive, inclusive, justice-oriented, loving, and aimed at liberation and cultivating good relations with our relatives and lands and waters—schooling, inextricably bound with systems of oppression, has to go. "Given the constraints and foundations of state-sanctioned violence as 'schooling,'" Stovall asks, "can education happen in the institution commonly known as 'school'?"[29] Stovall acknowledges that this critical question is a challenging one (not least because it leaves us to ask, "What do we call the places where education happens if we are abolishing 'school'?"),[30] but that doesn't make it any less imperative. He is pushing us to both "build and resist" in a manner that is both "imminent and in perpetuity."[31] Stovall is inviting us to understand abolition not as a destination or as an act of destruction, but as a set of experiments—as a type of creative and rebellious play. This requires a commitment not only to imagining an otherwise but to enacting that otherwise in every way imaginable, relentlessly, collectively, and in the spirit of pleasure and resilience. In this way, we stand to not only *take* power; we are able to *make* power.[32]

The movement to change how we think about teaching and learning is also bound up in how we think about land and sovereignty. Just as "Black Lives Matter" became a rallying cry to encapsulate decades of freedom struggles, "Land Back" has become a succinct way to talk about Indigenous sovereignty and rematriation.[33] On its face, Land Back involves a straightforward demand: return the lands comprising current settler states to the Indigenous nations that stewarded them for innumerable generations prior to colonization. But just as *abolition* calls on us to reimagine the entire power structure itself, so too does *Land Back* require us to think beyond mere transfer of ownership from private or government entities to tribal governance, and to actually strive for a fundamentally different relationship with our lands and waters. "When we say 'Land Back' we aren't asking for just the ground, or for a piece of paper that allows us to tear up and pollute the earth," write organizers Nickita Longman (Salteaux), Emily Riddle (Nehiyaw), Alex Wilson (Opaskwayak Cree Nation), and Saima Desai. "We want the system that is land to be alive so that it can perpetuate itself, and perpetuate us as an extension of itself. That's what we want back: our place in keeping land alive and spiritually connected."[34] Wilson specifies that transforming systems of teaching and learning are implicated in the idea of Land Back, because "with land comes knowledge. Our knowledge, cosmologies (how we understand ourselves within the wider multiverse), and all of the relational structures that connect to that knowledge have been impacted and, to some degree, severed by colonialism. When we say 'Land Back,' we are acknowledging and invoking those ancient knowledge systems and calling for a validation of them in our contemporary times."[35]

Through this lens, "land" is not the same as "property." In fact, we might understand it as the exact opposite. Property means private ownership, tied to enclosure and ultimately linked to capitalism. Scholar Mishuana Goeman (Tonawanda Band of Seneca) explains that we must "begin with land as meaning-making place because that is at the heart of indigenous identity, longing, and belonging. Indigenous peoples make place by relating both personal and communal experiences and histories to certain locations and landscapes—maintaining these spatial relationships is one of the most important components of politics and our identity."[36] In this sense, there is no way to build systems of education in which Indigenous learners can thrive without also cultivating right relation to the lands where that learning takes place, where lands, waters, and more-than-human relatives themselves are vital teachers, and the stories and peoples rooted in those lands are uplifted.

The call for Land Back is a call for Indigenous sovereignty, but not in a way that simply mirrors Western statecraft. Through the lens of Western state politics, the concept of "sovereignty" is rooted in the right to exclude, to mark out territorial borders, and to destroy, as Mohawk feminist scholar Audra Simpson has written—to "have absolute arbitrariness at one's disposal."[37] Indigenous ways of being and knowing offer different visions of what "sovereignty" can mean, where sovereignty is not a fixed term or concept but embedded in social relations that change over time and across place.[38] "Indigenous peoples define themselves through relatedness to each other as families, as clans and nations, in relationship to territory. . . . This fact renders sovereignty as a form of relationality rather than a violent claim of property, exclusion, and a right to kill."[39]

Leanne Betasamosake Simpson reminds us that matters of land, of stewardship and rematriation, are not parallel to matters of transformative education; from an Indigenous perspective, they are central. The land, she writes, is both the fundamental context on which learning occurs and the relational basis *through* which learning as a process occurs. "Indigenous education," Simpson writes, "is not Indigenous or education from within our intellectual traditions unless it comes through the land," which includes a relationship with the spiritual world and ancestral knowledge.[40] Thinking through the demands of Land Back as a lens on education, then, calls on us to envision modes of teaching, learning, and relationship in which children and elders and everyone in between are in a nourishing kinship with the land instead of an extractive one. It's a vision that centers care instead of violent exploitation; attentive listening instead of competition and domination; humility and wisdom instead of punishment, coercion, and belittlement; intergenerational study instead of hierarchy.

In this country, schools as institutions have never been for us. In their foundations they are places for Black and Indigenous personhood to be met with denial, disappearance, and repression, places where young people learn the language of a settler society built on racist hierarchies. That's a problem for Black and Indigenous youth—in some instances, it has destroyed their lives. But it's also a problem for anybody who doesn't want to be complicit in the ongoing maintenance of a violent social order.

The good news is that people made it, and people can unmake it—and make new things. Indeed, as Black feminist scholar Robyn Maynard makes clear, the *making* and the *unmaking* are two strands of the same double helix, happening at the same time. This is a basic premise of abolitionism.

> World-ending and world-making can occur, are occurring, have always occurred, simultaneously. Given that racial and ecological violence are interwoven and inextricable from one another, more now than ever, Black and Indigenous communities—who are globally positioned as "first to die" within the climate crisis—are also on the front lines of world-making practices that threaten to overthrow the current (death-making) order of things. Put otherwise, our communities, quite literally the post-apocalyptic survivors of world-endings already, are best positioned to imagine what this may be.[41]

We can make educational spaces that are not for the White supremacist settler state. We can make schools for *us*—schools that are loving and nourishing, schools that celebrate our languages and cultural histories and intergenerational bonds, schools that teach stewardship and care of the land and of one another. To Stovall's point about school abolition, these spaces might not even end up looking much like the "schools" we know; they might look like freedom schools, or survival schools, they might be outside in the meadow or on the block, they might have protest and grandparents and frybread and black-eyed peas and children teaching and teachers getting some damn rest. These might need to be fugitive schools—schools on the run.[42] But if we take seriously these two ideas, abolition and Land Back—at once movements, demands, political frameworks, and radical dreams—and if we take seriously the idea that schools are places where we build worlds, then we have to have really grand visions for building *schools for us*. A training on implicit bias, a tweak to the syllabus, a professional development where teachers read and discuss a book (even this one!) ain't gonna cut it. *Schools for us* means schools that are rooted in and exemplars of the systems of care at the core of the abolitionist demand, and that are rooted in and exemplars of right relations with the land and principles of Indigenous sovereignty. Or to put it as plainly as I possibly can: if you're going to be serious about transforming education, you have to be serious about transforming the world.

What does striving for those transformed relationships *look* like? What does it feel like? To answer that, I want to close by talking a little bit about braiding.

Tugging at the Roots

How can you have history without braids?

—RAYCH JACKSON[43]

In June 2020, I saw a piece of art by Sarah Ayaqi Whalen-Lunn (Iñupiaq) that I have thought about ever since. It's a drawing of two women, one Black and one Indigenous, standing back-to-back. Their chins are slightly lifted and they gaze off into the distance, surrounded by thinly outlined leaves and climbing flowers reminiscent of Whalen-Lunn's work as a skin-stitch practitioner. Each of them wears their hair in braids, and as their hair meets in the space between their backs, it is braided together.

In *Braiding Sweetgrass,* her love letter to botany, motherhood, and Indigenous ecology, Robin Wall Kimmerer opens by describing the titular process—twisting and plaiting sweetgrass, which is a sacred medicine:

> The sweetest way is to have someone else hold the end so that you pull gently against each other, all the while leaning in, head to head, chatting and laughing, watching each other's hands, one holding steady while the other shifts the slim bundles over one another, each in its turn. Linked by sweetgrass, there is reciprocity between you, linked by sweetgrass, the holder as vital as the braider.[44]

To close this book, I want to extend Kimmerer's metaphor of *braiding* as a way to think differently about spaces of teaching and learning. The poet in me can't help but note that *braiding* holds a bit of a slant rhyme with *banking*, another famous metaphor for thinking about teaching and learning practices. In his 1970 book *Pedagogy of the Oppressed,* Brazilian educator and critical theorist Paulo Freire critiqued what he called the "banking model" of education, in which the teacher is the sole keeper of knowledge. "Education thus becomes an act of depositing, in which the students are the depositories and the teacher is the depositor."[45] Freire's idea has long influenced educators precisely because the metaphor works so well, on multiple levels. It's not only that the concept of "banking" helps us understand the unidirectional passivity of this mode of learning. It's also that banking is bound up with so much else: capitalism, needless and heedless accumulation, the theft of land and bodies.

I humbly offer that *braiding* allows us a metaphor to think about a different mode of teaching and learning, a lens for reflecting on the ways we are connected to one another and as a practice that teaches us something about how we can be teachers and learners in community. Although braiding is by no means a universal practice among Black or Native people, it is a place where we converge; a braid can represent the relationship between mind, body, and spirit, or can represent pride in oneself and one's community, or can be an act of radical Lordeian self-care. As historian Robin D. G. Kelley tells us, braiding is, rather magically, "both a communal and intimate act."[46] Not coincidentally, it's a practice that has been subject to surveillance, banishment, and punishment. In firsthand accounts of boarding schools, many Native elders and memoirists describe braids being cut off as one of the first formative moments of trauma that would come to define the residential school experience.[47] "I cried aloud, shaking my head all the while until I felt the cold blades of the scissors against my neck, and heard them gnaw off one of my thick braids," wrote Zitkála-Šá in 1921. "Then I lost my spirit."[48] In the contemporary era, Native students and their families have had to go to court to fight against school district demands that they cut their hair or face punishment.[49] Black students wearing braids to school can be subject to mockery, being called dirty, or outright bans leading to detention or suspension.[50]

That braids have met such sanctions is telling. Damien Sojoyner observes that, in writing about the education system and its many harms against us, scholars and activists depict "the state in an offensive posture in relationship to a fledgling, reactionary group of helpless people." But, he asks, "What if the looking glass were reversed? That is, what if technologies of punishment and control were utilized by owners of capital, political leaders, and their ilk out of fear of what power relationships would look like in a society that was not built upon massive wealth disparities, racial terrorism, and sexual violence?"[51] If braiding—something so natural, quotidian, ancient, and lovely—requires such control, there must be something magic, dangerous, and insurgent about it. So what can we learn from braiding? Of hair, of sweetgrass, of stories? What can we learn from the many ways in which we are interwoven? What does braiding offer us—not as a prescriptive set of instructions, but as seeds scattered on a path through the woods, as a hand outstretched in invitation?

Braids have stayed with us, through it all. And so braiding teaches *survivance,* the term from Chippewa scholar Gerald Vizenor that nestles somewhere between survival, resistance, and "an active sense of presence over historical absence," a "continuance of stories"—being here, still, when you could have been anything but.[52] I think, for instance, of stories about enslaved people braiding seeds into their hair—grains of rice, seeds of okra or millet—something nourishing and familiar to carry across the Atlantic, the promise of continuance in the face of a fate worse than death.[53] A gift of the land. I think of these narratives as origin stories, parables, creation myths. They are meant to teach us something about the wisdom of mothers, who understood how to weave together art and body to ensure there would be something to hold on to, who used braids as a means to protect something cherished.

Braiding requires intimacy and attention to the *embodied self.* It requires leaning forward over a seated person who trusts you, or attending to how tight is too tight, covering your fingers in something sweet-smelling and touching it tenderly to the scalp—someone else's, or your own. Braids teach us to remember our bodies and the bodies of those around us: that before anything else, they require care. They require food to eat, water to drink, a safe place to rest when they are aching and tired. They are not monstrosities that require discipline and punishment; they are gifts—from God, from Creator, from the miracles of the land and evolution and childbirth—that require space to dance and music to dance to. Our physical selves move against the backdrop of the other bodies we share space with and the cradle of the more-than-human world and our relatives in it.

Braiding takes time, attention, skill, and forethought—and therefore braiding is an expression of love. Jas Morgan (Cree-Métis-Saulteaux) describes *sâkihitowask,* a Cree word for "love medicine," and what they see as the centrality of love in any Indigenous politics. "Like my kin before me, I would argue that the project of Indigenous survivance is nothing, is inanimate, without an ethics of love and kinship as a guiding principle."[54] I read Morgan's invocation of love not as "soft" and squishy, but as rigorous; I think of one of my great teachers, Sara Lawrence-Lightfoot, who told me that when we approach our work with love—with what she calls the "search for goodness"—it allows us a fuller picture of the people and places we are encountering: "I want to know what's good here. What's worthy here. What's strong here. What's resilient here. Where the survival roots come from, and where the creative and expressive roots come from that produced this community and these people."[55]

Thinking about love also encourages us to envision the many ways we can, do, and must relate to one another that are *not* rooted in shared struggle and pain. Sewsen Igbu, Shanna Peltier, Ashley Caranto Morford, and Kaitlin Rizarri—a working group of women of color in the humanities at the University of Toronto—wrote about this in a way that I found deeply moving when I first read it. They point out that Black and Indigenous scholars run the risk of talking and writing

> as if our kinship and collaboration can only, and do only, occur because of the violence of white supremacist structures and systems. . . . Certainly, the pain in our communities can bring us together in collective pursuits of justice. However, our kin-

> ship connections and desires to be in community are not—and should not be—inextricably bound to whiteness and violence.[56]

So, yes, if I love you, I have to make you conscious of the things you don't see, as James Baldwin says.[57] But also, if I love you, I want to take a walk with you, I want to bake you your favorite thing, I want to tell you about a really good movie I just saw. I want to see and celebrate all the ways you shine—the special gifts and talents that make you who you are. I want to see you jump and hug a tree and tap your toes. I want you to thrive, to prosper in your health and in the pursuit of your great joys. That's what love is. That's what braiding teaches us. And any teacher, any policymaker, any person in power who doesn't regard kids with love doesn't deserve to be near them. Love is the baseline. It's not extra, and it's not optional, and it's not something you learn from a professional development session or diversity workshop. Love is fundamental.

By now, maybe you see that I'm not talking only about hair, and I'm not talking only about braiding, but about weaving,[58] about all the things we tug, pull, tie, and knit together. Education scholars Gloria Snively and Wanosts'a7 Lorna Williams (Lil'wat of the St'at'yem'c First Nation) write that the structure of a braid itself represents a form of interdependency, each strand nestled with the others and defined in relation to the others. "Linked by braiding, there is a certain reciprocity amongst strands, all the strands hold together. Each strand remains a separate entity, a certain tension is required, but all strands come together to form the whole."[59]

I am seven years old. My mother sends me to Miss Agnes to braid my hair. She scolds me in her Belizean accent, working her fingers through the knots in my head. In our kitchen, I watch as my mother flicks a lighter and singes the ends of her own braids, and I feel that I am witnessing something secret and holy. In another woman's kitchen, my brother and I drink Kool-Aid and play with her son as she braids my mother's hair. Braiding calls us in close. When we are grown and my brother's heart is hurting, I take down his braids and wash his hair in the sink so that it can be done up again, and it's like seeing the back of my own neck for the first time. Braiding ushers in the impossible. My friends and I enter a new place and feel frightened, and we hold hands, braiding our fingers together. I am on the other side of the world from the lands where I was born, and poet Anne-Marie Te Whiu greets me with a smile and a basket she has woven, braiding flax into a vessel I will later use to hold a small altar after my grandmother becomes an ancestor. A friend has had a baby and the world is small and sick and she is having a hard time of it, and I think good thoughts for her and for her new daughter as I braid the puffy dough into a chocolate babka, something sweet among bitter days. My beloved looks over my scalp with a rattail comb and a squint, pulling the strands of the plaits free slowly, so as not to hurt me or snag my edges. My mother, now all gray, comes to my house with something good for me to eat, and has brought the spray bottle to sit between my knees.

We can, and must, build schools for us. They might be schools on the run—for now, or for a long time. But we have each other, and we have all the pieces we need. We just have to braid them together.

ACKNOWLEDGMENTS

Completing this book took me a long time, and so I'm even more terrified than usual to forget to thank someone. Nevertheless, it's still a joy to have the opportunity to thank the many people who helped me bring it to fruition.

Thanks to Elizabeth Méndez Berry for being on this journey with me, for taking a leap of faith, and for your immense trust. Many of my editors have become friends but it turns out to be a rarer thing for a friend to become an editor, and I'm glad it happened to me. Thanks to Chris Jackson, Oma Beharry, and everyone at One World—designers, copy editors, those whose labor is seen and unseen—who brought this book to life.

If you're like I was before I became an author, you may read acknowledgments and find yourself puzzled as to why people are thanking their agents so profusely. And then, if you're me, one day you win the agent lottery and find yourself with a champion like Chris Parris-Lamb. Steadfast believer, discerning thinker, exquisite reader, patient listener. Thank you.

Many brilliant and generous people read early versions of this manuscript in whole or in part and gave me their honest feedback. What a gift! Special thanks to those who participated in a manuscript workshop with me: Bryan McKinley Jones Brayboy, Eve Tuck, and Crystal Lynn Webster, and my very kind colleague and friend Ryan Jobson, who facilitated. Nadirah Farah Foley read early portions of this manuscript and offered generous feedback, and also assisted me in triple-checking Latin translations. Elizabeth Reese brought her legal expertise to bear in reading early portions as well, and offered crucial (and generous) analysis. Thanks to my other amazing readers: Hanif Abdurraqib, Bill Ayers, Mahogany Browne, Charlene Carruthers, Ta-Nehisi Coates, Caleb Gayle, Adrienne Keene, Nate Marshall, Reuben Miller, Shaun Ossei-Owusu, Laurence Ralph, Clint Smith, David O. Stovall, Amanda Tachine, Elizabeth Todd-Breland, and Tristan Walker. And my co-working buddies: Elizabeth Acevedo, Josie Duffy Rice, Safia Elhillo, and Clint Smith.

Samhitha Krishnan is one of the most amazing people I have ever worked with, for many reasons, but as it pertains to this project, she aided in an early literature review and once texted me offering to climb over a filing cabinet in the library to get to a book, which symbolizes so much about her.

Ena Alvarado did a phenomenal job fact-checking this text with a dizzying diligence and attention to detail. Without Kia Turner and Alyssa Mendez, my references for this book would be an unreadable mess peppered with bold highlighted notes that say things like "PAGE????" Kia also offered thoughtful, substantive comments on the manuscript. Becca Estrella very kindly made time to head to the Library Company of Philadelphia to track down the Josiah Clark Nott primary sources I needed.

Arianne Young makes all things possible, from helping me guard my time to write to managing the sprawling logistics of my calendar to lending a gentle nudge, good advice, and reminders to eat and sleep.

I was fortunate enough during the preparation of this manuscript to receive fellowships and support from the Spencer Foundation and the National Academy of Education, MacDowell, and New America.

Terrance Lafromboise, thank you to you and your mother for trusting me with Brendon's story, for speaking with me, for your kindness and honesty, and for all you do every day in your community.

I owe a debt of gratitude to the staff of the Georgia Archives and a special thanks to Kelly Zacovic of the City of Savannah Municipal Archives, both for helping me try to uncover details about the life and death of Julia Grant. Kelly, I may never meet you, but your kindness meant a lot. Thanks to the entire staff of the University of Chicago

Library for their assistance, and sorry for hoarding so many books for so long.

Thanks to all who have supported me at the University of Chicago, including my former colleagues at the School of Social Service Administration, my current colleagues in the Department of Race, Diaspora, and Indigeneity, and everyone at the Center for the Study of Race, Politics, and Culture. I'm especially thankful to my chair, Cathy Cohen, for securing funds for me to hold a manuscript workshop, and to my departmental writing buddies, Joyce Bell, Adrienne Brown, and Ryan Jobson. Thank you to all of my students for motivating me, inspiring me, keeping me sharp, and for co-creating the space for me to work through many of the ideas in this book over the course of years.

Thanks to Tabia Yapp and the team at Beotis for their years of support.

The folks who hold me down every day and keep me from spontaneously combusting: you know who you are, and I love you dearly, to the ends of the earth. My biological family, my chosen family, my ancestral and political family: I am because you are.

For Damon, no words could ever be enough.

BIBLIOGRAPHY

Adams, David Wallace. *Education for Extinction: American Indians and the Boarding School Experience, 1875–1928.* Lawrence: University Press of Kansas, 1995.

Adams, William, and Julie Samuels. *Tribal Youth in the Federal Justice System.* Washington, D.C.: Urban Institute Justice Policy Center, May 2011. www.urban.org/sites/default/files/publication/27426/412369-Tribal-Youth-in-the-Federal-Justice-System.PDF.

Addams, Jane. "Why Women Should Vote." *Ladies' Home Journal,* January 1910. digital.janeaddams.ramapo.edu/items/show/6155.

Agassiz, Louis. "The Diversity of Origin of the Human Races." *Christian Examiner* (Boston), July 1850. tile.loc.gov/storage-services/service/ll/llmlp/Diversity-of-Origin/Diversity-of-Origin.pdf.

Ajilore, Olugbenga. "Native Americans Deserve More Attention in the Police Violence Conversation." Urban Institute, December 4, 2017. www.urban.org/urban-wire/native-americans-deserve-more-attention-police-violence-conversation.

Akee, Randall, Sue K. Stockly, William Darity Jr., Darrick Hamilton, and Paul Ong. "The Role of Race, Ethnicity and Tribal Enrolment on Asset Accumulation: An Examination of American Indian Tribal Nations." *Ethnic and Racial Studies* 40, no. 11 (September 2017): 1939–60. doi.org/10.1080/01419870.2016.1216141.

Alagraa, Bedour. "The Interminable Catastrophe." *Offshoot,* March 1, 2021. offshootjournal.org/the-interminable-catastrophe.

Alderman, Michael. "Effectively Keep Students Engaged with SLANT." KIPP NJ (blog), April 3, 2014. blog.kippnj.org/2014/04/03/effectively-keep-students-engaged-with-slant.

Allen, Douglas W. "Establishing Economic Property Rights by Giving Away an Empire." *Journal of Law and Economics* 62, no. 2 (May 2019): 251–80. doi.org/10.1086/703464.

Alperin, Elijah, and Jeanne Batalova. "European Immigrants in the United States." Migration Policy Institute, August 1, 2018. www.migrationpolicy.org/article/european-immigrants-united-states-2016.

Alvarado, Gabriela. "The Penn Museum Must End Abuse of the Morton Collection." *Daily Pennsylvanian,* June 25, 2020. www.thedp.com/article/2020/06/penn-museum-samuel-morton-collection-repatriation-nagpra-skulls-racist-science.

American Civil Liberties Union. "RE: Loleta Union School District's Violations of Title VI of the Civil Rights Act of 1964, Title II of the Americans with Disabilities Act, and Section 504 of the Rehabilitation Act of 1973." Memo to the U.S. Department of Education, Office for Civil Rights, December 18, 2013. www.aclunc.org/sites/default/files/2013.12.18%20Loleta%20OCR%20Complaint.pdf.

American Psychological Association Zero Tolerance Task Force. "Are Zero Tolerance Policies Effective in the Schools? An Evidentiary Review and Recommendations." *American Psychologist* 63, no. 9 (2008): 852–62. doi.org/10.1037/0003-066X.63.9.852.

American Tract Society. *The Freedman's Third Reader.* Boston: American Tract Society, 1866.

Anderson, Gary Clayton. *Massacre in Minnesota: The Dakota War of 1862, the Most Violent Ethnic Conflict in American History.* Norman: University of Oklahoma Press, 2019.

Anderson, James D. *The Education of Blacks in the South, 1860–1935.* Chapel Hill: University of North Carolina Press, 1988.

Anderson, Linnea M. "'The Playground of Today Is the Republic of Tomorrow': Social Reform and Organized Recreation in the USA, 1890–1930's." *Encyclopedia of Pedagogy and Informal Education* (blog), 2006. infed.org/mobi/social-reform-and-organized-recreation-in-the-usa/.

Anderson, Melinda D. "Will the Push for Coding Lead to 'Technical Ghettos'?" *The Atlantic,* February 29, 2016. www.theatlantic.com/education/archive/2016/02/will-the-push-for-coding-lead-to-technical-ghettos/471300/.

Andrews, Benjamin F. *The Land Grant of 1862 and the Land-Grant Colleges.* Bulletin 1918, no. 13. Washington, D.C.: Government Printing Office, 1918.

Appiah, Kwame Anthony. "The Case for Capitalizing the *B* in Black." *The Atlantic,* June 18, 2020. www.theatlantic.com/ideas/archive/2020/06/time-to-capitalize-blackand-white/613159.

Apple, Rima D. "Liberal Arts or Vocational Training? Home Economics Education for Girls." In *Rethinking Home Economics: Women and the History of a Profession,* edited by Sarah Stage and Virginia B. Vincenti, 79–95. Ithaca, N.Y.: Cornell University Press, 1997.

Army Reserve. "Native American Heritage." www.usar.army.mil/NativeAmericanHeritage/.

Arvin, Maile. "Indigenous Feminist Notes on Embodying Alliance Against Settler Colonialism." *Meridians: Feminism, Race, Transnationalism* 18, no. 2 (October 2019): 335–357. muse.jhu.edu/article/746123.

Austin, Algernon. "Native Americans and Jobs: The Challenge and the Promise." Briefing Paper #370. Economic Policy Institute, December 17, 2013. www.epi.org/publication/bp370-native-americans-jobs/.

Bailyn, Bernard. *Voyagers to the West: A Passage in the Peopling of America on the Eve of the Revolution.* New York: Vintage, 1988.

Baldwin, Davarian L. *In the Shadow of the Ivory Tower: How Universities Are Plundering Our Cities.* New York: Bold Type, 2021.

Baldwin, James. "*The Black Scholar* Interviews: James Baldwin." *The Black Scholar* 5, no. 4 (1973): 33–42.

Bang, Megan, C. Montaño Nolan, and N. McDaid-Morgan. "Indigenous Family Engagement: Strong Families, Strong Nations." In *Handbook of Indigenous Education,* edited by Elizabeth Ann McKinley and Linda Tuhiwai Smith, 789–810. Singapore: Springer, 2019. doi.org/10.1007/978-981-10-3899-0_74.

Banneker, Benjamin. "To Thomas Jefferson from Benjamin Banneker, 19 August 1791." *Founders Online,* National Archives. founders.archives.gov/documents/Jefferson/01-22-02-0049.

Barker, Joanne. *Red Scare: The State's Indigenous Terrorist.* Oakland: University of California Press, 2021.

———. "For Whom Sovereignty Matters." In *Sovereignty Matters: Locations of Contestation and Possibility in Indigenous Struggles for Self-Determination,* edited by Joanne Barker, 1–33. Lincoln: University of Nebraska Press, 2005.

Barrows, Isabel C., ed. *Proceedings of the Ninth Annual Meeting of the Lake Mohonk Conference of Friends of the Indian.* Lake Mohonk Conference, 1891.

Barsh, Russel, and J. Youngblood Henderson. "Tribal Courts, the Model Code, and the Police Idea in American Indian Policy." *Law and Contemporary Problems* 40, no. 1 (January 1976): 25–60.

Bell, Derrick. *Silent Covenants: Brown v. Board of Education and the Unfulfilled Hopes for Racial Reform.* New York: Oxford University Press, 2004.

Bellamy, Francis. Essay on immigration. *The Illustrated American* 22, no. 9 (August 28, 1897): 258.

Belsha, Kalyn. "States and Cities Are Banning Hair Discrimination. Here's How That's Affecting Schools." *Chalkbeat,* January 16, 2020. www.chalkbeat.org/2020/1/16/21121830/states-and-cities-are-banning-hair-discrimination-here-s-how-that-s-affecting-schools.

"Benjamin Smith (1756–1826)." In "Slavery and the University." *The Carolina Story: A Virtual Museum of University History,* University of North Carolina, 2006. museum.unc.edu/exhibits/show/slavery/benjamin-smith--1756-1826-.

Bernstein, Robin. *Racial Innocence: Performing American Childhood from Slavery to Civil Rights.* New York: New York University Press, 2011.

Berry, Daina Ramey. *The Price for Their Pound of Flesh: The Value of the Enslaved, from Womb to Grave, in the Building of a Nation.* Boston: Beacon Press, 2017.

Bhandar, Brenna. "Property, Law, and Race: Modes of Abstraction." *UC Irvine Law Review* 4, no. 1 (March 2014): 203–18.

Bhandar, Brenna, and Rafeef Ziadah. "Acts and Omissions: Framing Settler Colonialism in Palestine Studies." *Jadaliyya,* January 14, 2016. www.jadaliyya.com/Details/32857.

Bhutta, Neil, Andrew C. Chang, Lisa J. Dettling, Joanne W. Hsu, and Julia Hewitt. "Disparities in Wealth by Race and Ethnicity in the 2019 Survey of Consumer Finances." *FEDS Notes.* Washington, D.C.: Board of Governors of the Federal Reserve System, September 28, 2020. doi.org/10.17016/2380-7172.2797.

Bickford, Annette. "The Merciful Executioner: Spectacles of Sexual Danger and National Reunification in the George Stinney Case, 1944." *Southern Anthropologist* 35, no. 1 (July 2010). egrove.olemiss.edu/southern_anthropologist/vol35/iss1/4.

Blackhawk, Maggie. "Federal Indian Law as Paradigm Within Public Law." *Harvard Law Review* 132, no. 7 (May 2019): 1787–1877. harvardlawreview.org/print/vol-132/federal-indian-law-as-paradigm-within-public-law/.

Blackhawk, Ned. *The Rediscovery of America: Native Peoples and the Unmaking of U.S. History.* New Haven, Conn.: Yale University Press, 2023.

Blackhorse, Amanda. "One Year Later, and Still No Justice for Loreal Tsingine." *ICT News,* September 13, 2018. ictnews.org/archive/blackhorse-one-year-later-still-no-justice-loreal-tsingine.

"Black Indigenous Solidarity: Decolonize and Defund," January 21, 2021. www.youtube.com/watch?v=yWeAovybXNs.

Blake, Jamilia J., Verna M. Keith, Wen Luo, Huong Le, and Phia Salter. "The Role of Colorism in Explaining African American Females' Suspension Risk." *School Psychology Quarterly* 32, no. 1 (2017): 118–30. doi.org/10.1037/spq0000173.

Bokenkamp, Kirsten, and Laurie A. Walker, *Empty Desks: Discipline and Policing in Montana's Public Schools.* ACLU Montana and University of Montana, December 2019. www.aclumontana.org/sites/default/files/aclu-education-report-2019-v13.pdf.

Bonilla-Silva, Eduardo. *Racism Without Racists: Color-Blind Racism and the Persistence of Racial Inequality in the United States.* Lanham, Md.: Rowman & Littlefield, 2010.

Boston Primary School Committee. *Report to the Primary School Committee, June 15, 1846, on the Petition of Sundry Colored Persons, for the Abolition of the Schools for Colored Children: With the City Solicitor's Opinion.* Boston: J. H. Eastburn, City Printer, 1846.

Brayboy, Bryan McKinley Jones. "Toward a Tribal Critical Race Theory in Education." *Urban Review* 37, no. 5 (December 2005): 425–46. doi.org/10.1007/s11256-005-0018-y.

Brayboy, Bryan McKinley Jones, and Jeremiah Chin. "'On the Development of Terrortory.'" *Contexts* 19, no. 3 (August 2020): 22–27. doi.org/10.1177/1536504220950397.

Brayboy, Bryan McKinley Jones, and Amanda R. Tachine. "Myths, Erasure, and Violence: The Immoral Triad of the Morrill Act." *Native American and Indigenous Studies* 8, no. 1 (2021): 139–44. doi.org/10.1353/nai.2021.a784826.

Brigham, Carl Campbell. "Intelligence Tests of Immigrant Groups." *Psychological Review* 37, no. 2 (1930): 158–65. doi.org/10.1037/h0072570.

———. *A Study of American Intelligence.* Princeton: Princeton University Press, 1923.

Brooks, Gwendolyn. "Introduction to 'We Real Cool.'" Academy of American Poets, May 3, 1983. soundcloud.com/poets-org/gwendolyn-brooks-introduction-to-we-real-cool.

Brown, Dorothy A. *The Whiteness of Wealth: How the Tax System Impoverishes Black Americans—and How We Can Fix It.* New York: Crown, 2022.

Brunhouse, Robert L. "Apprenticeship for Civilizations: The Outing System at the Carlisle Indian School," May 1939. Carlisle Indian School Digital Resource Center, Dickinson College Archives. carlisleindian.dickinson.edu/publications/apprenticeship-civilizations-outing-system-carlisle-indian-school-robert-brunhouse.

Bruyneel, Kevin. *Settler Memory: The Disavowal of Indigeneity and the Politics of Race in the United States.* Chapel Hill: University of North Carolina Press, 2021.

Buchli, Zoë, and Skylar Rispens. "Missoula Jury Confirms Galbreath Died by Suicide During Police Chase, Officer Cleared." *Missoulian,* April 29, 2022.

Bureau of Indian Affairs. *Annual Report of the Commissioner of Indian Affairs to the Secretary of the Interior for the Year 1859.* Washington, D.C.: George W. Bowman, 1860.

———. *Annual Report of the Commissioner of Indian Affairs to the Secretary of the Interior for the Year 1880.* Washington, D.C.: Government Printing Office, 1880. www.doi.gov/sites/doi.gov/files/T-21915.pdf.

———. *Annual Report of the Commissioner of Indian Affairs to the Secretary of the Interior for the Year 1882*. Washington, D.C.: Government Printing Office, 1882. www.doi.gov/sites/doi.gov/files/T-21917.pdf.

———. *Annual Report of the Commissioner of Indian Affairs to the Secretary of the Interior for the Year 1888*. Washington, D.C.: Government Printing Office, 1888. digitalcommons.csumb.edu/cgi/viewcontent.cgi?article=1025&context=hornbeck_usa_2_e.

———. *Annual Report of the Commissioner of Indian Affairs to the Secretary of the Interior for Year 1895*. Washington, D.C.: Government Printing Office, 1896. www.doi.gov/sites/doi.gov/files/T-21927.pdf.

———. *Annual Report of the Commissioner of Indian Affairs to the Secretary of the Interior for Year 1902*. Washington, D.C.: Government Printing Office, 1903. collections.lib.utah.edu/details?id=374024.

Byrd, Jodi A. *The Transit of Empire: Indigenous Critiques of Colonialism.* Minneapolis: University of Minnesota Press, 2011.

Byun, Soo-yong, Matthew J. Irvin, and Bethany A. Bell. "Advanced Math Course Taking: Effects on Math Achievement and College Enrollment." *Journal of Experimental Education* 83, no. 4 (2015): 439–68. doi.org/10.1080/00220973.2014.919570.

Cabral, Brian. "Linguistic Confinement: Rethinking the Racialized Interplay Between Educational Language Learning and Carcerality." *Race Ethnicity and Education* 26, no. 3 (2023): 277–97. doi.org/10.1080/13613324.2022.2069742.

Calderon, Dolores. "Uncovering Settler Grammars in Curriculum." *Educational Studies* 50, no. 4 (July 2014): 313–38. doi.org/10.1080/00131946.2014.926904.

Carby, Hazel V. "The Limits of Caste." *London Review of Books,* January 21, 2021. www.lrb.co.uk/the-paper/v43/n02/hazel-v.-carby/the-limits-of-caste.

Carey, Anthony Gene. *Sold Down the River: Slavery in the Lower Chattahoochee Valley of Alabama and Georgia.* Tuscaloosa: University of Alabama Press, 2011.

Carlos, Ann M., Donna L. Feir, and Angela Redish. "Indigenous Nations and the Development of the U.S. Economy: Land, Resources, and Dispossession." *Journal of Economic History* 82, no. 2 (June 2022): 516–55. doi.org/10.1017/S0022050722000080.

Carney, Judith A. *Black Rice: The African Origins of Rice Cultivation in the Americas.* Cambridge, Mass.: Harvard University Press, 2002.

Carr, Sarah. "How Flawed IQ Tests Prevent Kids from Getting Help in School." *The Hechinger Report,* March 28, 2024. hechingerreport.org/how-flawed-iq-tests-prevent-kids-from-getting-help-in-school/.

Carroll, Stephanie Russo, Ibrahim Garba, Oscar L. Figueroa-Rodríguez, Jarita Holbrook, Raymond Lovett, Simeon Materechera, Mark Parsons, et al. "The CARE Principles for Indigenous Data Governance." *Data Science Journal* 19, no. 1 (November 2020): 43. doi.org/10.5334/dsj-2020-043.

Carson, Homer S. "Penal Reform and Construction of the Western North Carolina Railroad, 1875–1892." *Journal of Appalachian Studies* 11, nos. 1–2 (2005), 205–25.

Carter, J. Kameron. "Other Worlds, Nowhere (or, The Sacred Otherwise)." In *Otherwise Worlds: Against Settler Colonialism and Anti-Blackness,* edited by Tiffany Lethabo King, Jenell Navarro, and Andrea Smith, 158–210. Durham, N.C.: Duke University Press, 2020. doi.org/10.1515/9781478012023-009.

Chang, David A. Y. O. "Where Will the Nation Be at Home? Race, Nationalisms, and Emigration Movements in the Creek Nation." In *Crossing Waters, Crossing Worlds:*

The African Diaspora in Indian Country, edited by Tiya Miles and Sharon P. Holland, 88–99. Durham, N.C.: Duke University Press, 2006.

Channing, Henry. "God Admonishing His People of Their Duty, as Parents and Masters. A Sermon, Preached at New-London, December 20th, 1786. Occasioned by the Execution of Hannah Ocuish, a Mulatto Girl, Aged 12 Years and 9 Months. For the Murder of Eunice Bolles, Aged 6 Years and 6 Months." New London, Conn., 1787.

Chen, David W., Mark Walker, and Kenneth P. Vogel. "How Sports Betting Upended the Economies of Native American Tribes." *New York Times,* February 10, 2023. www.nytimes.com/2023/02/10/sports/sports-betting-native-american-tribes.html.

Chen, Duke. "Tribal Casino Revenue Sharing in Other States." Research report. Connecticut Office of Legislative Research, August 13, 2019. www.cga.ct.gov/2019/rpt/pdf/2019-R-0135.pdf.

Chetty, Raj, Nathaniel Hendren, Maggie R. Jones, and Sonya R. Porter. "Race and Economic Opportunity in the United States: An Intergenerational Perspective." *Quarterly Journal of Economics* 135, no. 2 (May 2020): 711–83. doi.org/10.1093/qje/qjz042.

Child, Brenda J. *Boarding School Seasons: American Indian Families, 1900–1940.* Lincoln: University of Nebraska Press, 2000.

Child, Lydia Maria. *The Freedmen's Book.* Boston: Ticknor and Fields, 1865.

Chin, Jeremiah. "Red Law, White Supremacy: Cherokee Freedmen, Tribal Sovereignty, and the Colonial Feedback Loop." *John Marshall Law Review* [*UIC Law Review*] 47, no. 4 (2014): 1227–68. repository.law.uic.edu/lawreview/vol47/iss4/5.

Chireau, Yvonne P. *Black Magic: Religion and the African American Conjuring Tradition.* Berkeley: University of California Press, 2006.

City of Savannah, Georgia, Records. Recorder's Court, 1903. City of Savannah Research Library and Municipal Archives.

Clowse, Barbara Barksdale. *Brainpower for the Cold War: The Sputnik Crisis and National Defense Education Act of 1958.* Westport, Conn.: Greenwood Press, 1981.

Coleman, Arica L. *That the Blood Stay Pure: African Americans, Native Americans, and the Predicament of Race and Identity in Virginia.* Bloomington: Indiana University Press, 2013.

Coles, Justin A., Esther O. Ohito, Keisha L. Green, and Jamila Lyiscott. "Fugitivity and Abolition in Educational Research and Practice: An Offering." *Equity & Excellence in Education* 54, no. 2 (2021): 103–11. doi.org/10.1080/10665684.2021.1972595.

Collins, Patricia Hill. *Black Feminist Thought: Knowledge, Consciousness, and the Politics of Empowerment.* 2nd ed. New York: Routledge, 2000.

Colmant, Stephen, Lahoma Schultz, Rockey Robbins, Peter Ciali, Julie Dorton, and Yvette Rivera-Colmant. "Constructing Meaning to the Indian Boarding School Experience." *Journal of American Indian Education* 43, no. 3 (2004): 22–40.

Committee of the Virginia General Assembly. "A Bill for the More General Diffusion of Knowledge," June 18, 1779. founders.archives.gov/documents/Jefferson/01-02-02-0132-0004-0079.

Conley, Alia, and Nancy Gaarder. "Man Who Died After Being Tased by Police Was Mentally Ill, Off His Medication and Lost in Omaha, His Mother Says." *Omaha World-Herald,* June 6, 2017. omaha.com/news/crime/man-who-died-after-being-tased-by-police-was-mentally-ill-off-his-medication-and/article_288c7d14-49d7-11e7-9ed4-83fc5e66d19e.html.

Connor, Carol McDonald, Shayne B. Piasta, Stephanie Glasney, Christopher Schatschneider, Elizabeth Crowe, Phyllis Underwood, Barry Fishman, and Frederick J. Morrison. "Individualizing Student Instruction Precisely: Effects of Child × Instruction Interactions on First Graders' Literacy Development." *Child Development* 80, no. 1 (2009): 77–100.

"Consul Asks for Troops." *Hattiesburg Daily News* (Mississippi), October 3, 1907.

Convict Leasing and Labor Project. "The Sugar Land 95." Last modified August 2020. www.cllptx.org/sugarland95.

Coolidge, Calvin. "Whose Country Is This?" *Good Housekeeping,* February 1921.

Cooper, Anderson. "KIPP Offers Learning with a Twist." Transcript. *Anderson Cooper 360*. CNN, April 12, 2006. https://transcripts.cnn.com/show/acd/date/2006-04-12/segment/01.

Cooper, Tanya Asim. "Racial Bias in American Foster Care: The National Debate." *Marquette Law Review* 97, no. 2 (2013): 215.

Copur-Gencturk, Yasemin, Joseph R. Cimpian, Sarah Theule Lubienski, and Ian Thacker. "Teachers' Bias Against the Mathematical Ability of Female, Black, and Hispanic Students." *Educational Researcher* 49, no. 1 (January 2020): 30–43. doi.org/10.3102/0013189X19890577.

Coulthard, Glen Sean. *Red Skin, White Masks: Rejecting the Colonial Politics of Recognition.* Minneapolis: University of Minnesota Press, 2014.

Covello, Leonard. *The Heart Is the Teacher.* John D. Calandra Italian American Institute, Queens College, City University of New York, 2013. First published 1958 by McGraw-Hill (New York).

Cravens, Hamilton. *The Triumph of Evolution: American Scientists and the Heredity-Environment Controversy, 1900–1941.* Philadelphia: University of Pennsylvania Press, 1978.

Crawley, Ashon T. "Stayed | Freedom | Hallelujah." In *Otherwise Worlds: Against Settler Colonialism and Anti-Blackness,* edited by Tiffany Lethabo King, Jenell Navarro, and Andrea Smith, 27–37. Durham, N.C.: Duke University Press, 2020. doi.org/10.1515/9781478012023-002.

Cremin, Lawrence A. *American Education: The Colonial Experience, 1607–1783.* New York: HarperCollins, 1970.

———. *American Education: The National Experience, 1783–1876.* New York: HarperCollins, 1980.

Cross, Terry L. "Native Americans and Juvenile Justice: A Hidden Tragedy." *Poverty and Race* (PRRAC Poverty & Race Research Action Council) 17, no. 6 (2008): 19–22.

"CrossGen Conversation: Eve L. Ewing and Sara Lawrence-Lightfoot." Harvard Graduate School of Education, January 15, 2021. www.youtube.com/watch?v=C4vfghQ_6Rc.

Cubberley, Ellwood Patterson. *Changing Conceptions of Education.* New York: Houghton Mifflin, 1909.

Curtis, Henry Stoddard. *Education Through Play.* New York: Macmillan, 1915.

Curtis, Michael G., Annika S. Karlsen, and Leslie A. Anderson. "Transmuting Girls into Women: Examining the Adultification of Black Female Sexual Assault Survivors Through Twitter Feedback." *Violence Against Women* 29, no. 2 (February 2023): 321–46. doi.org/10.1177/10778012221083334.

Curtis, Thomas D. *Riches, Real Estate, and Resistance: How Land Speculation, Debt, and Trade Monopolies Led to the American Revolution.* 3rd ed. Malden, Mass.: Wiley, 2014.

Darby, Derrick, and John L. Rury. *The Color of Mind: Why the Origins of the Achievement Gap Matter for Justice.* Chicago: University of Chicago Press, 2018.

D'Arcus, Bruce. "The Urban Geography of Red Power: The American Indian Movement in Minneapolis–Saint Paul, 1968–70." *Urban Studies* 47, no. 6 (May 2010): 1241–55. doi.org/10.1177/0042098009360231.

D'Arcy, Janice. "Salecia Johnson, 6, Handcuffed After Tantrum: What's Wrong with This Picture?" *Washington Post,* April 18, 2012. www.washingtonpost.com/blogs/on-parenting/post/salecia-johnson-6-handcuffed-after-tantrum-whats-wrong-with-this-picture/2012/04/18/gIQAiUitQT_blog.html.

Darity, William A., Jr., and A. Kirsten Mullen. *From Here to Equality: Reparations for Black Americans in the Twenty-First Century.* Chapel Hill: University of North Carolina Press, 2020.

Darity, William, Jr., Darrick Hamilton, Mark Paul, Alan Aja, Anne Price, Antonio Moore, and Caterina Chiopris. *What We Get Wrong About Closing the Racial Wealth Gap.* Samuel DuBois Cook Center on Social Equity and Insight Center for Community Economic Development, April 2018. socialequity.duke.edu/wp-content/uploads/2019/10/what-we-get-wrong.pdf.

Davenport, Charles Benedict. *Heredity in Relation to Eugenics.* New York: Henry Holt, 1911. www.biodiversitylibrary.org/item/118734#page/9/mode/1up.

Day, James R. "School Men of the Hour." *American Education* 5, no. 1 (1902): 207–9.

De Forest, John William. *A Union Officer in the Reconstruction.* Archon Books, 1968. First published 1948 by Yale University Press (New Haven).

Deloria, Philip J. *Playing Indian.* New Haven, Conn.: Yale University Press, 2022. First published 1998 by Yale University Press (New Haven).

Deloria, Vine, Jr. *Custer Died for Your Sins: An Indian Manifesto.* New York: Macmillan, 1969.

———. *We Talk, You Listen. New Tribes, New Turf.* Lincoln: University of Nebraska Press, 2007. First published 1970.

Deloria, Vine, Jr., and Clifford M. Lytle. *American Indians, American Justice.* Austin: University of Texas Press, 1983.

———. *The Nations Within: The Past and Future of American Indian Sovereignty.* New York: Pantheon, 1984.

Department of the Tennessee and State of Arkansas. *Report of the General Superintendent of Freedmen, Department of the Tennessee and State of Arkansas, for 1864.* Memphis: Office General Superintendent of Freedmen, 1865. www.loc.gov/item/13022184/.

Dewbury, Adam. "The American School and Scientific Racism in Early American Anthropology." *Histories of Anthropology Annual* 3, no. 1 (2007): 121–47. doi.org/10.1353/haa.0.0026.

Diamond, John B., Antonia Randolph, and James P. Spillane. "Teachers' Expectations and Sense of Responsibility for Student Learning: The Importance of Race, Class, and Organizational Habitus." *Anthropology & Education Quarterly* 35, no. 1 (2004): 75–98. doi.org/10.1525/aeq.2004.35.1.75.

Díaz, Natalie. *Postcolonial Love Poem.* Minneapolis: Graywolf, 2020.

Dippel, Christian, Dustin Frye, and Bryan Leonard. "Property Rights Without Transfer

Rights: A Study of Indian Land Allotment." Working Paper 27479. National Bureau of Economic Research, July 2020. doi.org/10.3386/w27479.

Disare, Monica. "'No Excuses' No More? Charter Schools Rethink Discipline After Focus on Tough Consequences." *Chalkbeat New York,* March 7, 2016. ny.chalkbeat.org/2016/3/7/21095867/no-excuses-no-more-charter-schools-rethink-discipline-after-focus-on-tough-consequences.

Doran, Michael F. "Negro Slaves of the Five Civilized Tribes." *Annals of the Association of American Geographers* 68, no. 3 (September 1978): 335–50. www.jstor.org/stable/2561972.

Dorsey, Allison. *To Build Our Lives Together: Community Formation in Black Atlanta, 1875–1906.* Athens: University of Georgia Press, 2004.

Du Bois, W. E. B. *Black Reconstruction in America, 1860–1880.* New York: Free Press, 1997. First published 1935 by Harcourt, Brace (New York).

———. "The Hampton Idea (1906)." In *The Education of Black People: Ten Critiques, 1906–1960,* edited by Herbert Aptheker, 5–16. Amherst: University of Massachusetts Press, 1973.

———. *The Souls of Black Folk.* New Haven, Conn.: Yale University Press, 2015.

———. "The Souls of White Folk." In *Darkwater: Voices from Within the Veil,* 29–52. New York: Harcourt, Brace and Howe, 1920.

Dumas, Michael J. "'Losing an Arm': Schooling as a Site of Black Suffering." *Race Ethnicity and Education* 17, no. 1 (January 2014): 1–29. doi.org/10.1080/13613324.2013.850412.

Dunbar-Ortiz, Roxanne. *An Indigenous Peoples' History of the United States.* New ed. Boston: Beacon Press, 2023.

———. *Not "A Nation of Immigrants": Settler Colonialism, White Supremacy, and a History of Erasure and Exclusion.* Boston: Beacon Press, 2021.

Dunn, Richard S. *The Laws and Liberties of Massachusetts: Reprinted from the Unique Copy of the 1648 Edition in the Henry E. Huntington Library.* San Marino, Calif.: Huntington Library Press, 1998.

Dye, Eva Emery. *The Conquest: The True Story of Lewis and Clark.* Chicago: A. C. McClurg, 1902.

Eagle, Adam Fortunate. *Pipestone: My Life in an Indian Boarding School.* Norman: University of Oklahoma Press, 2012.

Ebeling, Eric R. "Massachusetts Education Laws of 1642, 1647, and 1648." In *Historical Dictionary of American Education.* Westport, Conn.: Greenwood Press, 1999.

Educational Records Bureau. "AABL What to Expect Video for PreK Applicants." January 26, 2016. vimeo.com/153145448.

Edwards, Torrie K. "From the Editorial Board: Tangled Discrimination in Schools: Binding Hair to Control Student Identity." *High School Journal* 103, no. 2 (2020): 53–56.

Egerton, Douglas R. *The Wars of Reconstruction: The Brief, Violent History of America's Most Progressive Era.* New York: Bloomsbury, 2015.

Ehrlich, Isaac, Adam Cook, and Yong Yin. "What Accounts for the US Ascendancy to Economic Superpower by the Early Twentieth Century? The Morrill Act–Human Capital Hypothesis." *Journal of Human Capital* 12, no. 2 (June 2018): 233–81. doi.org/10.1086/697512.

Eisenhower, Dwight D. "Transcript of the President's News Conference on Foreign and Domestic Matters." *New York Times,* October 31, 1957.

Ellis, Clyde. *To Change Them Forever: Indian Education at the Rainy Mountain Boarding School, 1893–1920*. Norman: University of Oklahoma Press, 1996.

Ellis, Richard J. *To the Flag: The Unlikely History of the Pledge of Allegiance.* Lawrence: University Press of Kansas, 2005.

Eltis, David, and David Richardson. *Atlas of the Transatlantic Slave Trade.* New Haven, Conn.: Yale University Press, 2015.

Emery, Jacqueline, ed. *Recovering Native American Writings in the Boarding School Press.* Lincoln: University of Nebraska Press, 2020.

Epstein, Rebecca, Jamilia Blake, and Thalia González. "Girlhood Interrupted: The Erasure of Black Girls' Childhood." Washington, D.C.: Center on Poverty and Inequality, Georgetown Law, June 2017. papers.ssrn.com/abstract=3000695.

Erdrich, Louise. "Indian Boarding School: The Runaways." In *Original Fire: Selected and New Poems.* New York: HarperCollins, 2009.

Estes, Nick. *Our History Is the Future: Standing Rock Versus the Dakota Access Pipeline, and the Long Tradition of Indigenous Resistance.* London: Verso, 2019.

Estes, Nick, Uahikea Maile, and Leanne Betasamosake Simpson. "Indigenous Solidarity with Palestine w/ Uahikea Maile and Leanne Betasamosake Simpson." *The Red Nation* (podcast), November 6, 2023. https://www.youtube.com/watch?v=IRaFbSRqe-o.

Eugenics Record Office. "College Courses in Genetics and Eugenics." In *Eugenical News* 1. Lancaster, Penn./Cold Spring Harbor, N.Y.: American Eugenics Society, 1916.

Evans, William N., and Julie H. Topoleski. "The Social and Economic Impact of Native American Casinos." Working Paper 9198. National Bureau of Economic Research, September 2002. doi.org/10.3386/w9198.

Ewing, Eve L. "Blue Bloods: America's Brotherhood of Police Officers." *Vanity Fair,* August 25, 2020. www.vanityfair.com/culture/2020/08/americas-brotherhood-of-police-officers.

———. "I'm a Black Scholar Who Studies Race. Here's Why I Capitalize 'White.'" *ZORA* (blog), July 2, 2020. zora.medium.com/im-a-black-scholar-who-studies-race-here-s-why-i-capitalize-white-f94883aa2dd3.

Faber, Eli. *The Child in the Electric Chair: The Execution of George Junius Stinney Jr. and the Making of a Tragedy in the American South.* Columbia: University of South Carolina Press, 2021.

Fairlie, Robert W. "Private Schools and 'Latino Flight' from Black Schoolchildren." *Demography* 39, no. 4 (2002): 655–74. doi.org/10.2307/3180825.

Farrow, Anne, Joel Lang, and Jenifer Frank. *Complicity: How the North Promoted, Prolonged, and Profited from Slavery.* New York: Random House, 2007.

FDR Presidential Library and Museum. "Great Depression Facts." www.fdrlibrary.org/great-depression-facts.

Fear-Segal, Jacqueline. "The Man on the Bandstand at Carlisle Indian Industrial School: What He Reveals About the Children's Experiences." In *Boarding School Blues,* edited by Clifford E. Trafzer, Jean A. Keller, and Lorene Sisquoc, 99–122. Lincoln: University of Nebraska Press, 2006.

Fear-Segal, Jacqueline, and Susan D. Rose, eds. *Carlisle Indian Industrial School: Indigenous Histories, Memories, and Reclamations.* Lincoln: University of Nebraska Press, 2016.

Feir, Donn. L., Rob Gillezeau, and Maggie E. C. Jones. "The Slaughter of the Bison and

Reversal of Fortunes on the Great Plains." Working Paper 30368. National Bureau of Economic Research, August 2022. doi.org/10.3386/w30368.

Feir, Donna, and Maggie E. C. Jones. "Repaying a Debt? The Performance of Morrill Act University Beneficiaries as Measured by Native Enrollment and Graduation Rates." *Native American and Indigenous Studies* 8, no. 1 (2021): 129–38. doi.org/10.1353/nai.2021.a784825.

Feiveson, Laura, and John Sabelhaus. "How Does Intergenerational Wealth Transmission Affect Wealth Concentration?" *FEDS Notes*. Washington, D.C.: Board of Governors of the Federal Reserve System, June 1, 2018. doi.org/10.17016/2380-7172.2209.

Ferguson, Russell, Martha Gever, Trinh T. Minh-ha, and Cornel West, eds. *Out There: Marginalization and Contemporary Cultures*. Cambridge, Mass.: MIT Press, 1992.

Ficker, Douglas J. "From *Roberts* to *Plessy:* Educational Segregation and the 'Separate but Equal' Doctrine." *Journal of Negro History* 84, no. 4 (October 1999): 301–14. doi.org/10.2307/2649034.

Fields, Karen E., and Barbara J. Fields. *Racecraft: The Soul of Inequality in American Life*. London: Verso, 2014.

Findlay, John M. "An Elusive Institution: The Birth of Indian Reservations in Gold Rush California." In *State and Reservation: New Perspectives on Federal Indian Policy*, edited by George Pierre Castile and Robert L. Bee, 13–37. Tucson: University of Arizona Press, 1992.

Finley, Chris. "Building Maroon Intellectual Communities." In *Otherwise Worlds: Against Settler Colonialism and Anti-Blackness*, edited by Tiffany Lethabo King, Jenell Navarro, and Andrea Smith, 362–69. Durham, N.C.: Duke University Press, 2020. doi.org/10.1515/9781478012023-021.

Fisk, Clinton Bowen. *Plain Counsels for Freedmen: In Sixteen Brief Lectures*. Boston: American Tract Society, 1866. loc.gov/item/08013310/.

Fixico, Donald L. *The Invasion of Indian Country in the Twentieth Century: American Capitalism and Tribal Natural Resources*. 2nd ed. Boulder: University Press of Colorado, 2011.

Florio, Gwen. "Nation Mourns Cobell While Blackfeet Grieve for Kennerly." *Montana Standard*, October 18, 2011. mtstandard.com/news/state-and-regional/nation-mourns-cobell-while-blackfeet-grieve-for-kennerly/article_0f62cc7a-f96b-11e0-9321-001cc4c03286.html.

Foley, Douglas E. "The Silent Indian as a Cultural Production." In *The Cultural Production of the Educated Person: Critical Ethnographies of Schooling and Local Practice*, edited by Bradley A. Levinson, Douglas E. Foley, and Dorothy C. Holland, 79–92. Albany: State University of New York Press, 1996.

Foner, Eric. *Reconstruction: America's Unfinished Revolution, 1863–1877*. New York: Harper & Row, 1988.

———. *The Second Founding: How the Civil War and Reconstruction Remade the Constitution*. New York: W. W. Norton, 2019.

Ford, Paul Leicester, ed. *The New-England Primer: A History of Its Origin and Development*. New York: Dodd, Mead, 1897.

Forsdick, Charles, and Christian Høgsbjerg. *Toussaint Louverture: A Black Jacobin in the Age of Revolutions*. London: Pluto Press, 2017.

Foucault, Michel. *Discipline and Punish: The Birth of the Prison.* Translated by Alan Sheridan. New York: Vintage, 1995.

Fox, Lindsay. "Seeing Potential: The Effects of Student–Teacher Demographic Congruence on Teacher Expectations and Recommendations." *AERA Open* 2, no. 1 (January–March 2016). doi.org/10.1177/2332858415623758.

Francis, Dania, Angela Oliveira, and Carey Dimmitt. "Do School Counselors Exhibit Bias in Recommending Students for Advanced Coursework?" *B.E. Journal of Economic Analysis & Policy* 19, no. 4 (July 2019). doi.org/10.1515/bejeap-2018-0189.

Francis, Dania V., and William A. Darity Jr. "Separate and Unequal Under One Roof: How the Legacy of Racialized Tracking Perpetuates Within-School Segregation." *RSF: Russell Sage Foundation Journal of the Social Sciences* 7, no. 1 (February 2021): 187–202. doi.org/10.7758/RSF.2021.7.1.11.

Francis, Dania V., and Christian E. Weller. "Retirement Inequality by Race and Ethnicity." *Public Policy & Aging Report* 31, no. 3 (August 2021): 83–88. doi.org/10.1093/ppar/prab009.

Franklin, Benjamin. "The Formation of the Grand Ohio Company [June? 1769]." University of Virginia Press, June 1, 1769. *Founders Online,* National Archives. founders.archives.gov/documents/Franklin/01-16-02-0083.

———. "Remarks Concerning the Savages of North America [Before 7 January 1784]." *Founders Online,* National Archives. founders.archives.gov/documents/Franklin/01-41-02-0280.

"The Freedman's Bureau! An Agency to Keep the Negro in Idleness at the Expense of the White Man. Twice Vetoed by the President, and Made a Law by Congress. Support Congress & You Support the Negro Sustain the President & You Protect the White Man." Still image, Pennsylvania, 1866. www.loc.gov/pictures/item/2008661698/.

Freire, Paulo. *Pedagogy of the Oppressed.* Thirtieth-anniversary edition. Translated by Myra Bergman Ramos. New York: Bloomsbury, 2000.

Frost, Joe L. *A History of Children's Play and Play Environments: Toward a Contemporary Child-Saving Movement.* New York: Routledge, 2009.

Fuente, Alejandro de la, and Ariela J. Gross. *Becoming Free, Becoming Black: Race, Freedom, and Law in Cuba, Virginia, and Louisiana.* Cambridge, England: Cambridge University Press, 2020.

Fuller, A. James. "'I Whipped Him a Second Time, Very Severely': Basil Manly, Honor, and Slavery at the University of Alabama." In *Slavery and the University: Histories and Legacies,* edited by Leslie M. Harris, James T. Campbell, and Alfred L. Brophy, 114–30. Athens: University of Georgia Press, 2019.

Gaddis, S. Michael. "Discrimination in the Credential Society: An Audit Study of Race and College Selectivity in the Labor Market." *Social Forces* 93, no. 4 (2015): 1451–79.

Gallup, George. *The Gallup Poll: Public Opinion, 1935–1971.* New York: Random House, 1972.

Gamoran, Adam. "Tracking and Inequality: New Directions for Research and Practice." WCER Working Paper No. 2009-6. Wisconsin Center for Education Research, University of Wisconsin–Madison, 2009. eric.ed.gov/?id=ED506617.

Gamoran, Adam, and Robert D. Mare. "Secondary School Tracking and Educational Inequality: Compensation, Reinforcement, or Neutrality?" *American Journal of Sociology* 94, no. 5 (1989): 1146–83.

Garth, T. R. "The Intelligence of Mixed Blood Indians." *Journal of Applied Psychology* 11, no. 4 (1927): 268–75. doi.org/10.1037/h0073753.

Gates, Merrill E. "Addresses at the Lake Mohonk Conferences." In *Americanizing the Indian,* edited by Francis Paul Prucha, 331–44. Cambridge, Mass.: Harvard University Press, 1973. doi.org/10.4159/harvard.9780674435056.c53.

Gayle, Caleb. *We Refuse to Forget: A True Story of Black Creeks, American Identity, and Power.* New York: Riverhead, 2023.

Gaztambide-Fernández, Rubén A. *The Best of the Best: Becoming Elite at an American Boarding School.* Cambridge, Mass.: Harvard University Press, 2009.

General Assembly. "An Act for Suppressing Outlying Slaves (1691)." *Encyclopedia Virginia.* encyclopediavirginia.org/entries/an-act-for-suppressing-outlying-slaves-1691/.

Gentry, Marcia, C. Matthew Fugate, Jiaxi Wu, and Jaime A. Castellano. "Gifted Native American Students: Literature, Lessons, and Future Directions." *Gifted Child Quarterly* 58, no. 2 (April 2014): 98–110. doi.org/10.1177/0016986214521660.

Gershenson, Seth, Stephen B. Holt, and Nicholas W. Papageorge. "Who Believes in Me? The Effect of Student–Teacher Demographic Match on Teacher Expectations." *Economics of Education Review* 52 (June 2016): 209–24. doi.org/10.1016/j.econedurev.2016.03.002.

Gershoff, Elizabeth T., and Sarah A. Font. "Corporal Punishment in U.S. Public Schools: Prevalence, Disparities in Use, and Status in State and Federal Policy." *Social Policy Report* 30, no. 1 (2016).

Giago, Tim. "Deaths of Indian Homeless in Rapid City Still Unresolved." *Indianz,* April 3, 2017. www.indianz.com/News/2017/04/03/tim-giago-deaths-of-indian-homeless-in-r.asp.

Gilder, Richard Watson. "The Kindergarten: An Uplifting Social Influence in the Home and the District." *Kindergarten Review* 14, no. 1 (September 1903): 1–10.

Gilliam, Walter S., Angela N. Maupin, Chin R. Reyes, Maria Accavitti, and Frederick Shic. "Do Early Educators' Implicit Biases Regarding Sex and Race Relate to Behavior Expectations and Recommendations of Preschool Expulsions and Suspensions?" Research Study Brief, Yale Child Study Center, September 28, 2016. marylandfamiliesengage.org/wp-content/uploads/2019/07/Preschool-Implicit-Bias-Policy-Brief.pdf.

Gilligan, Carol. *In a Different Voice: Psychological Theory and Women's Development.* Cambridge, Mass.: Harvard University Press, 1993.

Gilmore, Ruth Wilson. *Golden Gulag: Prisons, Surplus, Crisis, and Opposition in Globalizing California.* Berkeley: University of California Press, 2007.

Gingold, Dennis M., and M. Alexander Pearl. "Tribute to Elouise Cobell." *Public Land and Resources Law Review* 33 (2012): 189–198.

Givens, Jarvis R. *Fugitive Pedagogy: Carter G. Woodson and the Art of Black Teaching.* Cambridge, Mass.: Harvard University Press, 2021.

Givens, Jarvis R., and Ashley Ison. "Toward New Beginnings: A Review of Native, White, and Black American Education Through the 19th Century." *Review of Educational Research* 93, no. 3 (2023): 319–52. doi.org/10.3102/00346543221105544.

Glaeser, Edward L. "A Nation of Gamblers: Real Estate Speculation and American History." *American Economic Review* 103, no. 3 (May 2013): 1–42. doi.org/10.1257/aer.103.3.1.

Glickman, Emily. "No More AABL: Kindergarten Admissions Test Trashed." *Abacus Guide* (blog), June 9, 2020. abacusguide.com/2020/06/09/no-more-aabl-kindergarten-admissions-test-trashed/.

Gliha, Lori Jane. "El Paso County 12-Year-Old Speaks About Suspension for Briefly Showing Toy Gun in Zoom Class." *FOX31 Denver,* September 5, 2020. kdvr.com/news/problem-solvers/el-paso-county-12-year-old-speaks-about-suspension-for-briefly-showing-toy-gun-in-zoom-class/.

Goeman, Mishuana. "Land as Life: Unsettling the Logics of Containment." In *Native Studies Keywords,* edited by Stephanie Nohelani Teves, Andrea Smith, and Michelle H. Raheja, 71–89. Tucson: University of Arizona Press, 2015. doi.org/10.2307/j.ctt183gxzb.9.

Goff, Phillip Atiba, Matthew Christian Jackson, Brooke Allison Lewis Di Leone, Carmen Marie Culotta, and Natalie Ann DiTomasso. "The Essence of Innocence: Consequences of Dehumanizing Black Children." *Journal of Personality and Social Psychology* 106, no. 4 (April 2014): 526–45. doi.org/10.1037/a0035663.

Golann, Joanne W. *Scripting the Moves: Culture and Control in a "No-Excuses" Charter School.* Princeton: Princeton University Press, 2021.

Gold, Douglas. "Intelligence and Achievement of Blackfeet Indians." Master's thesis, University of Montana, 1934. scholarworks.umt.edu/etd/2722.

Golden, Hallie. "A Pregnant Woman Was in Trouble. Cops Killed Her in Her Bed." *Daily Beast,* January 4, 2021. www.thedailybeast.com/renee-davis-of-washington-state-was-killed-by-cops-in-her-bed-in-2016-and-her-family-still-wants-justice.

Goldstein, Joseph. "'Testilying' by Police: A Stubborn Problem." *New York Times,* March 18, 2018. www.nytimes.com/2018/03/18/nyregion/testilying-police-perjury-new-york.html.

Gooch, William. "Denying Free Blacks the Right to Vote (1724, 1735)." *Encyclopedia Virginia.* encyclopediavirginia.org/entries/denying-free-blacks-the-right-to-vote-1724-1735/.

Gould, Lewis L. *America in the Progressive Era, 1890–1914.* New York: Routledge, 2014.

Gould, Stephen Jay. *The Mismeasure of Man.* 2nd ed. New York: W. W. Norton, 1996.

Gover, Kevin. "Foreword." In *The Land Has Memory: Indigenous Knowledge, Native Landscapes, and the National Museum of the American Indian,* edited by Duane Blue Spruce and Tanya Thrasher. Chapel Hill: Smithsonian/University of North Carolina Press, 2009.

Graham, Patricia Albjerg. *Schooling America: How the Public Schools Meet the Nation's Changing Needs.* New York: Oxford University Press, 2005.

Grande, Sandy. *Red Pedagogy: Native American Social and Political Thought.* Lanham, Md.: Rowman & Littlefield, 2004.

Granger, Gordon. "General Order #3. Headquarters, District of Texas, Galveston, Texas, June 19, 1865. Issued by Order of Major General Granger." NAID 182778372, RG 393. National Archives. catalog.archives.gov/id/182778372.

Greene-Santos, Aniya. "Corporal Punishment in Schools Still Legal in Many States." NEA Today, May 20, 2024. www.nea.org/nea-today/all-news-articles/corporal-punishment-schools-still-legal-many-states.

Greer, Allan. *Property and Dispossession: Natives, Empires and Land in Early Modern North America.* New York: Cambridge University Press, 2018.

Grimké, Charlotte Forten. "Life on the Sea Islands (Part I)." *The Atlantic,* May 1864. www.theatlantic.com/magazine/archive/1864/05/life-on-the-sea-islands/308758/.

Grissom, Jason A., Luis A. Rodriguez, and Emily C. Kern. "Teacher and Principal Diversity and the Representation of Students of Color in Gifted Programs: Evidence from National Data." *Elementary School Journal* 117, no. 3 (March 2017): 396–422. doi .org/10.1086/690274.

Grunwald, Lisa, and Stephen J. Adler, eds. *Women's Letters: America from the Revolutionary War to the Present.* New York: Dial Press, 2008.

Guz, Samantha, and Brianna Suslovic. "'She Must Be Experimental, Resourceful, and Have Sympathetic Understanding': Toxic White Femininities as a Persona and Performance in School Social Work." *Affilia: Feminist Inquiry in Social Work* 38, no. 4 (2023): 759–74. doi.org/10.1177/08861099231157337.

Habtom, Sefanit, and Megan Scribe. "To Breathe Together: Co-Conspirators for Decolonial Futures." Yellowhead Institute, June 2, 2020. yellowheadinstitute.org/2020/06/02/to-breathe-together/.

Haggerty, Melvin E., Lewis M. Terman, Edward L. Thorndike, Guy Montrose Whipple, and Robert M. Yerkes. "National Intelligence Tests." Yonkers, N.Y.: World Book Company, 1920.

———. "Two Psychological Tests with Manual and Key, National Intelligence Tests. Scale A. Form 1 and Scale B. Form 1." Yonkers, N.Y.: World Book Company, 1920. National Museum of American History. americanhistory.si.edu/collections/search/object/nmah_692383.

Haley, Sarah. *No Mercy Here: Gender, Punishment, and the Making of Jim Crow Modernity.* Chapel Hill: University of North Carolina Press, 2016.

Hall, Gwendolyn Midlo. *Slavery and African Ethnicities in the Americas: Restoring the Links.* Chapel Hill: University of North Carolina Press, 2005.

Haller, John S., Jr. "Race, Mortality, and Life Insurance: Negro Vital Statistics in the Late Nineteenth Century." *Journal of the History of Medicine and Allied Sciences* 25, no. 3 (July 1970): 247–61.

Hancock, Cornelia. *Letters of a Civil War Nurse: Cornelia Hancock, 1863–1865.* Edited by Henrietta Stratton Jaquette. Lincoln, Neb.: Bison Books, 1998.

Hansen, Elise. "The Forgotten Minority in Police Shootings." CNN, November 10, 2017. www.cnn.com/2017/11/10/us/native-lives-matter/index.html.

Harber, Kent D., Jamie L. Gorman, Frank P. Gengaro, Samantha Butisingh, William Tsang, and Rebecca Ouellette. "Students' Race and Teachers' Social Support Affect the Positive Feedback Bias in Public Schools." *Journal of Educational Psychology* 104, no. 4 (November 2012): 1149–61. doi.org/10.1037/a0028110.

Harden, Kathryn Paige. "Why Progressives Should Embrace the Genetics of Education." *New York Times,* July 24, 2018. www.nytimes.com/2018/07/24/opinion/dna-nature-genetics-education.html.

Harjo, Joy, and Gloria Bird, eds. *Reinventing the Enemy's Language: Contemporary Native Women's Writings of North America.* New York: W. W. Norton, 1998.

Harper, Helen. "White Women Teaching in the North: Problematic Identity on the Shores of Hudson Bay." *Counterpoints* 73 (2000): 127–43.

Harring, Sidney L. *Crow Dog's Case: American Indian Sovereignty, Tribal Law, and United States Law in the Nineteenth Century.* New York: Cambridge University Press, 1994.

Hart, Hastings H. *Social Progress of Alabama: A Second Study of the Social Institutions and Agencies of the State of Alabama.* New York: Russell Sage Foundation, 1922.

Hartman, Saidiya V. *Scenes of Subjection: Terror, Slavery, and Self-Making in Nineteenth-Century America.* New York: Oxford University Press, 1997.

Hartocollis, Anemona. "Michael Feinberg, a Founder of KIPP Schools, Is Fired After Misconduct Claims." *New York Times,* February 22, 2018. www.nytimes.com/2018/02/22/us/kipp-sexual-misconduct-michael-feinberg.html.

Hayes, Kelly. "On Korryn Gaines, Loreal Tsingine and Refusing to Surrender." *BGD* (blog), August 3, 2016. www.bgdblog.org/2016/08/gaines-tsingine/.

Hayes, Sarah Kathryn Pitcher. "The Experiment at Fort Marion: Richard Henry Pratt's Recreation of Penitential Regimes at the Old Fort and Its Influence on American Indian Education." *Journal of Florida Studies* 1, no. 7 (2018). www.journalofflorida studies.org/files/vol0107/HAYES.Fort.Marion.pdf.

Heitzeg, Nancy A. "'Whiteness,' Criminality, and the Double Standards of Deviance/Social Control." *Contemporary Justice Review* 18, no. 2 (April 2015): 197–214. doi.org/10.1080/10282580.2015.1025630.

Herbert, Bob. "A Chance to Learn." *New York Times,* December 16, 2002. www.nytimes.com/2002/12/16/opinion/a-chance-to-learn.html.

Hillison, John. "The Coalition That Supported the Smith-Hughes Act or a Case for Strange Bedfellows." *Journal of Vocational and Technical Education* 11, no. 2 (1995): 4–11.

Hirschfeld, Lawrence A. "Seven Myths of Race and the Young Child." *Du Bois Review: Social Science Research on Race* 9, no. 1 (2012): 17–39. doi.org/10.1017/S1742058X12000033.

Hobson, Will. "How 'Race-Norming' Was Built into the NFL Concussion Settlement." *Washington Post,* August 2, 2021. www.washingtonpost.com/sports/2021/08/02/race-norming-nfl-concussion-settlement/.

Hochschild, Jennifer, and Brenna Powell. "Racial Reorganization and the United States Census 1850–1930: Mulattoes, Half-Breeds, Mixed Parentage, Hindoos, and the Mexican Race." *Studies in American Political Development* 22, no. 1 (2008): 59–96.

Hoffman, Frederick Ludwig. *Race Traits and Tendencies of the American Negro.* New York: Macmillan and American Economic Association, 1896.

Hong, Nicole. "Rochester Officers Suspended After Pepper-Spraying of 9-Year-Old Girl." *New York Times,* February 1, 2021. www.nytimes.com/2021/01/31/nyregion/rochester-police-pepper-spray-child.html.

Hooker, Juliet, ed. *Black and Indigenous Resistance in the Americas: From Multiculturalism to Racist Backlash.* Translated by Giorleny Altamirano Rayo, Aileen Ford, and Steven Lownes. Lanham, Md.: Lexington Books, 2020.

Hudetz, Mary. "Native American Teens Stopped on College Tour Urge Changes." Associated Press, September 21, 2018. apnews.com/general-news-6b071ad029704583b36ab afcc562adca.

———. "Suspicions of Native American Teens Point to Cultural Disconnect." *Christian Science Monitor,* May 14, 2018. www.csmonitor.com/USA/Society/2018/0514/Suspicions-of-Native-American-teens-point-to-cultural-disconnect.

Igbu, Sewsen, Shanna Peltier, Ashley Caranto Morford, and Kaitlin Rizarri. "BIPOC Solidarities, Decolonization, and Otherwise Kinship Through Black Feminist Love." *WSQ: Women's Studies Quarterly* 50, nos. 1–2 (2022): 187–204. doi.org/10.1353/wsq.2022.0015.

Infante, Chad Benito. "Murder and Metaphysics: Leslie Marmon Silko's 'Tony's Story' and Audre Lorde's 'Power.'" In *Otherwise Worlds: Against Settler Colonialism and Anti-Blackness,* edited by Tiffany Lethabo King, Jenell Navarro, and Andrea Smith, 133–57. Durham, N.C.: Duke University Press, 2020. doi.org/10.1515/9781478012023-008.

Irmscher, Christoph. *Louis Agassiz: Creator of American Science.* Boston: Houghton Mifflin Harcourt, 2013.

Jackson, Jessica Barbata. *Dixie's Italians: Sicilians, Race, and Citizenship in the Jim Crow Gulf South.* Baton Rouge: Louisiana State University Press, 2020.

Jackson, Raych. "A Sestina for a Black Girl Who Does Not Know How to Braid Hair." *Poetry,* April 2018. www.poetryfoundation.org/poetrymagazine/poems/146235/a-sestina-for-a-black-girl-who-does-not-know-how-to-braid-hair.

Jacobs, Margaret D. *White Mother to a Dark Race: Settler Colonialism, Maternalism, and the Removal of Indigenous Children in the American West and Australia, 1880–1940.* Lincoln: University of Nebraska Press, 2009.

Jacobson, Matthew Frye. *Whiteness of a Different Color: European Immigrants and the Alchemy of Race.* Cambridge, Mass.: Harvard University Press, 1998.

Jager, Rebecca Kay. *Malinche, Pocahontas, and Sacagawea: Indian Women as Cultural Intermediaries and National Symbols.* Norman: University of Oklahoma Press, 2016.

Jefferson, Thomas. *Notes on the State of Virginia.* Philadelphia: Prichard and Hall, 1788. docsouth.unc.edu/southlit/jefferson/jefferson.html.

———. *Notes on the State of Virginia.* Edited by William Peden. Chapel Hill: Omohundro Institute and University of North Carolina Press, 1996.

———. "Notes of a Conversation with George Hammond, 4 June 1792." *Founders Online,* National Archives. founders.archives.gov/documents/Jefferson/01-24-02-0023.

———. "Notes on Arthur Young's Letter to George Washington, 18 June 1792." *Founders Online,* National Archives. founders.archives.gov/documents/Jefferson/01-24-02-0088.

———. "Thomas Jefferson to John Taylor, 26 November 1798." *Founders Online,* National Archives. founders.archives.gov/documents/Jefferson/01-30-02-0398.

———. "Thomas Jefferson to Pierre Samuel Du Pont de Nemours, 25 April 1802." *Founders Online,* National Archives. founders.archives.gov/documents/Jefferson/01-37-02-0263.

———. "To John Adams from Thomas Jefferson, 11 June 1812." *Founders Online,* National Archives. founders.archives.gov/documents/Adams/99-02-02-5806.

———. "Thomas Jefferson to Thomas Cooper, 10 September 1814." *Founders Online,* National Archives. founders.archives.gov/documents/Jefferson/03-07-02-0471.

———. "Thomas Jefferson to William Short, 8 September 1823." *Founders Online,* National Archives. founders.archives.gov/documents/Jefferson/98-01-02-3750.

———. "Thomas Jefferson to William Ludlow, 6 September 1824." *Founders Online,* National Archives. founders.archives.gov/documents/Jefferson/98-01-02-4523.

Jenkins, Sally. *The Real All Americans: The Team That Changed a Game, a People, a Nation.* New York: Anchor, 2008.

Jensen, Arthur R. "How Much Can We Boost IQ and Scholastic Achievement?" *Harvard Educational Review* 39 (1969): 1–123. doi.org/10.17763/haer.39.1.l3u15956627424k7.

Johnson, Corey G. "Female Inmates Sterilized in California Prisons Without Approval."

Reveal, July 7, 2013. revealnews.org/article/female-inmates-sterilized-in-california-prisons-without-approval/.

Johnston-Dodds, Kimberly. "Early California Laws and Policies Related to California Indians." California Research Bureau, California State Library, September 2002. www.courts.ca.gov/documents/IB.pdf.

Johnston-Goodstar, Katie, and Ross VeLure Roholt. "'Our Kids Aren't Dropping Out; They're Being Pushed Out': Native American Students and Racial Microaggressions in Schools." *Journal of Ethnic & Cultural Diversity in Social Work* 26, no. 1–2 (2017): 30–47. doi.org/10.1080/15313204.2016.1263818.

Jones, Jeffrey Owen, and Peter Meyer. *The Pledge: A History of the Pledge of Allegiance.* New York: Thomas Dunne, 2010.

Jones, Sharon Lynette, ed. *Conversations with Angela Davis.* Jackson: University Press of Mississippi, 2021.

Jones-Rogers, Stephanie E. *They Were Her Property: White Women as Slave Owners in the American South.* New Haven, Conn.: Yale University Press, 2019.

Jordan, June. *Directed by Desire: The Collected Poems of June Jordan.* Port Townsend, WA: Copper Canyon Press, 2007.

Jordan, Winthrop D. *White Over Black: American Attitudes Toward the Negro, 1550–1812.* 2nd ed. Chapel Hill: Omohundro Institute and University of North Carolina Press, 2012.

Josey, Christopher Steven. "Race and Stereotypes in New Media: An Examination of How Internet News Frames Persons of Color." PhD thesis, University of Illinois at Urbana-Champaign, 2015. hdl.handle.net/2142/88171.

Kaba, Mariame. "So You're Thinking About Becoming an Abolitionist." *LEVEL* (blog), October 30, 2020. level.medium.com/so-youre-thinking-about-becoming-an-abolitionist-a436f8e31894.

———. *We Do This 'Til We Free Us: Abolitionist Organizing and Transforming Justice.* Chicago: Haymarket, 2021.

———. "Working Toward Abolition . . ." *Prison Culture: How the PIC Structures Our World* (blog), October 5, 2015. www.usprisonculture.com/blog/2015/10/05/working-toward-abolition/.

Kaba, Mariame, and Kelly Hayes. "A Jailbreak of the Imagination: Seeing Prisons for What They Are and Demanding Transformation." *Truthout,* May 3, 2018. truthout.org/articles/a-jailbreak-of-the-imagination-seeing-prisons-for-what-they-are-and-demanding-transformation/.

Kaba, Mariame, and Andrea J. Ritchie. *No More Police: A Case for Abolition.* New York: New Press, 2022.

Kaestle, Carl. *Pillars of the Republic: Common Schools and American Society, 1780–1860.* New York: Hill and Wang, 1983.

Kamin, Debra. "Home Appraised with a Black Owner: $472,000. With a White Owner: $750,000." *New York Times,* June 21, 2023. www.nytimes.com/2022/08/18/realestate/housing-discrimination-maryland.html.

Kandé, Sylvie. "Look Homeward, Angel: Maroons and Mulattos in Haile Gerima's *Sankofa.*" Translated by Joe Karaganis. *Research in African Literatures* 29, no. 2 (1998): 128–46.

Kao, Grace, and Jennifer S. Thompson. "Racial and Ethnic Stratification in Educational

Achievement and Attainment." *Annual Review of Sociology* 29, no. 1 (2003): 417–42. doi.org/10.1146/annurev.soc.29.010202.100019.

Kaomea, Julie. "Reconceptualizing Indigenous Parent Involvement in Early Educational Settings: Lessons from Native Hawaiian Preschool Families." *International Indigenous Policy Journal* 3, no. 4 (2012). doi.org/10.18584/iipj.2012.3.4.4.

Kaplan, Sidney. "The 'Domestic Insurrections' of the Declaration of Independence." *Journal of Negro History* 61, no. 3 (1976): 243–55. doi.org/10.2307/2717252.

Karcher, Carolyn L., ed. *A Lydia Maria Child Reader.* Durham, N.C.: Duke University Press, 1997.

Karuka, Manu. *Empire's Tracks: Indigenous Nations, Chinese Workers, and the Transcontinental Railroad.* Oakland: University of California Press, 2019.

Katanski, Amelia V. *Learning to Write "Indian": The Boarding-School Experience and American Indian Literature.* Norman: University of Oklahoma Press, 2005.

Katznelson, Ira. *When Affirmative Action Was White: An Untold History of Racial Inequality in Twentieth-Century America.* New York: W. W. Norton, 2005.

Kauanui, J. Kēhaulani. "'A Structure, Not an Event': Settler Colonialism and Enduring Indigeneity." *Lateral* 5, no. 1 (Spring 2016). www.jstor.org/stable/48671433.

Keenan, Harper B. "Selective Memory: California Mission History and the Problem of Historical Violence in Elementary School Textbooks." *Teachers College Record* 121, no. 8 (August 2019): 1–28. doi.org/10.1177/016146811912100805.

Keene, Adrienne J. "College Pride, Native Pride: A Portrait of a Culturally Grounded Precollege Access Program for American Indian, Alaska Native, and Native Hawaiian Students." *Harvard Educational Review* 86, no. 1 (2016): 72–97. doi.org/10.17763/0017-8055.86.1.72.

Kelleher, Suzanne Rowan. "How a Museum's Human Skull Collection Sparked a Racial Reckoning." *Forbes,* April 16, 2021. www.forbes.com/sites/suzannerowankelleher/2021/04/16/penn-museum-samuel-morton-human-skull-collection-black-slaves-repatriation/.

Kelley, Robin D. G. "The Rest of Us: Rethinking Settler and Native." *American Quarterly* 69, no. 2 (2017): 267–76. doi.org/10.1353/aq.2017.0020.

Kennedy, John F. "Extract from John F. Kennedy's Remarks at a Dinner Honoring Nobel Prize Winners of the Western Hemisphere," April 29, 1962. Jefferson Quotes & Family Letters, Monticello. tjrs.monticello.org/letter/1856.

Kennedy, Randall. *Race, Crime, and the Law.* New York: Pantheon Books, 1997.

Kent-Stoll, Peter. "Dispossessory Citizenship: The Settler Colonial State and the Bureau of Indian Affairs' Relocation Program, 1952–1972." *Social Problems* 20 (2022): 1–18. doi.org/10.1093/socpro/spac054.

Keyssar, Alexander. *The Right to Vote: The Contested History of Democracy in the United States.* New York: Basic Books, 2009.

Khwaja, Maira, Trina Reynolds-Tyler, Dominique James, and Hannah Nyhart. "Our Year of Mutual Aid." *New York Times,* March 11, 2021. www.nytimes.com/2021/03/11/opinion/covid-mutual-aid-chicago.html.

Kidder, William C., and Jay Rosner. "How the SAT Creates Built-in Headwinds: An Educational and Legal Analysis of Disparate Impact." *Santa Clara Law Review* 43, no. 1 (January 2002): 131. digitalcommons.law.scu.edu/lawreview/vol43/iss1/3/.

Kim, Suzanne A. "'Yellow' Skin, 'White' Masks: Asian American Impersonations of

Whiteness and the Feminist Critique of Liberal Equality." *Asian Law Journal* 8 (2001): 89–110.

Kimmerer, Robin Wall. *Braiding Sweetgrass: Indigenous Wisdom, Scientific Knowledge, and the Teachings of Plants.* Minneapolis: Milkweed Editions, 2016.

King, Tiffany Lethabo. *The Black Shoals: Offshore Formations of Black and Native Studies.* Durham, N.C.: Duke University Press, 2019. doi.org/10.1215/9781478005681.

King, Wilma. *Stolen Childhood: Slave Youth in Nineteenth-Century America.* 2nd ed. Bloomington: Indiana University Press, 2011.

KIPP New Jersey. "Ep. 02—How to Teach Your Class to Line Up," 2013. www.youtube.com/watch?v=nDq71SoUyD8.

Kleinfeld, Judith, and G. Williamson McDiarmid. "Teacher Expectations as a Political Issue in Rural Alaska Schools." *Research in Rural Education* 4, no. 1 (1986): 9–12.

Klotz, Sarah. *Writing Their Bodies: Restoring Rhetorical Relations at the Carlisle Indian School.* Logan: Utah State University Press, 2021.

Koeninger, Kevin. "Arrested & Beaten for Dozing in Class." *Courthouse News Service,* May 7, 2013. www.courthousenews.com/arrested-beaten-for-dozing-in-class/.

Kohlbrenner, Richard J. "William Torrey Harris, Superintendent of Schools, St. Louis, 1868–1880." *History of Education Journal* 2, no. 1 (1950): 18–24.

Koretz, Daniel. *The Testing Charade: Pretending to Make Schools Better.* Chicago: University of Chicago Press, 2017.

Kraus, Michael W., Ivuoma N. Onyeador, Natalie M. Daumeyer, Julian M. Rucker, and Jennifer A. Richeson. "The Misperception of Racial Economic Inequality." *Perspectives on Psychological Science* 14, no. 6 (November 2019): 899–921. doi.org/10.1177/1745691619863049.

Krauthamer, Barbara. *Black Slaves, Indian Masters: Slavery, Emancipation, and Citizenship in the Native American South.* Chapel Hill: University of North Carolina Press, 2013.

Krishna, Priya. "Mass Grave Recalls the Ugly Past of a City Where 'Life Is Sweeter.'" *New York Times,* November 8, 2023. www.nytimes.com/2023/11/08/dining/sugar-land-texas.html.

Ladson-Billings, Gloria. "It Doesn't Add Up: African American Students' Mathematics Achievement." *Journal for Research in Mathematics Education* 28, no. 6 (1997): 697–708.

Lafromboise, Terrance (brother of Brendon Galbreath). Interview with Eve L. Ewing, August 17, 2023.

Lakota People's Law Project. "Native Lives Matter," February 2015. lakotalaw.org/resources/native-lives-matter.

Langhorne, Orra. "Southern Sketches: Colored People in the Capital." In *Southern Workman and Hampton School Record* 21, no. 5 (May 1892): 78–80.

Lannie, Vincent P. *Public Money and Parochial Education: Bishop Hughes, Governor Seward, and the New York School Controversy.* Cleveland: Press of Case Western Reserve University, 1968.

Lawrence, Jane. "The Indian Health Service and the Sterilization of Native American Women." *American Indian Quarterly* 24, no. 3 (2000): 400–19.

Lawrence, Quil. "Federal Home Loan Program Is Still Failing Native American Veterans After 30 Years." Minnesota Public Radio, August 25, 2022. www.npr.org/2022/08/25/1119164311/federal-home-loan-program-is-still-failing-native-american-veterans-after-30-yea.

Lawrence-Lightfoot, Sara, and Jessica Hoffmann Davis. *The Art and Science of Portraiture.* San Francisco: Jossey-Bass, 1997.

Lazerson, Marvin. "Urban Reform and the Schools: Kindergartens in Massachusetts, 1870–1915." *History of Education Quarterly* 11, no. 2 (1971): 115–42. doi.org/10.2307/367590.

Lee, Robert, and Tristan Ahtone. "Land-Grab Universities: Expropriated Indigenous Land Is the Foundation of the Land-Grant University System." *High Country News,* March 30, 2020. www.hcn.org/issues/52-4/indigenous-affairs-education-land-grab-universities.

Lee, Robert, Tristan Ahtone, Margaret Pearce, Kalen Goodluck, Geoff McGhee, Cody Leff, Katherine Lanpher, and Taryn Salinas. "Morrill Act of 1862 Indigenous Land Parcels Database." *High Country News,* March 2020. www.landgrabu.org/universities/.

Legg, Mark, Apostolos Ampountolas, and Murat Hancer. "Senior Leadership Succession and Market Share: An Econometric Case Study on Native American Casinos." *Tourism Economics* 28, no. 8 (December 2022): 2176–96. doi.org/10.1177/13548166211035579.

Lemann, Nicholas. *The Big Test: The Secret History of the American Meritocracy.* New York: Macmillan, 2000.

Lemov, Doug. *Teach Like a Champion 3.0: 63 Techniques That Put Students on the Path to College.* Hoboken, N.J.: Jossey-Bass, 2021.

Leroy, Justin. "Black History in Occupied Territory: On the Entanglements of Slavery and Settler Colonialism." *Theory & Event* 19, no. 4 (2016). muse.jhu.edu/pub/1/article/633276.

Levenstein, Harvey. "The New England Kitchen and the Origins of Modern American Eating Habits." *American Quarterly* 32, no. 4 (1980): 369–86. doi.org/10.2307/2712458.

Levine, Susan. *School Lunch Politics: The Surprising History of America's Favorite Welfare Program.* Princeton: Princeton University Press, 2011.

Lewinson, Paul. *Race, Class & Party: A History of Negro Suffrage and White Politics in the South.* New York: Russell & Russell, 1963.

Lewis, Amanda E., and John B. Diamond. *Despite the Best Intentions: How Racial Inequality Thrives in Good Schools.* New York: Oxford University Press, 2015.

Lewis, William B. "Professor Lewis M. Terman." *The British Journal of Statistical Psychology* 10, no. 2 (November 1957): 65–68.

Lewis-Kraus, Gideon. "Can Progressives Be Convinced That Genetics Matters?" *The New Yorker,* September 6, 2021. www.newyorker.com/magazine/2021/09/13/can-progressives-be-convinced-that-genetics-matters.

Library of Congress. "Immigrants in the Progressive Era." Classroom Materials at the Library of Congress. www.loc.gov/classroom-materials/united-states-history-primary-source-timeline/progressive-era-to-new-era-1900-1929/immigrants-in-progressive-era/.

Lindsey, Donal F. *Indians at Hampton Institute, 1877–1923.* Urbana: University of Illinois Press, 1995.

Lipsitz, George. *The Possessive Investment in Whiteness: How White People Profit from Identity Politics.* New ed. Philadelphia: Temple University Press, 2006.

Litt, Jonathan, and Heather Valdez Singleton. "American Indian/Alaska Native Youth & Status Offense Disparities: A Call for Tribal Initiatives, Coordination & Federal Funding." Coalition for Juvenile Justice and Tribal Law and Policy Institute, 2015. turtletalk.files.wordpress.com/2015/06/5e0511a9-1707-4ffa-83d0-082b339f9ad4.pdf.

Litwack, Leon F. *Trouble in Mind: Black Southerners in the Age of Jim Crow.* New York: Knopf, 1998.

Lomawaima, K. Tsianina. "Domesticity in the Federal Indian Schools: The Power of Authority over Mind and Body." *American Ethnologist* 20, no. 2 (1993): 227–40.

———. "Estelle Reel, Superintendent of Indian Schools, 1898–1910: Politics, Curriculum, and Land." *Journal of American Indian Education* 35, no. 3 (1996): 5–31.

———. *They Called It Prairie Light: The Story of Chilocco Indian School.* Lincoln: University of Nebraska Press, 1995.

Lomawaima, K. Tsianina, and Teresa L. McCarty. *"To Remain an Indian": Lessons in Democracy from a Century of Native American Education.* New York: Teachers College Press, 2006.

Longman, Nickita, Emily Riddle, Alex Wilson, Saima Desai. "'Land Back' Is More Than the Sum of Its Parts." *Briarpatch,* September 10, 2020. briarpatchmagazine.com/articles/view/land-back-is-more-than-the-sum-of-its-parts.

Lookingbill, Brad D. *War Dance at Fort Marion: Plains Indian War Prisoners.* Norman: University of Oklahoma Press, 2014.

Lorde, Audre. *Sister Outsider: Essays and Speeches.* New York: Crossing Press, 2007. First published 1984.

Love, Bettina. *We Want to Do More Than Survive: Abolitionist Teaching and the Pursuit of Educational Freedom.* Boston: Beacon Press, 2023.

Loveless, Tom. *The 2013 Brown Center Report on American Education: How Well Are American Students Learning?* Vol. 3, no. 2. Brookings Institution, 2013.

Low, Rob. "12-Year-Old Suspended over Toy Gun Seen in Virtual Class." *FOX 31 Denver,* September 3, 2020. kdvr.com/news/problem-solvers/12-year-old-suspended-over-toy-gun-seen-in-virtual-class/.

Lucas, Samuel R., and Mark Berends. "Sociodemographic Diversity, Correlated Achievement, and De Facto Tracking." *Sociology of Education* 75, no. 4 (2002): 328–48. doi.org/10.2307/3090282.

Lui, Meizhu, Bárbara Robles, Betsy Leondar-Wright, Rose Brewer, and Rebecca Adamson. *The Color of Wealth: The Story Behind the U.S. Racial Wealth Divide.* New York: New Press, 2006.

Mann, Horace. *Twelfth Annual Report of the Board of Education, Together with the Twelfth Annual Report of the Secretary of the Board.* Massachusetts Department of Education. Boston: Dutton and Wentworth, 1849. archives.lib.state.ma.us/handle/2452/204731.

Marshall, Nate. "when the officer caught me." In *Blood Percussion.* Minneapolis: Button Poetry, 2014.

Martinez-Cola, Marisela. "Visibly Invisible: TribalCrit and Native American Segregated Schooling." *Sociology of Race and Ethnicity* 6, no. 4 (October 2020): 468–82. doi.org/10.1177/2332649219884087.

Marx, Sherry, and Julie Pennington. "Pedagogies of Critical Race Theory: Experimentations with White Preservice Teachers." *International Journal of Qualitative Studies in Education* 16, no. 1 (2003): 91–110. doi.org/10.1080/0951839022000036381.

Mason, Michele R., and Gisela Ernst-Slavit. "Representations of Native Americans in Elementary School Social Studies: A Critical Look at Instructional Language." *Multicultural Education* 18, no. 1 (2010): 10–17.

Maxim, Robert, Randall Akee, and Gabriel R. Sanchez. "For the First Time, the Government Published Monthly Unemployment Data on Native Americans, and the Picture Is Stark." Brookings Institution, February 9, 2022. policycommons.net/artifacts/4143180/for-the-first-time-the-government-published-monthly-unemployment-data-on-native-americans-and-the-picture-is-stark/4952424/.

Maynard, Robyn, and Leanne Betasamosake Simpson. *Rehearsals for Living*. Chicago: Haymarket, 2022.

Mbilishaka, Afiya M., and Danielle Apugo. "Brushed Aside: African American Women's Narratives of Hair Bias in School." *Race, Ethnicity and Education* 23, no. 5 (2020): 634–53. doi.org/10.1080/13613324.2020.1718075.

McInnis, Maurie D. "Violence." In *Educated in Tyranny: Slavery at Thomas Jefferson's University,* edited by Maurie D. McInnis and Louis P. Nelson. Charlottesville: University of Virginia Press, 2019.

McKittrick, Katherine. *Dear Science and Other Stories.* Durham, N.C.: Duke University Press, 2021.

McLaughlin, Elliott C., and Tony Marco. "Teen Made 911 Report that Preceded Policeman Killing Him, Investigators Say." CNN, November 14, 2017. www.cnn.com/2017/11/13/us/wisconsin-police-kill-native-american-teen/index.html.

McNally, Michael D. *Defend the Sacred: Native American Religious Freedom Beyond the First Amendment.* Princeton: Princeton University Press, 2020.

McNeil, Linda. *Contradictions of School Reform: Educational Costs of Standardized Testing.* New York: Routledge, 2002.

Medin, Douglas L., and Megan Bang. *Who's Asking? Native Science, Western Science, and Science Education.* Cambridge, Mass.: MIT Press, 2014.

Meiners, Erica R. "Disengaging from the Legacy of Lady Bountiful in Teacher Education Classrooms." *Gender and Education* 14, no. 1 (2002): 85–94.

———. *Right to Be Hostile: Schools, Prisons, and the Making of Public Enemies.* New York: Routledge, 2007. doi.org/10.4324/9780203936450.

Melamed, Jodi. "Racial Capitalism." *Critical Ethnic Studies* 1, no. 1 (2015): 76–85. doi.org/10.5749/jcritethnstud.1.1.0076.

Mielke, Laura L. "Performative Cultures of Early America." In *The Cambridge History of Native American Literature,* edited by Melanie Benson Taylor, 74–88. Cambridge, England: Cambridge University Press, 2020.

Miles, Tiya. "Eating Out of the Same Pot?" In *Crossing Waters, Crossing Worlds: The African Diaspora in Indian Country,* edited by Tiya Miles and Sharon P. Holland, xv–xviii. Durham, N.C.: Duke University Press, 2006.

———. *Ties That Bind: The Story of an Afro-Cherokee Family in Slavery and Freedom.* Berkeley: University of California Press, 2005.

Miller, Robert J. *Native America, Discovered and Conquered: Thomas Jefferson, Lewis and Clark, and Manifest Destiny.* Lincoln: Bison Books, 2008.

Miller, Robert J., Jacinta Ruru, Larissa Behrendt, and Tracey Lindberg. *Discovering Indigenous Lands: The Doctrine of Discovery in the English Colonies.* Oxford, England: Oxford University Press, 2012.

Miller, Vivien M. L. *Hard Labor and Hard Time: Florida's "Sunshine Prison" and Chain Gangs.* Gainesville: University Press of Florida, 2012.

Million, Dian. "Policing the Rez: Keeping No Peace in Indian Country." *Social Justice* 27, no. 3 (2000): 101–19.

Mills, ShaVonte'. "An African School for African Americans: Black Demands for Education in Antebellum Boston." *History of Education Quarterly* 61, no. 4 (November 2021): 478–502. doi.org/10.1017/heq.2021.38.

Milson, Andrew J., Chara Haeussler Bohan, Perry L. Glanzer, and J. Wesley Null, eds. *American Educational Thought: Essays from 1640–1940*. 2nd ed. Charlotte, N.C.: Information Age Publishing, 2009.

Moll, Luis C., Cathy Amanti, Deborah Neff, and Norma Gonzalez. "Funds of Knowledge for Teaching: Using a Qualitative Approach to Connect Homes and Classrooms." *Theory into Practice* 31, no. 2 (1992): 132–41.

Montemayor, Constanza. "Friends and Family of Brendon Galbreath Remember Him for His Kindness, Drive." *Daily Bruin,* September 18, 2021. dailybruin.com/2021/09/18/friends-and-family-of-brendon-galbreath-remember-him-for-his-kindness-drive/.

Monument Lab. *National Monument Audit,* 2021. monumentlab.com/audit.

Morgan, Becky. "American Indian Veterans Have Highest Record of Military Service." National Indian Council on Aging, November 8, 2019. www.nicoa.org/american-indian-veterans-have-highest-record-of-military-service.

Morgan, Jas. "Visual Cultures of Indigenous Futurism." In *Otherwise Worlds: Against Settler Colonialism and Anti-Blackness,* edited by Tiffany Lethabo King, Jenell Navarro, and Andrea Smith, 332–42. Durham, N.C.: Duke University Press, 2020. doi.org/10.1515/9781478012023-019.

Morgan, Lewis Henry. *Ancient Society: Or, Researches in the Lines of Human Progress from Savagery, Through Barbarism to Civilization.* New York: Henry Holt, 1877.

Morgan, T. J. *Indian Education.* Bulletin No. 1 (1889), U.S. Bureau of Education. Washington, D.C.: Government Printing Office, 1890. catalog.hathitrust.org/Record/100764231.

Morris, Monique W. *Pushout: The Criminalization of Black Girls in Schools.* New York: New Press, 2016.

Morris, Robert C. *Reading, 'Riting, and Reconstruction: The Education of Freedmen in the South, 1861–1870.* Chicago: University of Chicago Press, 2010.

Morrison, Toni. "On the Backs of Blacks." *Time,* December 2, 1993. content.time.com/time/subscriber/article/0,33009,979736,00.html.

Morton, Samuel George. *Crania Americana; Or, a Comparative View of the Skulls of Various Aboriginal Nations of North and South America.* Philadelphia: Dobson, 1839.

Mosteller, Kelli. "Private Land Ownership Won't Solve Native American Poverty." *The Atlantic,* September 17, 2016. www.theatlantic.com/politics/archive/2016/09/for-native-americans-land-is-more-than-just-the-ground-beneath-their-feet/500462/.

Moulton, Gary E. *The Lewis and Clark Journals: An American Epic of Discovery.* Lincoln: University of Nebraska Press, 2003.

Muir, David. Interview with Quvenzhané Wallis. *ABC World News Tonight,* December 20, 2014. www.youtube.com/watch?v=MuaojMt4MEw.

Muller, Chandra, Catherine Riegle-Crumb, Kathryn S. Schiller, Lindsey Wilkinson, and Kenneth A. Frank. "Race and Academic Achievement in Racially Diverse High Schools: Opportunity and Stratification." *Teachers College Record* 112, no. 4 (April 2010): 1038–63.

Murdy, Anne-Elizabeth. *Teach the Nation: Pedagogies of Racial Uplift in U.S. Women's Writing of the 1890s.* New York: Routledge, 2018.

Murphree, Daniel S., ed. *Native America: A State-by-State Historical Encyclopedia.* Santa Barbara, Calif.: Greenwood, 2012.

Murphy, John, and Brent Huggins. "Retirement Income Among American Indians and Alaska Natives in the American Community Survey." Research and Statistics Note No. 2015-01. Social Security Office of Retirement and Disability Policy, February 2015. www.ssa.gov/policy/docs/rsnotes/rsn2015-01.html.

Murray, Charles. *Human Diversity: The Biology of Gender, Race, and Class.* New York: Grand Central, 2020.

Nash, Gary B. *The Unknown American Revolution: The Unruly Birth of Democracy and the Struggle to Create America.* New York: Penguin, 2006.

National Alliance to End Sexual Violence. "Where We Stand: Racism and Rape." endsexualviolence.org/where_we_stand/racism-and-rape/.

National Center for Education Statistics. "Percentage Distribution of Enrollment in Public Elementary and Secondary Schools, by Race/Ethnicity and State or Jurisdiction: Fall 2000 and Fall 2018." *Digest of Education Statistics,* 2020. nces.ed.gov/programs/digest/d20/tables/dt20_203.70.asp.

———. "Percentage of Public School Students Enrolled in Gifted and Talented Programs, by Sex, Race/Ethnicity, and State: Selected Years, 2004 Through 2020-21." *Digest of Education Statistics,* 2023. nces.ed.gov/programs/digest/d23/tables/dt23_204.90.asp.

———. "Preprimary, Elementary, and Secondary Education." *Condition of Education,* 2021. nces.ed.gov/programs/coe/preprimary-elementary-and-secondary.

———. "Search for Public Schools." nces.ed.gov/ccd/schoolsearch/index.asp.

———. "Table 223.40: Percentage of Students Suspended and Expelled from Public Elementary and Secondary Schools, by Sex, Race/Ethnicity, and State: 2013–14." *Digest of Education Statistics,* 2014. nces.ed.gov/programs/digest/d18/tables/dt18_233.40.asp.

National Congress of American Indians. *Becoming Visible: A Landscape Analysis of State Efforts to Provide Native American Education for All,* October 10, 2019. archive.ncai.org/policy-research-center/research-data/prc-publications/NCAI-Becoming_Visible_Report-Digital_FINAL_10_2019.pdf.

National Defense Education Act of 1958. Public Law No. 85–864, 72 Stat. (1958). www.loc.gov/item/uscode1958-004020017/.

National Indian Gaming Commission. "The Commission: FAQS," 2022. www.nigc.gov/commission/faqs.

National Women's Law Center. "Forced Sterilization of Disabled People in the United States," January 24, 2022. nwlc.org/resource/forced-sterilization-of-disabled-people-in-the-united-states/.

Nation's Report Card. "NAEP Mathematics: Mathematics Results," 2022. www.nationsreportcard.gov/mathematics/?grade=4.

———. "NAEP Reading: Reading Results," 2022. www.nationsreportcard.gov/reading/?grade=4.

NDN Collective. "LANDBACK Manifesto." landback.org/manifesto/.

Nelson, Barbara J. *Making an Issue of Child Abuse.* Chicago: University of Chicago Press, 1986.

Newland, Bryan. *Federal Indian Boarding School Initiative Investigative Report*. Office of the Assistant Secretary, Indian Affairs, U.S. Department of the Interior, May 2022. www.bia.gov/sites/default/files/dup/inline-files/bsi_investigative_report_may_2022_508.pdf.

Nicolas, Serge, and Rasyid Bo Sanitioso. "Alfred Binet and Experimental Psychology at the Sorbonne Laboratory." *History of Psychology* 15, no. 4 (November 2012): 328–63. doi.org/10.1037/a0028060.

Nobles, Melissa. *Shades of Citizenship: Race and the Census in Modern Politics*. Stanford: Stanford University Press, 2000.

NoiseCat, Julian Brave. "The Western Idea of Private Property Is Flawed. Indigenous Peoples Have It Right." *The Guardian*, March 27, 2017. www.theguardian.com/commentisfree/2017/mar/27/western-idea-private-property-flawed-indigenous-peoples-have-it-right.

Nott, Josiah Clark. "Letter to Samuel George Morton, June 27, 1849." Samuel George Morton Papers, Library Company of Philadelphia. Box 2, Folder 83 (7389 F 77).

———. "The Mulatto a Hybrid—Probable Extermination of the Two Races if the Whites and Blacks Are Allowed to Intermarry." *Boston Medical & Surgical Journal* 29, no. 2 (August 1843): 29–32.

Oast, Jennifer Bridges. "Negotiating the Honor Culture: Students and Slaves at Three Virginia Colleges." In *Slavery and the University: Histories and Legacies*, edited by Leslie M. Harris, James T. Campbell, and Alfred L. Brophy, 84–98. Athens: University of Georgia Press, 2019.

Office of the Surgeon General, Division of Psychology. "Group Examination Beta," 1918. National Museum of American History. americanhistory.si.edu/collections/search/object/nmah_1214569.

Oklahoma Historical Society. "Freedmen History." www.okhistory.org/learn/freedmen.

Omi, Michael, and Howard Winant. *Racial Formation in the United States*. 3rd ed. New York: Routledge, 2014.

Opportunity Insights. "The Opportunity Atlas." opportunityatlas.org/.

Ortiz, Erik. "Michigan Judge Denies Release of Teenage Girl Who Was Jailed After Not Doing Homework." *NBC News*, July 20, 2020. www.nbcnews.com/news/us-news/michigan-judge-denies-release-teenage-girl-who-was-jailed-after-n1234377.

Oshinsky, David. *"Worse Than Slavery": Parchman Farm and the Ordeal of Jim Crow Justice*. New York: Free Press, 1996.

Ossei-Owusu, Shaun. "Police Quotas." *New York University Law Review* 96 (May 2021): 529–605.

Pager, Devah, Bart Bonikowski, and Bruce Western. "Discrimination in a Low-Wage Labor Market: A Field Experiment." *American Sociological Review* 74, no. 5 (2009): 777–99. doi.org/10.1177/000312240907400505.

Paine, Thomas. *Common Sense: Addressed to the Inhabitants of America, on the Following Interesting Subjects*. Philadelphia: R. Bell, 1776. www.loc.gov/item/2006681076/.

Painter, Nell Irvin. *The History of White People*. New York: W. W. Norton, 2011.

———. *Sojourner Truth: A Life, A Symbol*. New York: W. W. Norton, 1997.

———. "Why 'White' Should Be Capitalized, Too." *West Central Tribune*, July 23, 2020. www.wctrib.com/opinion/nell-irvin-painter-why-white-should-be-capitalized-too.

Paris, Django, and H. Samy Alim. "What Are We Seeking to Sustain Through Culturally Sustaining Pedagogy? A Loving Critique Forward." *Harvard Educational Review* 84, no. 1 (March 2014): 85–100. doi.org/10.17763/haer.84.1.982l873k2ht16m77.

Park, K-Sue. "Self-Deportation Nation." *Harvard Law Review* 132, no. 7 (May 2019): 1878–1942. harvardlawreview.org/print/vol-132/self-deportation-nation/.

Patterson, Anita Haya. *From Emerson to King: Democracy, Race, and the Politics of Protest.* New York: Oxford University Press, 1997.

Pauker, Kristin, Nalini Ambady, and Evan P. Apfelbaum. "Race Salience and Essentialist Thinking in Racial Stereotype Development." *Child Development* 81, no. 6. (2010): 1799–1813. doi.org/10.1111/j.1467-8624.2010.01511.x.

Pauker, Kristin, Amanda Williams, and Jennifer R. Steele. "Children's Racial Categorization in Context." *Child Development Perspectives* 10, no. 1 (March 2016): 33–38. doi.org/10.1111/cdep.12155.

Pauker, Kristin, Yiyuan Xu, Amanda Williams, and Ashley M. Biddle. "Race Essentialism and Social Contextual Differences in Children's Racial Stereotyping." *Child Development* 87, no. 5 (2016): 1409–22. doi.org/10.1111/cdev.12592.

Payne, Charles M., and Carol Sills Strickland, eds. *Teach Freedom: Education for Liberation in the African-American Tradition.* New York: Teachers College Press, 2008.

Perry, Andre M., Jonathan Rothwell, and David Harshbarger. *The Devaluation of Assets in Black Neighborhoods: The Case of Residential Property.* Brookings Institution, November 2018. www.brookings.edu/articles/devaluation-of-assets-in-black-neighborhoods.

Peterson, Judy. "Los Gatos: Where Would You Build a California Mission?" *Mercury News,* February 24, 2016. www.mercurynews.com/2016/02/24/los-gatos-where-would-you-build-a-california-mission/.

Phenix, Lucy Massie, and Veronica Selver, dirs. "We Are Going to Learn Together." Excerpt from *You Got to Move: Stories of Change in the South.* Milliarium Zero, 1985. youtu.be/gcKOmL4x1c8.

Porter, Anthony Toomer. *Led On! Step by Step: Scenes from Clerical, Military, Educational, and Plantation Life in the South, 1828–1898.* New York: G. P. Putnam's Sons, 1898.

Pratt, Richard Henry. "The Advantages of Mingling Indians with Whites." In *Proceedings of the National Conference of Charities and Correction at the Nineteenth Annual Session Held in Denver, Colorado, 1892.* Carlisle Indian School Digital Resource Center, Dickinson College Archives. carlisleindian.dickinson.edu/sites/default/files/docs-resources/CIS-Resources_1892-PrattSpeech.pdf.

———. *Battlefield and Classroom: Four Decades with the American Indian, 1867–1904.* Edited by Robert M. Utley. Norman: University of Oklahoma Press, 2004.

Price, Desmond. "Remembering Brendon Galbreath." *Independent Thought* (podcast), October 11, 2021. podcasters.spotify.com/pod/show/indethought/episodes/Remembering-Brendon-Galbreath-e18k2fk.

Prucha, Francis Paul, ed. *Documents of United States Indian Policy.* 3rd ed. Lincoln: University of Nebraska Press, 2000.

Rae, Heather, dir. *Trudell.* Appaloosa Pictures, 2005.

Ramsden, Sue, Fiona M. Richardson, Goulven Josse, Clare Shakeshaft, Mohamed L. Seghier, and Cathy J. Price. "The Influence of Reading Ability on Subsequent Changes in Verbal IQ in the Teenage Years." *Developmental Cognitive Neuroscience* 6 (2013), 30–39.

Ramsey, Patricia G., and Leslie C. Myers. "Salience of Race in Young Children's Cognitive, Affective, and Behavioral Responses to Social Environments." *Journal of Applied Developmental Psychology* 11, no. 1 (1990): 49–67.

Ray, Victor. *On Critical Race Theory: Why It Matters and Why You Should Care.* New York: Random House, 2023.

Reeves, Richard V., and Eleanor Krause. "Raj Chetty in 14 Charts: Big Findings on Opportunity and Mobility We Should All Know." Brookings Institution, January 11, 2018. www.brookings.edu/articles/raj-chetty-in-14-charts-big-findings-on-opportunity-and-mobility-we-should-know/.

Reyhner, Jon. "American Indian Boarding Schools: What Went Wrong? What Is Going Right?" *Journal of American Indian Education* 57, no. 1 (2018): 58–78. doi.org/10.5749/jamerindieduc.57.1.0058.

Reyhner, Jon, and Jeanne M. Oyawin Eder. *American Indian Education: A History.* Norman: University of Oklahoma Press, 2006.

Rhodes, Dusty. "Feedback: Noble Charter Schools Story Hit a Nerve." NPR Illinois, April 30, 2018. www.nprillinois.org/education-desk/2018-04-30/feedback-noble-charter-schools-story-hit-a-nerve.

Rhodes, Karl. "Economic History: Free to Speculate." *Econ Focus,* 3Q (2014): 24–26.

Richards, Cindy Koenig. "Inventing Sacagawea: Public Women and the Transformative Potential of Epideictic Rhetoric." *Western Journal of Communication* 73, no. 1 (February 2009): 1–22. doi.org/10.1080/10570310802635013.

Roberts, Alaina E. *I've Been Here All the While: Black Freedom on Native Land.* Philadelphia: University of Pennsylvania Press, 2021.

———. "When Black Lives Matter Meets Indian Country: Using the Cherokee and Chickasaw Nations as Case Studies for Understanding the Evolution of Public History and Interracial Coalition." *American Indian Quarterly* 45, no. 3 (2021): 250–71. doi.org/10.1353/aiq.2021.0020.

Roberts, Dorothy. *Fatal Invention: How Science, Politics, and Big Business Re-Create Race in the Twenty-First Century.* New York: New Press, 2011.

———. *Killing the Black Body: Race, Reproduction, and the Meaning of Liberty.* New York: Vintage, 1998.

———. *Shattered Bonds: The Color of Child Welfare.* New York: Basic Books, 2009.

Roberts, Dorothy, and Lisa Sangoi. "Black Families Matter: How the Child Welfare System Punishes Poor Families of Color." *The Appeal,* March 26, 2018. theappeal.org/black-families-matter-how-the-child-welfare-system-punishes-poor-families-of-color-33ad20e2882e/.

Robertson, Dwanna L. "The Myth of Indian Casino Riches." *ICT News,* September 12, 2018. ictnews.org/archive/the-myth-of-indian-casino-riches.

Robinson, Cedric J. *Black Marxism: The Making of the Black Radical Tradition.* 2nd ed. Chapel Hill: University of North Carolina Press, 2020.

Rockman, Seth. "Negro Cloth: Mastering the Market for Slave Clothing in Antebellum America." In *American Capitalism: New Histories,* edited by Sven Beckert and Christine Desan, 170–94. New York: Columbia University Press, 2018. doi.org/10.7312/beck18524-008.

Roid, Gale H. *Stanford-Binet Intelligence Scales: Examiners Manual.* 5th ed. Austin, Tex.: Pro-Ed Inc., 2003.

———. *Stanford-Binet Intelligence Scales: Item Books 1–3*. 5th ed. Austin, Tex.: Pro-Ed Inc., 2003.

Roid, Gale H., and R. Andrew Barram. *Essentials of Stanford-Binet Intelligence Scales (SB5) Assessment.* Hoboken, N.J.: John Wiley & Sons, 2004.

Róisín, Fariha. *Who Is Wellness For? An Examination of Wellness Culture and Who It Leaves Behind.* New York: Harper Wave, 2022.

Romero, Mary E. "Identifying Giftedness Among Keresan Pueblo Indians: The Keres Study." *Journal of American Indian Education* 34, no. 1 (1994): 35–58.

Roosevelt, Franklin D. "Address at the Dedication of the Thomas Jefferson Memorial, Washington, D.C.," April 13, 1943. American Presidency Project, University of California Santa Barbara. www.presidency.ucsb.edu/documents/address-the-dedication-the-thomas-jefferson-memorial-washington-dc.

Rosenbloom, Susan Rakosi, and Niobe Way. "Experiences of Discrimination Among African American, Asian American, and Latino Adolescents in an Urban High School." *Youth & Society* 35, no. 4 (2004): 420–51. doi.org/10.1177/0044118X03261479.

Rosentel, Kris, Ileana López-Martínez, Richard A. Crosby, Laura F. Salazar, and Brandon J. Hill. "Black Transgender Women and the School-to-Prison Pipeline: Exploring the Relationship Between Anti-Trans Experiences in School and Adverse Criminal-Legal System Outcomes." *Sexuality Research and Social Policy* 18, no. 3 (2021): 481–94. doi.org/10.1007/s13178-020-00473-7.

Ross, Luana. *Inventing the Savage: The Social Construction of Native American Criminality.* Austin: University of Texas Press, 1998.

Rossi, Rosalind. "Students Given Freedom to Blossom." *Chicago Sun-Times,* March 13, 2007. www.pressreader.com/usa/chicago-sun-times/20070313/281831459276723.

Rothberg, Emma. "Elouise Cobell ('Yellow Bird Woman')." National Women's History Museum, 2020. www.womenshistory.org/education-resources/biographies/elouise-cobell-yellow-bird-woman.

Sabino, Pascal. "After West Side School Forces 4-Year-Old to Remove His Braids, Parents Ask: Why Are We Policing Black Children's Hair?" *Block Club Chicago,* March 18, 2021. blockclubchicago.org/2021/03/18/west-side-private-school-forces-4-year-old-boy-to-remove-his-braids-why-are-we-policing-black-childrens-hair/.

Sabzalian, Leilani. *Indigenous Children's Survivance in Public Schools.* New York: Routledge, 2019.

Sahagun, Louis. "Tangled Trust Funds Earn Wrath of Native Americans." *Los Angeles Times,* November 10, 1996. www.latimes.com/archives/la-xpm-1996-11-10-mn-63448-story.html.

Salinas, Elaine. "Still Grieving Over the Loss of the Land." In *Messengers of the Wind: Native American Women Tell Their Life Stories,* edited by Jane Katz. New York: Random House, 2009.

Samelson, Franz. "World War I Intelligence Testing and the Development of Psychology." *Journal of the History of the Behavioral Sciences* 13, no. 3 (1977): 274–82. doi.org/10.1002/1520-6696(197707)13:3<274::AID-JHBS2300130308>3.0.CO;2-K.

Samudzi, Zoé, and William C. Anderson. *As Black as Resistance: Finding the Conditions for Liberation.* Chico, Calif.: AK Press, 2018.

San Pedro, Timothy. *Protecting the Promise: Indigenous Education Between Mothers and Their Children.* New York: Teachers College Press, 2021.

Sánchez-Eppler, Karen. "'Remember, Dear, When the Yankees Came Through Here, I Was Only Ten Years Old': Valuing the Enslaved Child of the WPA Slave Narratives." In *Child Slavery Before and After Emancipation: An Argument for Child-Centered Slavery Studies,* edited by Anna Mae Duane, 27–49. Cambridge, England: Cambridge University Press, 2017. doi.org/10.1017/9781316412312.003.

Sanders, Eulanda. "The Politics of Textiles Used in African American Slave Clothing." In *Textiles and Politics: Textile Society of America 13th Biennial Symposium Proceedings,* September 2012. digitalcommons.unl.edu/tsaconf/740.

Saporito, Salvatore, and Deenesh Sohoni. "Coloring Outside the Lines: Racial Segregation in Public Schools and Their Attendance Boundaries." *Sociology of Education* 79, no. 2 (April 2006): 81–105. www.jstor.org/stable/25054306.

Saunt, Claudio. *Unworthy Republic: The Dispossession of Native Americans and the Road to Indian Territory.* New York: W. W. Norton, 2020.

Savannah Morning News. "Many Criminals to Face Judicial Music," March 20, 1903, 10.

———. "Will Graft Skin on Woman Convict," February 2, 1904.

Scholastic. "Lewis and Clark Student Activity." 2021. Originally located at scholastic.com/teachers/activities/teaching-content/lewis-and-clark-student-activity. While the page does not exist anymore, it can be located via the Wayback Machine.

Schroedel, Jean Reith, and Roger J. Chin. "Whose Lives Matter: The Media's Failure to Cover Police Use of Lethal Force Against Native Americans." *Race and Justice* 10, no. 2 (April 2020): 150–75. doi.org/10.1177/2153368717734614.

Schurz, Carl. "Present Aspects of the Indian Problem." *North American Review* 258, no. 4 (1973): 45–54.

Senkel, David P. "Constitutional Law—Equal Protection—Major Crimes Act, 18 U.S.C. §1153, Which Subjects Indian Convicted of Certain Offenses to Greater Sentence Than Non-Indian Convicted for Same Offense, Violates Equal Protection Principles Inherent in Fifth Amendment Due Process Clause." *Creighton Law Review* 9 (1976): 717–38.

Shange, Savannah. *Progressive Dystopia: Abolition, Antiblackness, and Race in the New San Francisco.* Durham, N.C.: Duke University Press, 2019.

Shanks, Trina Williams. "The Homestead Act: A Major Asset-Building Policy in American History." Working Paper 00-9. Center for Social Development, Washington University, St. Louis. September 2000. doi.org/10.7936/K7RR1XQM.

Shannon, E. Roe. "The Phoenix Indian School." *The Native American* 9, no. 18 (May 1908): 167–69.

Shapiro, Laura. *Perfection Salad: Women and Cooking at the Turn of the Century.* Berkeley: University of California Press, 2009.

Shapiro, Thomas M. *The Hidden Cost of Being African American: How Wealth Perpetuates Inequality.* New York: Oxford University Press, 2004.

Sharpe, Christina. *In the Wake: On Blackness and Being.* Durham, N.C.: Duke University Press, 2016.

Shedd, Carla. *Unequal City: Race, Schools, and Perceptions of Injustice.* New York: Russell Sage Foundation, 2015.

Shilling, Vincent. "Mohawk Brothers Detained on Colorado Campus Tour Gain National Attention." *ICT News,* May 10, 2018. ictnews.org/archive/mohawk-brothers-detained-police-colorado-campus-tour-gain-national-attention.

Shockley, William. "A 'Try Simplest Cases' Approach to the Heredity-Poverty-Crime Problem." *Proceedings of the National Academy of Sciences* 57, no. 6 (June 1967): 1767–74.

———. "Dysgenics, Geneticity, Raceology: A Challenge to the Intellectual Responsibility of Educators." *Phi Delta Kappan* 53, no. 5 (1972): 297–307.

Shotton, Heather J., Shelly C. Lowe, and Stephanie J. Waterman, eds. "Introduction." In *Developments Beyond the Asterisk: New Scholarship and Frameworks for Understanding Native Students in Higher Education.* New York: Routledge, 2023.

Siddons, Louise. "Red Power in the *Black Panther:* Radical Imagination and Intersectional Resistance at Wounded Knee." *American Art* 35, no. 2 (June 2021): 2–31. doi.org/10.1086/715823.

Silva, Antonio José Bacelar da. *Between Brown and Black: Anti-Racist Activism in Brazil.* New Brunswick, N.J.: Rutgers University Press, 2022.

Silverman, John. "The Miner's Canary: Tribal Control of American Indian Education and the First Amendment." *Fordham Urban Law Journal* 19, no. 4 (January 1992): 1019.

Simonton, Dean Keith. "Presidential IQ, Openness, Intellectual Brilliance, and Leadership: Estimates and Correlations for 42 U.S. Chief Executives." *Political Psychology* 27, no. 4 (2006): 511–26.

Simpson, Audra. "The Sovereignty of Critique." *South Atlantic Quarterly* 119, no. 4 (October 2020): 685–99. doi.org/10.1215/00382876-8663591.

Simpson, Leanne Betasamosake. *As We Have Always Done: Indigenous Freedom Through Radical Resistance.* Minneapolis: University of Minnesota Press, 2017.

———. "Land as Pedagogy: Nishnaabeg Intelligence and Rebellious Transformation." *Decolonization: Indigeneity, Education & Society* 3, no. 3 (2014): 1–25.

———. "The Place Where We All Live and Work Together: A Gendered Analysis of 'Sovereignty.'" In *Native Studies Keywords,* edited by Stephanie Nohelani Teves, Andrea Smith, and Michelle H. Raheja, 18–24. Tucson: University of Arizona Press, 2015. doi.org/10.2307/j.ctt183gxzb.5.

Smith, Ben. "I'm Still Reading Andrew Sullivan. But I Can't Defend Him." *New York Times,* August 31, 2020. www.nytimes.com/2020/08/30/business/media/im-still-reading-andrew-sullivan-but-i-cant-defend-him.html.

Smith, Gregory D. "Disparate Impact of the Federal Sentencing Guidelines of Indians in Indian Country: Why Congress Should Run the Erie Railroad into the Major Crimes Act." *Hamline Law Review* 27, no. 3 (January 2004): 483–533.

Smith, Mark M. *How Race Is Made: Slavery, Segregation, and the Senses.* Chapel Hill: University of North Carolina Press, 2008.

Smith, Tom W., Michael Davern, Jeremy Freese, and Stephen Morgan. *General Social Surveys, 1972–2018: Cumulative Codebook.* Chicago: NORC, 2019. library.uvm.edu/sites/default/files/gss/2018_GSS_Codebook.pdf.

Snively, Gloria, and Wanotsts'a7 Lorna Williams. "Braiding Indigenous Science with Western Science." In *Knowing Home: Braiding Indigenous Science with Western Science 2,* edited by Gloria Snively and Wanosts'a7 Lorna Williams, 3–11. University of Victoria Libraries ePublishing Services, 2018. pressbooks.bccampus.ca/knowinghome2/.

Snyderman, Mark, and Stanley Rothman. "Survey of Expert Opinion on Intelligence and Aptitude Testing." *American Psychologist* 42 no. 2 (1987): 137–44. doi.org/10.1037/0003-066X.42.2.137.

Sojoyner, Damien M. *First Strike: Educational Enclosures in Black Los Angeles.* Minneapolis: University of Minnesota Press, 2016.

Sorber, Nathan M. *Land-Grant Colleges and Popular Revolt: The Origins of the Morrill Act and the Reform of Higher Education.* Ithaca, N.Y.: Cornell University Press, 2018.

Southern Poverty Law Center. "Relf v. Weinberger." www.splcenter.org/seeking-justice/case-docket/relf-v-weinberger.

Special Subcommittee on Indian Education. *Indian Education: A National Tragedy—A National Challenge.* Committee on Labor and Public Welfare, U.S. Senate, November 3, 1969. files.eric.ed.gov/fulltext/ED034625.pdf.

Spillers, Hortense J. "Mama's Baby, Papa's Maybe: An American Grammar Book." *Diacritics* 17, no. 2 (1987): 65–81. doi.org/10.2307/464747.

Spiro, Jonathan. *Defending the Master Race: Conservation, Eugenics, and the Legacy of Madison Grant.* Lebanon, N.H.: University Press of New England, 2009.

Spring, Joel. *American Education.* 15th ed. New York: McGraw-Hill Education, 2011.

———. *The American School: From the Puritans to the Trump Era.* 10th ed. New York: Routledge, 2018.

Stage, Sarah, and Virginia B. Vincenti, eds. *Rethinking Home Economics: Women and the History of a Profession.* Ithaca, N.Y.: Cornell University Press, 1997.

Stanton, William Ragan. *The Leopard's Spots: Scientific Attitudes Toward Race in America, 1815–59.* Chicago: University of Chicago Press, 1960.

Starblanket, Gina. "Being Indigenous Feminists: Resurgences Against Contemporary Patriarchy." In *Making Space for Indigenous Feminism,* 2nd ed., edited by Joyce Green, 21–41. Halifax/Winnipeg: Fernwood, 2017.

Stark, Heidi Kiiwetinepinesiik. "Criminal Empire: The Making of the Savage in a Lawless Land." *Theory & Event* 19, no. 4 (2016). muse.jhu.edu/pub/1/article/633282.

Stern, Alexandra Minna. *Eugenic Nation: Faults and Frontiers of Better Breeding in Modern America.* Berkeley: University of California Press, 2015.

Stevenson, Brenda, ed. *The Journals of Charlotte Forten Grimké.* New York: Oxford University Press, 1988.

Stivers, Camilla. "Elouise Cobell and the Indian Trust Funds: Accountability and Trust in Public Administration." *Administrative Theory and Praxis* 39, no. 2 (2017): 157–69. doi.org/10.1080/10841806.2017.1293406.

Stokes, Stephannie, and Agnel Philip. "When Families Need Housing, Georgia Will Pay for Foster Care Rather Than Provide Assistance." *ProPublica,* January 18, 2024. www.propublica.org/article/georgia-housing-assistance-foster-care.

Stovall, David. "Are We Ready for 'School' Abolition? Thoughts and Practices of Radical Imaginary in Education." *Taboo: Journal of Culture and Education* 17, no. 1 (2018): 51–61. doi.org/10.31390/taboo.17.1.06.

Sullivan, Andrew. "Dear Ta-Nehisi." *The Dish* (blog), December 1, 2011. dish.andrewsullivan.com/2011/12/01/what-good-is-intelligence-research/.

———. "Race and IQ. Again." *The Dish* (blog), May 14, 2013. dish.andrewsullivan.com/2013/05/14/is-christopher-jencks-a-racist/.

Sullivan, Laura, and Amy Walters. "Incentives and Cultural Bias Fuel Foster System." NPR, October 25, 2011. www.npr.org/2011/10/25/141662357/incentives-and-cultural-bias-fuel-foster-system.

Sullivan, Winnifred Fallers. "'A History of America': Comments on *Johnson v M'Intosh.*"

In *Theologies of American Exceptionalism*, edited by Winnifred Fallers Sullivan and Elizabeth Shakman Hurd. Bloomington: Indiana University Press, 2021.

Swarns, Rachel L. "Insurance Policies on Slaves: New York Life's Complicated Past." *New York Times,* December 18, 2016. www.nytimes.com/2016/12/18/us/insurance-policies-on-slaves-new-york-lifes-complicated-past.html.

Szabo, Joyce M. *Art from Fort Marion: The Silberman Collection.* Norman: University of Oklahoma Press, 2009.

Tachine, Amanda, and Z. Nicolazzo, eds. *Weaving an Otherwise: In-Relations Methodological Practice.* New York: Routledge, 2022.

Tachine, Amanda R. *Native Presence and Sovereignty in College: Sustaining Indigenous Weapons to Defeat Systemic Monsters.* New York: Teachers College Press, 2022.

Takaki, Ronald. *A Different Mirror: A History of Multicultural America.* Boston: Little, Brown, 1993.

Talpade, Medha, and Salil Talpade. "Relevance of the Sankofa Teaching and Learning Approach: A Cultural Comparison." *North American Journal of Psychology* 18, no. 3 (2016): 453–68.

Teachers Pay Teachers. "About Us." TPT. www.teacherspayteachers.com/About-Us.

Terman, Lewis M. *The Measurement of Intelligence: An Explanation of and a Complete Guide for the Use of the Stanford Revision and Extension of the Binet-Simon Intelligence Scale.* Boston: Houghton Mifflin, 1916.

———. "Mental and Physical Traits of a Thousand Gifted Children." In *Child Behavior and Development: A Course of Representative Studies,* 279–306. New York: McGraw-Hill, 1943. doi.org/10.1037/10786-017.

Terman, Lewis M., Virgil E. Dickson, A. H. Sutherland, Raymond H. Franzen, C. R. Tupper, and Grace Fernald. *Intelligence Tests and School Reorganization.* Yonkers, N.Y.: World Book Company, 1922.

Thomas, Evan. *Ike's Bluff: President Eisenhower's Secret Battle to Save the World.* New York: Back Bay Books, 2013.

Thomas, Hugh. *The Slave Trade: The Story of the Atlantic Slave Trade: 1440–1870.* New York: Simon & Schuster, 1997.

Thornton, Russell. *American Indian Holocaust and Survival: A Population History Since 1492.* Norman: University of Oklahoma Press, 1990.

Torpy, Sally J. "Native American Women and Coerced Sterilization: On the Trail of Tears in the 1970s." *American Indian Culture and Research Journal* 24, no. 2 (2000): 1–22. escholarship.org/uc/item/2254n09g.

Trafzer, Clifford E., and Joel R. Hyer, eds. *Exterminate Them! Written Accounts of the Murder, Rape, and Enslavement of Native Americans During the California Gold Rush.* East Lansing: Michigan State University Press, 1999.

Trask, Haunani-Kay. *From a Native Daughter: Colonialism and Sovereignty in Hawaii.* 2nd ed. Honolulu: University of Hawai'i Press, 1999.

Trennert, Robert A. "From Carlisle to Phoenix: The Rise and Fall of the Indian Outing System, 1878–1930." *Pacific Historical Review* 52, no. 3 (August 1983): 267–91. doi.org/10.2307/3639003.

———. *The Phoenix Indian School: Forced Assimilation in Arizona, 1891–1935.* Norman: University of Oklahoma Press, 1988.

Tuck, Eve, and K. Wayne Yang. "Decolonization Is Not a Metaphor." *Decolonization: In-*

digeneity, Education & Society 1, no. 1 (September 2012). jps.library.utoronto.ca/index.php/des/article/view/18630.

Tyack, David, and Larry Cuban. *Tinkering Toward Utopia: A Century of Public School Reform.* Cambridge, Mass.: Harvard University Press, 1995.

University of Lethbridge. "School of Liberal Education Celebrates Blackfoot Heritage by Accepting Image of the Turtle as an Official Symbol." *UNews* (Campus Life), September 25, 2018. www.ulethbridge.ca/unews/article/school-liberal-education-celebrates-blackfoot-heritage-accepting-image-turtle-official.

Urban, Wayne J. *More Than Science and Sputnik: The National Defense Education Act of 1958.* Tuscaloosa: University of Alabama Press, 2018.

U.S. Bureau of the Census. "Negroes in the United States." Washington, D.C.: Government Printing Office, 1904.

U.S. Congress House Committee on the Judiciary. *Indian Religious Freedom Issues: Hearing Before the Subcommittee on Civil and Constitutional Rights.* June 10, 1982.

U.S. Congress Joint Select Committee on the Condition of Affairs in the Late Insurrectionary States. *Report of the Joint Select Committee to Inquire into the Condition of Affairs in the Late Insurrectionary States, Made to the Two Houses of Congress February 19, 1872.* Washington, D.C.: Government Printing Office, 1872.

U.S. Department of the Interior. *Annual Reports of the Department of the Interior for the Fiscal Year Ended June 30, 1898.* Indian Affairs. Washington, D.C.: Government Printing Office, 1898.

U.S. Department of Justice. *Criminal Resource Manual 601–699. 679.* The Major Crimes Act—18 U.S.C. § 1153. www.justice.gov/archives/jm/criminal-resource-manual-679-major-crimes-act-18-usc-1153.

U.S. Government Accountability Office. *Indian Trust Funds: Improvements Made in Acquisition of New Asset and Accounting System But Significant Risks Remain,* September 2000. www.gao.gov/assets/aimd-00-259.pdf.

———. *Native American Youth: Involvement in Justice Systems and Information on Grants to Help Address Juvenile Delinquency,* September 2018. www.gao.gov/assets/gao-18-591.pdf.

U.S. National Park Service. "Sacagawea." Lewis and Clark National Historic Trail, Lewis and Clark National Historical Park. www.nps.gov/people/sacagawea.htm.

U.S. Sentencing Commission, *Native American Advisory Group Public Hearing.* November 4, 2003. www.ussc.gov/sites/default/files/NAAGhear.pdf

U.S. Supreme Court. *Oliphant v. Suquamish Indian Tribe.* 435 U.S. 191 (1978).

Vara-Orta, Francisco. "Fits and Starts: Inside KIPP's School-by-School Discipline Transformation." *Chalkbeat,* November 8, 2018. www.chalkbeat.org/2018/11/8/21106138/fits-and-starts-inside-kipp-s-school-by-school-discipline-transformation.

Vaught, Sabina, Bryan McKinley Jones Brayboy, and Jeremiah Chin. *The School-Prison Trust.* Minneapolis: University of Minnesota Press, 2022.

Vizenor, Gerald. *Native Liberty: Natural Reason and Cultural Survivance.* Lincoln: University of Nebraska Press, 2009.

Vogel, Howard J. "Rethinking the Effect of the Abrogation of the Dakota Treaties and the Authority for the Removal of the Dakota People from Their Homeland." *William Mitchell Law Review* 39, no. 2 (2013): Article 5. open.mitchellhamline.edu/cgi/viewcontent.cgi?article=1491&context=wmlr.

Walch, Michael C. "Terminating the Indian Termination Policy." *Stanford Law Review* 35, no. 6 (1983): 1181–1215. doi.org/10.2307/1228583.

Wald, Johanna, and Daniel J. Losen. "Defining and Redirecting a School-to-Prison Pipeline." *New Directions for Youth Development,* no. 99 (2003): 9–15. doi.org/10.1002/yd.51.

Walker, Francis A. "Restriction of Immigration." *The Atlantic,* June 1896. www.theatlantic.com/magazine/archive/1896/06/restriction-of-immigration/306011/.

Wallace, Anthony F. C. *Jefferson and the Indians: The Tragic Fate of the First Americans.* Cambridge, Mass.: Belknap Press, 2001.

Wang, Leah. "The U.S. Criminal Justice System Disproportionately Hurts Native People: The Data, Visualized." Briefing, Prison Policy Initiative, October 8, 2021. www.prisonpolicy.org/blog/2021/10/08/indigenouspeoplesday/.

Warren, Chezare A. *Urban Preparation: Young Black Men Moving from Chicago's South Side to Success in Higher Education.* Cambridge, Mass.: Harvard Education Press, 2021.

Weber, Max. *The Protestant Ethic and the Spirit of Capitalism.* London: Routledge, 2001. First published 1905; in English translation, 1930.

Webster, Crystal. " 'Hanging Pretty Girls': The Criminalization of African American Children in Early America." *Journal of the Early Republic* 42, no. 2 (2022): 253–76. doi.org/10.1353/jer.2022.0027.

Webster, Crystal Lynn. *Beyond the Boundaries of Childhood: African American Children in the Antebellum North.* Chapel Hill: University of North Carolina Press, 2021.

Webster, Noah. *The American Spelling Book: Containing an Easy Standard of Pronunciation. Being the First Part of a Grammatical Institute of the English Language. To Which Is Added an Appendix Containing a Moral Catechism, and a Federal Catechism.* Wilmington, Del.: Bonsal & Niles, 1800. www.merrycoz.org/books/spelling/SPELLING.xhtml.

———. "On the Education of Youth in America." In *A Collection of Essays and Fugitiv[e] Writings on Moral, Historical, Political and Literary Subjects.* Boston: I. Thomas and E. T. Andrews, 1790.

Weld, Theodore Dwight, Angelina Grimké, and Sarah Grimké. *American Slavery as It Is: Testimony of a Thousand Witnesses.* New York: American Anti-Slavery Society, 1839.

Whitty, Julia. "Elouise Cobell's Accounting Coup." *Mother Jones,* September/October 2005. www.motherjones.com/politics/2005/09/accounting-coup-0.

"Who We Are: Boston Immigration Then and Now." Exhibition. May 24 to October 31, 2017. Norman B. Leventhal Map & Education Center, Boston Public Library. collections.leventhalmap.org/exhibits/19.

Wichgers, Chuck. *Joint Hearing on Education: Chuck Wichgers Testimony.* Wisconsin State Assembly, August 11, 2021. weac.org/wp-content/uploads/2021/10/AB-411-Testimony-Wichgers.pdf.

Widoktadwen Center for Native Knowledge. "Our Philosophy," July 15, 2020. widoktadwen.org/our-philosophy/.

Wildeman, Christopher, and Natalia Emanuel. "Cumulative Risks of Foster Care Placement by Age 18 for U.S. Children, 2000–2011." *PLoS ONE* 9, no. 3 (March 2014): e92785. doi.org/10.1371/journal.pone.0092785.

Wilder, Craig Steven. *Ebony & Ivy: Race, Slavery, and the Troubled History of America's Universities.* New York: Bloomsbury, 2013.

Wilhelm, Mark O. "The Role of Intergenerational Transfers in Spreading Asset Ownership." In *Assets for the Poor: The Benefits of Spreading Asset Ownership,* edited by Thomas M. Shapiro and Edward N. Wolff, 132–62. New York: Russell Sage Foundation, 2001.

William & Mary. "The Brafferton Building." www.wm.edu/about/history/historic campus/brafferton/index.php.

Williams, Heather Andrea. *Self-Taught: African American Education in Slavery and Freedom.* Chapel Hill: University of North Carolina Press, 2005.

Willis, Paul. *Learning to Labour: How Working Class Kids Get Working Class Jobs.* London: Routledge, 2017.

Wilson, Douglas L. "The Evolution of Jefferson's *Notes on the State of Virginia.*" *Virginia Magazine of History and Biography* 112, no. 2 (2004): 98–133.

Wilson, Keith. "Education as a Vehicle of Racial Control: Major General N. P. Banks in Louisiana, 1863–64." *Journal of Negro Education* 50, no. 2 (1981): 156–70. doi.org/10.2307/2294849.

Wister, Owen. *Roosevelt: The Story of a Friendship, 1880–1919.* New York: Macmillan, 1930.

Wolfe, Patrick. "Settler Colonialism and the Elimination of the Native." *Journal of Genocide Research* 8, no. 4 (December 2006): 387–409. doi.org/10.1080/14623520601056240.

Wolff, Megan J. "The Myth of the Actuary: Life Insurance and Frederick L. Hoffman's *Race Traits and Tendencies of the American Negro.*" *Public Health Reports* 121, no. 1 (2006): 84–91.

Woodson, Carter Godwin. *The Mis-Education of the Negro.* Washington, D.C.: Associated Publishers, 1933.

Wright, Carroll Davidson. *The History and Growth of the United States Census.* Washington, D.C.: Government Printing Office, 1900.

Wynter, Sylvia. "1492: A New World View." In *Race, Discourse, and the Origin of the Americas: A New World View,* edited Vera Lawrence Hyatt and Rex Nettleford, 5–57. Washington, D.C.: Smithsonian Institution Press, 1995.

Yoakum, Clarence S., and Robert M. Yerkes, eds. *Army Mental Tests.* New York: Henry Holt, 1920. doi.org/10.1037/11054-000.

Zagorsky, Jay L. "Native Americans' Wealth." In *Wealth Accumulation and Communities of Color in the United States: Current Issues,* edited by Jessica Gordon Nembhard and Ngina S. Chiteji, 133–54. Ann Arbor: University of Michigan Press, 2006.

Zahniser, Timothy. "Alabama & Coushatta Tribes v. Big Sandy School District: The Right of Native American Public School Students to Wear Long Hair." *American Indian Law Review* 19, no. 1 (January 1994): 217–39.

Zaw, Khaing, Jhumpa Bhattacharya, Anne Price, Darrick Hamilton, and William Darity Jr. "Women, Race, & Wealth." Research Brief Series Volume 1. Samuel DuBois Cook Center on Social Equity and Insight Center for Community Economic Development, January 2017. assetfunders.org/wp-content/uploads/womenraceandwealth_partner_material.pdf.

Zenderland, Leila. *Measuring Minds: Henry Herbert Goddard and the Origins of American Intelligence Testing.* Cambridge, England: Cambridge University Press, 1998.

Zimmer, Amy. "QUIZ: Are You Smart Enough to Get into Private Kindergarten?" *DNAinfo New York,* July 7, 2014. www.dnainfo.com/new-york/20140707/upper-east-side/quiz-are-you-smart-enough-get-into-private-kindergarten/.

Zitkála-Šá. *American Indian Stories.* Glorieta, N.M.: Rio Grande Press, 1976. First published 1921 by Hayworth (Washington, D.C.).

Zotigh, Dennis. "Native Perspectives on the 40th Anniversary of the American Indian Religious Freedom Act." *Smithsonian Voices,* November 30, 2018. www.smithsonianmag.com/blogs/national-museum-american-indian/2018/11/30/native-perspectives-american-indian-religious-freedom-act/.

NOTES

EPIGRAPH

1. Spillers, "Mama's Baby, Papa's Maybe," 65.
2. Simpson, *As We Have Always Done*, 6.

INTRODUCTION

1. Díaz, *Postcolonial Love Poem*, 46.
2. Mann, *Twelfth Annual Report of the Board of Education*, 42.
3. Countless authors have referred to slavery as the "original sin" of the United States, and in *Red Pedagogy* Sandy Grande refers to Indigenous genocide as the nation's original sin (48). Maggie Blackhawk does the same in her 2019 article "Federal Indian Law as Paradigm Within Public Law," which refers to both slavery and colonialism as original sins. However, as Ned Blackhawk points out in *The Rediscovery of America* (3), more often than not Indigenous genocide is left out of this framing. "Leading scholarship considers [slavery] both America's original sin and its foundational institution. 'In the American book of genesis,' we are told in a recent best-selling history of the United States, 'liberty and slavery became the American Abel and Cain.' But can we imagine an American Eden that is not cultivated by its original caretakers? Exiled from the American origin story, Indigenous peoples await the telling of a history that includes them. It was their garden homelands, after all, that birthed America."

   I maintain, to quote Jodi Byrd, that "there must be the possibility of the originary in the new world" (*Transit of Empire*, xiv). Not because I am a believer in the linear march of time—I definitively am not—but because I think that origin stories give us a shared place from which to understand one vision of how and where we find ourselves.
4. For more on the many diverse peoples who were captured and transported in the transatlantic slave trade, see Hall, *Slavery and African Ethnicities in the Americas*.
5. Cf. Pauker, Ambady, and Apfelbaum, "Race Salience and Essentialist Thinking in Racial Stereotype Development"; Ramsey and Myers, "Salience of Race in Young Children's Cognitive, Affective, and Behavioral Responses to Social Environments."
6. Hirschfeld, "Seven Myths of Race and the Young Child"; Pauker, Williams, and Steele, "Children's Racial Categorization in Context"; Pauker, Xu, Williams, and Biddle, "Race Essentialism and Social Contextual Differences in Children's Racial Stereotyping."

7. "In our society dominant discourse tries never to speak its own name. Its authority is based on absence. The absence is not just that of the various groups classified as 'other,' although members of these groups are routinely denied power. It is also the lack of any overt acknowledgment of the specificity of the dominant culture, which is simply assumed to be the all-encompassing norm. This is the basis of its power" (Ferguson, Gever, and Minh-ha, *Out There,* 11).

   I capitalize "White" and "Whiteness" here and throughout this book because to be White in the United States is to have a racial identity that shapes one's experiences, worldview, and life trajectories, as does any other racial identity. I believe that one of the ways White supremacy maintains power in our culture is through the occlusion of this fact; White people are endowed with the privilege of believing that race is something other people are burdened with and not something that should trouble them.

   The question of whether to capitalize "White" has sparked a fair amount of debate in recent years, and I wrote about it in a short essay for popular audiences with the comically straightforward title "I'm a Black Scholar Who Studies Race. Here's Why I Capitalize 'White.'" On this matter I am in agreement with Nell Irvin Painter in "Why 'White' Should Be Capitalized, Too," and Kwame Anthony Appiah in "The Case for Capitalizing the *B* in Black."

   One of the critiques I've encountered from peers about this style decision is that it "centers Whiteness," meaning that by capitalizing "White" we are giving White people disproportionate attention and therefore replicating the patterns of a world in which they are allocated disproportionate wealth, power, and visibility. While I have the utmost respect for many of the colleagues offering this point, I do not agree, as capitalization in English is generally intended to denote specificity, not necessarily respect. When we capitalize "Oreos" or "Dick Cheney" or "Walmart," the intention is to be descriptive and specific, not to indicate love or pride. When we do not capitalize bell hooks or adrienne maree brown or will.i.am, as per their preferences, this is not seen as disrespect.

   Ultimately, though, I do not think the question of capitalization warrants dogma. I believe that social scientists, journalists, and all writers should make style decisions that are in accordance with their opinions about race and how it functions. In fact, in general, I wish people would spend less energy thinking about the "right" or "wrong" way to use racial descriptors and more about how these descriptors reflect one's own theories and assumptions about what a given identity is and how it is made and remade.

8. Omi and Winant, *Racial Formation in the United States,* 109.
9. Fields and Fields, *Racecraft,* 146.
10. There have been remarkable points in history where individuals have tried to challenge those boundaries, exposing their fundamental illogic. Homer Plessy became one such figure when he was selected by a group of fellow activists in New Orleans to intentionally get arrested. To challenge the law that forced Black passengers to sit in separate cars, he made use of the self-contradictions of Jim Crow. Plessy tactically deployed the fact that his strictly hierarchal social world defined him as a Black man, even though his skin color made him look to be what newspapers at the time described as "as white as the average white southerner," laying bare the arbitrary contradictions and inconsistencies that make up the boundaries of race and leading to the hallmark *Plessy v. Ferguson* decision that would cement the doctrine of "separate but equal" for generations to come.

    Japanese American Takao Ozawa was also trying to test the edges of the Race Machine when in 1922 he petitioned the Supreme Court to seek naturalized citizenship, pointing out that the law permitted citizenship for "free white persons" and that his skin was in fact lighter than Italian or Spanish immigrants who enjoyed the privileges of citizenship. The court didn't buy it, arguing that "mere color of the skin" didn't make Ozawa into a White person, because he was "clearly of a race which is not Caucasian."

Spotting an opportunity in jurisprudence, Bhagat Singh Thind, who was born in Punjab and enlisted in the U.S. Army during the First World War, argued before the Supreme Court that he ought to have the right to citizenship. After all, early anthropologists classified "Caucasian" to include people from the Indian subcontinent, making Thind "Caucasian." The court pivoted again, denying Thind's claim. "It may be true that the blond Scandinavian and the brown Hindu have a common ancestor in the dim reaches of antiquity," they wrote, "but the average man knows perfectly well that there are unmistakable and profound differences between them today." No further "scientific" evidence was needed, it turns out; the judicial standard for Whiteness was basically *I know it when I see it.* See Smith, *How Race Is Made,* chapter 4, and Kim, "'Yellow' Skin, 'White' Masks," 96–97.

11. Deloria, *Playing Indian,* 3–5.
12. Roberts, *Fatal Invention,* 4. Emphasis mine.
13. Woodson, *The Mis-Education of the Negro,* 29.
14. Woodson, *The Mis-Education of the Negro,* 34.
15. Throughout this book, I use a variety of terms to refer to the first peoples of the lands currently comprising the settler entity of the United States. These terms include: "Indian," "Indigenous," "Native," and specific tribal affiliations. These decisions can be complex to navigate, especially as a non-Native person. When I use the word "Indian," it is either in citation of historical sources or to refer to a culturally constructed figure rather than to an individual person. "The Indian is simultaneously, multiply, a colonial, imperial referent that continues to produce knowledge about the indigenous as 'primitive' and 'savage' otherness" (Byrd, *Transit of Empire,* 19). I do so with the understanding that many Native people use this term for themselves, in various modes—from affinity marker to tongue-in-cheek aside to political reclamation—but that is not in my purview as a non-Native person.

    I use "Native" as a general descriptor while understanding that it is an imperfect choice, because it is an all-encompassing term to describe a diverse range of peoples with different histories, languages, cultural practices, forms of governance, and relations to lands and waters. The same is true of its corollary used in the context of the Canadian settler state, "First Nations." Therefore, where possible, I have strived to use specific tribal designations. When I use the word "Indigenous," I do so with an understanding of the term as a global political identifier that unites first peoples across the world in order to have transnational discussions about processes of colonization and decolonization.
16. "We have been reminded by Hartman and many others that the repetition of the visual, discursive, state, and other quotidian and extraordinary cruel and unusual violences enacted on Black people does not lead to a cessation of violence, nor does it, across or within communities, lead primarily to sympathy or something like empathy. Such repetitions often work to solidify and make continuous the colonial project of violence" (Sharpe, *In the Wake,* 116–17).
17. I'd like to flag some things about the uses of the word "human" or its corollary "subhuman" in this book.

    As many Indigenous thinkers have reminded us, the fellow travelers who make up the non-human, more-than-human, or other-than-human world are our kin. They are sacred neighbors and teachers on the planet we share, relatives on the land in which we find ourselves. Throughout this book I will discuss the ways that Black and Native people have been viewed as subhuman through the lens of European colonial expansion and racial hierarchy, a worldview in which the category of "Man" is the ultimate expression of goodness, worthiness, and power. But to be clear, this is not to suggest that our aspirational goal ought to be for Black and Native people to be elevated to a concept of humanity that just means we get the privilege of participating in the violent domination of the lands and waterways around us. Nothing about that is desirable or aspirational. Nor is my intention to romanticize the notion of the "human," which as many theorists in the field of Black studies have articulated could be considered constitutionally antithetical to Blackness; the figure of the Black is the "symbol, par excellence, for the less-than-human being condemned to death" (Sharpe, *In the Wake,* 21). Through this lens, the figure of humanity—the modern concept itself—is always constructed against the foil of Black people; Black people therefore can never be "human." From this disciplinary perspective, some might feel that the historical and sociological narratives laid out in this book are a bit of a fool's errand, as understanding them will do nothing to undo a fundamentally permanent set of social relations. I don't personally agree with that worldview, but I understand it.

I find this all to be a bit of a terminological puzzle, because in my view "human" remains the best colloquial and accessible way to signify what I'm trying to describe, and the idea of "dehumanization" will resonate with most readers of this book, as will the aspiration toward something like inclusion in the project of "humanity" . . . even as the concept inherently has problems. No answer to this puzzle is forthcoming at the end of this note, but I'd like to be transparent about this conundrum.

18. Noting tribal membership is a common practice when citing Native authors. At times throughout this book I have also added identifiers of various kinds for other authors I cite. To construct these, I have referred to the publicly available information about each individual at the time of writing (self-identified when possible, as on a faculty website). I do so with respectful deference to their wisdom and apologies for the fact that none of us is easily reducible in all our multitudinous work and ways of being in a way that allows for a quick summary. The practice of citation is inherently political; to cite someone is to afford them space in the story I am trying to tell and to invite them in as a co-constructor of that story and its meaning (or, in rarer cases, to name them as an antagonistic conversation partner). I hope that the descriptors I include can serve as one piece of information for the careful reader trying to understand how I have sewn together the pieces that I hope will build an argument across this book.
19. Habtom and Scribe, "To Breathe Together."
20. As my friend Amanda Tachine put it to me, we are "curators of futures."
21. Martinez-Cola, "Visibly Invisible."
22. "As settler conquest and chattel slavery sanctif[y] the white body, they simultaneously cast Indianness and Blackness as its malefic other," writes Chad Benito Infante ("Murder and Metaphysics," 147). Omi and Winant call this casting a process that "combined to form a template, a master frame, that has perniciously shaped the treatment and experiences of other subordinated groups as well" (Omi and Winant, *Racial Formation in the United States,* 107).
23. I believe that, as Bryan McKinley Jones Brayboy argues, Native people in the United States occupy "a liminal space" that straddles, at once, a position "as both racial and legal/political groups and individuals" ("Toward a Tribal Critical Race Theory in Education," 427). Within this liminal space, questions of sovereignty and colonization remain central even as folks move through the world as racialized beings.

At the same time, I want to resist the narrative whereby "transforming American Indians into a minority within a country of minorities is the fait accompli of the colonial project that disappears sovereignty, land rights, and self-governance as American Indians are finally, if not quite fully, assimilated *into* the United States" (Byrd, *Transit of Empire,* 137). Or, to quote Joanne Barker: "Within these identificatory practices, 'indigenous people' are marked as yet another ethnic group within the larger national melting pot, where the goal is to boil out cultural differences and the national jurisdictions and territorial boundaries of indigenous groups by boarding schools, farming programs, citizenship, and adoption. . . . The *making ethnic* or *ethnicization* of indigenous peoples has been a political strategy of the nation-state to erase the sovereign from the indigenous" ("For Whom Sovereignty Matters," 16).

I also recognize what Glen Sean Coulthard (Yellowknives Dene) has described as the dangers inherent in the politics of recognition, whereby settler colonial state governments use promises of mere recognition or even "reconciliation" as a cover for extending their own legitimacy, "reproduc[ing] the very configurations of colonialist, racist, patriarchal state power that Indigenous peoples' demands for recognition have historically sought to transcend" (*Red Skin, White Masks,* 3).

In sum, I write from what I view as these multiple truths, which are contradictory and yet coexisting and overlapping: first, that Indigenous peoples in the United States occupy a specific social location with a distinct relationship to both the state apparatus and (more important) the lands and waters; second, that Indigenous peoples simultaneously have been and continue to be racialized; third, that responding to that racialization and marginalization with projects of social or civic "inclusion" is both woefully inadequate and a surreptitious form of erasure; and yet, fourth, Indigenous peoples have in many instances formed political coalitions within formations of people of color in recognition of solidarity and shared struggle.

24. Estes, *Our History Is the Future,* 6.
25. Cf. Hooker et al., *Black and Indigenous Resistance;* Silva, *Between Brown and Black.*
26. Because it already took me way too long to write just about the United States context, this book is also not an effort to explain or account for global systems of racism or settler colonialism. This is a major limitation, to be sure. The imperialism America perfected on its own shores is but a piece of the global imperialism that has, in turn, created new racial categories through capitalism and displacement. Everything I will describe in this book also has intimate ties to international and transnational phenomena. As Hazel Carby has written, subjugation has known no borders: "The trade in commodified human beings was, however, integral to a global, not national, project of colonial modernity. As African and Indigenous peoples were dispossessed and subjugated, a multiplicity of complex, entangled racial formations were created across the Americas" ("The Limits of Caste").
27. San Pedro, *Protecting the Promise,* 9. This reflection is based on a conversation San Pedro had with Amanda Tachine and Adrienne Keene.
28. King, *The Black Shoals,* 166–67.
29. To quote Christina Sharpe, "The archive, too, is invention" (*In the Wake,* 51).
30. This quotation was featured in the exhibit *The Anishinaabe Universe* at the National Museum of the American Indian, which I visited and recorded on December 17, 2021. The quotation is also viewable on the website of the Widoktadwen Center for Native Knowledge ("Our Philosophy"), where it is attributed to Garry Raven.
31. Kandé, "Look Homeward, Angel"; Talpade and Talpade, "Relevance of the Sankofa Teaching and Learning Approach." Kandé also reminds us of a less often cited but equally important interpretation of the Sankofa symbol: "One must not be afraid to redeem one's past mistakes" (136).

PART I: WHAT ARE SCHOOLS FOR?

1. Deloria, *Custer Died for Your Sins,* 8.
2. Jones in Bureau of Indian Affairs, *Annual Report of the Commissioner, 1902,* 2.
3. *Wall Street Journal,* August 8, 1912, 1.
4. United States Office of Education, *Report of the Commissioner of Education for the Year 1889–90,* vol. 2, 1075. Washington, D.C.: Government Printing Office, 1893.

CHAPTER 1: JEFFERSON'S GHOST

1. Du Bois, *The Souls of Black Folk,* 3.
2. Jefferson, *Notes on the State of Virginia,* 150.
3. National Center for Education Statistics, "Search for Public Schools."
4. Turtle Island is a name for what is sometimes called the continent of North America, derived from the creation stories of multiple Indigenous nations of these lands. I use this term both as a tacit acknowledgment of the blurry boundaries and often overlapping policies and experiences that link together the United States and Canada, and in recognition of the fact that naming something is one of the ways we give it power; these lands had countless names and peoples long before there was such a thing as the United States.
5. Simonton, "Presidential IQ." If you are a professor or statistics teacher interested in teaching students about the use and misuse of quantitative methods to maintain a veil of "objectivity" in work that is in fact deeply subjective, I implore you to look up this paper. Seriously. Put down this book, go read the paper, and come back. Thank me later.
6. Kennedy, "Extract from John F. Kennedy's Remarks."
7. Jefferson, *Notes on the State of Virginia,* ed. Peden, v, xi.

   For a text that would prove to be so influential, the *Notes* began innocuously enough. François Barbé-Marbois, a French diplomat, circulated a twenty-two-question survey to representatives of each of the thirteen brand-new United States. What was the history of each former colony? Who lived there? What natural resources and geographical features did it harbor? What were its systems of education, religion, and commerce? Barbé-Marbois sent the questionnaire to Virginia congressman Joseph Jones, and Jones in turn passed it along to the person he believed to be most knowledgeable about the state: Thomas Jefferson. Jefferson was enthralled by the project. In a 1780 letter, he wrote, "I am at present busily employed for Monsr. Marbois without his knowing it; and have to acknolege [sic] to him the mysterious obligation for making me much better acquainted with my own country than I ever was before. His queries as to this country put into my hands by Mr. Jones I take every occasion which presents itself of procuring answers to." See Wilson, "The Evolution of Jefferson's *Notes.*"
8. Coleman, *That the Blood Stay Pure,* 11.
9. Jefferson, *Notes on the State of Virginia,* ed. Peden, 138. This use of "veil" is ironic, for it was also W. E. B. Du Bois's metaphor for the boundary separating White and Black life.
10. Jefferson, *Notes on the State of Virginia,* ed. Peden, 139.
11. Jefferson, *Notes on the State of Virginia,* ed. Peden, xii–xiii.
12. Wilson, "The Evolution of Jefferson's *Notes,*" 101.
13. Jefferson, *Notes on the State of Virginia,* ed. Peden, 143, 146.
14. In considering this claim, we should first understand that Jefferson was born and raised in a society in flux. As a Virginian born in 1743, Jefferson entered into a world that was at the front line of evolving racial hierarchy. Between the arrival of enslaved people on the coast of Virginia in 1619 and the time when Jefferson was born, Virginia law shifted significantly in ways that concretized the legal link between Blackness and enslavement. As early as the 1640s, there are records of Black people being privately emancipated without interference from the law, owning livestock, being deeded lands, filing lawsuits and testifying in courts, and purchasing their own freedom. During this period, many of the enslaved people arriving in Virginia had first spent time in Brazil or in Spanish colonies in the Caribbean, where it was more common for enslaved Africans to make use of the legal system to buy their freedom, and some of them brought that knowledge with them to Turtle Island (Fuente and Gross, *Becoming Free, Becoming Black,* 53–56). For decades, Black people becoming free was

considered quotidian enough that county court decisions declaring their emancipation often kept very little record of the reason; their freedom was unremarkable. Other enslaved individuals who had been baptized as Christians specifically used that fact as the basis for a successful legal appeal.

But beginning in 1691, when the state assembly passed a set of slave codes, everything would change. For a generation to come, the Virginia legal structure would steadily erode possibilities for Black freedom, equating the condition of Blackness with the condition of slavery. Fuente and Gross point to three reasons for this shift: political, economic, and demographic. The political reason is perhaps the best known: Bacon's Rebellion. In 1676, wealthy White property owner Nathaniel Bacon rallied a militia against the governor of Virginia, and his group of rebels succeeded in torching Jamestown. Bacon's militia was a multiracial band of White, African, and Native people, with free and enslaved and indentured people fighting alongside one another—a terrifying prospect for Virginia's landholding elite. The second reason was demographic, in turn driven by economics: by the 1680s, there were increased opportunities for gainful employment back in England, and other, newer American colonies such as Pennsylvania were proving increasingly attractive, decreasing the number of White indentured servants arriving in Virginia and increasing their cost by 60 percent—while, at the same time, the price of enslaved Africans was dropping. See Fuente and Gross, *Becoming Free, Becoming Black,* 58–59.

First, interracial marriage had to go, as that might be a pathway through which an "abominable mixture" could arise and through which people of color could make civic claims: "It is hereby enacted, that for the time to come, whatsoever English or other white man or woman being free shall intermarry with a negroe, mulatto, or Indian man or woman bond or free shall within three months after such marriage be banished and removed from this dominion forever." If any White woman were to be found to have a child with a Black father, she would have to pay a fee to the local church wardens, who would keep the child in indentured servitude.

Next came the justification that "great inconveniences may happen to this country by the setting of negroes and mulattoes free." Therefore, from then on, no Black person was to be "set free by any person or persons whatsoever, unless such person or persons, their heires, executors or administrators pay for the transportation of such negro or negroes out of the countrey within six moneths after such setting them free" (General Assembly, "An Act for Suppressing Outlying Slaves").

In 1723, it became illegal for Black people or Native people to vote or hold elected office, even if they were legally free. In 1724, legal counsel for the English governing body charged with regulating colonial trade noted in a letter that while surely a slave master could decide what his property could and could not do, it would seem that the matter of free people should be different—did they not have rights? In response, Virginia's lieutenant governor wrote that there were conspiracies suspected among enslaved and free Black people, and based on their "insolence," the assembly had deemed it necessary "to fix a perpetual Brand upon Free-Negros & Mulattos by excluding them from that great Priviledge of a Freeman, well knowing they always did, and ever will, adhere to and favour the Slaves. And 'tis likewise said to have been done with design, which I must think a good one, to make the free-Negros sensible that a distinction ought to be made between their offspring and the Descendants of an Englishman, with whom they never were to be Accounted Equal." In other words, the legislature deemed it necessary to remind these insolent Negros that despite their alleged *legal* freedom, they could never be *socially* free—that they were marked forever with a "brand," a scarlet letter symbolizing that neither they nor their children could ever fully participate in civic life. Otherwise, a free Black person might make the mistake of believing himself to be "as good a Man as the best of his Neighbours" (Gooch, "Denying Free Blacks the Right to Vote"). By the 1770s, when Jefferson was in his thirties, the association between Blackness and enslavement was nearly seamless—fewer than 2 percent of Black people in the state were free (Fuente and Gross, *Becoming Free, Becoming Black,* 73).

15. Jordan, *White Over Black,* 429.
16. "We know that among the Romans, about the Augustan age especially, the condition of their slaves was much more deplorable than that of the blacks on the continent of America," Jefferson says in the *Notes.* Roman slave masters, he wrote, were needlessly cruel, torturing the enslaved or selling them off when they were sick. "We are told of a certain Vedius Pollio, who, in the presence of Augustus, would have given a slave as food to his fish, for having broken a glass," he wrote. This point served not only to suggest that Jefferson and his contemporaries were relatively kind, but also to reinforce the idea that Black inferiority was inherent, fundamental, and absolute, not merely a result of disadvantage—since, after all, enslaved people of the Roman era had gone on to create great works the likes of which Black people were incapable of conceiving. "Notwithstanding these and other discouraging circumstances among the Romans, their slaves were often their rarest artists. They excelled too in science, insomuch as to be usually employed as tutors to their master's children. Epictetus, Terence, and Phædrus, were slaves. But they were of the race of whites. It is not their condition then, but nature, which has produced the distinction." (Jefferson, *Notes on the State of Virginia,* 152.)
17. Wilson, "The Evolution of Jefferson's *Notes,*" 124.
18. Wilson, "The Evolution of Jefferson's *Notes,*" 124–25.
19. Wilson, "The Evolution of Jefferson's *Notes,*" 125.
20. Jefferson, "Thomas Jefferson to Thomas Cooper." In some popular tellings of Jefferson's life story, we are reminded of this fact and invited to consider his personal investment in the institution as a canonical example of how complex and intriguing he was as a figure, and how relatable. After all, have we not all experienced the personal struggle of being part of institutions we theoretically abhor but do not know how to escape? Jordan wrote of Jefferson that he "genuinely hated" slavery and that "for a man of Jefferson's convictions, entanglement in Negro slavery was genuinely tragic." Franklin D. Roosevelt obliquely nods at this contradiction during the dedication address for Jefferson's memorial: "We judge him by the application of his philosophy to the circumstances of his life," he told the assembled crowd. "But in such applying we come to understand that his life was given for those deeper values that persist throughout all time." *Yes,* in other words, *he was the guardian of freedom who kept a class of people unfree. But he gave his life for the* principle *of freedom—and isn't that what really counts?* See Jefferson, "Thomas Jefferson to Thomas Cooper" and "From Thomas Jefferson to William Short"; Jordan, *White Over Black,* 430; and Roosevelt, "Address at the Dedication of the Thomas Jefferson Memorial."
21. Jefferson, "Notes on Arthur Young's Letter to George Washington." We might see this as an example of what Bedour Alagraa has called "cruel mathematics" ("The Interminable Catastrophe").
22. Jefferson, "Thomas Jefferson to John Taylor, 26 November 1798."
23. Banneker, "To Thomas Jefferson from Benjamin Banneker, 19 August 1791."
24. Banneker, "To Thomas Jefferson from Benjamin Banneker, 19 August 1791." I think of "But Sir how pitiable is it to reflect" as the eighteenth-century version of "I just think it's funny how . . ."
25. Coleman, *That the Blood Stay Pure,* 57–60.
26. Coleman, *That the Blood Stay Pure,* 52.
27. This population estimate comes from Thornton, *American Indian Holocaust and Survival,* 133.
28. Adams, *Education for Extinction,* 5.
29. Miller et al., *Discovering Indigenous Lands,* 1.

30. Dunbar-Ortiz, *An Indigenous Peoples' History*. The doctrine by no means originates with Jefferson, or even in the United States—it was established centuries earlier, defined in part by Portuguese colonization of the Canary Islands in the 1400s. Seeking support from the Pope and the right to conquer this archipelago off the northwestern coast of the African continent, the king of Portugal proclaimed that conquest was necessary and desirable "for the salvation of the souls of the pagans of the islands." See Miller et al., *Discovering Indigenous Lands*, 10–11.
31. As legal scholar Robert J. Miller argues, Jefferson "demonstrated an understanding and avid use of Discovery throughout his legal and political careers," drawing upon it strategically and methodically to accomplish his goals for establishing the fortunes of the United States (*Native America, Discovered and Conquered*, 59). One of the most famous instances of this understanding occurred in 1792, in a conversation with British diplomat George Hammond. Recounting the conversation in his papers, Jefferson recalled that Hammond asked him what he believed to be the rights of the United States to Indian land. Ever the scrupulous archivist for posterity, Jefferson made record of his responses to Hammond (Jefferson, "Notes of a Conversation with George Hammond"):

> 1. A right of preemption of their lands, that is to say the sole and exclusive right of purchasing from them whenever they should be willing to sell. 2. A right of regulating the commerce between them and the Whites.—Did I suppose that the right of preemption prohibited any individual of another nation from purchasing lands which the Indians should be willing to sell?—Certainly. We consider it as established by the usage of different nations, into a kind of Jus gentium [international law] for America, that a White nation setting down and declaring that such and such are their limits, makes an invasion of those limits by any other White nation an act of war, but gives no right of soil against the native possessors.

In this brief passage, Jefferson lays down a set of ideas in clear terms. It's important to note that this is not a personal journal of his philosophical musings, nor a chat with a friend. Acting in his official capacity as secretary of state, speaking with his counterpart from a newly allied nation, Jefferson is establishing the key terms upon which the new country will conduct itself. As he made plain to Hammond, the United States had "sole and exclusive" rights to Indian lands—the rights to buy them and the right to regulate their commerce—reflecting a view that Native tribes were substantively different from European nations and did not possess the same rights to sovereignty or free trade among peers. Hammond was none too pleased with Jefferson's assertions: "He said they apprehended our intention was to exterminate the Indians and take the lands.—I assured him that, on the contrary, our system was to protect them," wrote Jefferson.

Jefferson's pointed claims to Hammond made the Doctrine of Discovery explicit, but his stake in the conversation drew upon ideas he held from earlier in his life—years before he ever sat down with the British diplomat.

32. Wallace, *Jefferson and the Indians*, 79.
33. The James Cameron films, of course. Not the good *Avatar*.
34. As Dakota historian Philip J. Deloria describes in his classic analysis *Playing Indian* (4), the idea of the noble savage "both juxtaposes and conflates an urge to idealize and desire Indians and a need to despise and dispossess them. . . . Two interlocked traditions: one of self-criticism, the other of conquest. They balance perfectly, forming one of the foundations underpinning the equally intertwined history of European colonialism and the European Enlightenment."
35. Through its recitation in popular culture, the noble savage has become what Black

feminist philosopher Patricia Hill Collins calls a "controlling image"—an image that, through its circulation and frequent reinscription, creates the illusion that harm against an oppressed group is a natural, inevitable part of the social world. See Collins, *Black Feminist Thought,* 5.

36. Wallace, *Jefferson and the Indians,* 1.
37. Mielke, "Performative Cultures of Early America," 79.
38. Jefferson begins the passage by briefly recounting the story of Logan. His story begins when two Shawnee robbed and murdered a White Virginian. "The neighbouring whites, according to their custom, undertook to punish this outrage in a summary way," searching for Indians to kill as vengeance. "Unfortunately a canoe of women and children, with one man only, was seen coming from the opposite shore, unarmed, and unsuspecting an hostile attack from the whites. . . . This happened to be the family of Logan, who had long been distinguished as a friend of the whites. This unworthy return provoked his vengeance." In the battle that ensued, the Indians were defeated, but Logan, seeing himself as having been wronged, refused to participate in the surrender. Instead, he sent the following speech via messenger to Virginia's governor, Lord Dunmore; Jefferson presents it at length in *Notes on the State of Virginia* (67–68):

> I appeal to any white man to say, if ever he entered Logan's cabin hungry, and he gave him not meat; if ever he came cold and naked, and he clothed him not. During the course of the last long and bloody war, Logan remained idle in his cabin, an advocate for peace. Such was my love for the whites, that my countrymen pointed as they passed, and said, "Logan is the friend of white men." I had even thought to have lived with you, but for the injuries of one man. Col. Cresap, the last spring, in cold blood, and unprovoked, murdered all the relations of Logan, not sparing even my women and children. There runs not a drop of my blood in the veins of any living creature. This called on me for revenge. I have sought it: I have killed many: I have fully glutted my vengeance. For my country, I rejoice at the beams of peace. But do not harbour a thought that mine is the joy of fear. Logan never felt fear. He will not turn on his heel to save his life. Who is there to mourn for Logan?—Not one.

39. See Wallace, *Jefferson and the Indians,* 2.
40. The framing of Native people as savages had deadly consequences. John G. Heckewelder, a missionary who arrived in eastern Ohio in 1772, wrote that White people on the frontier would "rove through the country in search of land, either to settle on, or for speculation . . . [they] maintained that to kill an Indian, was the same as killing a bear or a buffalo" (Nash, *The Unknown American Revolution,* 169).

Jefferson's investment in this violent colonialist expansion was not only a reflection of his role as elder statesman. It was also a personal and economic investment. Jefferson held an interest in the land claims of the Loyal Land Company and the Greenbrier Company, and was closely associated with others engaged in land speculation. In the eighteenth century, these companies were the equivalent of hedge funds—a route for people of great means and elite political connections to trade their prestige for access to a form of investment that could yield lucrative rewards. Working as a conglomerate of shareholders, land speculators purchased vast tracts of land that they believed would make them rich in the long run. It was an unprecedented land grab, and one in which many of the men we refer to as Founding Fathers handily lined their pockets.

"Everyone, it seems, was involved," writes historian Bernard Bailyn. "The population movement into uncultivated and legally unclaimed land excited feverish ambitions in land speculators in every corner of the Anglo-American world. . . . Among them were most of the officials of colonial America, a large phalanx of British politicians and merchants, and planters and merchants everywhere in America, who were determined to get a substantial piece of the pie." Benjamin Franklin was an investor in the Grand Ohio Company, later called the Vandalia Company, which petitioned the King of England to receive almost 2.5 million acres of land—uncultivated and legally unclaimed. The key, of course, was the "legally unclaimed" part, which had the prerequisite of denying Native people any legitimate claim to their land. In this regard, the Doctrine of Discovery benefited not just Jefferson's aspirations for the new nation, but his personal financial investments. The United States in its early days was what economist Edward Glaeser has characterized as a "nation of gamblers," and Jefferson was firmly among them. The Loyal Land Company was directed by three men: surveyor Joshua Fry, physician Thomas Walker, and Jefferson's father, Peter Jefferson. Walker had been one of Thomas Jefferson's guardians when the latter was young. Jefferson had been friends with Patrick Henry (of "Give me liberty or give me death" fame) since he was seventeen years old; Henry would go on to become one of the colonies' leading land speculators. And another familiar name associated with Jefferson was engaged in land speculation: George Washington, who used his early career as a military surveyor to scope out lands that could become lucrative sources of investment and eventually significant wealth and social status.

From 1769 to 1777, Jefferson made attempts to acquire about 35,000 acres of land west of the Appalachian Mountains. Despite this, in 1783 he wrote a letter to James Madison fiercely denying that he had ever had any such interests, admitting only that he had joined others in their land applications without taking leadership or showing enthusiasm. What Jefferson said was patently untrue; he may have been motivated to lie by his desire to have his pending appointment to serve as a cultural minister in France confirmed without incident. He was also under suspicion for having allegedly dedicated resources during the Revolutionary War to the western part of the state—where he and his close associates had financial interests—at the expense of the eastern part of Virginia. For Jefferson as well as for these other Founding Fathers, the claim on Indigenous land was an opportunity for personal gain through financial investment. For some reason, he felt the need to obscure this material interest in the *Notes,* arguing adamantly that White settlers had obtained Native lands fairly in arrangements between equals. "I find in our historians and records, repeated proofs of purchase, which cover a considerable part of the lower country; and many more would doubtless be found on further search. The upper country we know has been acquired altogether by purchases made in the most unexceptionable form." It was important to Jefferson to put forth this narrative, legitimizing the displacement of Native peoples. In an earlier version of the *Notes* manuscript, Jefferson wrote: "It is true that these purchases were sometimes made with the price in one hand and the sword in the other." He crossed it out, and the caveat never made it into the final published version of the *Notes*. See Bailyn, *Voyagers to the West;* Curtis, *Riches, Real Estate, and Resistance;* Franklin, "The Formation of the Grand Ohio Company"; Glaeser, "A Nation of Gamblers"; Rhodes, "Economic History"; Wallace, *Jefferson and the Indians.*

41. In an earlier draft of the document, Jefferson (with the approval of John Adams and Benjamin Franklin) spelled out more explicitly what he meant by "domestic insurrections": those of enslaved people. Governor Dunmore had promised them their freedom if they joined the British side and rose in arms against their masters, an idea that must have been terrifying to Jefferson and his contemporaries. In the earlier draft, Jefferson accused King George of launching the slave trade, profiting from it, and then "exciting those very people to rise in arms among us, and to purchase that liberty of which *he* has deprived them" (emphasis in the original; see Kaplan, "'Domestic Insurrections,'" 244). This complaint does not appear in the final version of the Dec-

laration, which refers only to "domestic insurrections" and the "merciless Indian savages." In both complaints—the retained portion about violent attacks at the hands of Native people and the deleted portion about violent threats from enslaved Black people goaded into rising up against their masters—the Founding Fathers conveniently omit any of their own culpability, placing blame squarely on the shoulders of the king and making use of rhetoric that would appeal to aspiring patriots regardless of whether it maintained any kind of internal consistency with their own actions. Thomas Paine's *Common Sense,* often viewed alongside the Declaration as a document that spurred the spirits of great men toward revolution, made use of the same rhetoric: "There are thousands and tens of thousands, who would think it glorious to expel from the Continent, that barbarous and hellish power, which hath stirred up the Indians and the Negroes to destroy us; the cruelty hath a double guilt, it is dealing brutally by us, and treacherously by them" (Paine, *Common Sense,* 99).

42. William & Mary, "The Brafferton Building."
43. The Doctrine of Discovery became the law of the land through the 1823 case of *Johnson v. McIntosh* (or *M'Intosh*), a dispute over a land claim that was the first of the "Marshall trilogy" cases. William McIntosh, a White man, asserted that he owned a piece of land in what is currently Illinois via a federal land grant from the U.S. government. In turn, the government claimed to have purchased the land via treaty. Meanwhile, two other companies claimed that they had purchased the lands from the Illinois and Piankeshaw Nations years before the government entered into that treaty.

The questions before the Supreme Court were: Who had a more legitimate claim to the land? Was the tribes' earlier sale valid? Did tribal nations have the right to sell their land directly to private entities?

The case presented an inherent tension for the project of the settler state. The issue at hand was not just about settling this land dispute, but about maintaining broader American ambitions to fulfill Jefferson's dream of holding the entire continent. If the Supreme Court ruled that the initial sale had been valid, establishing that tribes *did* have the right to freely sell their lands—meaning that they truly *owned* their lands—that would undermine the project of westward expansion, which depended upon forcing Native land sales to the U.S. government via treaty. On the other hand, if the court ruled that Native people did *not* have the right to sell their lands, the decision could invalidate the patchwork of treaties and sales that the government had been engaging in since the Jefferson presidency. Either decision would seem to challenge legal precedent and establish a new foundation that could threaten the American colonial project.

So Chief Justice John Marshall took a simpler route. Rather than just addressing these competing claims, he also told a story. It was a comfortable story, one that began with the arrival of Europeans on the shores of what would become a new nation and that ended with the inevitability of America's destiny as a land governed by White settlers. Marshall first recounted the narrative of European colonists seizing as much of the continent as they could, generously allowing Native people to remain there "as occupants" while asserting "the ultimate dominion" to themselves, in the way a landlord allows a renter to temporarily take up space:

> On the discovery of this immense continent, the great nations of Europe were eager to appropriate to themselves so much of it as they could respectively acquire. Its vast extent offered an ample field to the ambition and enterprise of all; and the character and religion of its inhabitants afforded an apology for considering them as a people over whom the superior genius of Europe might claim an ascendency. . . . While the different nations of Europe respected the right of the natives, as occupants, they asserted the ultimate dominion to be in themselves; and claimed and

> exercised, as a consequence of this ultimate dominion, a power to grant the soil, while yet in possession of the natives. These grants have been understood by all to convey a title to the grantees, subject only to the Indian right of occupancy.

Marshall went on to assert that the United States, once a collection of territories governed by distant European crowns, inherited the "ultimate dominion" of those crowns when it became an independent nation. Native people did not have true ownership. They could sell their lands and cede their right of occupancy, but not to just anybody, nor could they engage in a competitive market-based process to seek the highest bidder. They could *only* cede this right to the United States.

> [The United States] maintain, as all others have maintained, that discovery gave an exclusive right to extinguish the Indian title of occupancy, either by purchase or by conquest; and gave also a right to such a degree of sovereignty as the circumstances of the people would allow them to exercise. . . . These claims have been maintained and established as far west as the river Mississippi, by the sword. The title to a vast portion of the lands we now hold, originates in them. It is not for the courts of this country to question the validity of this title, or to sustain one which is incompatible with it.

While Marshall admitted that, in ideal circumstances, a conquered people should maintain their property rights, should not be oppressed, and should be governed fairly, he expressed sympathy for the actions of European settlers and determined that Native people should not be subject to the same consideration as "civilized" people:

> The tribes of Indians inhabiting this country were fierce savages, whose occupation was war, and whose subsistence was drawn chiefly from the forest. To leave them in possession of their country was to leave the country a wilderness; to govern them as a distinct people was impossible, because they were as brave and as high spirited as they were fierce, and were ready to repel by arms every attempt on their independence.
>
> What was the inevitable consequence of this state of things? The Europeans were under the necessity either of abandoning the country, and relinquishing their pompous claims to it, or of enforcing those claims by the sword, and by the adoption of principles adapted to the condition of a people with whom it was impossible to mix, and who could not be governed as a distinct society, or of remaining in their neighborhood and exposing themselves and their families to the perpetual hazard of being massacred.

Marshall went on to express some self-awareness of the obvious absurdity of declaring that anyone can show up on the shores of a land they've never seen, inhabited by people they've never met, and declare it their own. Nevertheless, he wrote, what's done is done, and now it's the law, because it must be.

> However extravagant the pretension of converting the discovery of an inhabited country into conquest may appear, if the principle has been asserted in the first instance, and afterwards sustained; if a country has been acquired and held under it; if the property of the great mass of the community originates in it, it becomes the law of the land, and cannot be questioned.

Incidentally, in another point for the legacy of land speculation, the "Johnson" side of the case represented Thomas Johnson—one of the first justices of the Supreme Court, who had bought the land and left it to his descendants, who then leased the land.

For more on this case, see Sullivan, "'A History of America.'"

This summary and my understanding of this case owe a great debt to Elizabeth Hidalgo Reese, Yunpoví (Nambé Pueblo), who generously reviewed it and provided feedback, clarification, and suggested edits.

44. Jefferson, "Thomas Jefferson to William Ludlow, 6 September 1824."
45. The Supreme Court's decision in 1823 had much earlier roots—in Jefferson's writings in the *Notes* four decades earlier. As Robert J. Miller and other legal scholars have written, Jefferson "personifies the use of Discovery against American Indians because he understood the Doctrine and used it regularly in his work as a private lawyer, state official, Secretary of State, Vice-President, and President" (Miller et al., *Discovering Indigenous Lands,* 66).

Even before his conversation with Hammond, Jefferson articulated an earlier version of the Doctrine in the *Notes* themselves, writing that the state held "a sole and exclusive power of taking conveyances of the Indian right of soil: since, according to them, an Indian conveyance alone could give no right to an individual, which the laws would acknowledge." (Jefferson, *Notes on the State of Virginia,* 145.)

46. Jefferson, "To John Adams from Thomas Jefferson, 11 June 1812."
47. Jefferson, "Thomas Jefferson to Pierre Samuel Du Pont de Nemours, 25 April 1802."
48. Scholastic, "Lewis and Clark Student Activity." This set of activities is designated as taking seventeen class periods, which seems like . . . a lot?
49. As historian Rebecca Kay Jager points out in *Malinche, Pocahontas, and Sacagawea,* Sacagawea is rarely considered through the lens of her own time or identity. Rather, she and women like her are "pliable legends," conscripted into a pleasing mythology intended to "clarify how Natives and Europeans came together willingly. . . . Native Americans and Euro-Americans endured the frontier together, and this shared experience became the ideological foundation for nationhood" (18). Inspiring stories of teamwork united on a shared adventure across social boundaries fit neatly into romantic American values such as multiculturalism, inclusion, and "strong, independent women," as described by the U.S. National Park Service ("Sacagawea").

Sacagawea, much like Logan or cartoon Columbus, belongs in the category of what historian Nell Irvin Painter calls "invented greats"—"glorious" individuals "known purely through the agency of others, who have constructed and maintained their legends . . . consumed as a signifier and beloved for what we need her to have said" (Painter, *Sojourner Truth,* 285; and see Richards, "Inventing Sacagawea," 4). It's no coincidence that the story of Sacagawea rose to mainstream prominence through the efforts of the National American Woman Suffrage Association, which raised money to commemorate a statue of her to be unveiled in Oregon at the 1905 centennial celebration of the expedition. At the dedication, Susan B. Anthony called Sacagawea "one of the greatest American heroines," and Eva Emery Dye—author of the book *The Conquest: The True Story of Lewis and Clark,* published in 1902 to wild popularity—called her "a reminder and inspiration to duty and to progress," comparing her to the Pilgrims and their voyage to Plymouth Rock.

In *The Conquest* (290), Dye described Sacagawea as a paragon of Euro-American ideals of femininity, a keystone in the bridge to a new future: "Sacajawea, modest princess of the Shoshones, heroine of the great expedition, stood with her babe in arms and smiled upon them from the shore. So had she stood in the Rocky Mountains pointing out the gates. So had she followed the great rivers, navigating the continent. Sacajawea's hair was neatly braided, her nose was fine and straight, and her skin pure copper like the statue in some old Florentine gallery. Madonna of her race, she had led the way to a new time."

Dye refers to Sacagawea as a princess multiple times, and specifically a "modest princess" twice. As Vine Deloria Jr. has noted, the figure of the "Indian princess" provides an image at once aspirational and familiar—"royalty for the taking." Elsewhere in the book (227), Dye describes Sacagawea's reunion with an old friend: "They wandered off and talked and talked of the wonderful fortune that had come to Sacajawea, the wife of a white man." Elevating Sacagawea to the level of partnership with the other great discoverer of the land, she writes: "Across North America a Shoshone Indian Princess touched hands with Jefferson, opening her country."

At a time when Susan B. Anthony and her fellow suffragettes were campaigning for the rights of White women to vote, the statue and the novel and the speeches neatly served a twofold purpose: to reaffirm the legitimacy of Manifest Destiny while also making a compelling argument that proper, princessly women were necessary for the thriving of the republic and should be included as leaders in the nation's march toward progress. The statue portrays Sacagawea much as Dye described her, in the tradition of Delacroix's *Liberty Leading the People* or Gast's *American Progress:* proud, chest partly bared, dressed in flowing garments. Looking bravely into the future of the expanding nation, Sacagawea holds her head high and points at the possible. The sculpture is titled *Sacajawea and Jean-Baptiste,* and she holds her baby on her back—a child of the New World. The inscription reads: "Erected by the women of the United States in memory of the only woman in the Lewis & Clark expedition, and in honor of the pioneer mother of Oregon."

"The rhetorical invention of Sacagawea as a symbol of American leadership and progress characterized the conquest of the West in a manner that affirmed US expansion and asserted a leading role for women in the public realm," writes communication scholar Cindy Koenig Richards. Sacagawea and her counterparts are "gracious Indian women and nurturing mothers of new civilizations," at the center of "sentimental creation stories [that] have expressed the grand theme of cross-cultural respect and admiration."

We know that Sacagawea, a Shoshone woman, was born in what is now referred to as Idaho, at a time when her nation was experiencing hunger and uncertainty and had taken on a nomadic way of life out of necessity. When she was twelve years old, she was captured along with several other women and children by Hidatsa men who took her hundreds of miles east. After a few years, the Hidatsa gave her as a token of political alliance to a French Canadian trader, Toussaint Charbonneau. When Lewis and Clark brought Charbonneau into their corps to serve as an interpreter, a pregnant Sacagawea joined them. Historian Gary Moulton, who edited a definitive collection of Lewis and Clark's journals, observes that the precise details of what happened next have elicited fierce debate and controversy. "Most of what we know about her is found in expedition journals," Moulton writes, "and it is very meager material on which to build a legend" (xxviii). Sacagawea's presence may have been reassuring to Native people who saw the party arrive, as a woman with a baby signified that their intentions were not immediately violent. (Only, as it turns out, eventually violent, in the form of dispossession and empire.)

She also provided guiding insight to the party when they arrived in the region where she had grown up, as Clark recorded in his journal:

> The Indian woman wife to Shabono [Charbonneau] informed me that she had been in this plain frequently and knew it well that the Creek which we decended was a branch of Wisdom river and when we assended the higher part of the plain we would discover a gap in the moun-

> tains in our direction to the Canoes, and when we arrived at that gap we would See a high point of a mountain covered with snow in our direction the canoes. . . . I discovered one at a distance very high covered with Snow which bore S. 80° E. The Squ*r pointed to the gap through which she said we must pass which was S. 56° E. She said we would pass the river before we reached the gap.

Did Sacagawea single-handedly guide the intrepid band of pioneers over treacherous unknown lands, soothing animosities and paving the way toward ensuring that the United States enact its godly fortune? Almost certainly not. Do the facts of her role matter? In a way, not really. "Sacagawea's story," writes Jager, "supports one of America's most compelling national myths: that Americans had a divine mission to erect a new social order on the frontier and to extend its boundaries to the continent's national geographical borders. Sacagawea's commitment to the American cause (later defined as Manifest Destiny) positioned her at the center of American frontier myth. . . . [She] clarified European dominance by illustrating how loving Native women embraced the outsiders, gave birth to mixed-blood children, and symbolically offered the newcomers inheritance rights to Indian land" (19).

By no means does this assessment minimize Sacagawea's life, her agency, or her significance. But she was significant by virtue of being a person: a woman, a mother, and a Shoshone; an autonomous being with thoughts and feelings, who navigated the world in the best way she could in order to survive. By recruiting her into the service of Manifest Destiny, mythologies about her belie that simple fact. See Deloria, *Custer Died for Your Sins;* Jager, *Malinche, Pocahontas, and Sacagawea;* Dye, *The Conquest;* and Richards, "Inventing Sacagawea."

50. Cover image from *In Their Own Words: Lewis and Clark* by George Sullivan. Cover illustration copyright © 1999 by Scholastic Inc. Reprinted by permission of Scholastic Inc. Cover image from *The Lewis and Clark Expedition: A True Book* by John Perritano. Cover illustration copyright © 2010 by Scholastic Inc. Reprinted by permission of Children's Press, an imprint of Scholastic Inc. Cover image from *Cornerstones of Freedom: The Lewis and Clark Expedition* by Teresa Domnauer. Cover illustration copyright © 2012 by Scholastic Inc. Reprinted by permission of Children's Press, an imprint of Scholastic Inc.
51. Trask, *From a Native Daughter,* 18, 25.
52. Wolfe, "Settler Colonialism and the Elimination of the Native," 388. Though Wolfe is the most frequently cited scholar in efforts to explain settler colonialism, the idea did not originate with him. Arvin's "Indigenous Feminist Notes on Embodying Alliance Against Settler Colonialism" (2019) and Kauanui's "'A Structure, Not an Event': Settler Colonialism and Enduring Indigeneity" (2016) helpfully recall that this citational practice reflects how White male scholars often gain academic recognition in ways that others may not.

As Bhandar and Ziadah have written in the context of Palestine studies ("Acts and Omissions"), there is a risk that "a politics of citation is developing that reinscribes different forms of gender-race privilege. It often marginalizes scholars who have been writing about the effects of settler colonialism for decades, but perhaps not using the analytic of settler colonialism to describe the colonization and occupation of their land."

Other scholars have built upon, critiqued, and complicated Wolfe's writings on settler colonialism to illustrate the complex set of relationships created by the settler state, particularly the role of enslaved Black people and their descendants. Historian Robin D. G. Kelley, for instance, points out that some of Wolfe's insights, though intended to be global, arise out of the specific historic context of Australia, not the United States—rendering the role of slavery in the construction of the modern world an afterthought. Kelley writes in "The Rest of Us: Rethinking Settler and Native" (268):

> I want to suggest that by not incorporating more of the globe in his study, Wolfe's particular formulation of settler colonialism delimits more than it reveals. As he writes in the introduction: "The role that colonialism has assigned to Indigenous people is to disappear. By contrast, though slavery meant the giving up of Africa, Black Americans were primarily colonised for their labour rather than for their land." The statement is problematic for two reasons. First, it presumes that indigenous people exist only in the Americas and Australasia. African indigeneity is erased in this formulation because, through linguistic sleight of hand, Africans are turned into Black Americans. The Atlantic Slave Trade rips Africans from their homeland and deposits them in territories undergoing settlement and dispossession, but renaming severs any relationship to their land and indigenous communities. . . . Consequently, settler colonialism on the African continent falls out of Wolfe's purview.

53. Trask, *From a Native Daughter*, 26.
54. Tuck and Yang, "Decolonization Is Not a Metaphor," 5.
55. Tuck and Yang, "Decolonization Is Not a Metaphor," 6–7.
56. Clowse, *Brainpower for the Cold War*, 6–8.
57. Thomas, *Ike's Bluff*, 253.
58. Clowse, *Brainpower for the Cold War*, 4.
59. Gallup, *The Gallup Poll*, 1525.
60. Eisenhower, "Transcript of the President's News Conference."
61. Historian Barbara Barksdale Clowse makes the important point that many in education policy circles had been agitating for greater federal financing of schools for some time prior to this. The inflection point created by Sputnik provided not a brand-new catalyst for this group, but rather opportunity in crisis, allowing them to overcome political opponents who decried the possibility of federal overreach in local administration of school affairs. See Clowse, *Brainpower for the Cold War*, chapter 4.
62. Urban, *More Than Science and Sputnik*, 3; National Defense Education Act of 1958.
63. National Defense Education Act of 1958. The value in today's dollars was calculated using the U.S. Bureau of Labor Statistics Consumer Price Index calculator.
64. National Defense Education Act of 1958.
65. National Defense Education Act of 1958.
66. Graham, *Schooling America*, 2.
67. Givens and Ison astutely refer to these three threads as "symbiotic," pointing out that the usual narrative of early American education history, which centers White students and tangentially mentions Black and Native students as having been simply "excluded," is woefully inaccurate: "The history of formal U.S. education is fundamentally a story where White education developed in contradistinction to the educational domination of Black and Native peoples; and the relationships between White, Native, and Black education were based on terms of violent extraction and extermination. . . . One group's experience held a symbiotic relationship to the ideological and institutional development of education for the others" ("Toward New Beginnings," 320).

CHAPTER 2: MAKING CITIZENS: SCHOOLS FOR WHITE PEOPLE

1. As historian Matthew Frye Jacobson observes, "Between the 1840s and the 1920s it was not altogether clear just where that line ultimately would be drawn" (*Whiteness of a Different Color*, 7).

2. Specifically, for Jefferson it meant "Saxon" (Painter, *History of White People,* 111, 125).
3. Painter, *History of White People,* 34.
4. Painter, *History of White People,* 133.
5. Emerson as cited in Painter, *History of White People,* 139.
6. Painter, *History of White People,* 147–48.
7. Alperin and Batalova, "European Immigrants in the United States."
8. Painter, *History of White People,* 206, 211.
9. Walker, "Restriction of Immigration."
10. Painter, *History of White People,* 250.
11. Wister, *Roosevelt,* 66.
12. Coolidge, "Whose Country Is This?"
13. Ebeling, "Massachusetts Education Laws of 1642, 1647, and 1648."
14. Dunn, *The Laws and Liberties of Massachusetts.*
15. Spring, *The American School.*
16. Ford, *The New-England Primer,* 19.
17. Ford, *The New-England Primer,* 69.
18. Committee of the Virginia General Assembly, "A Bill for the More General Diffusion of Knowledge."
19. Spring, *American Education,* 13.
20. Spring, *The American School.*
21. Milson et al., *American Educational Thought.*
22. Milson et al., *American Educational Thought,* 73.
23. Webster, "On the Education of Youth in America."
24. Spring, *The American School.*
25. Cremin, *American Education: The National Experience,* 569.
26. Webster, *The American Spelling Book,* 148–49.
27. Cremin, *American Education: The Colonial Experience,* 260.
28. Cremin, *American Education: The Colonial Experience,* 261.
29. Lannie, *Public Money and Parochial Education,* 21.
30. Lannie, *Public Money and Parochial Education,* 24, 26, 240.
31. Lannie, *Public Money and Parochial Education,* 241–42.
32. Lannie, *Public Money and Parochial Education,* 243.
33. Spring, *The American School.*
34. Spring, *The American School.*
35. Kaestle, *Pillars of the Republic,* 80.
36. Kaestle, *Pillars of the Republic,* 80.
37. Spring, *The American School,* Table 8.1.
38. Library of Congress, "Immigrants in the Progressive Era."
39. For a critique of the "nation of immigrants" language, see Dunbar-Ortiz, *Not a "Nation of Immigrants."*
40. Cubberley, *Changing Conceptions of Education,* 14.
41. Cubberley, *Changing Conceptions of Education,* 15–16.
42. You can find an account of this story in Jackson, *Dixie's Italians,* 98–99; it was also covered in the *Hattiesburg Daily News* (see "Consul Asks for Troops," 1907).
43. Covello, *The Heart Is the Teacher,* 70.
44. Covello, *The Heart Is the Teacher,* 43–44.
45. Ellis, *To the Flag,* 40; 4.
46. Jones and Meyer, *The Pledge,* 70–71.
47. Jones and Meyer, *The Pledge,* 71.
48. Ellis, *To the Flag,* 15.
49. Ellis, *To the Flag,* 16.
50. Ellis, *To the Flag,* 29–31.
51. Jones and Meyer, *The Pledge,* 71.

52. Ellis, *To the Flag*, 19.
53. Ellis, *To the Flag*, 22.
54. Bellamy, Essay on immigration, 258.
55. Spoiler: he was racist.
56. "Foreign-Born Share of the Population 1840–2015," Boston Planning & Development Agency and the U.S. Census Bureau, cited in "Who We Are: Boston Immigration Then and Now."
57. Levenstein, "The New England Kitchen."
58. Levenstein, "The New England Kitchen."
59. Stage and Vincenti, *Rethinking Home Economics*, 24.
60. Shapiro, *Perfection Salad*, 150–51.
61. Levenstein, "The New England Kitchen."
62. Levine, *School Lunch Politics*, 32.
63. Levine, *School Lunch Politics*, 32.
64. Levenstein, "The New England Kitchen."
65. Levine, *School Lunch Politics*, 30.
66. Stage and Vincenti, *Rethinking Home Economics*, 27.
67. Apple, "Liberal Arts or Vocational Training?," 81.
68. Hillison, "The Coalition That Supported the Smith-Hughes Act."
69. Apple, "Liberal Arts or Vocational Training?," 84.
70. Apple, "Liberal Arts or Vocational Training?," 87.
71. Apple, "Liberal Arts or Vocational Training?," 90.
72. Levine, *School Lunch Politics*, 21–22.
73. Addams, "Why Women Should Vote."
74. Lazerson, "Urban Reform and the Schools," 116.
75. Lazerson, "Urban Reform and the Schools," 122.
76. Gilder, "The Kindergarten," 2.
77. Gilder, "The Kindergarten," 3.
78. Lazerson, "Urban Reform and the Schools," 121.
79. Frost, *A History of Children's Play and Play Environments*.
80. Anderson, "'The Playground of Today.'"
81. Not exactly a banger.
82. Curtis, *Education Through Play*, 80.
83. Curtis, *Education Through Play*, 78–79.
84. Curtis, *Education Through Play*, 82.
85. Curtis, *Education Through Play*, 75.
86. Curtis, *Education Through Play*, 182–83.
87. I'm deeply indebted to Joel Spring's classic *The American School* for its discussion of these examples as instruments for creating (White) national cohesion, and Spring's broader discussion of other constructs of the schooling environment (e.g., kindergarten, summer school), which he argues serve a function of social control and that persist, mostly uninterrogated, in everyday life.
88. Morrison, "On the Backs of Blacks."
89. Jacobson, *Whiteness of a Different Color*, 8.

CHAPTER 3: SAVIORISM AND SOCIAL CONTROL: SCHOOLS FOR BLACK PEOPLE

1. Mills, "An African School for African Americans."
2. Ficker, "From *Roberts* to *Plessy*," 301–2.
3. Boston Primary School Committee, *Report*, 10.
4. Boston Primary School Committee, *Report*, 7.
5. The distinction between schooling and education is an important one that many have

made, but it first came to me as an insight via the teaching of my mentor and graduate adviser Sara Lawrence-Lightfoot.

6. Du Bois, *Black Reconstruction in America;* Egerton, *The Wars of Reconstruction,* 151.
7. Egerton, *The Wars of Reconstruction,* 145.
8. Lewinson, *Race, Class & Party,* 36; Du Bois, *Black Reconstruction in America.*
9. Du Bois, *Black Reconstruction in America.*
10. Morris, *Reading, 'Riting, and Reconstruction,* ix.
11. Morris, *Reading, 'Riting, and Reconstruction,* xi.
12. Morris, *Reading, 'Riting, and Reconstruction,* 6.
13. Quoted in Morris, *Reading, 'Riting, and Reconstruction,* 6.
14. Quoted in Morris, *Reading, 'Riting, and Reconstruction,* 150.
15. Quoted in Morris, *Reading, 'Riting, and Reconstruction,* 11.
16. Department of the Tennessee and State of Arkansas, *Report,* 75.
17. De Forest, *A Union Officer in the Reconstruction,* 116–17.
18. Eberhart to Hunt, 1866, quoted in Morris, *Reading, 'Riting, and Reconstruction,* 41.
19. Quoted in Morris, *Reading, 'Riting, and Reconstruction,* 42.
20. Givens, *Fugitive Pedagogy,* 4; Morris, *Reading, 'Riting, and Reconstruction,* 68.
21. Hancock, *Letters of a Civil War Nurse,* 44.
22. Morris, *Reading, 'Riting, and Reconstruction,* 57–58.
23. Quoted in Morris, *Reading, 'Riting, and Reconstruction,* 59.
24. Quoted in Morris, *Reading, 'Riting, and Reconstruction,* 62.
25. Quoted in Morris, *Reading, 'Riting, and Reconstruction,* 143.
26. Morris, *Reading, 'Riting, and Reconstruction,* 143.
27. Quoted in Morris, *Reading, 'Riting, and Reconstruction,* 146–47.
28. Porter, *Led On!,* 70–71.
29. Morris, *Reading, 'Riting, and Reconstruction,* 140.
30. Quoted in Morris, *Reading, 'Riting, and Reconstruction,* 141–42.
31. Quoted in Morris, *Reading, 'Riting, and Reconstruction,* 151.
32. American Tract Society, *The Freedman's Third Reader,* 51.
33. American Tract Society, *The Freedman's Third Reader,* 54.
34. Forsdick and Høgsbjerg, *Toussaint Louverture,* 17.
35. American Tract Society, *The Freedman's Third Reader,* 82.
36. American Tract Society, *The Freedman's Third Reader,* 83.
37. American Tract Society, *The Freedman's Third Reader,* 84–85.
38. American Tract Society, *The Freedman's Third Reader,* 86.
39. Child, *The Freedmen's Book,* 241–242.
40. Child, *The Freedmen's Book,* 270.
41. Child, *The Freedmen's Book,* 271–72.
42. Child, *The Freedmen's Book,* 273.
43. Child, *The Freedmen's Book,* 274.
44. Child, *The Freedmen's Book,* 275.
45. Child, *The Freedmen's Book,* 276.
46. Karcher, *A Lydia Maria Child Reader.*
47. See Guz and Suslovic, "'She Must Be Experimental.'"
48. Harper, "White Women Teaching in the North," 131.
49. Meiners, "Disengaging from the Legacy of Lady Bountiful," 87.
50. Meiners, "Disengaging from the Legacy of Lady Bountiful," 88.
51. "The persistence of this Lady-icon contributes to a climate that makes addressing white supremacy, heteronormativity, and class issues in teacher education difficult, if not impossible. I also suggest that the endurance of this image as it is subtly (and often not so subtly) reinforced in popular culture, in teacher education programs, and beyond, actively prohibits certain bodies from entering the field" (Meiners, "Disengaging from the Legacy of Lady Bountiful," 90).

It's important to note that the image of White Lady Bountiful is not a liberatory or empowering image for the individuals bound within it. It is also a form of patriarchal control enacted upon White women, conscripting them into a specific mode of femininity that serves the aims of the state. As Vaught, Brayboy, and Chin put it: "This was a race-gender worldmaking labor by which white possession, again, relied on dispossession and disappearance. . . . To make women of white women, they sought to rupture the maternity or parenthood of Indigenous women, and leave them dispossessed of their children and Indigenous futures." Meanwhile, these women served as "the paramilitary force entrenching conquest power" (*The School-Prison Trust*, 36–37).

52. National Center for Education Statistics, "Preprimary, Elementary, and Secondary Education." As of this writing, the most recent year for which these figures are available is the 2020–2021 academic year.
53. Marx and Pennington, "Pedagogies of Critical Race Theory," 101.
54. Quoted in Morris, *Reading, 'Riting, and Reconstruction*, 89.
55. Chireau, *Black Magic*, 130.
56. Quoted in Morris, *Reading, 'Riting, and Reconstruction*, 89.
57. Morris, *Reading, 'Riting, and Reconstruction*, 99–100.
58. Quoted in Morris, *Reading, 'Riting, and Reconstruction*, 90–91.
59. Quoted in Morris, *Reading, 'Riting, and Reconstruction*, 92.
60. Morris, *Reading, 'Riting, and Reconstruction*, 126–27.
61. U.S. Congress Joint Select Committee, *Report*, 46.
62. Stevenson, *Journals of Charlotte Forten Grimké*, 397. Entry dated November 13, 1862.
63. Grimké, "Life on the Sea Islands."
64. Anderson, *The Education of Blacks in the South*.
65. Anderson, *The Education of Blacks in the South*.
66. Du Bois, "The Hampton Idea," 11–12.

CHAPTER 4: DISAPPEARANCE BY DESIGN: SCHOOLS FOR NATIVE PEOPLE

1. Kohlbrenner, "William Torrey Harris."
2. Bureau of Indian Affairs, *Annual Report of the Commissioner, 1895*, 34. I would be remiss not to point out that, amid the general goofiness of Harris's ideology, the idea that no Asian civilization had experienced feudalism stands out as especially ill-informed.
3. Bureau of Indian Affairs, *Annual Report of the Commissioner, 1895*, 34.
4. Bureau of Indian Affairs, *Annual Report of the Commissioner, 1880*, 7–8.
5. Bureau of Indian Affairs, *Annual Report of the Commissioner, 1880*, 7–8.
6. For more on the relationship between railroad expansion, the theft of Native land, and American imperialism, see Karuka, *Empire's Tracks*.
7. Schurz was also the namesake of the locally zoned high school in the neighborhood I grew up in, and his wife, Margaret, was another well-regarded kindergarten reformer.
8. Schurz, "Present Aspects of the Indian Problem."
9. Quoted in Adams, *Education for Extinction*, 15, though Hiram Price is referred to as "Henry."
10. Momaday, in Fear-Segal and Rose, *Carlisle Indian Industrial School*, 46.
11. Barrows, *Annual Meeting of the Lake Mohonk Conference*, 9.
12. Bureau of Indian Affairs, *Annual Report of the Commissioner, 1882*, 92.
13. Pratt, *Battlefield and Classroom*, 109.
14. Lookingbill, *War Dance at Fort Marion*, chapter 1.
15. Pratt, *Battlefield and Classroom*, 92.
16. Pratt, *Battlefield and Classroom*, 113.
17. Pratt, *Battlefield and Classroom*.

18. Pratt, *Battlefield and Classroom*, 117, 118.
19. Pratt was not the only educational "missionary" who practiced the craft of civilization on both Black and Native people. Frederick Ayer worked as a missionary in Ojibwe territory in Minnesota from the 1840s to 1863, then went to Atlanta and ran two schools for freedmen, which later became Atlanta University. Richard Sloan was a teacher in Comanche territory who, during Reconstruction, then opened a school for Black people in Texas. See Morris, *Reading, 'Riting, and Reconstruction*, 65–66.
20. Hayes, "The Experiment at Fort Marion," 4.
21. Pratt, *Battlefield and Classroom*, 120. Emphasis mine.
22. The term "panopticon" originates with the writings of English theorist Jeremy Bentham at the end of the eighteenth century.
23. Foucault, *Discipline and Punish*, 201.
24. Foucault, *Discipline and Punish*, 201.
25. Woodson, *The Mis-Education of the Negro*, 31.
26. For more analysis of Fort Marion and its surveillance regime through both a spatial and Foucauldian lens, see Hayes, "The Experiment at Fort Marion."
27. Jacobs, *White Mother to a Dark Race*, 283; Lindsey, *Indians at Hampton Institute*, 28; Jenkins, *The Real All Americans*, 48.
28. Pratt, *Battlefield and Classroom*, 155.
29. Pratt, *Battlefield and Classroom*, 156.
30. Pratt, *Battlefield and Classroom*, 162.
31. Lookingbill, *War Dance at Fort Marion*, 8.
32. See Szabo, *Art from Fort Marion*.
33. Lookingbill, *War Dance at Fort Marion*, 12.
34. Emery, *Recovering Native American Writings in the Boarding School Press*.
35. Adams, *Education for Extinction*, 44.
36. Adams, *Education for Extinction*.
37. Adams, *Education for Extinction*, 45–47.
38. Pratt, *Battlefield and Classroom*, 214.
39. Pratt, *Battlefield and Classroom*, 215.
40. Pratt, *Battlefield and Classroom*, 215–17.
41. Klotz, *Writing Their Bodies*, ix.
42. Child, *Boarding School Seasons*, 6.
43. Quoted in Adams, *Education for Extinction*, 55.
44. Child, *Boarding School Seasons*, 81–82.
45. Brunhouse, "Apprenticeship for Civilizations."
46. Katanski, *Learning to Write "Indian,"* 56.
47. Klotz, *Writing Their Bodies*, 77.
48. Quoted in Fear-Segal, "The Man on the Bandstand," 101.
49. Katanski, *Learning to Write "Indian,"* 54.
50. Yes, this is the first "elf on a shelf."
51. Quoted in Katanski, *Learning to Write "Indian,"* 55.
52. Quoted in Katanski, *Learning to Write "Indian,"* 57.
53. Pratt, "Advantages of Mingling Indians with Whites."
54. Quoted in Adams, *Education for Extinction*, 274.
55. Adams refers to him as "Plenty Kill." He is listed in the school records as Luther Standing Bear or Kills Plenty, according to the digital archives maintained by Dickinson College in Carlisle, Pennsylvania.
56. Quoted in Adams, *Education for Extinction*, 98–99.
57. Quoted in Adams, *Education for Extinction*, 101.
58. Adams, *Education for Extinction*, 103.
59. For more on Plains Sign Talk, Pratt's orientation toward it (which changed between his time at Fort Marion and his time at Carlisle), and the relationship between Car-

lisle and the pedagogical approaches toward teaching Deaf students at that time, see chapter 2 of Klotz, *Writing Their Bodies*.

60. Klotz, *Writing Their Bodies*, 77–78.
61. Quoted in Adams, *Education for Extinction*, 141. Age from Carlisle digital archives, Dickinson College.
62. Emery, *Recovering Native American Writings in the Boarding School Press*, 73.
63. Prior to this, many treaties with individual tribes also required compulsory education.
64. Adams, *Education for Extinction*, 57.
65. Pratt, *Battlefield and Classroom*, xii.
66. Grande, *Red Pedagogy*, 186.
67. Quoted in Adams, *Education for Extinction*, 211.
68. Murphree, *Native America*, 44.
69. Murphree, *Native America*, 44.
70. Quoted in Adams, *Education for Extinction*, 215.
71. Quoted in Adams, *Education for Extinction*, 221.
72. Morgan, *Indian Education*, 9–10.
73. Lomawaima and McCarty, *"To Remain an Indian,"* 47.
74. Findlay, "An Elusive Institution," 16.
75. Zitkála-Šá, *American Indian Stories*, 98.

PART II: DEFECTIVE STRAINS

1. Quoted in Patterson, *From Emerson to King*, 131.
2. Lemann, *The Big Test*, 34.
3. Jordan, *Directed by Desire*, 274–75.

CHAPTER 5: THE GOSPEL OF INTELLECTUAL INFERIORITY

1. Rarely in this conversation does anyone bother noting Asian American students, who perform better than their White counterparts on tests such as the NAEP. This more complex and nuanced narrative would in turn become even more complex and nuanced if we look at disaggregated data on educational outcomes for students from different ethnic backgrounds within the broad umbrella "Asian American."
2. Nation's Report Card, "Reading Results."
3. Nation's Report Card, "Mathematics Results."
4. Darby and Rury, *The Color of Mind*, 10–12.
5. Bell, *Silent Covenants*, 100.
6. Bell, *Silent Covenants*, 105. Thanks to Elizabeth Todd-Breland for suggesting that I include this point about the history of *Brown* and reminding me that these critiques of the NAACP's approach were prevalent at the time this battle was being fought. By the way, *Silent Covenants* is one of my all-time favorite books on race and education if you're looking for something else to read.
7. Cf. Diamond, Randolph, and Spillane, "Teachers' Expectations and Sense of Responsibility"; Fox, "Seeing Potential"; Gershenson, Holt, and Papageorge, "Who Believes in Me?"; Kleinfeld and McDiarmid, "Teacher Expectations as a Political Issue."
8. Kleinfeld and McDiarmid, "Teacher Expectations as a Political Issue."
9. National Center for Education Statistics, "Percentage of Public School Students Enrolled in Gifted and Talented Programs."
10. Gentry et al., "Gifted Native American Students."
11. At just under five-foot-four, I am precisely average in height. I just have a lot of tall friends.
12. Grissom, Rodriguez, and Kern, "Teacher and Principal Diversity."
13. Romero, "Identifying Giftedness."

14. Simpson, "Land as Pedagogy," 11.
15. Jordan, *Directed by Desire.*
16. Bryan McKinley Jones Brayboy shared with me that this point made him think of a story Benjamin Franklin told, of a 1744 meeting between Haudenosaunee leaders and a group of White government representatives from Virginia. The Virginians offered to take six Native youth to attend college in Virginia. The Haudenosaunee leaders replied that, in the past, some of their youth had been educated by White people. "When they came back to us they were bad Runners, ignorant of every means of living in the Woods, unable to bear either Cold or Hunger, knew neither how to build a Cabin, take a Deer, or kill an Enemy, spoke our Language imperfectly; were therefore neither fit for Hunters, Warriors, or Counsellors; they were totally good for nothing." Instead, the Haudenosaunee leaders offered, the Virginians ought to send a dozen of their sons, and the Native leaders would care for them and "instruct them in all we know" (Franklin, "Remarks Concerning the Savages of North America").
17. Hobson, "How 'Race-Norming' Was Built into the NFL Concussion Settlement."
18. Snyderman and Rothman, "Survey of Expert Opinion." These experts included members of the American Educational Research Association and the American Sociological Association, both organizations of which I am a member. A fun game is to think about which of the current members who were present in 1984 answered what on this survey.
19. Smith et al., *General Social Surveys, 1972–2018.*
20. Smith et al., *General Social Surveys, 1972–2018.*
21. Bonilla-Silva, *Racism Without Racists,* 11.
22. Murray, *Human Diversity,* chapter 6.
23. Sullivan, "Dear Ta-Nehisi."
24. Sullivan, "Race and IQ. Again."
25. Sullivan, "Race and IQ. Again." Presumably, this was the logic Sullivan had in mind when he emailed journalist Linda Villarosa to ask her about what evidence she had that stereotypes regarding Black people having "large sex organs" were untrue. Defending the email on Twitter on January 6, 2020, Sullivan wrote that "as a test to see just how fact-checked these essays were, I merely asked her what sources she had that this is indeed a 'myth.'"
26. Smith, "I'm Still Reading Andrew Sullivan."
27. Gould, *The Mismeasure of Man,* 27.
28. Harden herself has been an advocate for using genetic testing as part of an agenda for educational reform—not for eugenics, she insists, but for social justice. "Knowing which genes are associated with educational success," she wrote in a 2018 *New York Times* op-ed, "will help scientists understand how different environments also affect that success. The eventual development of a polygenic score that statistically predicts educational outcomes will allow researchers to control for genetic differences between people, so that the causal effects of the environment are thrown into sharper focus. Understanding which environments cause improvements in children's ability to think and learn is necessary if we want to invest wisely in interventions that can truly make a difference" ("Why Progressives Should Embrace the Genetics of Education").

    Never mind the fact that there are plenty of nongenetic variables we know convincingly to have deleterious effects on young people's learning—everything from food insecurity and lack of stable housing to air pollution and inadequate dental care—none of which seem to inspire massive efforts at social welfare or to stop people from blaming children for their own alleged deficiencies. Nor does Harden's argument acknowledge, as Dorothy Roberts puts it, that "there's just no way that genetic testing is going to lead to a restructuring of society in a just way in the future—we have a hundred years of evidence for what happens when social outcomes are attributed to genetic differences, and it is always to stigmatize, control, and punish the people predicted to have socially devalued traits." See Lewis-Kraus, "Can Progressives Be Convinced That Genetics Matters?"

29. Gould, *The Mismeasure of Man*, 28.
30. Nott, "Letter to Samuel George Morton, June 27, 1849."
31. Dewbury, "The American School and Scientific Racism."
32. *Oxford English Dictionary*, 3rd ed. (oed.com), s.v. "mulatto."
33. Quoted in Nobles, *Shades of Citizenship*, 37.
34. Nott, "The Mulatto a Hybrid."
35. Quoted in Nobles, *Shades of Citizenship*, 40.
36. Nobles, *Shades of Citizenship*, 37–42.
37. Wright, *The History and Growth of the United States Census*, 157.
38. Hochschild and Powell, "Racial Reorganization."
39. Wolff, "The Myth of the Actuary."
40. Hoffman, *Race Traits and Tendencies*, 188.
41. For more on Hoffman's report, eugenics, and the insurance industry, see Wolff's excellent article "The Myth of the Actuary."
42. Haller, "Race, Mortality, and Life Insurance," 248–49.
43. Stanton, *The Leopard's Spots*, 144; quoted in Gould, *The Mismeasure of Man*, 83.
44. Morton, *Crania Americana*, 6.
45. Morton, *Crania Americana*, 64.
46. Morton, *Crania Americana*, 76–77.
47. Morton, *Crania Americana*, 82.
48. Morton, *Crania Americana*, 66.
49. Some scholars have also contended that Morton's calculations of averages were actually wrong.
50. According to Paul Wolff Mitchell, quoted in Kelleher, "How a Museum's Human Skull Collection Sparked a Racial Reckoning." The skulls were removed, and an apology issued with an accompanying plan to repatriate the human remains, only in 2020 when Penn undergraduate Gabriela Alvarado wrote an excoriating critique of the collection. In "The Penn Museum Must End Abuse of the Morton Collection," Alvarado wrote: "After Morton's death, the Academy held onto the collection of 918 crania for some years. In that time, the collection grew to 1,355. In 1966, the Penn Museum obtained the collection, and it now remains in its basement in 'open storage.'"
51. Gould, *The Mismeasure of Man*, 75; Irmscher, *Louis Agassiz*, 3–7.
52. Translated and quoted in Gould, *The Mismeasure of Man*, 76–7.
53. Agassiz, "The Diversity of Origin of the Human Races," 4.
54. Agassiz, "The Diversity of Origin of the Human Races," 36.
55. Ironically enough, eugenicist William Shockley (discussed in chapter 7) compared himself to Galileo and Darwin: "Galileo and Darwin brought new knowledge that was incompatible with the then-cherished interpretation of humanity's unique place in the universe." He saw Galileo, Darwin, and himself as impeded by "thought-blockers and unsearch dogmatism." I can only assume that Shockley meant "unsearch" to be an Orwellian Newspeak remix of "research"? I don't know.
56. Quoted in Lomawaima, "Estelle Reel," 14.
57. Quoted in Lomawaima, "Estelle Reel," 14.
58. Lomawaima, "Estelle Reel," 14.
59. Day, "School Men of the Hour," 207.
60. Day, "School Men of the Hour," 208.
61. Roberts, *Fatal Invention*, 27–28.

CHAPTER 6: A NATION FOR THE FITTEST: ENDLESS MEASUREMENT AND THE ARCHITECTS OF PROGRESS

1. Gould, *America in the Progressive Era.*
2. Davenport, *Heredity in Relation to Eugenics,* 1.
3. Davenport, *Heredity in Relation to Eugenics,* 3.
4. Spiro, *Defending the Master Race,* 126–31.
5. Spiro, *Defending the Master Race,* 131.
6. Spiro, *Defending the Master Race,* 185–86.
7. Cravens, *The Triumph of Evolution,* 53.
8. I am indebted to Kirt von Daacke for bringing William Heck at UVA to my attention, which led me to this 1916 list.
9. Eugenics Record Office, "College Courses," 26–27.
10. Fittingly, during this period the "mulatto" category briefly reappeared on the census, after Cornell University statistician Walter Willcox argued that there might be value in reinstating it. Though he admitted that there might be some errors in calculation, as some enumerators in the North were "less familiar with the racial characteristics of the negro and less able to judge of the question of intermixture of blood," he viewed the attempts as being at least "a step away from ignorance" (U.S. Bureau of the Census, "Negroes in the United States," 16).

    In 1930, as the social tides turned away from the questions of Nott's era and toward a dogged determination to draw the lines of Jim Crow clearly and above dispute, the mulatto question went away again. See Hochschild and Powell, "Racial Reorganization and the United States Census 1850–1930."
11. Nicolas and Sanitioso, "Alfred Binet."
12. Gould, *The Mismeasure of Man,* 149.
13. Zenderland, *Measuring Minds,* 96.
14. Gould, *The Mismeasure of Man,* 180.
15. Quoted in Gould, *The Mismeasure of Man,* 184.
16. Quoted in Gould, *The Mismeasure of Man,* 181.
17. Lewis, "Professor Lewis M. Terman," 66.
18. Terman, *The Measurement of Intelligence,* vii–viii.
19. Gould, *The Mismeasure of Man,* 185.
20. Terman, *The Measurement of Intelligence,* 4.
21. Terman, *The Measurement of Intelligence,* 6–7.
22. Terman, *The Measurement of Intelligence,* 19–20.
23. All of the above quotes from Terman, *The Measurement of Intelligence.*
24. Terman, *The Measurement of Intelligence,* 17–18.
25. Samelson, "World War I Intelligence Testing," 275.
26. Samelson, "World War I Intelligence Testing," 275.
27. Samelson, "World War I Intelligence Testing," 276–77.
28. Yoakum and Yerkes, *Army Mental Tests,* 261.
29. Yoakum and Yerkes, *Army Mental Tests,* 251.
30. Samelson, "World War I Intelligence Testing," 277.
31. Haggerty et al., "Two Psychological Tests."
32. Haggerty et al., "National Intelligence Tests."
33. Terman, "Mental and Physical Traits," 55.
34. Terman et al., *Intelligence Tests and School Reorganization,* 20–21.
35. Loveless, *2013 Brown Center Report,* 16–17.
36. Garth, "The Intelligence of Mixed Blood Indians," 268.
37. Gold, "Intelligence and Achievement of Blackfeet Indians," 44.
38. Garth, "The Intelligence of Mixed Blood Indians," 275.
39. Brigham, *A Study of American Intelligence,* 190.

40. Brigham, *A Study of American Intelligence*, 192.
41. Lemann, *The Big Test*, 30.
42. Brigham, *A Study of American Intelligence*.
43. Quoted in Lemann, *The Big Test*, 33.
44. Kidder and Rosner, "How the SAT Creates Built-in Headwinds," 135; see pp. 152 and 154 for the discussion of the 1998 SAT analysis and the experimental items.
45. Brigham, "Intelligence Tests of Immigrant Groups," 164.
46. Brigham, "Intelligence Tests of Immigrant Groups," 165.
47. Quoted in Darby and Rury, *The Color of Mind*, 65.
48. I was an editor of the *Harvard Educational Review* beginning in 2013 and later was co-chair of the journal. The legacy of Jensen and this article was taken so seriously that new editors had to read a brief history of the uproar it caused as part of our onboarding.
49. Jensen, "How Much Can We Boost?," 28, 29.
50. Jensen, "How Much Can We Boost?," 79.
51. Jensen, "How Much Can We Boost?," 82.
52. Jensen, "How Much Can We Boost?," 95.
53. Shockley, "A 'Try Simplest Cases' Approach," 1767.
54. Shockley described his statement as being inspired by a familiar source: the army's intelligence exams, in which he had observed that Negro scores had dropped since World War I; he hypothesized that this decline was due to "higher birth rates of disadvantaged, improvident people" ("A 'Try Simplest Cases' Approach").
55. Presaging Jensen, Shockley argued that Black people, more than anyone, should *want* to cast light on this area of research: "If study shows that ghetto birthrates are actually lowering average Negro intelligence, objectively facing this fact might lead to finding ways to prevent a form of genetic enslavement that could provoke extremes of racism. I feel that no one should be more concerned with this possibility than Negro intellectuals" ("A 'Try Simplest Cases' Approach," 1771).
56. Shockley, "A 'Try Simplest Cases' Approach," 1771.
57. Shockley, "Dysgenics, Geneticity, Raceology," 297.
58. Shockley dismissed potential criticism of his ideas as "unsearch" (again, a nod to Orwell?) held in place by "thought-blockers." He also urged his critics to consider an analysis of the "great work" completed by Lewis Terman as a model for why conversations about IQ are so critical to society's functioning.
59. Shockley, "Dysgenics, Geneticity, Raceology," 303.
60. Shockley, "Dysgenics, Geneticity, Raceology," 307.
61. Shockley, "Dysgenics, Geneticity, Raceology," 304.
62. Shockley, "Dysgenics, Geneticity, Raceology," 306.
63. Gould, *The Mismeasure of Man*, 52. Gould is quoting Nicolas de Condorcet.
64. Lawrence, "The Indian Health Service and the Sterilization," 406–7.
65. Lawrence, "The Indian Health Service and the Sterilization."
66. Roberts, *Killing the Black Body*.
67. Roberts, *Killing the Black Body*.
68. National Women's Law Center, "Forced Sterilization of Disabled People."
69. Johnson, "Female Inmates Sterilized in California."

CHAPTER 7: WHOSE KNOWLEDGE?

1. McNeil, *Contradictions of School Reform*, 248.
2. Office of the Surgeon General, "Group Examination Beta."
3. Darby and Rury, *The Color of Mind*, 10.
4. Stern, *Eugenic Nation*, 2.

5. Roid and Barram, *Essentials of Stanford-Binet Intelligence Scales,* 76.
6. Roid, *Stanford-Binet Intelligence Scales: Examiners Manual,* 3.
7. Roid, *Stanford-Binet Intelligence Scales: Item Books 1–3.*
8. Ramsden et al., "The Influence of Reading Ability."
9. Carr, "How Flawed IQ Tests Prevent Kids."
10. Glickman, "No More AABL."
11. Educational Records Bureau, "AABL What to Expect Video."
12. Zimmer, "QUIZ: Are You Smart Enough?" As of this writing, Horace Mann is using an admissions test from a different company, First Look Insights, to evaluate applicants to kindergarten and first grade.
13. Koretz, *The Testing Charade,* 11.
14. Shotton, Lowe, and Waterman, "Introduction."
15. Tachine, *Native Presence and Sovereignty in College,* 10.
16. I am grateful to Nicole for giving me permission to share this story.
17. For more on the distinction between the bogeyman labeled "critical race theory" and the actual Critical Race Theory, cf. Ray, *On Critical Race Theory.*
18. Quoted in Ross, *Inventing the Savage,* 66–67. Emphasis in the original.
19. Wichgers, *Joint Hearing on Education.*
20. Although, if you've read Part I, you'll know that we can't properly call Columbus "White," I feel confident that Wichgers would claim him.
21. Wolfe, "Settler Colonialism and the Elimination of the Native."
22. Thank you to Bryan McKinley Jones Brayboy for making the point to me that the Doctrine of Discovery also has epistemological implications. For more on "funds of knowledge," see Moll et al., "Funds of Knowledge for Teaching."
23. Collins, *Black Feminist Thought,* 252.
24. Grande, *Red Pedagogy,* 101.
25. Gregory A. Cajete, "Where There Is No Name for Science: Response 1," in Grande, *Red Pedagogy.*
26. Carroll et al., "CARE Principles for Indigenous Data Governance."
27. Kimmerer, *Braiding Sweetgrass,* 42, 158.
28. Lorde, *Sister Outsider,* 38.
29. Collins, *Black Feminist Thought,* 265.
30. See Payne and Strickland, *Teach Freedom,* chapter 3.
31. Payne and Strickland, *Teach Freedom,* 3.
32. Phenix and Selver, "We Are Going to Learn Together."
33. Williams, *Self-Taught,* chapter 1.
34. McKittrick, *Dear Science,* 4.
35. McKittrick, *Dear Science,* 5.
36. Medin and Bang, *Who's Asking?,* 183.
37. Medin and Bang, *Who's Asking?,* 182.
38. As education scholar Django Paris and linguistic anthropologist H. Samy Alim point out, this pedagogical orientation goes deeper than simply seeing the home cultures of students of color as flat, static "assets" that are above critique; it requires a "culturally sustaining pedagogy" that sees heritage practices and community practices as complex and fluid. See Paris and Alim, "What Are We Seeking to Sustain Through Culturally Sustaining Pedagogy?"

PART III: HANDS CLASPED

1. Grande, *Red Pedagogy,* xvi.
2. Hong, "Rochester Officers Suspended."
3. Marshall, "when the officer caught me."

CHAPTER 8: CARCERAL LOGICS

1. All of these names are pseudonyms.
2. Webster, "'Hanging Pretty Girls.'"
3. Channing, "God Admonishing His People of Their Duty."
4. Webster, "'Hanging Pretty Girls.'"
5. Bickford, "The Merciful Executioner"; Faber, *The Child in the Electric Chair.*
6. Bickford, "The Merciful Executioner."
7. Faber, *The Child in the Electric Chair,* 35.
8. Faber, *The Child in the Electric Chair,* 5.
9. Wald and Losen, "Defining and Redirecting a School-to-Prison Pipeline," 11. Other scholars who were early contributors to this work include Garrett Albert Duncan, Pedro Noguera, and Russ Skiba.
10. Meiners, *Right to Be Hostile,* 31–32. In addition to the metaphors of the "pipeline" (movement from one place to the other) and the "nexus" (an intersection between two sites), sociologist Brian Cabral has made a valuable contribution to this conversation by suggesting "educational carcerality" as a more broadly encompassing idea that schools and prisons can be distinct places but carcerality moves betwixt and between, a set of "complex manifestations of carcerality within and outside schooling" ("Linguistic Confinement").
11. Meiners, *Right to Be Hostile,* 4.
12. "Carceral" comes from Latin *carcer,* meaning "prison" or "jail."
13. Kaba, "So You're Thinking About Becoming an Abolitionist."
14. Kaba, "Working Toward Abolition . . ."
15. Kaba and Hayes, "Jailbreak of the Imagination."
16. Kaba and Hayes, "Jailbreak of the Imagination."
17. Kaba and Hayes, "Jailbreak of the Imagination."
18. Sojoyner, *First Strike,* 35. Emphasis mine.
19. Shedd, *Unequal City,* 82–84.
20. Shedd, *Unequal City,* 93.
21. Foucault, *Discipline and Punish,* 136.
22. Foucault, *Discipline and Punish,* 136–37.
23. Lomawaima, "Estelle Reel," 13.
24. Foucault, *Discipline and Punish,* 187.
25. Gliha, "El Paso County 12-Year-Old Speaks."
26. Low, "12-Year-Old Suspended."
27. Low, "12-Year-Old Suspended."
28. American Civil Liberties Union, "RE: Loleta Union School District's Violations."
29. American Psychological Association Zero Tolerance Task Force, "Are Zero Tolerance Policies Effective?," 5.
30. Jones, *Conversations with Angela Davis,* 127.
31. As Vaught, Brayboy, and Chin put it, incarceration is therefore "a removal project" akin to other forms of Indian "removal" (*The School-Prison Trust,* 4).
32. National Center for Education Statistics, "Table 223.40: Percentage of Students Suspended and Expelled . . . 2013-2014."
33. Bokenkamp and Walker, *Empty Desks.*
34. Wang, "The U.S. Criminal Justice System Disproportionately Hurts Native People."
35. Lakota People's Law Project, "Native Lives Matter."
36. Heitzeg, "'Whiteness,' Criminality, and the Double Standards," 201.

CHAPTER 9: TO RESIST IS TO BE CRIMINAL

1. Adams, *Education for Extinction,* 337.
2. Rae, *Trudell.*

3. As described by Blackfoot elder Mike Oka in University of Lethbridge, "School of Liberal Education Celebrates Blackfoot Heritage."
4. Terrance Lafromboise, in interview with Price, "Remembering Brendon Galbreath."
5. Montemayor, "Friends and Family of Brendon Galbreath."
6. Montemayor, "Friends and Family of Brendon Galbreath."
7. Price, "Remembering Brendon Galbreath."
8. Lafromboise interview with Ewing, August 17, 2023.
9. Lafromboise interview with Ewing, August 17, 2023.
10. Lafromboise interview with Ewing, August 17, 2023. I have written elsewhere about the notion of police, especially police unions, as a brotherhood (Ewing, "Blue Bloods").
11. Buchli and Rispens, "Jury Confirms Galbreath."
12. If Terrance and his family did not believe the official version of the story, that would also be understandable. Even as more and more people across the United States have become aware of the epidemic of police-involved shootings, data on when, how, and where they happen remains unreliable and undercounted. A *New York Times* investigative report comparing police testimony in court with surveillance cameras and other evidence revealed that police lie on the witness stand about all kinds of incriminating details—whether someone had a weapon, whether suspects approached them, and even whether someone was present at the scene of the crime. These findings will be unsurprising to anyone who has paid attention to high-profile cases where initial reports denying all police wrongdoing have later been disproved. See Goldstein, "'Testilying' by Police."
13. Lafromboise interview with Ewing, August 17, 2023.
14. Ajilore, "Native Americans Deserve More."
15. Hansen, "The Forgotten Minority in Police Shootings." The CDC figure is from the period between 1999 and 2015.
16. McLaughlin and Marco, "Teen Made 911 Report that Preceded Policeman Killing Him, Investigators Say."
17. Golden, "A Pregnant Woman Was in Trouble."
18. Blackhorse, "One Year Later."
19. Conley and Gaarder, "Man Who Died After Being Tased by Police."
20. Hansen, "Forgotten Minority in Police Shootings."
21. Schroedel and Chin, "Whose Lives Matter."
22. Josey, "Race and Stereotypes in New Media"; population figure is based on the 2020 Census, inclusive of those who checked "American Indian and Alaska Native" and some other racial group.
23. Giago, "Deaths of Indian Homeless in Rapid City."
24. Ross, *Inventing the Savage,* 29.
25. Barsh and Henderson, "Tribal Courts," 33.
26. Ross, *Inventing the Savage,* 18.
27. Harring, *Crow Dog's Case,* 206.
28. Deloria and Lytle, *The Nations Within,* 4.
29. Deloria and Lytle, *The Nations Within,* 29. The seven original "major crimes" were: murder, manslaughter, rape, assault with intent to kill, arson, burglary, larceny. The current list includes: murder, manslaughter, kidnapping, maiming, a felony under chapter 109a (i.e., sexual abuse), incest, a felony assault under section 113 (e.g., assault with intent to commit murder or assault with a dangerous weapon), an assault against an individual who has not attained the age of sixteen years, felony child abuse or neglect, arson, burglary, robbery, a felony under section 661 of this title (i.e., larceny). See U. S. Department of Justice, *Criminal Resource Manual.*
30. Senkel, "Constitutional Law," 725.
31. Asserting that Native people are inherently lawless handily deflects attention from the state's own "major crimes" committed in the service of what political scientist

Heidi Kiiwetinepinesiik Stark (Turtle Mountain Ojibwe) calls a "criminal empire" (Stark, "Criminal Empire").

32. One of the reasons cited by the court was the "presumption, commonly shared by Congress, the Executive Branch, and lower federal courts, that tribal courts have no power to try non-Indians." In other words, tribal courts have no jurisdiction over non-Native people because most people assume that tribal courts have no jurisdiction over non-Native people. Justice Thurgood Marshall issued a dissenting opinion, arguing that "Indian tribes enjoy, as a necessary aspect of their retained sovereignty, the right to try and punish all persons who commit offenses against tribal law within the reservation" (U.S. Supreme Court, *Oliphant v. Suquamish Indian Tribe*).
33. Native communities "are restrained from asserting their own jurisdictions and customs to combat racism, violence, and deteriorating social conditions while the surrounding, non-Indian community is free to criminalize Indians' proactive responses" (Million, "Policing the Rez," 102).
34. Deloria, *Custer Died for Your Sins*, 9.
35. Smith, "Disparate Impact of the Federal Sentencing Guidelines," 485. The double standard of the Major Crimes Act has resulted in offenses involving Native people being a drastically overrepresented share of federal cases. In 2003, the United States Sentencing Commission found, staggeringly, that cases involving tribal jurisdiction comprised nearly half of all murder and assault cases in the federal caseload, over sixty percent of sexual abuse cases, and over *eighty* percent of manslaughter cases. (See Smith, "Disparate Impact of the Federal Sentencing Guidelines," 487.) "Hence," as Luana Ross writes, "in their lurch to possess Indian Country, Euro-Americans in Congress defined crime differently for Natives than for themselves, with the Native definition requiring less proof for conviction" (*Inventing the Savage*, 19).

    The commission's investigation also found that "there is a significant negative disparity in sentencing of Native American people." Alas, the commission insisted, these disparities could not possibly be considered racist—they were merely a misfortune of jurisdiction. "It appears truly not to be a racial bias," testified one committee member. "We are looking at a jurisdictional framework that throws Native Americans disproportionately into federal court where they receive stiffer sentences." "We don't believe that there is a racial animus behind the number of people who are in the system," testified another. (See U.S. Sentencing Commission, *Native American Advisory Group Public Hearing*.)

    This finding offers a tidy example of what sociologist Eduardo Bonilla-Silva has termed "racism without racists": racial hierarchies and inequalities persist through "practices that are subtle, institutional, and apparently nonracial," in a " 'now you see it, now you don't' fashion." If a Native person spends more time in prison than a White person for committing the same crime, *c'est la vie*—can't blame anyone in particular. See Bonilla-Silva, *Racism Without Racists*, 3.
36. U.S. Government Accountability Office, *Native American Youth*, 31.
37. Adams and Samuels, *Tribal Youth in the Federal Justice System*, 76.
38. Litt and Singleton, "American Indian/Alaska Native Youth," 1.
39. Cross, "Native Americans and Juvenile Justice."
40. McNally, *Defend the Sacred*, 40.
41. Prucha, *Documents of United States Indian Policy*, 159. This is another area of intersection in the histories of Black and Native peoples; enslaved Black people were sometimes forbidden from singing or dancing, as these activities were seen as opportunities for them to be riled up toward insurrection or refusal to work. See Sojoyner, *First Strike*, 20–21.
42. Jones in Bureau of Indian Affairs, *Annual Report of the Commissioner, 1902*, 13–14.
43. Jones in Bureau of Indian Affairs, *Annual Report of the Commissioner, 1902*, 15–16.

    In a 1921 memorandum, seeking to clarify that these prohibitions were in no way antithetical to supposed principles of American freedom, the Commissioner of Indian Affairs reassured superintendents that he had no problem with dancing per se. After all, White people dance. The problem, he insisted, involved dances that happened "under most primitive and pagan conditions," dances that encouraged unforgivable acts such as "immoral relations between the sexes," giving property away, or coming together from across a great distance "to the neglect of their crops, livestock, and home interests." Any dancing that was "disorderly or plainly excessive" or that promoted superstition, idleness, or shiftlessness . . . all of that *type* of dancing should be controlled "by educational processes as far as possible, but if necessary, by punitive measures when its degrading tendencies persist." He also recommended that anyone under fifty years old be prohibited from dancing, and that dances should in particular be banned between March and August lest they interfere with agricultural productivity. (See U.S. Congress House Committee on the Judiciary, *Indian Religious Freedom Issues,* 43.)

44. This is a legislative remedy that only "permits" Native people the right to enact sacred practices that predate the United States through an appeal to the logics and language that it deems legible: the notion of "freedom of religion" protected by the Constitution. In a 2018 commentary on the anniversary of the act, Ponca actress and activist Casey Camp-Horinek called it "an oxymoron": "Can we live freely within the Natural Laws and honor our one true Mother, the Earth? No, not when laws created by man are defining our relationship with Her. Balance must be restored through prayer and ceremony, not by written words in man's attempt to override the Great Mystery's original instructions." Coquille woodcarver Shirod Younker noted that while legal protections were meaningful, "our ceremonial ways all come from the earth. We cannot effectively understand their importance or details until we restore the environment that helps sustain us physically and spiritually." See Zotigh, "Native Perspectives on the 40th Anniversary."
45. Barker, *Red Scare,* 40. In one especially visible example, water protectors who held space at the Oceti Sakowin Camp in opposition to the Dakota Access Pipeline and in celebration of the principle of *mní wičóni* (water is life) were subject to surveillance by militarized police forces, strip searches, beatings, detainment in freezing chain-link cages, water hoses, tear gas, infiltration by private security forces working undercover to sow conflict, and incarceration because they were deemed "murderable."
46. Barker, *Red Scare,* 37.
47. Vaught, Brayboy, and Chin, *The School-Prison Trust,* 55.
48. Wynter, "1492," 28–29.
49. Thomas, *The Slave Trade,* 82.
50. I feel obliged to note that dill is *not,* strictly speaking, a spice. Dill is an herb.
51. Blackhawk, *The Rediscovery of America,* 2.
52. Monument Lab, *National Monument Audit,* 12.
53. Teachers Pay Teachers.
54. As of this writing, this paper is still forthcoming. I'm extremely proud of my co-author, Maggie Rivera, and grateful for her efforts. As an undergraduate student, she was undaunted when I asked her to spend the summer coding thousands of lesson plans, and ultimately developed a nuanced coding scheme and training materials to teach other research assistants how to evaluate the lessons and code them.
55. Bruyneel, *Settler Memory,* 13.
56. Wynter, "1492," 11; Takaki, *A Different Mirror,* 30.
57. "In effect," Wynter explains, "we are co-identified only with those with whom our origin narratives and their systems of symbolic representations, or cultural programs, have socialized us to be symbolic conspecifics of, and therefore to display altruistic behaviors toward those who constitute the *nos* on whose behalf we collectively act" (Wynter, "1492," 30–31).

Wynter's use of the Latin *nos* is a reference to the phrase *propter nos*, "for us" or "for our sake." Who is "us"? Who are "we"? Who among us gets to belong within the confines of the pronoun? If our origin narratives, the symbols we use to relay those narratives, and the cultural programs in which we take part exclude certain people from the *nos*—from the "us," the "we"—we are fundamentally hindered in our ability to see those who lie outside those narratives to be part of our frame of humanity.

58. Keenan, "Selective Memory," 2. The role of state-sanctioned colonial violence is conspicuously absent in the invocation of what Barker describes as the trope of the savage prone to "irrational and unprovoked violence against guiltless whites . . . this Indian has dominated colonial and U.S./Canadian writings for centuries as the barbaric savage who wantonly rapes, tortures, and kills whites without cause or purpose, even in reports involving invasions and attacks on Indians themselves" (*Red Scare*, 41).
59. Peterson, "Where Would You Build a California Mission?"
60. Keenan, "Selective Memory," 13–14.
61. Quoted in National Congress of American Indians, *Becoming Visible*, 9.
62. National Congress of American Indians, *Becoming Visible*, 8.
63. Bruyneel, *Settler Memory*, xiii.
64. Mason and Ernst-Slavit, "Representations of Native Americans," 13.
65. Calderon, "Uncovering Settler Grammars in Curriculum."

One way to counter settler grammars, as education scholar Leilani Sabzalian (Alutiiq) points out, is to create systems wherein "knowledge of Native survivance, settler colonialism, and Native studies [are] requisite teacher knowledge to counter deficit thinking, detect and interrupt settler colonial discourses in educational policy and practice, and imagine and enact anticolonial and decolonial educational alternatives in public schools"; it's not enough to have a simplified and "safe" version of Indigenous inclusion that can make non-Native educators feel good while re-creating forms of tokenism (*Indigenous Children's Survivance in Public Schools*, 14).

66. Brayboy and Chin, "'On the Development of Terrortory.'"
67. Brayboy and Chin, "'On the Development of Terrortory.'"
68. Adams, *Education for Extinction*, 121.
69. Federal investigators have concluded that these schools stayed open until 1969 (see Newland, *Federal Indian Boarding School Initiative Investigative Report*). However, many Native people have shared accounts of attending boarding schools later than that. As of this writing, the Department of the Interior is only now starting to do a more thorough reckoning of boarding schools' legacies; cultures of abuse and secrecy make it unlikely that we will ever fully understand the scope of their footprint, and we will never be able to fully account for their harms.
70. Lomawaima, "Domesticity in the Federal Indian Schools," 210.
71. Lomawaima, "Domesticity in the Federal Indian Schools," 204.
72. Ellis, *To Change Them Forever*, 102. In his memoir, *Pipestone*, Adam Fortunate Eagle describes hearing that the blue denim coveralls he wore during his time at boarding school were actually made by men incarcerated at Stillwater State Prison, in an instance of tragic irony.
73. Ellis, *To Change Them Forever*, 101–2.
74. Lomawaima, "Domesticity in the Federal Indian Schools," 232.
75. Ellis, *To Change Them Forever*, 105.
76. Trennert, *The Phoenix Indian School*, 48.
77. Shannon, "The Phoenix Indian School," 167.
78. Eagle, *Pipestone*, 73–74.
79. Quoted in Adams, *Education for Extinction*, 228.
80. Ellis, *To Change Them Forever*, 102–3.
81. Ellis, *To Change Them Forever*, 103.

82. Ellis, *To Change Them Forever,* 105.
83. Ellis, *To Change Them Forever,* 105–7.
84. Trennert, *The Phoenix Indian School,* 68.
85. Lomawaima, *They Called It Prairie Light,* 23.
86. Salinas, "Still Grieving Over the Loss of the Land," 102–3.
87. Ross, *Inventing the Savage,* 40.
88. Ellis, *To Change Them Forever,* 99.
89. Ellis, *To Change Them Forever,* 108.
90. Trennert, *The Phoenix Indian School,* 77.
91. Harjo and Bird, *Reinventing the Enemy's Language.*
92. Quoted in Reyhner, "American Indian Boarding Schools," 67.
93. Johnston-Goodstar and VeLure Roholt, "'Our Kids Aren't Dropping Out,'" 32. See the Truth and Reconciliation Commission's reports at nctr.ca/records/reports/#trc-reports.
94. Newland, *Federal Indian Boarding School Initiative Investigative Report.*
95. Special Subcommittee on Indian Education, *Indian Education: A National Tragedy,* 62.
96. Special Subcommittee on Indian Education, *Indian Education: A National Tragedy,* 64, 67.
97. The Indian Education Act is formally known as Title IV of Public Law 92-318, and reauthorized as Part A, Title IX of the Education Amendments of 1994.
98. Hudetz, "Suspicions of Native American Teens"; Hudetz, "Native American Teens Stopped."
99. Foley, "The Silent Indian."
100. Shilling, "Mohawk Brothers."
101. Hudetz, "Native American Teens Stopped."
102. Shilling, "Mohawk Brothers."
103. Wildeman and Emanuel, "Cumulative Risks of Foster Care Placement."
104. Cooper, "Racial Bias in American Foster Care."
105. Nelson, *Making an Issue of Child Abuse,* 3.
106. Roberts, *Shattered Bonds,* v, 18. In 2024, *ProPublica* reported on the state of Georgia's record of taking children into foster care in over seven hundred cases where inadequate housing was listed as the cause, despite advocates arguing that simply housing the families would be less expensive (Stokes and Philip, "When Families Need Housing, Georgia Will Pay for Foster Care").
107. Roberts, *Shattered Bonds,* 9; Roberts and Sangoi, "Black Families Matter."
108. Sullivan and Walters, "Incentives and Cultural Bias."

CHAPTER 10: ABSOLUTE OBEDIENCE AND PERFECT SUBMISSION

1. Eltis and Richardson, *Atlas of the Transatlantic Slave Trade.*
2. Quoted in Carey, *Sold Down the River,* 112.
3. As legal scholar Randall Kennedy has written, other states had similar provisions to ensure that the law never impeded a slave master's right to injure or kill any enslaved person, in the name of maintaining the total submission that was the hallmark of the racial order. In 1798, for example, a North Carolina statute declared the killing of a slave to be a felony, but then added that the statute should not extend "to any person killing . . . any slave in the act of resistance to his lawful owner or master, or any slave dying under moderate correction." The Mississippi Supreme Court declared in 1860 that "the master may use just such force as may be requisite to reduce his slave to obedience, even to the death of the slave, if that become[s] necessary . . . to maintain his lawful authority." In a case involving an enslaver who shot an enslaved woman, the North Carolina Supreme Court made clear that "we cannot allow the right of the master to be brought into discussion in the Courts of Justice. The slave, to remain a

slave, must be made sensible that there is no appeal from his master; that his power is in no instance, usurped; but is conferred by the laws of man at least, if not by the law of God." See Kennedy, *Race, Crime, and the Law,* 30–33.

4. As Brenna Bhandar writes, the sociolegal position of an enslaved person as property also involved some contradiction—namely, that an enslaved person was an object belonging to someone else but, unlike an object, could be held liable for their crimes; one in this position had the burdens but not the autonomous privileges of personhood: "This form of property thus produced a hybrid legal form that has both the status of object and human" ("Property, Law, and Race," 206).
5. Grunwald and Adler, *Women's Letters,* 307.
6. Carey, *Sold Down the River,* 114.
7. Carey, *Sold Down the River,* 115.
8. Jones-Rogers, *They Were Her Property,* 102.
9. Jones-Rogers, *They Were Her Property,* 106.
10. Quoted in Jones-Rogers, *They Were Her Property,* 16.
11. Sánchez-Eppler, "'Remember, Dear,'" 29.
12. King, *Stolen Childhood,* 71.
13. Quoted in King, *Stolen Childhood,* 75.
14. King, *Stolen Childhood,* 76–77.
15. Kennedy, *Race, Crime, and the Law,* 42–43.
16. King, *Stolen Childhood,* 251–52.
17. Webster, *Beyond the Boundaries of Childhood,* 10.
18. Cf. Foner, *The Second Founding;* Haley, *No Mercy Here;* Litwack, *Trouble in Mind.*
19. Hart, *Social Progress of Alabama,* 38.
20. Haley, *No Mercy Here,* 17, discusses Fears; her source is the 1900 Census, which lists the others.
21. Haley, *No Mercy Here,* 172.
22. Carson, "Penal Reform and Construction," 217.
23. Oshinsky, *"Worse Than Slavery,"* 46–47.
24. Oshinsky, *"Worse Than Slavery,"* 47–48.
25. Litwack, *Trouble in Mind,* 272–74.
26. Krishna, "Mass Grave Recalls the Ugly Past"; Convict Leasing and Labor Project, "The Sugar Land 95."
27. Miller, *Hard Labor and Hard Time,* 19.
28. Haley, *No Mercy Here,* 195. In the rare instances when White girls were convicted of crimes, they earned press attention and sympathy amid fears that they should not be trapped in the prison camps with "negro women who are foul with crime and disease" (Haley, *No Mercy Here,* 168).
29. Haley, *No Mercy Here,* 126.
30. *Savannah Morning News,* "Many Criminals to Face Judicial Music."
31. City of Savannah, Georgia, Recorder's Court, Police Court Docket Books (1903) and Fine Docket Book (1903). I am deeply obliged to Kelly Zacovic, senior archivist, for locating these records for me.
32. On Julia's contracting pneumonia: *Savannah Morning News,* "Will Graft Skin on Woman Convict." Her death from pneumonia is recorded in the City of Savannah vital records and death registry; information on her interment is publicly viewable in the city cemetery database at savannah.cemsites.com. Once more, I am indebted to City of Savannah senior archivist Kelly Zacovic for locating this information as I attempted to puzzle out what happened to Julia.
33. Brooks, "Introduction to 'We Real Cool.'"
34. Dorsey, *To Build Our Lives Together,* 150.
35. Haley, *No Mercy Here,* 174–75.
36. Bernstein, *Racial Innocence,* 34.

37. Muir, interview with Quvenzhané Wallis.
38. Sharpe, *In the Wake,* 80. Elsewhere in this source, Sharpe puts it this way: "Blackness disrupts the figure of the child" (97).
39. Gilliam et al., "Do Early Educators' Implicit Biases?," 6.
40. Greene-Santos, "Corporal Punishment in Schools Still Legal in Many States."
41. Gershoff and Font, "Corporal Punishment in U.S. Public Schools."
42. Gershoff and Font, "Corporal Punishment in U.S. Public Schools."
43. National Center for Education Statistics, "Percentage Distribution of Enrollment in Public Elementary and Secondary Schools."
44. Gershoff and Font, "Corporal Punishment in U.S. Public Schools."
45. Kennedy, *Race, Crime, and the Law,* 47.
46. Hartman, *Scenes of Subjection,* 140. Emphasis mine.
47. To quote Foucault: "He who is subjected to a field of visibility, and who knows it, assumes responsibility for the constraints of power; he makes them play spontaneously upon himself; he inscribes in himself the power relation in which he simultaneously plays both roles; he becomes the principle of his own subjection" (*Discipline and Punish,* 202–3).
48. KIPP New Jersey, "How to Teach Your Class to Line Up."
49. Vara-Orta, "Fits and Starts"; see also Disare, "'No Excuses' No More?"
50. Cooper, "KIPP Offers Learning with a Twist"; Hartocollis, "Michael Feinberg, a Founder of KIPP Schools, Is Fired."
51. Herbert, "A Chance to Learn."
52. Goff et al., "The Essence of Innocence."
53. Blake et al., "The Role of Colorism."
54. Epstein, Blake, and González, "Girlhood Interrupted."
55. Curtis, Karlsen, and Anderson, "Transmuting Girls into Women."
56. Sojoyner, *First Strike,* 107. As Michael Dumas has aptly pointed out (see "'Losing an Arm,'" 3), schools are often normalized as sites of suffering for Black students (as well as teachers and families). "I want to suggest that Black suffering is a kind of constant traveling between historical memory and current predicament, that there is a psychic link between the tragedy of antebellum African bondage and post–civil rights (indeed, "post-racial") Black suffering in schools. Like Dana in Octavia Butler's *Kindred* (a sci-fi protagonist who is transported at random moments back and forth through time from slavery to the present), Black educators, children, and families are never quite sure when they will be taken (back) to this place of trauma, nor can they determine when or if the pain will end."
57. Golann, *Scripting the Moves,* 6. Emphasis in the original.
58. Golann, *Scripting the Moves,* 31.
59. Ossei-Owusu, "Police Quotas."
60. Golann, *Scripting the Moves,* 32, 141.
61. Golann, *Scripting the Moves,* 34.
62. Alderman, "Effectively Keep Students Engaged with SLANT."
63. Warren, *Urban Preparation.*
64. Lemov, *Teach Like a Champion 3.0,* chapter 10, footnote 10.
65. Gaztambide-Fernández, *The Best of the Best,* 79.
66. Warren, *Urban Preparation.*
67. Rossi, "Students Given Freedom to Blossom." Go Mustangs.
68. Morris, *Pushout.*
69. Koeninger, "Arrested & Beaten for Dozing in Class."
70. D'Arcy, "Salecia Johnson, 6, Handcuffed."
71. Rhodes, "Noble Charter Schools Story Hit a Nerve."
72. Ortiz, "Michigan Judge Denies Release of Teenage Girl."

73. Rosentel et al., "Black Transgender Women and the School-to-Prison Pipeline."
74. National Alliance to End Sexual Violence, "Racism and Rape."
75. Morris, *Pushout,* 2.
76. As a non-Indigenous person, I won't be using this disparaging epithet for Native women.
77. Ross, *Inventing the Savage,* 240–43.
78. For more on the horrifying history of forced sterilization in Native communities, see Torpy, "Native American Women and Coerced Sterilization."
79. Southern Poverty Law Center, "Relf v. Weinberger."
80. Hayes, "On Korryn Gaines, Loreal Tsingine and Refusing to Surrender."
81. Sharpe, *In the Wake,* 77.
82. Deloria and Lytle, *American Indians, American Justice,* 111.
83. Ross, *Inventing the Savage,* 30.
84. Shange, *Progressive Dystopia,* 56.

PART IV: SOMEBODY'S GOT TO MOW THE LAWN

1. Gates, "Addresses at the Lake Mohonk Conferences."
2. Cited in Child, *The Freedmen's Book,* 260.
3. Melamed, "Racial Capitalism," 77.

CHAPTER 11: A CROOKED PLAYING FIELD

1. Darity and Mullen, *From Here to Equality,* 31. Much of this quote is Darity quoting his coauthored work with Darrick Hamilton, "Can 'Baby Bonds' Eliminate the Racial Wealth Gap in Putative Post-Racial America?"
2. Bhutta et al., "Disparities in Wealth by Race and Ethnicity."
3. Darity et al., *What We Get Wrong.*
4. Brown, *The Whiteness of Wealth,* 112.
5. Darity et al., *What We Get Wrong,* 6.
6. Zaw et al., "Women, Race, & Wealth," 3.
7. Pager, Bonikowski, and Western, "Discrimination in a Low-Wage Labor Market."
8. Gaddis, "Discrimination in the Credential Society"; cited in Darity and Mullen, *From Here to Equality,* 45–46.
9. Opportunity Insights, "The Opportunity Atlas."
10. Reeves and Krause, "Raj Chetty in 14 Charts."
11. Chetty et al., "Race and Economic Opportunity."
12. Chetty et al., "Race and Economic Opportunity." Emphasis in the original.
13. Feiveson and Sabelhaus, "How Does Intergenerational Wealth Transmission Affect Wealth Concentration?" This analysis was based on the Survey of Consumer Finances, which is conducted by the Fed every three years. The authors note: "Using a real interest rate of 5 percent, the estimated share of wealth accounted for by intergenerational transfers jumps to 51 percent. The choice of interest rate clearly matters for the aggregate estimates of the extent to which intergenerational transfers can account for total wealth, and indeed, that is one of the main points of contention in the older literature."
14. Wilhelm, "The Role of Intergenerational Transfers."
15. For more on intergenerational wealth transfer going from children to parents, see Brown, *The Whiteness of Wealth,* chapter 5.
16. Shapiro, *The Hidden Cost of Being African American,* 75.
17. Shapiro, *The Hidden Cost of Being African American,* 80.
18. Francis and Weller, "Retirement Inequality by Race and Ethnicity."

19. Murphy and Huggins, "Retirement Income Among American Indians and Alaska Natives."
20. Perry, Rothwell, and Harshbarger, *The Devaluation of Assets in Black Neighborhoods.*
21. Kamin, "Home Appraised."
22. Fairlie, "Private Schools and 'Latino Flight'"; Saporito and Sohoni, "Coloring Outside the Lines."
23. Brown, *The Whiteness of Wealth,* 215.
24. Shapiro, *The Hidden Cost of Being African American,* 76.
25. Brown, *The Whiteness of Wealth,* 215.
26. Kraus et al., "The Misperception of Racial Economic Inequality."
27. Shapiro, *The Hidden Cost of Being African American,* 60.

CHAPTER 12: SLAVERY, SETTLER COLONIALISM, AND AMERICAN WEALTH

1. Farrow, Lang, and Frank, *Complicity,* 13–14.

   Northern textile mills happily churned out a product that was actually known as "negro cloth"—fabric made specifically to dress enslaved people. Isaac P. Hazard of Providence, Rhode Island, hailing from a family of prominent industrialists, professed that "it is our intention to make cheap goods for Southern planters," and once they figured out the most profitable formula for doing so, they would turn their factory over entirely to this sole lucrative pursuit. "Northern manufacturers would come to have a stake in the price of cotton comparable to that of their slaveholding customers," writes historian Seth Rockman, "and just as next year's cotton crop financed speculation in lands and slaves along the plantation frontier, so too did it shape the prospects of Connecticut tool manufacturers, Massachusetts shoemakers, and the families braiding palm-leaf hats in New Hampshire." See Rockman, "Negro Cloth," 170–72.

   The specific types of fabric that enslaved people were allowed to wear were also, at times, used as a form of social control. For instance, the 1735 South Carolina Negro Act authorized citizens to seize textiles from enslaved people if they were found to be "wearing any sort of garment or apparel whatsoever, finer, other or of greater value than Negro cloth." See Sanders, "The Politics of Textiles."
2. Swarns, "Insurance Policies on Slaves."
3. Farrow, Lang, and Frank, *Complicity,* 4–5.
4. Weld, Grimké, and Grimké, *American Slavery as It Is,* 110. Emphasis in the original.
5. Berry, *The Price for Their Pound of Flesh,* 35.
6. Allen, "Establishing Economic Property Rights."
7. And any story of how the United States ascended to the status of global superpower is incomplete without an understanding of how European colonizers not only stole Native land, but also delegitimized and desecrated the very *relation* to the land that defined the cultures of the continent prior to their arrival. The economic history of Turtle Island does not begin with European contact; Native peoples prior to the fifteenth century had systems of agriculture, organized movement on roads, irrigation, production, and exchange. In contrast to the myth of empty land—the idea of *terra nullius*—Turtle Island was inhabited prior to European colonization by people who turned it, tilled it, dwelled upon it, and held it in different notions of relation long before the era of conquest. Thus, not only the fact of European ownership but, more fundamentally, the notion that they *could* own it, required violent disruption of Native social worlds and ways of being. See Carlos, Feir, and Redish, "Indigenous Nations and the Development of the U.S. Economy," 517.

   The decimation of bison alone had a devastating impact on the communities that had depended on them for generations; as Europeans slaughtered millions of bison to near extinction, nations that had previously had among the highest standards of living and well-being in the world were suddenly driven into widespread malnutrition. See Feir, Gillezeau, and Jones, "The Slaughter of the Bison."

8. Quoted in Trafzer and Hyer, *Exterminate Them,* 1.
9. Johnston-Dodds, "Early California Laws," 8.
10. Saunt, *Unworthy Republic,* 136.
11. Saunt, *Unworthy Republic,* 207. We might also think of such actions as contributing to what legal scholar K-Sue Park has referred to as "self-deportation," which she defines as "the removal strategy of making life so unbearable for a group that its members will leave a place" ("Self-Deportation Nation").
12. Saunt, *Unworthy Republic,* 202.
13. Saunt, *Unworthy Republic,* 217.
14. Quoted in Saunt, *Unworthy Republic,* 206.
15. Saunt, *Unworthy Republic,* 188–89.

    It's also worth thinking about this period as an example of how settler colonialism and racial capitalism destroy lands and waters. Saunt writes compellingly of Native people's original stewardship of these lands, cultivating them in a way that fostered ecological diversity and sustainability. Peaches, apples, blueberries, blackberries, persimmons, and mushrooms provided sustenance. Complex biological relationships among farms, forests, and prairies allowed game animals to thrive. The plantation system replaced this biodiversity with a monoculture, preferring a cash crop that could be a global export, and destroying forests and prairies in favor of vast swaths of cotton fields that would serve as the site of suffering for countless individuals (192–95).
16. Dippel, Frye, and Leonard, "Property Rights Without Transfer Rights," 6.
17. Roberts, *I've Been Here All the While,* 43.

    The Dawes Act also had the effect of formally erasing the Native identity of many Afro-Indigenous people. Households received land based on whether they were on an official tribal enrollment list. However, these lists were subject to the decisions of the Department of the Interior and a political ideology that viewed the coexistence of Blackness and Indigeneity as an impossibility. Appearing Black in the judgment of the Dawes Rolls panelists was often sufficient for an individual to be labeled as a formerly enslaved person, regardless of their actual status, ancestry, or tribal relationships. See Miles, *Ties That Bind,* 191.
18. Lui et al., *The Color of Wealth,* 30; Dippel, Frye, and Leonard, "Property Rights Without Transfer Rights."
19. Dippel, Frye, and Leonard, "Property Rights Without Transfer Rights," 5.
20. Dippel, Frye, and Leonard, "Property Rights Without Transfer Rights," 6.

    And despite the federal government's condescending pretense that holding assets in trust is a necessity for tribes' own protection, internal documents concede that the management of these assets "has long been plagued by inadequate financial management, such as poor accounting and information systems; untrained and inexperienced staff; backlogs in appraisals, determinations of ownership, and record-keeping; lack of a master lease file or accounts-receivable system; inadequate written policies and procedures; and poor internal controls" (U.S. Government Accountability Office, *Indian Trust Funds*).
21. Dippel, Frye, and Leonard, "Property Rights Without Transfer Rights," 38.
22. Mosteller, "Private Land Ownership."
23. Rothberg, "Elouise Cobell ('Yellow Bird Woman')." I'm indebted to Bryan McKinley Jones Brayboy for suggesting that I write in this chapter about Elouise Cobell and her incredible fight for justice.
24. Sahagun, "Tangled Trust Funds."
25. Stivers, "Elouise Cobell and the Indian Trust Funds," 158.
26. Stivers, "Elouise Cobell and the Indian Trust Funds," 159.
27. Whitty, "Elouise Cobell's Accounting Coup."

28. Stivers, "Elouise Cobell and the Indian Trust Funds," 157.
29. Stivers, "Elouise Cobell and the Indian Trust Funds," 158; Gingold and Pearl, "Tribute to Elouise Cobell," 192.
30. Whitty, "Elouise Cobell's Accounting Coup."
31. Whitty, "Elouise Cobell's Accounting Coup."
32. Florio, "Nation Mourns Cobell While Blackfeet Grieve for Kennerly."
33. To add insult to injury, historically the United States government has sought to dissolve the trustee relationship when it is convenient to do so—and in the messiest, most cavalier, most destructive possible way. Consider the Klamath Reservation in the Pacific Northwest. In the 1940s and 1950s, the land was lush with towering ponderosa pines and abundant fish. The pines, along with white fir trees, made Klamath the source of more valuable timber than any other tribally held lands in the country. In 1954, Congress passed the Klamath Termination Act in the name of hastening assimilation, ending its formal relationship with the Klamath Tribes—essentially declaring that such a thing as the Klamath Tribe no longer existed. It was thereby terminated. Termination of Klamath and other tribes in the 1950s and 1960s left their people with the worst of all possible worlds economically: tribal sovereignty dissipated, state tax exemptions disappeared, benefits from federal programs ended, and new tax liability appeared. And the "termination" of the tribe meant the termination of treaty rights—in the case of Klamath, conveniently opening commercial access to over $80 million worth of ponderosa pines, a lucrative commodity in the timber industry. The Klamath people thereafter saw a rise in unemployment and poverty, and had to fight to have their tribal rights restored in 1986.

    See Fixico, *The Invasion of Indian Country*, 79–82; Walch, "Terminating the Indian Termination Policy."
34. Lui et al., *The Color of Wealth*, 32.
35. Maxim, Akee, and Sanchez, "For the First Time."
36. Maxim, Akee, and Sanchez, "For the First Time"; FDR Presidential Library, "Great Depression Facts."
37. Austin, "Native Americans and Jobs."
38. Akee et al., "The Role of Race, Ethnicity and Tribal Enrolment." To quote Zagorsky ("Native Americans' Wealth," 134), "The premier source of individual wealth data in the United States is the Survey of Consumer Finances, sponsored every three years by the Federal Reserve. While this survey provides exceptional detail on families' wealth and debt holdings, it provides relatively little detail on the respondents' racial background. In particular, while the survey asks respondents if they are 'American Indian' or 'Alaska Native,' the public data release combines Asians, Native Americans, Native Hawaiians, and the catchall 'other' individuals into a single category, preventing researchers from using this preeminent source to study Native Americans."
39. Zagorsky, "Native Americans' Wealth."

    What about tribally run casinos, one of the most visible means of potential Native wealth generation? Such gaming operations bring in over $33 billion in annual revenues. (Legg, Ampountolas, and Hancer, "Senior Leadership Succession," 2.)

    But the purpose of the 1988 Indian Gaming Regulatory Act, which allowed for the growth of casinos, is to generate income for the tribe—not necessarily to enrich individual families. Federal law stipulates that funds from tribal gaming enterprises must be used to fund tribal government operations, promote the general welfare, promote tribal economic development, donate to charities, and support the operations of local government agencies. Native-run casinos are not a universal income source among Indigenous communities: they operate in twenty-nine states, and out of 574 federally recognized tribes, only 243 tribes—fewer than half—have gaming facilities. (Robertson, "The Myth of Indian Casino Riches"; National Indian Gaming Commission,

"FAQS"; Chen, Walker, and Vogel, "How Sports Betting Upended the Economies of Native American Tribes.")

Further, states sometimes collect a hefty share of gaming revenue—in some cases as high as 25 percent. (Chen, "Tribal Casino Revenue Sharing in Other States.") One economic analysis found that opening tribal casinos results in a 26 percent rise in employment four years later, but also increases in bankruptcy, violent crime, auto theft, and larceny in surrounding communities. (Evans and Topoleski, "The Social and Economic Impact of Native American Casinos.")

40. Tachine, *Native Presence and Sovereignty in College,* 139.
41. Tachine, *Native Presence and Sovereignty in College,* 108.
42. Lee et al., "Morrill Act of 1862 Indigenous Land Parcels Database." The publication of this database was accompanied by the tremendous journalistic efforts of Tristan Ahtone (Kiowa). It's a truly remarkable collaborative public data project.
43. Sorber, *Land-Grant Colleges and Popular Revolt,* 48–49.
44. Ehrlich, Cook, and Yin, "What Accounts for the US Ascendancy?"
45. Lee et al., "Morrill Act of 1862 Indigenous Land Parcels Database."
46. Feir and Jones, "Repaying a Debt?"
47. Lee and Ahtone, "Land-Grab Universities."
48. Vogel, "Rethinking the Effect of the Abrogation," 544–47.
49. Vogel, "Rethinking the Effect of the Abrogation," 548.
50. Anderson, *Massacre in Minnesota,* 262.
51. Andrews, *The Land Grant of 1862,* 25–26.
52. Lee et al., "Morrill Act of 1862 Indigenous Land Parcels Database."
53. Brayboy and Tachine, "Myths, Erasure, and Violence."
54. Shanks, "The Homestead Act," 32.
55. Baldwin, *In the Shadow of the Ivory Tower,* 6.
56. Baldwin, *In the Shadow of the Ivory Tower,* 6.
57. Wilder, *Ebony & Ivy,* 9.
58. Wilder, *Ebony & Ivy,* chapter 3.
59. Wilder, *Ebony & Ivy,* 114.
60. Wilder, *Ebony & Ivy,* 100; "Benjamin Smith," *The Carolina Story.*
61. Wilder, *Ebony & Ivy,* 118.
62. Wilder, *Ebony & Ivy,* 105.
63. Wilder, *Ebony & Ivy,* 109.
64. Wilder, *Ebony & Ivy,* 114. Emphasis mine.
65. Wilder, *Ebony & Ivy,* chapter 4.
66. Wilder, *Ebony & Ivy,* 142.
67. McInnis, "Violence." See also Oast ("Negotiating the Honor Culture"), who writes that such students "could take liberties with slaves working on campus that they rarely would have with another man's slaves because institutionally owned or controlled slaves were overseen by men and women with a limited interest (economic or otherwise) in them."
68. Fuller, "'I Whipped Him a Second Time.'"

CHAPTER 13: A PLACE TO LEARN YOUR PLACE: EDUCATION AND RACIAL CAPITALISM

1. Kao and Thompson, "Racial and Ethnic Stratification"; Keene, "College Pride, Native Pride." The Kao and Thompson data is older; more research is needed in this area.
2. On Native student enrollment in AP math, see Francis and Darity, "Separate and Unequal Under One Roof," 193. On AP math enrollment and academic outcomes, see Byun, Irvin, and Bell, "Advanced Math Course Taking."

3. Anderson, "Will the Push for Coding Lead to 'Technical Ghettos'?"
4. Robinson, *Black Marxism,* 2.
5. Willis, *Learning to Labour.*
6. Lucas and Berends, "Sociodemographic Diversity, Correlated Achievement, and De Facto Tracking." Other research has suggested that these newer forms of tracking are more tightly correlated to class than they are to race, and that when controlling for socioeconomic status, high-achieving students of color are offered high-level academic opportunities. While this point allows for important analytic specificity, in real life race and class are tightly coupled. See Gamoran and Mare, "Secondary School Tracking and Educational Inequality."
7. Connor et al., "Individualizing Student Instruction Precisely."
8. Summarized in Gamoran, "Tracking and Inequality," 214.
9. Summarized in Gamoran, "Tracking and Inequality," 217–18.
10. Muller et al., "Race and Academic Achievement."
11. Fox, "Seeing Potential."
12. Harber et al., "Students' Race and Teachers' Social Support."
13. Francis, Oliveira, and Dimmitt, "Do School Counselors Exhibit Bias?"
14. Copur-Gencturk et al., "Teachers' Bias Against the Mathematical Ability."
15. Ladson-Billings, "It Doesn't Add Up," 698.
16. Katznelson, *When Affirmative Action Was White,* 163.
17. Thank you to Bryan McKinley Jones Brayboy for making this point to me. See Morgan, "American Indian Veterans Have Highest Record of Military Service"; Army Reserve, "Native American Heritage."
18. Lawrence, "Federal Home Loan Program."
19. Katznelson, *When Affirmative Action Was White,* 163.
20. Lewis and Diamond, *Despite the Best Intentions,* 123.
21. Lewis and Diamond, *Despite the Best Intentions,* 125.
22. Lewis and Diamond, *Despite the Best Intentions,* 128.
23. Bang, Montaño Nolan, and McDaid-Morgan, "Indigenous Family Engagement," 793.
24. Kaomea, "Reconceptualizing Indigenous Parent Involvement."
25. Weber, *The Protestant Ethic,* 17. Emphasis mine.
26. Weber, *The Protestant Ethic,* 19.
27. Quoted in Keyssar, *The Right to Vote,* 1.
28. Keyssar, *The Right to Vote,* 5.
29. Carter, "Other Worlds, Nowhere." Here Carter is glossing W. E. B. Du Bois, "The Souls of White Folk": "I do not laugh. I am quite straight-faced as I ask soberly: 'But what on earth is whiteness that one should so desire it?' Then always, somehow, some way, silently but clearly, I am given to understand that whiteness is the ownership of the earth forever and ever, Amen!"
30. Róisín, *Who Is Wellness For?*
31. "The Freedman's Bureau!" See a brief discussion of this poster in Egerton, *The Wars of Reconstruction,* chapter 3.
32. Foner, *Reconstruction,* 134. Emphasis in the original.
33. Quoted in Murdy, *Teach the Nation.*
34. Child, *The Freedmen's Book,* 262.
35. Fisk, *Plain Counsels for Freedmen,* 23.
36. Fisk, *Plain Counsels for Freedmen,* 41–42.
37. Fisk, *Plain Counsels for Freedmen,* 54. In reading this passage, my friend Clint Smith points out that it is reminiscent of a detail included in "General Order #3," the edict issued by Union general Gordon Granger in Galveston, Texas, declaring that enslaved people were now free—the catalyst for what we celebrate today as Juneteenth. After establishing "an absolute equality of personal rights and rights of property be-

tween former masters and slaves," General Granger's pronouncement immediately adds that "freedmen are advised to remain quietly at their present homes, and work for wages," not to gather at military bases, and that "they will not be supported in idleness either there or elsewhere" (Granger, "General Order #3").

38. American Tract Society, *The Freedman's Third Reader*, 131.
39. Foner, *Reconstruction*, 108.
40. Foner, *Reconstruction*, 109.
41. Langhorne, "Southern Sketches," 78. Emphasis mine.
42. Quoted in Wilson, "Education as a Vehicle of Racial Control," 160.
43. Wilson, "Education as a Vehicle of Racial Control," 164.
44. Wilson, "Education as a Vehicle of Racial Control."
45. NoiseCat, "The Western Idea of Private Property Is Flawed."
46. Greer, *Property and Dispossession*.
47. Gover, "Foreword," xi–xiii.
48. Morgan, *Ancient Society*, 6.
49. Reyhner and Eder, *American Indian Education*, 143.
50. Harris in Bureau of Indian Affairs, *Annual Report of the Commissioner, 1895*, 1017.
51. Quoted in Ross, *Inventing the Savage*, 39.
52. Ross, *Inventing the Savage*, 40.
53. Ross, *Inventing the Savage*, 40.
54. Oberly in Bureau of Indian Affairs, *Annual Report of the Commissioner, 1888*, lxxxix.
55. Schurz, "Present Aspects of the Indian Problem," 9.
56. Schurz, "Present Aspects of the Indian Problem," 17.
57. Oberly in Bureau of Indian Affairs, *Annual Report of the Commissioner, 1888*, lxxxix.
58. U.S. Department of the Interior. *Annual Reports of the Department of the Interior for the Fiscal Year Ended June 30, 1898*, 353.
59. Trennert, "From Carlisle to Phoenix," 278.
60. Trennert, "From Carlisle to Phoenix," 279.
61. Trennert, "From Carlisle to Phoenix," 280.
62. Quoted in Lomawaima, "Estelle Reel," 13. The focus on housekeeping was also a central component of the Bureau of Indian Affairs relocation programs of the 1950s and 1960s, which moved Native people from reservations to urban centers under coercive pretenses. "Once on relocation, the BIA also directed women to keep their families' homes tidy and clean to facilitate social acceptance by the new community. . . . The BIA surveilled these expected performances of femininity and motherhood by making unannounced home visits and cutting funding or increasing the scrutiny of visits when families received poor evaluations" (Kent-Stoll, "Dispossessory Citizenship," 9).
63. Adams, *Education for Extinction*, 162.
64. Quoted in Adams, *Education for Extinction*, 162.
65. Trennert, "From Carlisle to Phoenix," 283.

CONCLUSION: STRANDS TOGETHER: IMAGINATION, LIBERATION, AND BRAIDING

1. Erdrich, "Indian Boarding School: The Runaways."
2. "Black Indigenous Solidarity."
3. Finley, "Building Maroon Intellectual Communities."
4. Barker, *Red Scare*, 128.
5. Ultimately, Leroy argues, "The United States emerged as a racial capitalist settler state through the *simultaneous* operation of colonialism and anti-blackness. For all their differences, settler colonialism and slavery are violent justifications for extermination—of bodies, of sovereignty, of self-possession. Suspending claims to exceptionalism

allows us to see how such forms of extermination blend into one another." (Emphasis mine.)

Leroy then asks a vital question: "What intellectual pathways are foreclosed when slavery and settler colonialism vie for primacy as the violence most foundational to the modern social order?" If you've read this far, hopefully you've come to understand the "slippages" Leroy is describing: the ways that the experiences of Black and Native peoples continue to be intimately entwined—not identical, not interchangeable, but inextricably bound together.

To Leroy's question above, I would add: What pathways toward thriving, joy, and love are foreclosed? What pathways toward kinship and robust political relationships are foreclosed? To put it as plainly as I can: intellectual debates that are more concerned with the absolute supremacy of one historical form of shattering cruelty over another risk perpetuating a lie that we cannot work together against the ways those cruelties persist now, right now, in the immediate present. The assertion that the United States has been shaped first and foremost by anti-Blackness and chattel slavery *or* by anti-Indigeneity and settler colonialism, but never *both,* is only one heuristic for thinking about history and the future. In the academy, we are often trained that the way to perform smartness is through rhetorical practice that is, at its core, rooted in competition, violence, and domination. A "good" book, a "smart" person, or a "convincing" intellectual is defined by their ability to smash their foes. Destruction is valued over construction, the pretense of certainty is valued over the admission of vulnerability, and saying that you are mostly in accord with someone is admission of your own weakness or irrelevance.

I get why it's tempting to start from that place, even those of us who recognize that the Western traditions of the academy were not built to serve our best interests. We start there because we are people who have been hurt, who have had so much taken from us, who have learned the hard way that it is dangerous to rely on anyone other than ourselves. But this view on intellectual production occludes the many other pathways through which we might make knowledge. Further, if feelings of antagonism are the natural result of being persistently hurt, I can't help but be curious about what might be undone if we swam upstream toward the source of those feelings rather than allowing them to draw us away from one another. Would doing so lead us to the source of the power that has harmed us, and lend us the power to undo it? I can't help but wonder.

6. Leroy, "Black History in Occupied Territory."
7. Cf. D'Arcus, "The Urban Geography of Red Power"; Siddons, "Red Power in the *Black Panther*."
8. Lipsitz, *The Possessive Investment in Whiteness*, 3.
9. In *We Do This 'Til We Free Us,* there is a conversation among Mariame Kaba, adrienne maree brown, and Autumn Brown in which Kaba shares the following: "My friend Danielle Sered has said and written this thing that really made a difference for me . . . which was that 'no one enters violence for the first time by committing it.' No one enters violence for the first time by committing it. And it just—I was like—Jesus Christ. If that's true, then all this shit that we talk about, these binaries about victims and perpetrators—that explodes it all. At heart it's the harm that exists, that has motivated and transformed us and allowed us to continue, and if we're not intervened with, will keep harming people in bigger and bigger ways. When we know we're all going to harm each other, it's a matter of degrees."
10. Bureau of Indian Affairs, *Annual Report of the Commissioner, 1859,* 172. The full quotation, which I have abbreviated here for the sake of space, reads: "I am clearly of the opinion that the rapid advancement of the Cherokees is owing in part to the fact of their being slaveholders, which has operated as an incentive to all industrial pursuits; and I believe, if every family of the wild roving tribes of Indians were to own a negro

man and woman, who would teach them to cultivate the soil, and to properly prepare and cook their food, stock cattle given them, and a school master appointed for every district, it would tend more to civilize them than any other plan that could be adopted; for it is a well established fact that all wild tribes have an aversion to manual labor, and when thrown in contact with those who will work, they will gradually acquire industrious habits." I have seen other texts where this passage is quoted and the part about the enslaved people teaching soil cultivation is omitted, but I think it is important to include here. It hearkens back to Pratt's argument that slavery was the best thing that happened to Black people because it allowed them to learn "civilization." In other words, the implication is that owning slaves would bring Native people closer to "civilization" because that's what White people do, but also because Black people would teach them the tools of "civilization."

For more on the implications of this history for contemporary political solidarity movements, see Roberts, "When Black Lives Matter Meets Indian Country."

11. Doran ("Negro Slaves of the Five Civilized Tribes") estimates the number of people enslaved in the Creek, Chickasaw, Choctaw, Cherokee, and Seminole Nations in the 1830s to have been 4,162. The Oklahoma Historical Society ("Freedmen History") cites the number as being 8,000 to 10,000 by 1861.

One of the most notable ways in which policy and perception have painted Blackness and Indigeneity as incommensurable is the term "freedman" itself, which is applied in the Creek Nation even to descendants of Black people who *were never enslaved.* This creates a semantic tie between Blackness and the condition of slavery, even though, as David A. Y. O. Chang writes, "free men and women of African descent had been members of the Creek Nation since its emergence in the eighteenth century. . . . They thereby erased the free Creeks of African descent from the history of the Creek nation and remapped its racial boundaries" ("Where Will the Nation Be at Home?," 82). And, of course, White assessors putting people on the Dawes Rolls could decide that you were a "freedman" based solely on your looks, regardless of lineal descent. In *We Refuse to Forget* (chapter 9), for instance, Caleb Gayle tells the story of two siblings, Jane and Louisa, both Black Creeks; one was marked by the Dawes Commission as "full-blood" (Creek) and one as "Freedman" based solely on their complexions.

For more on histories of enslavement, freedpeople, and descendant rights among the Five Tribes, see Chin, "Red Law, White Supremacy"; Gayle, *We Refuse to Forget;* Krauthamer, *Black Slaves, Indian Masters;* Miles, *Ties That Bind;* Roberts, *I've Been Here All the While.*

12. For a terrific discussion of how this classification led to the Rappahannock Tribe losing federal recognition, see Coleman, *That the Blood Stay Pure.*
13. Miles, "Eating Out of the Same Pot?," xvii.
14. King, *The Black Shoals,* xi.
15. Infante, "Murder and Metaphysics," 150.
16. Tuck and Yang, "Decolonization Is Not a Metaphor."
17. The term "ethic of care" most famously comes from Carol Gilligan's *In a Different Voice,* in which she argues that women use notions of care as an inherent good as the foundation of their ethical reasoning (as opposed to notions of "justice" or abstract fairness). The premise of care is also a central idea in both Black and Indigenous feminist traditions, as I discuss further in the text.
18. Some of the thinkers from whom I have received this teaching include Patricia Hill Collins, bell hooks, Mariame Kaba, Audre Lorde, and Barbara Ransby.
19. For more on mutual aid as a microcosm of "a society where we meet one another's needs, not with shame but with the sense that contributing is an essential thing we do for one another," see Khwaja et al., "Our Year of Mutual Aid."
20. Starblanket, "Being Indigenous Feminists."

21. Crawley, "Stayed | Freedom | Hallelujah."
22. Tyack and Cuban, *Tinkering Toward Utopia.*
23. Estes, Maile, and Simpson, "Indigenous Solidarity with Palestine."
24. Shange, *Progressive Dystopia,* 70.
25. Kaba and Ritchie, *No More Police,* 14.
26. Kaba and Ritchie, *No More Police,* 14–15. Coles et al. ("Fugitivity and Abolition in Educational Research and Practice") point out that "visions of abolition" require "untethering education from the carceral state grounded in punishment and confinement [and] can work as a catalyst for enacting methods of escape, becoming fugitive, in ways that allow one to do the actual work for constructing old-new educational ways of being."
27. Love, *We Want to Do More Than Survive,* 2.
28. Stovall, "Are We Ready for 'School' Abolition?," 51.
29. Stovall, "Are We Ready for 'School' Abolition?," 52–53.
30. Stovall, "Are We Ready for 'School' Abolition?," 57.
31. Stovall, "Are We Ready for 'School' Abolition?," 57.
32. This idea of *taking* versus *making* power is one gleaned from Ruth Wilson Gilmore's classic *Golden Gulag,* 248.
33. It would be easy to see the call for Land Back as being at odds with visions of Black uplift that see land ownership and private property as central (e.g., as represented in the aphorism "I'm still owed my forty acres and a mule!"). Samudzi and Anderson (*As Black as Resistance,* 17) call on Black folks to approach calls for land-based reparations with a critical eye, arguing that "championing the creation of a Black majoritarian nation-state, where the fate of Indigenous people is ambiguous at best, is an idea rooted in settler logic. Is settler adjacency what a truly intersectional framework and multifaceted approach to Black liberation entails? . . . Black American land politics cannot simply be built on top of centuries-old exterminatory settler logic of Indigenous removal and genocide. Rather, the actualization of truly liberated land can only come about through dialogue and co-conspiratorial work with Native communities and a shared understanding of land use outside of capitalistic models of ownership." On the website Landback.org, created by the NDN Collective, the "LANDBACK Manifesto" specifies that Land Back includes "a future where Black reparations and Indigenous LANDBACK co-exist."
34. Longman et al., "'Land Back' Is More Than the Sum of Its Parts."
35. Longman et al., "'Land Back' Is More Than the Sum of Its Parts."
36. Goeman, "Land as Life," 73–74.
37. Simpson, "The Sovereignty of Critique," 686.
38. Barker, "For Whom Sovereignty Matters."
39. Simpson, "The Sovereignty of Critique," 689. Sandy Grande puts it this way: "The task is to detach and dethink the notion of sovereignty from its connection to Western understandings of power and relationships and base it on Indigenous notions of power" (*Red Pedagogy,* 70). I'm also thinking of Simpson's gendered reading of sovereignty, in which she articulates that an Indigenous understanding of sovereignty is never coercive, and necessarily includes "not only the freedom to make decisions about our land but also the freedom to make decisions about our bodies" ("The Place Where We All Live and Work Together").

    Interestingly, in *We Talk, You Listen,* Vine Deloria Jr. suggests that *all* people of color minoritized in the United States inherently have some form of sovereignty. See chapter 8, "Power, Sovereignty, and Freedom." Thanks to Bryan McKinley Jones Brayboy for bringing this chapter to my attention.
40. Simpson, "Land as Pedagogy," 9. I also want to make note here of another passage from Simpson, from *As We Have Always Done* (19): "It became clear to me that *how* we live, *how* we organize, *how* we engage in the world—the process—not only frames

the outcome, it is the transformation. *How* molds and then gives birth to the present. The *how* changes us. *How* is the theoretical intervention."

41. Maynard and Simpson, *Rehearsals for Living,* 26.
42. Here, I am gesturing toward Jarvis R. Givens's book *Fugitive Pedagogy* (see p. viii), which in turn is drawing from the poet and literary critic Nathaniel Mackey's notion of the fugitive spirit that imbues Black educational projects.
43. Jackson, "A Sestina for a Black Girl Who Does Not Know How to Braid Hair."
44. Kimmerer, *Braiding Sweetgrass,* ix.
45. Freire, *Pedagogy of the Oppressed,* 72.
46. In Maynard and Simpson, *Rehearsals for Living,* 270.
47. See, for instance, Colmant et al., "Constructing Meaning."
48. Zitkála-Šá, *American Indian Stories,* 91.
49. Silverman, "The Miner's Canary"; Zahniser, "Alabama & Coushatta Tribes."
50. Belsha, "States and Cities Are Banning Hair Discrimination. Here's How That's Affecting Schools"; Edwards, "Tangled Discrimination in Schools"; Mbilishaka and Apugo, "Brushed Aside"; Rosenbloom and Way, "Experiences of Discrimination"; Sabino, "After West Side School Forces 4-Year-Old to Remove His Braids."
51. Sojoyner, *First Strike,* 71.
52. Vizenor, *Native Liberty,* 1.
53. Carney, *Black Rice,* 153–54.
54. Morgan, "Visual Cultures of Indigenous Futurism."
55. "The search for goodness" comes from Lawrence-Lightfoot and Davis, *The Art and Science of Portraiture,* 146. The extended quotation can be found in "CrossGen Conversation: Eve L. Ewing and Sara Lawrence-Lightfoot."
56. Igbu et al., "BIPOC Solidarities, Decolonization, and Otherwise Kinship Through Black Feminist Love."
57. Baldwin, "*The Black Scholar* Interviews."
58. As in Tachine and Nicolazzo, *Weaving an Otherwise.*
59. Snively and Williams, "Braiding Indigenous Science with Western Science," 4.

INDEX

ABOUT THE AUTHOR

Eve L. Ewing is a writer, scholar, and cultural organizer from Chicago. She is the award-winning author of four books: the poetry collections *Electric Arches* and *1919*, the nonfiction work *Ghosts in the Schoolyard: Racism and School Closings on Chicago's South Side*, and a novel for young readers, *Maya and the Robot*. She is the co-author (with Nate Marshall) of the play *No Blue Memories: The Life of Gwendolyn Brooks* and co-wrote the short story "Timebox" with Janelle Monáe as part of the queer Afrofuturist short story collection *The Memory Librarian*. She also co-wrote the young adult graphic novel *Change the Game* with Colin Kaepernick, illustrated by Orlando Caicedo. Ewing has written several projects for Marvel Comics, most notably the series *Ironheart*, *Black Panther*, and *Exceptional X-Men*. She is an associate professor in the Department of Race, Diaspora, and Indigeneity at the University of Chicago. Her work has been published in *The New Yorker*, *The Atlantic*, *The New York Times*, and many other venues.

eveewing.com

ABOUT THE TYPE

This book was set in Caslon, a typeface first designed in 1722 by William Caslon (1692–1766). Its widespread use by most English printers in the early eighteenth century soon supplanted the Dutch typefaces that had formerly prevailed. The roman is considered a "workhorse" typeface due to its pleasant, open appearance, while the italic is exceedingly decorative.